# China's Digital Nationalism

# Oxford Studies in Digital Politics

Series Editor: Andrew Chadwick, Professor of Political Communication in the Centre for Research in Communication and Culture and the Department of Social Sciences, Loughborough University

# China's Digital Nationalism

FLORIAN SCHNEIDER

OXFORD
UNIVERSITY PRESS

Oxford University Press is a department of the University of Oxford. It furthers
the University's objective of excellence in research, scholarship, and education
by publishing worldwide. Oxford is a registered trade mark of Oxford University
Press in the UK and certain other countries.

Published in the United States of America by Oxford University Press
198 Madison Avenue, New York, NY 10016, United States of America.

Library of Congress Cataloging-in-Publication Data
Names: Schneider, Florian, 1977– author.
Title: China's digital nationalism / Florian Schneider.
Description: New York, NY : Oxford University Press, [2018] |
Series: Oxford studies in digital politics | Includes bibliographical references and index.
Identifiers: LCCN 2018003759 (print) | LCCN 2018020114 (ebook) | ISBN 9780190876814 (Updf) |
ISBN 9780190876821 (Epub) | ISBN 9780190876807 (pbk. : alk. paper) |
ISBN 9780190876791 (hardcover : alk. paper)
Subjects: LCSH: Internet—Political aspects—China. | Cyberspace—Politicalaspects—China. |
Internet—Government policy—China. | Nationalism—China.
Classification: LCC HM851 (ebook) | LCC HM851 .S274 2018 (print) | DDC004.67/80951—dc23
LC record available at https://lccn.loc.gov/2018003759

9 8 7 6 5 4 3 2 1

Paperback printed by Sheridan Books, Inc., United States of America
Hardback printed by Bridgeport National Bindery, Inc., United States of America

```
01001110
01100001
01110100
01101001
01101111
01101110
01100001
01101100
01101001
01110011
01101101
```

*For Foteini.*

*The 1 to all my 0s.*

# Contents

# Tables and Illustrations

## Tables

## Figures

# Acknowledgements

This book is the result of a three-year research project titled 'Digital Nationalism in China', which lasted from 2013 to 2016, and which has involved a number of institutions and people to whom I am deeply grateful for their advice, help, and support. None of the persons or institutions mentioned here are, of course, responsible for any shortcomings in the book, and any remaining errors are entirely my own.

Institutionally, the project was financed by the Netherlands Organization for Scientific Research (NWO), with a generous VENI grant (project no. 275-63-005). The project was hosted at the Leiden University Institute for Area Studies (LIAS). I thank the former LIAS directors Maghiel van Crevel and Frank Pieke for their support of the project. I am in perpetual awe of their dedication to their colleagues and to academic research. Both Maghiel and Frank provided invaluable advice in the run-up to the grant application, and they have been supportive ever since. The financial officers Ine Goedegebuur and Alex van der Meer accompanied the project and helped me manage the grant. During the project, I had the pleasure of visiting China numerous times for fieldwork, with the kind support of my colleagues Yana Zuo and Marc Blanchard at Shanghai Jiaotong University, Huang Dianlin and Zhang Qing at the Communication University of China in Beijing, and Lena Scheen at the New York University Shanghai Campus. On these occasions, many scholars, journalists, media workers, and administrators shared their thoughts with me during formal or informal interviews. For reasons of anonymity, I cannot list their names here, but I am truly grateful for their willingness to share their knowledge and views.

Before the start of this project, as I was developing the ideas for this study, the team around Chris Goto-Jones's research project 'Beyond Utopia' offered me a place to prepare my research. Chris has been incredibly kind in his support of my work, not only by including me in his VICI project as a post-doc but also by continuously providing me with a sounding board for ideas. I have benefitted immensely from working with him and the project's PhD graduates Carl Li, Mari Nakamura, and Martin Roth.

At Leiden University, I have had the pleasure of working in a rich and engaging academic environment that is home to many excellent East Asia scholars, and our conversations over recent years have shaped this book in countless ways. My thanks go to Lindsay Black, Remco Breuker, Javier Cha, Rogier Creemers, Kasia Cwiertka, Koen de Ceuster, Alice de Jong, Ans de Rooij, Hilde De Weerdt, Aya Ezawa, Ed Frettingham, Marc Gilbert, Han Namhee, Hwang Yih-jye, Erik Herber, Anne-Sytske Keijser, Svetlana Kharchenkova, Nadia Kreeft, Stefan Landsberger, Luo Ting, Ewa Machotka, Ethan Mark, Oliver Moore, Kiri Paramore, Park Saeyoung, Fresco Sam-Sin, Ivo Smits, Daniela Stockmann, Rint Sybesma, Teh Limin, Paul van Els, Paul Vierthaler, Bryce Wakefield, Wang Jue, Wang Ying-Ting, Jeroen Wiedenhof, Guita Winkel, and Zhang Yinzhi. I also want to thank my colleagues in Utrecht and Amsterdam for our conversations about digital media and digital methods, especially Anne Helmond, Richard Rogers, and Mirko Schäfer.

While I was preparing and later working on this project, Russ Glenn and Taru Salmenkari took over my teaching duties, and I am in their debt for all the hard work and dedication they showed during what must have frequently seemed like a thankless task: to pick up someone else's teaching obligations on short notice and supervise such a large number of undergraduate and graduate projects. Our students have benefitted enormously from their excellent teaching, and I have profited time and time again from their input and feedback on this project.

Also at Leiden University, Jacqueline Hicks did a tremendous job organizing the Digital Asia Conference of 2016, and it was a pleasure working with her and Bart Barendregt during that event. Jacky and Bart have also been invaluable members of our editorial team for the journal *Asiascape: Digital Asia*, and I thank everyone involved in helping launch that journal and creating such a lively community of scholars interested in digital communication and Asia. Our exchanges of ideas and our work on journal-related issues have provided me with an important and fruitful context for my own work. In addition to Bart and Jacky, I thank Azman Azwan Azmawati, Ian Condry, Jens Damm, Fu King-wa, Chris Goto-Jones, David Herold, Dal Yong Jin, Thomas Looser, Nissim Otmazgin, Martin Roth, Barbara Schulte, Martin Slama, Ross Tapsell, Takayuki Tatsumi, Kyong Yoon, and Elaine Yuan for all their excellent work. Hugo Dobson, Christopher Hughes, Jeroen de Kloet, Thomas Lamarre, Mark McLelland, Jack Linchuan Qiu, Éric Sautedé, Yang Guobin, and Zhang Xiaoling have been tremendously helpful as our advisory board, and I thank them for their unwavering support. It has been wonderful being part of this community while working on this book.

In recent years, I had the pleasure of attending a series of academic events to present parts of this book, and many of my fellow participants provided invaluable constructive feedback and advice. This included colleagues at the annual China Internet Research Conference (CIRC), which I joined in 2013 at the Oxford Internet Institute, in 2014 at the Hong Kong Polytechnic University, and in 2016 at Shanghai's Fudan University. I especially thank David Herold for inviting me to teach workshops at the 12th CIRC in Hong Kong. At various CIRC events, I have been particularly grateful for thoughtful comments from and inspiring conversations with David Herold, Ang Peng Hwa, Séverine Arsène, Gilian Bolsover, Gabriele de Seta, William Dutton, Margaret Hillenbrand, Fang Kecheng, Fu King-wa, Hu Yong, Jiang Min, Randy Kluver, Liao Han-teng, Silvia Lindtner, Tom McDonald, Gianluigi Negro, Jack Qiu, Clément Renaud, Maria Repnikova, Marcella Szablewicz, Cara Wallis, Yang Guobin, Peter Yu, Elaine Yuan, Zhang Weiyu, and Zhou Baohua. In addition, Yang Guobin was kind enough to let me join the 2015 conference on Social Media and Public Engagement in Hangzhou, and Randy Kluver included me in his panel at the International Communication Association's annual meeting in Fukuoka in 2016, for which I am deeply grateful.

Also in Hangzhou, I am indebted to Shi Xu for including me in the International Conference on Multicultural Discourse in 2013, at a time when I was in the middle of preparing the research project, and Cao Qing, Lutgard Lams, and Johann Unger provided feedback on the pilot study that would later become the foundation of this project. At the London School of Economics (LSE), I would like to thank the Association for the Study of Ethnicity and Nationalism (ASEN) for inviting me to their annual meeting in 2014. ASEN is a wonderful community of scholars working at the cutting-edge of nationalism studies, and I have very much enjoyed the many enlightening exchanges that take place at the LSE. Incidentally, the LSE's William A. Callahan later caught a translation error of mine, just as the book was about to go to press, and I thank him for his keen eye and his last-minute assistance.

In the same year as the ASEN meeting, the American Political Science Association (APSA) included me in its annual meeting, and I thank Brock Tessman for hosting our panel on East Asian territorial conflicts. In late 2014, at Lund University, Marina Svensson invited me to join one of her Digital China workshops, and my thanks go to her and her colleagues Gladys Chicharro, Christian Göbel, Annika Pissin, Jesper Schlaeger, Barbara Schulte, and Wang Ning for making this such a successful event.

In 2015, Karl Gustafsson and Linus Hagström invited me to Stockholm to present my work at the Swedish Institute of International Affairs, and I thank them and their colleagues for the opportunity to share my thoughts with them, and especially Astrid Nordin and Joakim Edvardsson Reimar for their helpful feedback. At Cambridge University and Oxford University, my sincere gratitude goes to Barak Kushner and Rana Mitter for inviting me to join their thought-provoking international conferences on media and history in East Asia. The conversations with Barak, Rana, and the participants of the 2015 and 2016 Toshiba International Foundation conferences have deeply shaped my thinking about historiography in a time of digital mediation. At New York University (NYU), my thanks go to Lena Scheen for our many exciting conversations about contemporary China; Lena and Constance Bruce also organized my 2016 visit to the Shanghai Campus, which provided me with the chance to discuss my research with the NYU colleagues and students. I also thank NYU's Clay Shirky for sharing his thoughts on the project with me on numerous occasions. His expansive knowledge of digital media and his commitment to life-long learning are truly inspiring.

I am grateful to Hugo Dobson and his colleagues at Sheffield University for including me in their White Rose workshops on international relations in East Asia. Hugo has rightly insisted that we look beyond the traditional actors in international relations and explore how celebrities, journalists, intellectuals, and others influence politics, and the events he created to discuss these activities have provided a great opportunity for thinking about social media celebrities in China. I also thank Jamie Coates, Adrian Campbell, Andrew Cooper, Elena Denezhkina, Mark Jones, and Mark Wheeler for our conversations on politics, power, and celebrity.

Some of the studies this book is based on have appeared in peer-reviewed journals (see Schneider 2016a, 2017, 2018), and I would like to thank the editors of *New Media and Society, Celebrity Studies,* and the *Journal of Asian Studies* for their help and feedback. Jonathan Sullivan kindly included some of my thoughts on cyberpolitics in the online journal of Nottingham's China Policy Institute. I am also grateful to the anonymous peer-reviewers who have shared their insights on nationalism, media, politics, and China throughout the various review processes. And, of course, I am grateful to my series editor at Oxford University Press (OUP), Andrew Chadwick, for being so supportive of this project, and to OUP's publishing editor Angela Chnapko and assistant editor Alexcee Bechthold for taking the project forward and being available with helpful comments and advice during the publishing process. Lincy Priya and Holly Haydash accompanied the manuscript during the final production stages, and I thank them for all their hard work creating the final book. In three cases, I have kindly been granted permission to use other people's artwork in this book: Figure 1.1 was provided by a photographer who has asked to remain anonymous, but who of course has my sincere thanks; Cristóbal Schmal has allowed me to reproduce his artwork for Figure 1.2; and Transport for London has granted me permission to use their London tube map in Figure 4.2. Finally, Anna Yeadell has again done a tremendous job copyediting the manuscript. I cannot express how thankful I am for her professional advice on writing, and her ability to make me seem eloquent. At OUP, Sylvia Cannizzaro provided a helpful, final round of copy-editing, and I am thankful to her for giving the text its final form.

A number of colleagues need to be mentioned here specifically, for their input, their help, and their friendship. After a chance encounter in a Beijing elevator, Christian Göbel spent many evenings discussing Chinese politics and digital communication with me and has generously shared his ongoing research in the years since. My teacher Marion Müller has taught me everything I know about visual communication, and she continues to inspire me with her enthusiasm for research and teaching. Peter Gries has shared so much of his knowledge on nationalism and group psychology with me over the years, but, more importantly, he has also been an amazing friend. Finally, Lindsay Black, Ed Frettingham, Jay Hwang, Mari Nakamura, and Bryce Wakefield joined a manuscript reading group towards the end of the project. They did an excellent job helping me with the earlier draft of the book, providing insightful feedback and crucial reality checks, and all they received in return were small bribes in the form of food and drink. To all of you: thank you.

Of course, this project has benefitted from the many conversations I have had with my students at Leiden University, especially the participants of my graduate class on the Politics of Digital China, and my graduate and post-graduate research students Anna Fiedler, Milan Ismangil, Manya Koetse, Nie Yuxi, Gina van Ling, Wang Qing, and Zhang Qiaoqi. I have learned so much from you.

Finally, I thank my parents Heike and Michael Schneider for their love and support, and my friends Gina van Ling, Vincent Onken, and Dimitris Froudakis for keeping me sane with various gamic distractions during the hot phase of finishing this book. Joost Hillringhaus, my best man and indeed the best man, has been there for me at every step of the way, and I suspect he will recognize our conversations in many parts of this book. Most importantly, I thank Foteini Poimenidi. Her keen eye as a psychologist and her unbeatable bullshit detector have kept my meandering thoughts on track, and it is fair to say that her critical questions and relentless scepticism have shaped every idea in this book. For that, for her unwavering love and support, and for so much more, I am forever grateful.

# Note on Conventions

In this book, Asian names follow the local convention of placing the last name first and the given name second, for example, 'Mao Zedong'. I have only made exceptions where another rendition is more commonly accepted, for example, 'Jackie Chan'.

For Chinese names and phrases, I have used the Pinyin transliteration that is prevalent in mainland China. Where I have used Chinese characters, I have generally provided the simplified version commonly used on the mainland, unless the discussion warranted mention of the traditional script, for instance in online posts that mix both writing systems.

All English translations from Chinese sources are my own, unless noted otherwise.

A short note on references: throughout, I have quoted and referenced a number of e-books, specifically texts in Amazon's Kindle format. In such cases, I have used Kindle's page location in place of the hard copies' page number to indicate where a quote, factoid, or argument is located. I have also spelled out all given names in the list of references rather than using initials as convention frequently dictates. This is to make it less cumbersome for readers to identify authors with Asian names, especially considering how the relatively low number of common Chinese surnames can lead to many authors sharing the same last name and initial.

# Abbreviations

| | |
|---|---|
| CAC | Cyberspace Administration of China |
| CCP | Chinese Communist Party |
| CFDD | Chinese Federation for Defending the Diaoyus |
| CNNIC | China Internet Network Information Centre Online |
| ICANN | Internet Corporation for Assigned Names and Numbers |
| ICT | Information and Communication Technology |
| IT | Information Technology |
| KMT | Kuomintang (National Party) |
| NGO | Non-Governmental Organization |
| PLA | People's Liberation Army |
| PRC | People's Republic of China |
| ROC | Republic of China (Taiwan) |
| SAR | Special Administrative Region |
| SIIO | State Internet Information Office |
| WCADDL | World Chinese Alliance in Defence of the Diaoyus |

# China's Digital Nationalism

# 1

# Introduction

Devils and traitors:

In the sweltering heat of the 2012 summer, passions are running high in China. After Japanese right-wing activists land on contested islands in the East China Sea, known as the Diaoyu Islands in China, the Chinese internet erupts with angry posts. 'It feels like when your wife is raped yet you can only stand at a distance cursing the culprit, "dare you do it again?"', concludes one user on the popular Chinese messaging service QQ. The online anger quickly spills into the streets as protesters march through major Chinese cities. Some carry picket signs reading 'resist the devils' (*kangji guizi* 抗击鬼子), others burn Japanese flags. The situation escalates further when the Japanese government decides to purchase the islands from their private owner in a bid to outmanoeuvre a nationalist politician at home. The resulting riots across China see Japanese factories and stores set on fire. Japanese restaurants are flying Chinese national flags to discourage vandalism.

On 15 September 2012, a particularly gruesome scene plays itself out in the central-Chinese city of Xi'an: second-hand car dealer Li Jianli is driving his family to a homewares market when he encounters a crowd of protesters smashing and overturning Japanese cars. The mob encircles his vehicle and trashes it with clubs and bricks. When the 51-year-old Mr. Li attempts to protect his car, a rioter smashes his skull in with a bicycle lock. His wife drags him from a pool of blood to a nearby taxi, which rushes Li to a hospital. Emergency brain surgery saves him, but he and his family are scared for life. Mr. Li's offense: he was driving a Nissan.

Four years after the attack, Li and his wife are trending again on social media, following a video report of him and his continuing health problems. In the report, his wife draws her own conclusions from the event: 'Perhaps Japan is all to blame for this, for stealing our Diaoyu Islands. If they wouldn't have done that, there would have been no protests.'[1]

Events like the 2012 riots in the People's Republic of China (PRC) highlight how important popular nationalism is in contemporary Chinese society. They also highlight how strongly this nationalism remains tied to anti-Japanese sentiments, and how those sentiments, in turn, inform political discussions and actions (Figure 1.1). Importantly, the events illustrate that present-day nationalism is a different animal than the nationalism of earlier centuries. Nationalism itself is, of course, not a new phenomenon. From 17th-century Europe, the institution of the nation state has spread to all corners of the world.[2] Today, the United Nations recognizes nearly 200 autonomous nation states. This success story has been made possible by the innovative idea that human beings should be viewed as members of nations—of territorially bound, politically sovereign ethnic communities that share self-proclaimed cultural and historical ties. The nation has become so ubiquitous that it seems nearly impossible to imagine human identity without recourse to a person's nationhood. Indeed, most nationals are passionate about belonging to 'their' nation. It matters to be American or Australian, Chinese or Japanese, Dutch or South African. Sometimes, it matters in seemingly banal ways, for instance during international sporting events or when a border guard requests a traveller's passport. In other instances, such

*Figure 1.1* Japanese Restaurant in Beijing Makes Nice. With kind permission from an anonymous photographer, 30 September 2012.

as during the events outlined earlier, it matters in ways that have broad and, at times, grave consequences.

If we are to understand the social and political complexities of the 21st century, we need to ask: what happens to nationalism when it goes digital? Nationalism today is shared through digital information and communication technologies (ICTs). It is adopted, filtered, transformed, enhanced, and accelerated through digital networks. Moreover, nationalism in digital spheres interacts in complicated ways with nationalism 'on the ground', challenging simple dichotomies of online versus offline politics. All of these dynamics are on display in the rich cultural and political environment that is digital China.

## Chinese Nationalism in the 21st Century

Communication in digital China has been diversifying since the PRC established its first fully functional linkage to the internet in 1994 (see CERNET 2001). Yet, diverse and pluralist as many interactions in digital China may be, political content on the Chinese web is clustered around a small number of recurring themes, and nationalism remains 'the primary online political discourse' (Breslin & Shen 2010: 6).[3] In digital China, internet users commenting on international affairs frequently denounce perceived humiliations of the nation (*guochi* 国耻) while advocating patriotism (*aiguo zhuyi* 爱国主义), thereby contributing to the construction of a national community. For the PRC leadership, taking control of this construction process is a political imperative. Since the 1980s, and especially since the fall of the Soviet Union, China's leaders have been implementing a 'patriotic education' campaign (*aiguo zhuyi jiaoyu* 爱国主义教育) that aims 'to stimulate national pride and cohesion' by 'teaching China's history of resisting foreign aggression as a collective experience of suffering, struggle and glory' (He 2007a: 57).[4]

The Party hopes that patriotic education will inspire 'pragmatic nationalism' (Zhao 2004: 218) and legitimate the Party's rule. Yet, a national community does not exist in a vacuum. Every in-group requires out-groups (Billig 2009: 55–59), and the Chinese leadership has staked its claim as the sole guarantor of the nation's prosperous future on strong 'us versus them' narratives. China's education policies not only 'reeducate the youth (as in the past)', but also 'redirect protest towards the foreigners as the primary enemy' (Callahan 2010: 35).

In the Chinese case, one of the most important foreign others is Japan. It provides the crucial foil against which the Chinese Communist Party (CCP) projects its vision of national cohesion. Of course, not all digital representations of Japan are negative, and especially Chinese interests in Japanese popular culture sit awkwardly alongside more chauvinistic views of the PRC's neighbour.

An example of this complicated relationship is the role the Japanese adult film actress and pop idol Sola Aoi played during the 2012 territorial dispute. Her so-cial media calls for peace between the Chinese and Japanese people brought the patriotic sentiments of many Chinese fans in conflict with their love for Japanese pornography (see Coates 2014). As the ensuing debates over who should be permitted to speak on issues of national self and other suggest, and as the online anger and rioting of 2012 also demonstrate more generally, 'relations between Japan and China continue to be overshadowed by the history of war between them' (Austin & Harris 2001: 48). Routinely resurfacing issues show how deep historical conflicts run: Japanese history textbooks, political rituals, and claims to disputed territories have repeatedly outraged Chinese internet users.[5] While nationalist voices also target other perceived enemies of China, the 'fiercest comments and suggestions are reserved for Japan' (Breslin & Shen 2010: 8).

For the Chinese government, anti-Japanese sentiments are a mixed blessing. On the one hand, they help construct a sense of national unity, and the lead-ership has consequently fostered the idea of a malicious Japan through school curricula (Wang 2012: ch.4), museum exhibits (Denton 2014), and a wide range of media products such as books, TV programmes, computer games, maps, and paraphernalia (Callahan 2010; Nie 2013). Through propaganda strategies old and new (Brady 2008: 125–149), the CCP reminds its citizens to 'never forget' the atrocities of the Second Sino-Japanese War (Mitter 2003), and to view modern Chinese history through the lens of national humiliation (Cohen 2002; Wang 2012). As Carrico and Gries argue (2016: 430), the fre-quently racist anti-Japanese views of contemporary Chinese nationalists 'cannot be understood apart from their socialization in the PRC into a view of Japan as a fascist state perpetually frozen in time in 1945'. Indeed, Japan as an antagonist has become deeply engrained in the CCP's attempt to legitimate its rule over China. On the other hand, as He (2007b: 2) points out, 'the visceral nation-alist sentiment' that these 'pernicious mythos in the national collective memory' often lead to also endanger political and economic cooperation, and in extreme cases they have the potential to harm the political legitimacy of the CCP. In heated current affairs debates, Chinese internet users at times bypass official in-formation policies and shape the meaning of patriotism in ways that do not nec-essarily serve the leadership.[6]

Japanese planes in China's skies:

One of the most devastating earthquakes in human history strikes the Chinese province of Sichuan on 12 May 2008. Over 70,000 people are killed or missing, hundreds of thousands more are injured. Neighbouring Japan is quick to offer aid to the disaster-stricken region, which China's leaders gladly accept. Japan issues 500 million Yen in funding and dispatches responders—the first foreign relief workers to operate on Chinese soil since 1949. Yet after the Japanese government accepts an informal request by the Chinese authorities to also send military aircraft to deliver much needed supplies, the situation threatens to deteriorate online. One user echoes popular sentiments: 'if military planes of Japan fly in [the] sky of China to transport goods to relieve the disaster, this can't stop us from remembering the scenes 60 years ago'. Concerned about this online 'backlash and aversion to Japan', the Japanese ministry of defence shelves its original plans for a military air bridge. The urgently needed supplies are delayed. Private planes must be chartered instead. While Russian and US military planes begin delivering aid, one Japanese air force official comments that 'only Japan was rejected by China, because it is still in the shadow of war'.[7]

It may seem as though Chinese nationalism is designed and implemented by the state and its governing Party, and that it then becomes a run-away phenomenon as state-educated Chinese nationalists confront complex regional and international issues with internalized nationalist scripts. The active role that China's political elites take in shaping national narratives indeed lends itself to such an interpretation, which I discuss in more detail in chapter 2. However, it would be a mistake to conclude that nationalism is simply a form of 'top-down' indoctrination—an argument that is pervasive in popular accounts of Chinese history and memory, particularly when it comes to controversial episodes in PRC history such as the Sino-Japanese War, the Cultural Revolution, or the 1989 Tiananmen Protests. Louisa Lim thus concludes that China is suffering 'amnesia' at the hands of the government (Lim 2014), and the Beijing-based writer Yan Lianke similarly writes in the *New York Times* that the Chinese state is systematically 'deleting memories' and 'utilizing state power to shackle people's minds' (Yan 2013). Cristóbal Schmal has beautifully illustrated this argument in the artwork that accompanies Yan's opinion piece, showing stylized hands that reach into people's heads to pluck out 'memories' like flash cards from an archive (Figure 1.2).

There are, of course, good reasons to be critical of the way that the PRC government treats its own recent history, but stories of 'brainwashing' are nonetheless unhelpful. While they no doubt resonate with problematic American and European threat-perceptions of China as a quasi-totalitarian Communist state, they obscure how politics, media, and psychology are connected.

As I argue in this book, national histories and patriotic sentiments are not passively consumed but are actively constructed in a creative interplay between different stakeholders. This includes the authorities, but also commercial enterprises and private internet users, all of whom benefit in one way or another

*Figure 1.2*  Media and Minds in Popular China Discourses. Cristóbal Schmal/artnomo 2013.

from engaging in nationalism, but without any single actor directly designing the national narratives that ultimately emerge. Importantly, these interactions between stakeholders are mediated through digital technologies, and these technologies sit on top of our human psychological propensities to form social ties, see ourselves as members of groups, and make sense of our world in terms of imagined communities. To understand these dynamics, I propose that we update concepts like nation and nationalism in two important ways.

First, I believe we need to treat political concepts like the nation and its state as technologies in their own right. They are designed by people, in specific socio-historical contexts, to solve perceived problems of their time, for instance how to assure large-scale economic production and political organization. As with any technology, coming up with such solutions is 'path dependent', meaning that the perceived problems as well as their solutions are grounded in specific socio-historical conditions. The process is also highly idiosyncratic, reflecting the messiness of human creativity and lived experiences. Technologies like the nation are imperfect human innovations that have evolved over time, and that are by no means inevitable. Moreover, technologies act on social processes, for instance by changing how we gather knowledge, store information, share cultural artefacts, or engage in debate; technologies also act upon each other, for instance when a transportation technology like the airplane creates incentives for conceptual changes about spatial organization, or when political technologies such as the nation state regulate how a communication technology like the internet is governed. As I show throughout this book, such interactions between technologies are at the heart of how ICTs shape nationalism, and how nationalism, in turn, shapes ICTs.

Secondly, I make a case for updating concepts like nations by treating them as networks. The idea of the network is itself a metaphor, but I believe it is a useful one that draws much needed attention to the features of complex communities, for instance what roles real or potential network linkages play in such communities, how the nature of power changes when people and things are networked, and how important the architecture of a network is for shaping the behaviour of its members. In addition, the network idea forces us to take complexity seriously. In networks, actors behave in bounded ways, but these bounded interactions are 'complex' in the sense that they create outcomes that are impossible to predict. Network theories explain these dynamics by pointing out how networks give rise to so-called emergent properties: unpredictable macroscopic behaviour, based on simple micro-processes that combine to become more than the sum of their parts (see Mitchell 2009: 13). In this sense, nationalism is an emergent property of communication networks. It is the outcome of complex interactions that are bound by the network, but that ultimately construct community discourses and sentiments outside of any single actor's direct control.

Much of this construction process is deeply human, rooted in the psychology of group affiliation; consequently, it translates from the Chinese case to social interactions elsewhere, for instance in Europe, Australia, or America, where nationalist confrontations, for instance over migration issues, are increasingly shaping public discussion. Rather than trying to explain these dynamics through simple indoctrination stories, it would be wise to opt for a nuanced view of how digitally networked nationalism generally works today.

## China's Digital Revolution

China is a particularly compelling place to explore this issue. This is not simply because the PRC is an increasingly important power in world politics. Granted, the country's geopolitical and economic relevance make Chinese nationalism reverberate throughout the East Asian region and beyond, with far-reaching implications. Sino-Japanese historical animosities are one example of how strong nationalist sentiments can threaten peace and prosperity in an entire region. However, this is not a book about Sino-Japanese relations, even though I draw several conclusions about East Asian regional politics in its final chapter. More importantly, views of Japan in digital China serve as an excellent window onto the complex dynamics that characterize digital nationalism more broadly. In that sense, digital nationalism in the PRC can tell us about far more than just the situation in China or developments in East Asia.

The PRC has witnessed a profound transition from an agrarian, socialist past to a hyper-modern, capitalist present. This transition has taken place at historically unprecedented speeds and scales. It has been informed by a pragmatic approach on how to manage a complex system like Chinese society, and it has been implemented by a strong and highly creative political elite—an elite that is comfortable with both cautious policies and heavy-handed measures, depending on what a particular situation seems to call for (see Pieke 2016). Reflecting in 2003 on such complexities of digital development in the PRC, Jack Qiu argued that the Chinese internet is an 'invaluable' object of study that 'calls into question many existing conceptions of technology-society relations formulated in the western context of late capitalism' (2003: 1). This sentiment is as true today as it was then. Indeed, contemporary China is far more than a simple case. It is a vast laboratory for social, cultural, and political change.

The scale and speed of China's transition frequently elicit hyperbole from scholars and journalists alike, particularly with regard to digital technology. The anthropologist David Herold (2012: 2) points out that almost every introduction or paper dealing with digital developments in China stresses that 'the Chinese Internet is huge, it is diverse, and it is different from the Internet elsewhere'. Indeed, the transformations that have taken place in China at times provoke a sense that digital media 'could change absolutely everything', as Liz Carter writes in her discussion of social media in the PRC (Carter 2015: 13). It is easy to see why. When the first e-mail was sent from China in 1987, the vast majority of Chinese citizens would not have been able to afford a computer with which to read it.[8] Indeed, when the PRC published its first statistics on Chinese internet usage 10 years later, only about 620,000 people were accessing China's internet via 300,000 computers, and the country's web consisted of only 1,500 websites (CNNIC 2009). At the time of writing, the PRC's internet population had surpassed the population of the entire European Union: 731 million Chinese internet users had been surfing the web in 2016, using desktop computers (60.1%), laptops (36.8%), tablets (31.5%), and, most importantly, mobile phones (95.1%) to access roughly 4.8 million Chinese websites (CNNIC 2017). Carter concludes, 'if Chinese netizens formed a sovereign country, it would be the world's third largest' (Carter 2015: 2).

These numbers surely obscure many of the uneven developments in digital China, particularly in poorer rural regions of the country.[9] They also suggest that China's digital spheres form one, large community akin to a country in its own right—an allegory that may not capture the full complexity of online developments in the PRC. This can also legitimately be said of the term 'digital China', which is a shorthand that I employ throughout this book to mean all digital information and networks in the PRC, including the digitally enabled actors who access and interact in these networks. Talk of 'digital China' should emphatically not imply a monolithic, homogeneous virtual space; an idea that writers like Ethan Zuckerman (2013) and Michael Stevenson (2012) have rightly criticized for not capturing the many ways in which 'online' and 'offline' phenomena are actually connected. Nevertheless, despite these valid caveats, the scope of developments in the PRC is indeed impressive. Take China's web space: in 2014, Chinese websites took up a staggering 9.3 petabytes of data storage (CNNIC 2015). To get a sense of the scale, imagine all of that data were printed out and then stored in conventional file cabinets. It would take about 26 million cabinets to accommodate all the paper, and if the cabinets were placed in a row, they would reach from Beijing to Rome. Meanwhile, China's web space is still growing by another quarter of its size each year, and each month millions of new users join the digitally connected population (CNNIC 2015), producing e-mails, sending text messages, posting blogs, uploading photos, and streaming videos. Indeed, digital communication in China has been expanding so rapidly that trying to provide accurate numbers of current developments is like trying to hit a target mounted onto one of China's high-speed trains. By the time this book goes to print, the numbers provided here will already be anachronistic.

The impressive dynamics in digital China are accompanied by complex and often seemingly contradictory policy choices. On the one hand, China's authorities hope to create a fruitful business environment for Chinese cultural and technology industries. Next-generation ICTs are one of China's designated 'pillar industries' (Han 2012), and it is a matter of both national pride and economic reasoning for the state to support national champions like the three 'BAT' enterprises Baidu, Alibaba, and Tencent.[10] In 2015, Chinese spending on ICTs alone was estimated to reach 465 billion US dollars (Welitzkin 2014), which is equivalent to the GDP of a mid-sized country like Austria. China's booming e-commerce sector reportedly generated more revenue in 2014 than the entire economy of India (EU SME Centre 2015: 19). During the 2016 Chinese e-commerce day that Alibaba organizes every 11 November (called 'single's day', i.e., 11/11), Chinese shoppers reportedly spent 17.8 billion US dollars, which was more than online shoppers in Brazil spent throughout that entire year (Lavin 2016).

While China's digital capitalism continues to gain momentum, the state keeps a careful eye out for any information it deems inappropriate. Such unwanted information includes so-called yellow content like pornography or gambling, but also 'black' topics like political controversies that might threaten 'social stability' or challenge the leadership. To stay ahead of public opinion, the Chinese authorities closely monitor, guide, censor, and often directly engineer the information that circulates through China's networks (Han 2013; King, Pan, & Roberts 2017; MacKinnon 2009; Wright 2014). I examine this governance strategy in detail in chapter 8 of this book; suffice to say here that the Chinese authorities have taken their overarching model of media management (see Brady 2008; Lieberthal 2003, ch.7; Schneider 2012, ch.7; Shambaugh 2007, 2008; Stockmann 2013) and have creatively extended it to digital China. One particularly visible example of this was the 2011 establishment of the central State Internet Information Office (*Guojia hulianwang xinxi bangongshi* 国家互联网信息办公室; Reuters 2011), which is dedicated to managing digital China and protecting the PRC's 'internet sovereignty' (Sheehan 2015), often heavy-handedly so. The seemingly contradictory Chinese mix of liberal and conservative politics, of participatory media and state-mandated restrictions, has led to a continuously growing body of research on digital China.

## Making Sense of Digital China

The dynamics of digital China promise to shine a spotlight on the social and political implications of digital communication, not just in China but elsewhere as well. Regrettably, scholarship on the internet in China rarely reflects this. As Herold (2012) found in his meta-study of 590 English-language publications that appeared between 1990 and 2012, much of this scholarship treats the Chinese situation as unique. The questions asked of digital processes in China echo this. Scholars based in the United Kingdom and United States overwhelmingly ask whether digital technologies have the potential to 'democratize' China. In Herold's corpus, 88 contributions from the United States and 13 from the United Kingdom asked this question, while only 17 contributions from China and 10 from Hong Kong were interested in this line of inquiry. Agreeing with James Leibold (2011: 1036) and Evgeny Morozov (2011: 241) that much of the English-language scholarship is bogged down in a pervasive 'digital Orientalism', Herold provocatively asks, 'is politics and the pursuit of democracy really the most important issue for Chinese Internet users, or is it just the most important issue for us researchers?' (Herold 2012: 11; see also Arora 2012, for similar criticism).

This is not to say that how people use technologies is not potentially empowering. As Clay Shirky has pointed out, the wide-ranging adoption of novel ICTs around the world 'changes the way groups function', leading to 'profound ramification from everything from commerce and government to media and religion' and transforming 'the world everywhere groups of people come together to accomplish something, which is to say everywhere' (2008: 16, 24). Evidence from China appears to confirm Shirky's assessment. Digital technologies such as mobile phones (Guo & Wu 2009; Liu 2014), blogs (Giese 2003; Esarey & Qiang 2008), and microblogging services (Huang & Sun 2014; Tong & Zuo 2014) afford Chinese citizens with opportunities to challenge perceived social injustices, environmental problems, and political failings, whether through subtle acts of resistance or high-profile protests. Yang Guobin (2009: 217), in his seminal study of online activism, interprets these unprecedented developments as 'the emergence of a citizen's discourse space', and other studies have similarly highlighted how contentious, and often empowering, the diverse interactions in this 'discourse space' can be.[11]

An open question, however, is whether such diversity should be interpreted as 'expanding citizen's unofficial democracy' (Yang 2009: 212). A frequent argument among scholars is that digital technologies in the PRC are tools that empower citizens against the state. Carter, for instance, makes the case that 'social-media users—and companies—push the envelope and the government pushes back' (2015: 3). Lagerkvist similarly argues that a 'domestic tug-of-war between the Party-state and society in China' is playing itself out on the internet (2010: 20), and that this struggle is 'facilitating normative change, and transforming China towards its ultimate horizon—inclusive democracy' (2010: 39). Such claims assume that Chinese society will transition to a liberal democratic system, and that the question is merely how and when. In this view, the internet becomes the harbinger of a Habermasian public sphere (Gang & Bandurski 2011; Lagerkvist 2010: 24) that sets the stage for broader democratization.

Indeed, discussion between diverse actors is not only *possible* in digital China, but in many ways *encouraged* (Sullivan 2014; Tsang 2009)—at least, as long as these actors do not call on internet users to mobilize (King, Pan, & Roberts, 2013). It should come as no surprise that much of this discussion is political (Stockmann 2013): interest in politics is as common in China as it is elsewhere in the world, with heated discussions taking place on a daily basis in classrooms, restaurants, and teahouses across the PRC, and this interest extends to online spheres. But is it accurate to call these digital spaces 'public spheres'? Is the internet to China what salons and cafés were to early Enlightenment Europe (see Habermas 1962/1990)? Are Chinese social media groups the digital teahouses of the 21st century?

I hesitate to agree with assessments that view digital technologies as stepping-stones on a path to liberal democracy. In my view, the arguments surrounding new ICTs in China tend to continue discussions from the 20th century, when it was so-called free markets and the privatization of the economy that allegedly heralded a move towards democracy; now, the supposed free flow of information that advanced digital technologies afford is believed to have the same effect. However, such a focus on democracy and democratization is based on assumptions that misrepresent how political and digital technologies intersect today. Asking how the PRC will become a liberal democracy is, for several reasons, asking the wrong question.

For one thing, discussions about politics and digital technologies often ignore that most digital activities are not political (Arora 2012). Chinese internet users, for instance, are just as interested in whimsical or trivial exchanges as their peers elsewhere. Of course, the fact that digital media users crave entertainment does not obviate the possibility that they also use the medium for political ends. It does, however, raise the question under what conditions banal everyday activities deserve to be interpreted as meaningful civic engagement (see Leibold 2011). In the Chinese case, the assumption that China's internet users are, by default, politically engaged citizens has led to the prolific practice of calling these users 'netizens' (*wangmin* 网民)—a term that frequently suggests struggle for liberty, rights, and justice on China's web, but that is ultimately misleading (Herold 2014; also see Marolt 2011). Much of what happens through digital technologies in China is not about civic engagement. Studying how one family in small-town China uses the internet, Tom McDonald concludes that their concerns 'centre not on issues of democracy or freedom, but rather on the effects of internet use on family, kinship, children's education and achievement' (2015: 28). Such detailed ethnographic studies provide important reminders that internet users in China, like internet users everywhere else, are primarily interested in connecting with friends and family, posting selfies, buying cheap consumer products, exchanging funny pictures of pets, and sharing what they had for lunch. If these interactions are to be understood as a 'public sphere', then this would require a radical overhaul of Habermas's concept, which is originally built around the idea of a contentious and critical civil society, with equal access for all, that challenges state power.[12]

Another problem related to claims about China's supposed digital 'public spheres' is that such claims are vulnerable to the same criticism leveraged against earlier interpretations of the net as an egalitarian civic space (see Dean 2003). Even where digitally enabled actions are indeed contentious, it may be unhelpful to view them through the lens of democratization. Contentious publics are not necessarily egalitarian. While the activities of those who inhabit the much-evoked 'public spheres' are often well-meaning, they tend to follow the reasoning of prosperous (mainly male) elites that consist of 'academia, activists, corporate, and state power' (Hoofd 2012: 50). This is also true in the Chinese context, where many of the famous cases of collective action reflect the interests and worries of an affluent, property-owning class of urbanites. The 2011 high-speed train crash in the rich coastal province of Zhejiang captures the anxieties of this demographic, as does the 2015 Tianjin Blast with its iconic images of shattered urban life (Figure 1.3).

Hot-button issues like plans to build waste disposal sites or chemical factories are often topics that drive members of China's 'moderately well-off society' (*xiaokang shehui* 小康社会) to the streets in protest. However, the same cannot

*Figure 1.3* Shattered Vision of Capitalist Urbanism. A field of cars, burned-out by the massive industrial explosions that shook the harbour city of Tianjin on 12 August 2015. Karl-Ludwig Poggemann/Flickr 2015, available at https://www.flickr.com/photos/hinkelstone/19926727424/in/photolist-wmRFPW-xz5n9k/.

be said for China's frequent mining catastrophes, the plight of the Chinese floating population of migrant labourers, or the often dismal living conditions in poor rural areas. Public discourse in China is shaped by highly plugged-in elites, and it remains an open question whether their activism contributes to 'democracy'. In advanced capitalist societies, the projects that these 'speed elites' (Hoofd 2012: 11) are engaged in tend to be fuelled by concerns over property rights and the wish to maintain a privileged lifestyle, and they tend to be informed by the same arguments for liberty and self-actualization that also provide the foundation for neoliberalism. Active personal engagement, digital literacy, and political responsibility are at the core of these activities; disengagement and laziness are considered irresponsible. Thus, a valid question is whether digital activism ultimately perpetuates the very rationale of the systemic neoliberal problems it frequently claims to be fighting (Hoofd 2012).

Optimistic accounts of emancipatory technology tend to ignore the degree to which digital spheres are connected to the logic of contemporary capitalism. As Dan Schiller (2014: 1727) writes, 'virtual spaces are, in fact, bolted to the material world through spatially organized infrastructures', and within these infrastructures traditional stakeholders like capitalist enterprises retain much of their power. Companies like Apple, Facebook, or Google collaborate closely with state authorities in their quest for profit, often censoring and controlling what happens through their products. Try uploading a photo of a woman breastfeeding her child to a social media account for a practical example of such corporate censorship. Where digital technologies do indeed facilitate change, it is because the interests of progressive social groups align with the interest of the profit-oriented enterprises that provide the technologies. In this, Chinese companies are no different from large corporations elsewhere. Companies 'such as Baidu, Sina Weibo and Renren are capitalist companies whose operations and economic structures are very similar to the ones of Google, Twitter and Facebook', writes Christian Fuchs; all of these companies rely on 'the influx of investments on finance markets and the confidence of advertisers' (2015: 21, 23). 'Bolted' as they are to existing power relations and institutions of 'digital capitalism' (Schiller 1999), it is not clear to me why social media platforms, proprietary mobile phone software, or financially motivated search engines should inevitably be viewed as 'liberation technologies' (Diamond 2010).

Finally, the strong research focus on contentious politics risks underemphasizing the power that nation-state institutions exert over the rules of political communication, and the many ways in which these institutions are successfully addressing the challenges of governing a complex and dynamic network society in the 21st century. The many new ways in which ICTs allow people to organize today does not imply that digital technologies are a death knell to the institutions of the nation state. Digital technologies strengthen established political stakeholders as much as they strengthen the much-evoked 'multitude' of newly empowered media users.[13] The Chinese example is again instructive. The PRC's internet is one of the most heavily policed in the world (Deibert, Palfrey, Rohozinski, & Zittrain, 2010: 449–487). The national infrastructure remains firmly in the hands of three large state-owned conglomerates (China Telecom, China Unicom, and China Mobile) and four public internet service providers, all of which 'assume heavy and important responsibilities of internet regulation' (Hu 2011: 523–524) in close collaboration with the authorities. As it turns out, John Gilmore's famous claim that 'the Net interprets censorship as damage and routes around it' is a myth.[14] The CCP has effectively proven that controlling the internet is not 'like trying to nail jello to the wall', as former US president William J. Clinton (2000) put it. Chinese leaders have been very successful at managing digital media, and they unapologetically justify their interventions as safeguards against the 'harmful effects of illegal information', claiming that unfettered information flows would jeopardize their efforts to create a 'healthy and harmonious Internet environment' (Information Office 2010).

Contrary to accounts that portray these interventions as wholly unpopular and that focus primarily on confrontations between citizens and state, the PRC's attempts to manage digital communication are part of wider governance practices that are negotiated and coordinated between diverse, networked actors. Frequently, these governance practices are not implemented against China's citizens, but in collaboration with them. Much of this process is not an antagonistic struggle between citizens and the state. As Christian Göbel (2015: 7) points out, digital technologies potentially reduce 'the likelihood of such struggles to appear in the first place'. Throughout this book, I view digital media as technologies through which various stakeholders in China construct networks and deploy power to achieve their individual political and commercial ends. Indeed, digital politics are shaped by negotiations, collaborations, and persuasions. In China, various actors have actively created and nurtured spaces for open discussion. These spaces benefit internet users as they connect with each other and exchange information. They benefit enterprises as they profit financially from internet traffic, user-generated content, and e-commerce. They also benefit the Chinese state and the CCP as these authorities integrate online discussions into their system of policy feedback and strategic planning (see the contributions in Damm & Thomas 2006). This includes so-called e-governance initiatives (see Göbel 2015; Kluver 2005; Lollar 2006; Schlæger 2013; and Wu 2009), but also 'cultural governance' strategies (Callahan 2010; Schneider 2016b) that aim to regulate society by regulating the cultural parameters in which social interactions take place. As Kirk Denton (2014: 4) has rightly pointed out, 'to dismiss this state presence as nothing but propaganda is to fail to understand the complexity of the state/people relationship'. This complex relation deserves close attention, particularly if we wish to understand how nation states adapt to the shifting terrain of the digital age. The Chinese state's interactions with popular nationalism is an example of these adaptive capabilities.

## Studying Digital Nationalism

When branding goes wrong:

Embarrassment at Toyota. Advertisers Saatchi & Saatchi have released their campaign for the Prado Land Cruiser in the Beijing magazine *Auto Fan*, but Beijing's auto fans are not amused. The double-spread shows the Prado driving past two Chinese stone lions that are saluting the vehicle. The caption reads: 'The Prado. You can't help but respect it'. A flood of outrage ensues on China's web. More than 200,000 internet users log their protest online. 'It is unbelievable to see that today, fifty-eight years since the Chinese drove the Japanese invaders out of China in 1945, a stone lion [is] saluting Japan', writes one commentator. For many, the lions provoke bitter associations with the stone statues along Beijing's Marco Polo Bridge. The site saw the beginning of Japan's brutal war in China. That the Chinese name for 'Prado' (*Badao* 霸道) can also mean 'tyrannical way' or 'rule by force' is further oil on the flames of digital fury. The advertisements are shared widely online. Amidst calls to 'boycott little Japan' (*dizhi xiao Riben* 抵制小日本), Chinese bloggers post digitally altered images of the car, now trampled by over-sized lion statues. The advertisement campaign is quickly banned by the Chinese state for 'hurting the nation's feeling', and Toyota issues a 'sincere apology for the unpleasant feelings [the ads] have generated among Chinese readers'.[15]

This book explores the issue of digital nationalism by looking at online discourses and networks in China. While a number of path-breaking studies have explored nationalism in China (Gries 2004; Zhao 2004), including cyber-nationalism (Jiang 2012; Leibold 2010; Shen 2008; Shen & Breslin 2010; Weiss 2014, Xu 2007), these works usually bracket the question of how the digital technology itself enables certain interactions. To my knowledge, none of the influential contributions on Chinese nationalism place the medium in the centre of their empirical work, nor do they re-conceptualize nationalism in the digital age. Where innovative studies address technological issues, they tend to do so within the confines of specific platforms or digital practices, for example, specific social media platforms (Benney 2014), online encyclopaedias (Liao 2013), blog posts and online articles (Leibold 2011, 2016a), or search engines (Jiang 2014), but they do not systematically connect findings from such disparate media sites. What is currently missing in the study of nationalism is an approach that integrates these two crucial dimensions: the discourses and the digital technologies.

To explore this connection, I draw on research in multiple disciplines, sketching controversies that surround digital politics and national communities in fields like area studies, communication and media studies, political science, psychology, and sociology. At the same time, I analyse digital China first-hand, by empirically examining what search engines, online encyclopaedias, websites, digital networks, and social media can tell us about the way that different actors construct and manage a crucial topic in contemporary Chinese politics: the protracted historical relationship with neighbouring Japan. As I have outlined earlier, Japan provides an important foil for contemporary Chinese nationalism. What is more, the focus on Japan as an antagonist to China's national success happens to coincide with the popularization of the internet in the PRC. As on-line discussions became possible and indeed widespread in China, discourses on Japan were also highly en vogue, and they remain so today.[16] It is for these reasons that this book provides an account of digital nationalism by asking, how do networked actors use ICTs to shape nationalist discourse in the PRC, vis-à-vis Japan as foreign Other?

To answer this question, I focus on two specific cases. The first case is the Nanjing Massacre of 1937. The Nanjing Massacre is an important topic in contemporary Chinese historiography.[17] The event marks a particularly gruesome episode of the Second Sino-Japanese War (Mitter 2013: ch.7), which saw Japanese imperial forces engaged in months of unrestrained pillaging, rape, and murder in the former capital of Republican China. The atrocities that the Japanese invaders committed during the winter of 1937 have been central to the patriotic education campaign discussed earlier, and Callahan rightly concludes that 'the "rape" of Nanjing defines the relationship between China and Japan' to this day (2010: 165).[18] The Nanjing Massacre consequently makes for a good case to check how an established political discourse works on the web. While there are recurring disagreements between Chinese and Japanese intellectuals about the exact interpretation of the event, particularly about the number of civilians who were murdered by the Japanese invaders, the topic is largely uncontroversial in China, and one might expect its online representation to be relatively stable.

My second case is the ongoing East China Sea dispute, which revolves around the aforementioned group of uninhabited islands that are situated north-east of Taiwan and are called Diaoyu (钓鱼) in Chinese and Senkaku (尖閣) in Japanese.[19] Sovereignty over these islands has long been an issue of contention between the governments of China, Japan, and Taiwan. The conflict dates back to the First Sino-Japanese War (1894–1895), when the Japanese empire took control of the islands. The dispute gained momentum in the late 1960s, when fossil fuels were discovered in the region, and again in the early 1970s, when the American government transferred administrative control over the islands to Japan (Blanchard 2000). While the dispute is indeed a historical conflict, it came to the fore in the 1990s, and then again in recent years (Stockmann 2010), most visibly during the 2012 anti-Japanese protests in the PRC (Wallace & Weiss 2015; Weiss 2014). This volatile security issue serves as a contrast to the more established historical discourse of the Nanjing Massacre, promising to reveal how a dynamic current affairs topic is presented in digital China.

I explore these cases by taking a two-step approach, which combines elements of traditional qualitative analyses with recent innovations in digital methods research. This means that I am exploring and, at times, generating novel data about various parts of digital China. My approach covers the logic behind the algorithms that govern digital spheres, the interfaces that guide our perceptions, and the network infrastructures that shape how information is constructed, accessed, and shared online. Using digital methods thus means taking media technologies and the objects they produce seriously. If we understand nationalism as the emergent property of communication networks, then we require research tools that can study such networks on their own terms. Combining digital methods with more traditional, qualitative means of analysis then promises to capture the complexity of digital networks, by exploring their technological properties, their discursive effects, and their contextual meanings.

This mixed-methods approach frequently involves non-trivial choices about what counts as data; how to attribute social and political meaning to techno-logical elements like search rankings, hyperlinks, IP addresses, or social media buttons; and how to visualize findings. I draw attention to such issues of research methods throughout the book as they arise, specifically to highlight how meth-odological choices often affect the conclusions one might draw from particular data. A brief summary suffices here to give an impression of what the empirical studies involved.

To study the kinds of statements that circulate through China's digital networks, I have taken a discourse analysis approach. Discourse here means communication practices that systematically construct our knowledge of reality and reinforce commonly accepted truths—an issue that is intricately linked to how people construct social institutions like the nation, and to which I conse-quently return in more detail in the next chapter.[20] Studying discourse means asking questions like: What themes do specific cultural sources prominently cover, what positions do they relay, and what strategic moves do the creators make to frame the topic? It usually entails detailed linguistic analysis of spe-cific statements in their relevant contexts, with the goal of establishing what assumptions and world-views inform the statements.[21] For instance, phrasing a sentence in active or passive voice either emphasizes or de-emphasizes who the main agent in the sentence is. It makes a difference, for example, whether I write 'the Chinese state regulates the web in China', or whether I write 'the web in China is regulated'—the first phrase assigns responsibility to a specific agent, the second phrase deletes that agent. Discourse analysis tries to systemat-ically uncover such communication choices and assess their social and political implications.

Much of the discourse analysis I provide focuses on web content. In prac-tice, studying discourse on the web means first identifying websites dedicated to the relevant topic and then collecting the content on those websites through a combination of manual and computer-assisted archiving (e.g., preserving screenshots of relevant sites and stripping pages of text and media elements). It then means deploying a combination of computer tools to narrow down the corpus of data and check pages for representative or outlying keyword results. The actual qualitative analysis then draws from the toolbox of discourse anal-ysis, but it also takes into account that a complex medium like the website is not simply 'text'. Like most human communication, digital media do not solely consist of linguistic statements. They are 'multi-modal' (Kress & Van Leeuwen 2001: 2), which means they are communication practices that work on multiple levels, for instance through written language, pictures and layout choices, moving images, sounds, and so on.[22] This also includes so-called natively digital features like hyperlinks, scroll-overs, or social media buttons, and these elements must consequently be taken into account.[23]

While studying discourses on China's web is itself useful for mapping out what beliefs and ideas circulate through digital China, such an approach focuses on content alone. To explore the broader digital infrastructures within which the discourse exists, I am adopting an approach that 'follows the medium', as Richard Rogers (2013: 27) puts it. Using a combination of traditional and digital research methods, I have traced the two cases through China's online spheres. This includes comparing what happens when specific keywords are entered into different Chinese search engines (chapter 3). What can search rankings tell us about the way that the discourse is framed on China's web? What are the entry points to the topic? Exploring the websites that deal with the two cases, a crucial question is how these sites are connected to each other through hyperlinks (chapter 4). Which online networks are involved in producing discourse on Sino-Japanese history? Are these networks stable over time or do they change frequently? Who are the actors in these networks, and what are their roles? In practice, answering these questions involved two digital tools: the first is the IssueCrawler software, developed and hosted by Rogers and the Digital Methods Initiative (DMI) in Amsterdam (see Rogers 2010). The IssueCrawler is an open access analytical programme that can be run from a browser interface in order to locate linked sites and map online networks.[24] The second tool is the network visualization programme Gephi, which I have used to represent the network data and highlight the most pertinent features.[25]

As I show, by analysing digital media and the discourses they affect—in this case, on topics related to Japan—it becomes possible not only to explore the specific topic at hand, but also to establish more broadly which communication models inform governance in media ecologies.[26] Exploring such governance strategies in the Chinese context is notoriously difficult. While the authorities regularly publish official announcements regarding the PRC's cyber regulations, their general scope and vagueness only offer superficial purchase on the issue. Overall, the Party remains secretive about the practical details of how it attempts to 'guide public opinion' on China's internet. Bar the occasional informal conversations with officials or leaked memos (NYT 2010), researchers thus do not normally have insight into the intricate workings of the CCP's propaganda and censorship system, which consists of shadowy leadership groups and personal networks that crisscross the PRC's state and societal institutions at all levels of administration, making it 'virtually invisible on China's organization charts' (Lieberthal 2003: 233). However, through their active management of digital discourses, the authorities are leaving traces of their cultural governance approach within the artefacts and digital infrastructures they are managing. As this book demonstrates, an approach that 'follows the medium' can be a fruitful way to reverse-engineer contemporary politics in national webs (Rogers 2013: ch.6).

In addition to this medium-centric approach, I have also conducted qualitative interviews with industry insiders and academics to explore in more detail how Chinese media management works, how Chinese experts make sense of recent developments in digital China, and what the political economy of digital China looks like. Conducting these interviews has been challenging, as I was repeatedly confronted with the chilling effects that politics under Xi Jinping have had on public debate in China. The practical implication is that, over the course of this project, the majority of my conversations on digital issues in China had to remain informal. Only in ten out of about a hundred cases have I been able to conduct formal, semi-structured interviews. While these interviews have been with highly informed and well-situated individuals, they can only serve here to provide general texture for the rest of the analysis. I have consequently quoted from them to add context and illustrate specific views from China, but not in order to provide stand-alone evidence on digital issues.

## Structure of This Book

In this book, I trace discourses on Japan through various parts of digital China. Following this introductory chapter, the book continues with a discussion of how we might think about nations and nationalism in the digital age. In this second chapter, I briefly review how scholars have discussed nationalism in the past, and I attempt to convince readers that the most useful way to view nations and their states is as modern technologies. I will make the case, as scholars like Benedict Anderson and Michael Billig have done before me, that human beings 'imagine' nations, and that they do so largely through communication practices. To make better sense of these communication practices, I propose that we view social groups as networked communities, and I examine what network theory and network analysis can tell us about the workings of imagined communities like nations.

This second chapter further discusses why the modern nation often seems rooted in primordial human nature. To this end, I discuss the social and psychological mechanisms that are at work in various kinds of communities. My argument is that the modern technology of nationalism draws from universal human desires and aspirations, but that this does not make nations primordial. It does, however, make such communities extremely seductive, based as they are in the human propensity to feel strongly about the kind of social ties that nations evoke. Following this excursion into the social psychology of nations and nationalism, the chapter examines how we need to rethink the construction of networked communities like nations in light of recent shifts in communication practices. I conclude by reviewing the scholarship on nationalism in China, drawing attention to core debates in contemporary Chinese studies, and finally making the case that a diverse range of actors today 'programme' the networks of national communities through discursive practices in order to shift what the nation means. Nationalism, then, becomes an emergent property of these networked activities.

Following this conceptual discussion, the third chapter looks at the most common access route into digital networks: the search engine. I first present how scholarship has been making sense of web queries and their social relevance. This includes a look at state-of-the-field research on the world's most ubiquitous search engine, Google, but also at recent work on China's search engines. Next, I take a tour through China's different search engines, experimenting with various platforms to see what happens when they are used to search for issues related to Japan. As this chapter shows, China's search engines reproduce many of the biases that scholars have identified for other search engines, but they also generate additional biases through the commercial imperatives under which they labour. I argue that this outcome is owed to a 'digital bias' that is produced when algorithms draw from material, social, and subjective elements in order to generate effective search results for users. Overall, the way in which search algorithms in China set the stage for digital inquiries into knowledge is linked to several factors, including China's political economy, state interventions, technical and design choices of the companies themselves, and the psychology of users. This combination of factors actively contributes to the construction of the Chinese nation and makes China's search engines extremely warped windows onto knowledge about Japan.

Chapter 4 examines the online networks between Chinese websites. I start by discussing what the social and political meanings of hyperlinks might be, and what mapping out so-called issue networks on the web can tell us about digital ecologies. Next, I discuss how linking practices work in China's web spaces. As I show, the websites that deal with the Nanjing Massacre and the Diaoyu Islands make only limited use of the web's interactive affordances, for instance of hyperlinks. An analysis of link structures and sitemaps reveals that issue websites on Sino-Japanese issues resemble traditional archives more than they resemble interactive information hubs. Following this discussion of links, I provide an analysis of how these issue sites tie into wider digital networks. This includes an examination of the actors that dominate the two issue spaces. As I show, the main players in these networks are large corporations, state agencies, and Party institutions, which together form a national web space that reflects many of the governance mechanisms that are at work 'offline'. While it may seem as though China's web is primarily 'national' due to the control that the authorities exert, similar 'nationalizing' effects are also visible in other networks across the region, for instance in Taiwan or Hong Kong. A short excursion into the networks of self-proclaimed cosmopolitan academic institutions from three major cities in 'Greater China' demonstrates this. I conclude by arguing that, in the case of the web, the way in which contemporary digital technologies and human psychology interact predisposes communication practices to take place within highly parochial boundaries. Rather than breaking these boundaries down, the central actors in digital China exacerbate these tendencies through their policies and design choices.

The fifth and sixth chapters of this book each turn to the digital discourse surrounding one of the cases. Chapter 5 examines the Nanjing Massacre on China's web, chapter 6 the East China Sea dispute. I first analyse how Chinese-language online encyclopaedias present the Nanjing Massacre, and how Wikipedia's Chinese entries compare to entries in Encyclopaedia Baidu (*Baidu Baike* 百度百科). I then turn to the major websites that cover the respective issue. In the case of the Nanjing Massacre, this includes a large commemoration portal on Sina.com as well as the website of the Nanjing Massacre Memorial Hall. For the East China Sea dispute, it includes various military news portals and the web presence of non-governmental advocacy groups. In all of these cases, my focus is on the language with which the issues are presented as well as on visual materials and digital features. As I show, both discourses are overall in line with the CCP's official narratives. In fact, the Nanjing Massacre discourse draws mostly from authoritative, vetted sources and is presented in a static way that offers very little space for discussion. On China's web, the history of the Nanjing Massacre resembles a shrine rather than a forum. The Diaoyu Island issue is more dynamic, and notably involves more commercial actors who commodify the discourse, but overall these sites also fall back on traditional mass-media scripts. My argument is that both cases offer an intriguing glimpse into how China's web works; specifically, how it is today essentially an info-web: a traditional mass communication space that offers accredited information by established stakeholders, who shape nationalist discourse for their own political and commercial purposes. This can have unanticipated effects, for instance when misogynist arguments start to develop a digital life of their own, ultimately constraining how a political discourse can be articulated online.

In chapter 7, I turn to user-generated content and social media. This includes first a discussion of 'Web 2.0' technologies, which is followed by a look at message boards and comment sections in digital China. The cases I examine show that while narratives on the Nanjing Massacre and the Diaoyu Islands frequently provide a nuanced picture of how to make sense of China and its relation with Japan, the overarching discursive patterns of what is appropriate discourse on the issue combine with digital mechanisms such as 'likes' and algorithmic popularity rankings to push the discussion into nationalist media scripts. In contrast to message boards and online comment sections, China's microblogging and messaging spheres at first sight offer a different story: discussions on Weibo or Weixin are highly diverse, extremely dynamic, and can have impressive reach. Also, they at times seem to elude attempts at censorship and control. Yet, the nature of such social networks ultimately either skews them in favour of a few influential users (as in the case of Weibo and its 'Big-V' celebrities) or pushes discussions into the walled gardens of small social groups (as in the case of Weixin). In each instance, the technology, the design choices, and the political framework that govern these networks interact seamlessly with the human psychology of group behaviour. The effect is that nationalist discourse reverberates through the echo chambers of China's social media, which contribute directly and in visceral ways to the sense of a shared nationhood.

Following these various empirical studies of Chinese digital spheres, chapter 8 is again conceptual. Stepping away from nationalist discourses about Japan, the chapter examines what the findings can tell us about information and communication governance in the PRC more broadly. This question is closely linked to debates about Chinese politics in the 21st century, which are often associated with the idea of authoritarianism. There has indeed been a host of concepts that are meant to make sense of this seemingly peculiar brand of politics, and the Chinese case has been labelled an example of 'authoritarian resilience', 'authoritarian consolidation', 'responsive authoritarianism', or 'adaptive authoritarianism'. Transferred to the digital age, the concept of authoritarianism has informed debates about China's 'authoritarian informationalism', 'authoritarian deliberation', and 'authoritarianism 2.0'. In this chapter, I review these discussions, arguing that while such concepts may highlight certain state–society dynamics, they nevertheless risk underemphasizing important aspects of Chinese politics and ultimately obscure how communication governance and political legitimacy work in general. This is, in part, because discussions about authoritarianism potentially draw attention away from the degree of participation and collaboration that takes place in Chinese politics. It is also partly because such a focus creates unwarranted boundaries between a perceived authoritarian China and an ostensibly democratic 'West'. Such boundaries fail to acknowledge how politics around the world are increasingly intertwined with information management and control, and how the Chinese case is not as peculiar as it is often made out to be. The Chinese leadership may be in the process of developing a governance approach 'with Chinese characteristics', but the issues that this approach addresses and the strategies it deploys are by no means 'Chinese'. Instead, I propose that we view politics more generally as practices that selectively draw from both democratic and authoritarian governing techniques. I conclude this chapter by showing how important stakeholders in the PRC are reworking networks to create hierarchical structures, and I make the case that this governance approach has much in common with governance in neoliberal democracies, which, in turn, has important implications for how we assess politics in the 21st century.

Each of these chapters includes a short conclusion, and the final chapter of this book then draws together these fragments to retrace the central findings and arguments of this study. This conclusion first summarizes how digital nationalism works across different Chinese online spheres, and it then discusses how digital discourses are managed in China today. Next, it considers what implications digital nationalism has for the PRC and its regional relations. Following this discussion on East Asia, the chapter turns to more general findings about imagined communities and networked societies, and it summarizes how nationalism changes in a time of ubiquitous digital media use. My main argument is that advanced ICTs 'update' the nation, its state, and the sentiments that people attach to imagined communities and their institutions. In essence, nationalism thrives in current digital networks, because the design choices behind network architectures, the technical properties of the medium, and the political economies of the societies we live in seamlessly connect with human psychology to create group sentiments that are not under the control of any single stakeholder. This fundamentally challenges our assumptions about technology and politics, and I show how China is the perfect place to explore these issues empirically, especially if we turn to representations of China's most important 'other': Japan. One of my main contentions is that the findings from China translate to other contexts and are crucial if we are to understand, for instance, the rise of populism in Europe and the United States. The book concludes with a personal, normative assessment, in which I argue that, without serious rethinking on the part of policymakers, information gatekeepers, tech innovators, and ICT users, the 21st century is bound to again be a century of nations and nationalism, now filtered through the networks of neoliberal digital capitalism. Without intervention, this will turn out to be a parochial world that is ultimately ill-equipped to handle the daunting challenges humanity faces today.

# 2

# Nationalism and Its Digital Modes

The martial-arts actor Jackie Chan is on a mission. It does not involve fighting, but it involves a good deal of singing. Touring through talk shows and media events across China, Chan is promoting his own brand of nationalism. During the 60-year anniversary of the PRC, the superstar from Hong Kong presented his sentiments in the song 'Country':

> A home (*jia* 家) is the smallest country (*guo* 国),
> A country is ten million homes . . .
> This country is my country,
> This home is my home,
> I love this country,
> I love this home,
> I love this nation state (*guojia* 国家).

Chan's unerring support for the central government has attracted criticism, both in China and abroad, and crude songs like this one are probably doing little to mend his image.[1] Yet, regardless of how one feels about Jackie Chan and his performances, the lyrics of this song are telling, even if some of the wordplay is arguably lost in my somewhat awkward translation of terms like 'country', 'home', and 'nation state': The Chinese word for country or nation state combines the character for 'state' (confusingly, sometimes also translated as 'country') and the character for 'home' or 'family'. The play on words in Chan's song illustrates one of the basic mechanisms in nationalism: the fusion of a political unit with a 'homeland'. In this, Chinese language is not alone.

This chapter sets the stage for the analyses and discussions that follow throughout this book. I first explore how we might make sense of nations and nationalism in contexts that are shaped by ubiquitous digital communication. This book deals with nationalism and communication technologies, and my goal in this chapter is to connect theories of nationalism with theories of such technologies. Much of early thinking about digital media assumed that the kind of cheap, easy, and widespread communication that digital technologies afford would contribute to an age of transnational interaction and cosmopolitan understanding, or in Habermas's words (2001), a 'post-national constellation'.[2] However, as digital media have become ever more available to ever more people, the cosmopolitan shift in humanity's understanding of the world has yet to materialize. Nations, and the nationalist sentiments that sustain them, remain strong.

To make sense of this seemingly contradictory situation, and to ultimately show that nationalism and digital communication are not at odds with one another, I first discuss why it makes sense to see nations and states as modern technologies. This perspective is important if we are to understand what physical tools and technical devices have in common with conceptual and institutional innovation. Moreover, such a view also highlights how technologies are created and deployed by human beings for specific purposes, in specific contexts, and how the use of such technologies is consequently neither inevitable, nor self-evident.

In the case of the nation and its state, these technologies are closely connected to modernity, and the subsequent section reviews this connection. Next, I outline what national communities have in common with other social groups, and what sets them apart. This includes a discussion of how scholars have traditionally made sense of nations, and it also includes my own definitions of concepts like nation, nation state, nationalism, and patriotism. My goal in this section is to explain what makes nations 'tick', and to show that they are intimately linked to the social and psychological dynamics of human groups.

It is these psychological foundations of group behaviour that the chapter turns to next. I make the argument that the various psychological factors that prompt human beings to seek security in groups provide the foundations on which national communities are constructed. As the chapter then discusses, communication plays a crucial role in this construction process. I review how communities are created and maintained through the circulation of shared symbols, and what this has to do with mass communication and ICTs. Finally, I revisit how scholarship on China has made sense of nationalism there, and I outline some of the debates that characterize this scholarship. First, however, allow me to start with a discussion of how we might make sense of technology more generally.

## Technology and Its Uses

In popular definitions, technology tends to refer to 'the application of scientific knowledge to the practical aims of human life' (Britannica, n.d.). Such a view of technology highlights the importance of scientific progress, but it remains rooted in a modern European understanding of innovation that does not fully capture how human ingenuity has worked across time and space. If we were to follow such a definition, then the meaning of technology would hinge on whether or not an application was based on scientific processes, leading to paradoxical situations: imagine someone in premodern China mixing a number of substances with peculiar properties and realizing that the result can be ignited to create magnificent explosive effects. Yet, this substance, if discovered without a scientific rationalization of how its components interact, would not constitute a technology. On the other hand, if, a millennium later, the same discovery were accompanied by a systematic attempt to explore how sulphur, charcoal, and saltpetre combine to form 'gunpowder', then it would qualify as a technology. In such an understanding, there could never be a premodern or non-scientific technology.[3] This strikes me as wrong. Surely, the core idea that the term 'technology' needs to capture is that humans tend to apply their understanding of the world they inhabit to solve problems they face. How such understanding came about is not the main issue.

To capture the full range of ingenuity, creativity, and knowledge application that humans have exhibited throughout history, I am using a broad definition of technology in this book, where 'technology' refers to any systematic, practical application of human knowledge. In this view, Neolithic stone tools, medieval agricultural techniques, modern transportation vehicles, or contemporary digital computation devices are all technologies. However, such a focus on tools alone still falls short. In his epic study of human development throughout history, the sociologist and philosopher of technology Lewis Mumford (1966) takes issue with the idea that technology should refer chiefly to physical applications. To Mumford, innovations like the stone axe, the plough, the airplane, or the computer are not the most notable human technologies. In fact, finding technical solutions that make our physical environment more liveable is not a uniquely human activity, but rather one that humans share with many fellow animal species. Instead of viewing toolmaking alone as the pinnacle of human development, Mumford argues, we should connect this activity to the conceptual meaning-making capacities of human beings. Creating tools and devices is truly innovative because these creations are 'modified by linguistic symbols, aesthetic designs, and socially transmitted knowledge' (Mumford 1966: 5).

According to Mumford, the impressive revolution of the human nervous system has seen a similarly impressive evolution of the human capacity for symbolic representation and communication, which made the human being 'preeminently a mind-making, self-mastering, and self-designing animal' (1966: 9) that was able to 'outsource' its mind to cultural artefacts and to other minds.[4] As Mumford writes (1966: 28):

> the mind reproduces itself by transmitting its symbols to other intermediaries, human and mechanical, than the particular brain that

first assembled them. Thus in the very act of making life more meaningful, minds have learned to prolong their own existence, and influence other human beings remote in time and space, animating and
vitalizing ever larger portions of experience.

This view of technical innovation is in line with arguments that technologies are
not always straightforward, intentional solutions to the real-world problems that
humans encounter. The wish to solve specific challenges indeed often plays an
important role, but innovation also involves a large degree of playful tinkering,
unaccredited copying, and incremental tweaking. Necessity is not always the
'mother of invention', and technologies are rarely tailored solutions to a specific problem; they are 'inventions in search of a use' (Diamond 1999: 243). It
is only through communication processes that human conceptual work turns
into commonly accepted, systematic usage (Sperber 1996: 82), and it is through
human institutions and social power relations that certain innovations rather
than others become entrenched as seemingly inevitable outcomes. This is true
of diverse innovations ranging from horseback riding to agriculture, from music
trends to video games, from computer keyboards to electric cars (Rogers 2003).
It is also true of social institutions, for instance hospitals and prisons (Foucault
1965/1988, 1978/1995), debt and money (Graeber 2011b), nations and states
(Shapiro 2004).

As discussed in the introduction, it makes little sense to view technologies in
a deterministic fashion. Innovations like ICTs are not essential for the construction of specific social and political systems, for example, democracies. Also, they
are not agents with their own will. Contrary to claims by tech writers like Kevin
Kelly (2010), technology does not 'want' anything specific. It does not have the
same kind of agency that human beings possess. A more plausible argument
about technology's capacity to have 'agency' comes from proponents of actor-
network theory, most notably its founder Bruno Latour (2005). Latour views
cultural artefacts as mediators, and he suggests that we should ask how they
'act upon' other artefacts. In this sense, Latour's view of 'agency' can be a useful
heuristic device for studying contemporary technical phenomena, for instance
how ICTs 'act upon' the nation and its state. Such a perspective is particularly
valuable where independently acting algorithms are involved, for instance the
crawlers upon which internet search engines are built (a topic that I return to in
the next chapter). That said, Latour provocatively takes his case to the extreme
when he writes, 'there is hardly any doubt that [ . . . ] knifes [sic] "cut" meat' (
2005: 71). His argument is that since we can formulate an active sentence that
has as its subject the knife, we should then conclude that the knife is the agent.
Aside from playing rather fast and loose with linguistic conventions, Latour's
argument completely removes from the picture the human agent who wields

the knife. Michael Billig (2013: 3094) has sharply criticized such practice as an 'error of describing how things happen in the social world without mentioning how people might make them happen, or, indeed, who the people are who make  them happen'—a critique with which I concur.

However strongly one wants to attribute agency to cultural artefacts, it does not follow that technology 'naturally' creates clearly determined outcomes, for instance by making societies generally better, as Kelly (2010) argues. It also does not follow that certain technologies inevitably make life worse, as Sherry Turkle (2011) claims in her study of how social media and mobile technologies supposedly isolate us from other human beings. Turkle is not alone with her scepticism. Popular writers like Nicholas Carr (2010) or Susan Greenfield (2015) claim that ICTs affect our brains and societies in ways that make human beings stupid and human interactions shallow. In China, popular science books and self-improvement manuals frequently focus on the controversial issue of 'internet addiction' (*wangyin* 网瘾; e.g., Wang 2011), at times making alarmist comparisons between digital technologies and opium (e.g., Ying & Yue 2008). In Chinese academia, as Qiu and Bu (2013) have shown, the dominant framework for understanding ICTs remains technological determinism.

Such perspectives frequently rely on problematic understandings of human psychology and the brain, a conservative view of culture and change, and an often blatant disregard of empirical evidence.[5] The neuroscientist and comedian Dean Burnett (2013) has criticized such arguments in his brilliant self-help guide on how to write technophobic newspaper articles, pointing out how concerns over ICTs are by no means novel:

> Previous examples include video games, online porn, social networking, anything with a screen, the internet in general, television, books, typewriters, the printing press, the internal combustion engine, carrier pigeons, and that hot orange stuff you get when you rub sticks together that makes raw food dangerously edible. Not newspapers, though. Never ever newspapers!

A reasonable reaction to one-sided claims about innovation might therefore be that technologies are not beneficial or harmful in their own right, but that they are inherently neutral; their value lies in how they are ultimately used. Jill Walker Rettberg, in her discussion of blogging technologies, makes use of the popular example of the knife to argue that 'blogs, knives and most other tools can be used for good or for evil' (2014: 2770). In this view, technologies can be used for numerous purposes; a knife can be used to stab someone, or it can be used to cut a birthday cake. This is indeed an interpretation that is frequently and rightly mustered against simple deterministic views of technologies, but I ultimately find it wanting. As the historian of technology Melvin Kranzberg famously phrased it, 'technology is neither good or bad, *nor is it neutral*' (quoted in Pariser 2012: 2342, my emphasis). How technologies are ultimately used is highly contingent on three factors: design, social structures, and human psychology. To illustrate this, it is worth dwelling on the example of the knife, especially considering how frequently this particular tool is used as a metaphor in debates about technology.

Take, for instance, how design choices and technological properties guide the use of technology along specific paths. The technical properties of a knife make it very unlikely that it will be repurposed to eat soup. There are many things for which one might 'misappropriate' a knife, but its usage has limits. I cannot use it to make a phone call, or to travel to work, or to power my refrigerator. In short: design matters. Consider the difference between a butter knife and a dagger. Each has been designed for specific purposes: one for spreading dairy products on staple foods, the other for physically harming living creatures. This is not to say that either of these designs *pre-determines* what the knife will be used for (it is entirely possible to deploy a dagger to make a sandwich or to wield a butter knife to deadly effect), but the design choices *imply* certain uses rather than others. This also means that certain technologies can have specific applications. Automatic weapons, for instance, are designed to intimidate, wound, or kill; they are not meant to soothe the anxieties of a potential opponent, and they cannot be deployed to heal or bring to life. However one might feel about such technologies of violence, they are decidedly and often unapologetically *not* neutral.

Second, the use of technology takes place in a political and economic environment that precludes specific choices. There are rules, for instance, that govern the purposes for which knives should or should not be used. Stabbing others is punished by modern societies, at least outside of specifically sanctioned interactions such as wars. Similarly, what kinds of knives can be made or owned is regulated. Double-edged knives or knives with retracting blades are prohibited in many places. Then, there are the economic dynamics that make producing specific technologies and designs more attractive than others. In modern capitalist societies, knives have a price tag, which means that affluent buyers will be able to afford different knives than destitute buyers, and this, in turn, creates incentives for producers to favour specific devices and designs. Finally, the use of knives is guided by social conventions. In many cultures, handing someone a knife edge-first is impolite, as is licking a knife at the dinner table. In some places, knives are used during a meal, in others they are traditionally used only in kitchens to prepare the meal. The use of technology is shaped by structural factors. These factors may, at times, be complex and hard to trace, but they shape technological uses nonetheless.

Third, within these structural confines, human psychology prompts us to deploy technology in certain ways. The psychological patterns that shape how we use tools, as well as the meanings we attribute to certain technologies, can be profoundly important. If someone is able to convince me, for example, that only the 'iKnife' truly represents my personality, then this specific device becomes part of larger need structures and identity practices that can be very powerful. How I then use that knife is not at all straightforward. Following social conventions is often easier than breaking through those conventions, and some usages are psychologically more rewarding. Others are more taxing: stabbing someone, for instance, is mentally difficult for anyone who is not suffering from a mental disorder, is placed in a life-or-death situation, or is generally hardened to the task of physically harming another living being. This is precisely why military organizations deploy training methods designed to de-sensitize recruits to otherwise socially unacceptable and psychologically strenuous behaviour.

In summary, certain technological uses turn out to be more plausible than others, and a range of factors have to come together before someone uses a butter knife to stab their friend rather than to make them a peanut-butter sandwich. This is why the use of technologies is never 'good or bad, nor is it neutral', to again quote Kranzberg. It is *conditional*. This is true not only of knives, but also of smartphones and tablets, search algorithms and computer operating systems, websites and social networking services. Throughout this book, I will repeatedly provide examples of how usage is guided along specific paths. What is important here is that the factors that shape technologies and their uses also apply to what Mumford calls conceptual 'technics' like social and political innovations. How technologies work is the outcome of design choices, socio-political and economic conditions, and psychological processes, and, in this sense, a knife is no different from, for instance, nations and their states.

## Nations and Their States: Core Technologies of Modernity

The nation state is one of modernity's core technologies (Gluck 2011: 676). It is a form of political organization that takes the premodern concept of the 'state', that is, a collection of political institutions that claim a legitimate monopoly on the power to govern a territory, and makes it coterminous with the idea of the 'nation', or what Shapiro (2004: 49) describes as a set of people who see themselves as part of a larger ethnic community, based on perceived cultural, linguistic, civic, and/or physiological commonalities. To scholars of modernity, the nation state is a political technology that addresses a specific problem of the modern condition: how to arrange the complexity of social life in a way that makes large-scale political and economic organization possible (Gellner 1983/2006: 5). The rise of nation states is thus intimately linked with increased capitalist industrialization, as Anthony Giddens (1985/2002) has shown. In its numerous iterations and variations, this political technology has proven so successful at enabling large-scale social cooperation that it now seems to be an indispensable part of political life the world over.

Yet, despite this success story, it would be misleading to view the nation state as an inevitable or 'natural' outcome of human progress. It is rather the result of a lengthy process of construction, innovation, and negotiation, driven in no small part by elites and their self-interests (Gellner 1983/2006). In this sense, capitalist modernity is not a revolutionary break with premodern times that can be traced to a specific moment and place, but rather a general mindset that grew out of several centuries of attempts to innovate how human societies operate, and that ultimately justified a range of practices and institutions such as the nation and its nation state. It is consequently problematic to talk about human history in terms of developmental periods, in 'stages' and 'revolutions', 'waves' or 'ages, as 19th-century thinkers like Hegel, Marx, or Kierkegaard tended to do, and as is still commonly done today. The anthropologist David Graeber points out, correctly I believe, that ' "societies" are constantly reforming, skipping back and forth between what we think of as different evolutionary stages' (Graeber 2004: 54).

It seems much more prudent to speak of social, political, and economic 'modes' rather than 'ages'. The institutions of modernity are part of one partic-ular mode, but this is not to say that this mode was predestined in a teleolog-ical fashion, or that it constitutes an evolutionary improvement. It is part of the success of modern institutions to suggest that the modes by which we live are the inevitable outcome of 'progress', even though there is no progressive movement 'forward' through history, and societies often switch modes or combine them creatively. This is important to keep in mind, especially considering how modern generations tend to describe their world as the unique and inevitable outcome of technology's march forward. An example of this is the recent work of the psy-chologist Steven Pinker (2012), who links the overall decline in physical vio-lence throughout human history to evolving social structures, making what is essentially a modernist claim about the inevitability of human progress. Lewis Mumford remained sceptical of such views. Writing in the mid-20th century, he noted the following (Mumford 1966: 22):

> During the last half century, this short period has been described as the Machine Age, the Power Age, the Steel Age, the Concrete Age, the Air Age, the Electronic Age, the Nuclear Age, the Rocket Age, the Computer Age, the Space Age, and the Age of Automation. One would

hardly guess from such characterizations that these recent technological triumphs constitute but a fraction of the immense number of
highly diversified components that enter into present-day technology,
and make up but an infinitesimal part of the entire heritage of human
culture.

Mumford's assessment extends to our present, which is frequently described
as a unique 'information age' (Castells 2010), and which I have also referred
to in the introduction of this book as a 'digital age'. Such terms deserve careful
qualification. There is no single moment in time at which the 'digital age' begins.
Instead, a lengthy historical process that spans centuries has led to a collection
of innovations surrounding computational devices and to the introduction
of 'digital modes' to politics, economics, and society. Historians of computation rightly place a strong emphasis on 20th-century innovations in micro-
processing, as well as on the computational and cryptographic work of Alan Turing
in the 1940s. However, important precursors to this work date back to at least
the 19th century, when mathematicians like Charles Babbage and Ada Lovelace
conceptualized their analytical machine. This conceptual work, in turn, continued even earlier algorithmic endeavours, for instance by 17th-century natural philosophers like Gottfried Wilhelm Leibniz.[6] The history of computation
thus shows that the 'digital age' is not a neat developmental stage that follows
the 'modern age', but that digital modes have crisscrossed with modern and premodern modes throughout history (see Thompson 1995: 19). The result has
been a 'suite' of technologies (Swaminathan 2015: 239–240) that is deployed in
varying ways and combinations in different places. Just as ostensibly premodern
institutions and practices have carried over into the 'modern age', so, too, do
premodern and modern modes still operate in today's 'digital age'. Modern
technologies like nation states or capitalism have not disappeared. Quite the op-
posite is the case: they have become updated.

In short, modernity is not a period in time, and most certainly not a human
reality that is the inevitable outcome of innovation. It is instead a set of organizational principles and technologies. These technologies happen to have first been
popularized and institutionalized in specific times and places, and they then
spread as stakeholders in different societies became convinced, through observation, interaction, and communication, that these technologies were worth
deploying. Some technologies were rejected, others were initially adopted and
later abandoned, and yet others became ubiquitous (see Diamond 1999: 257–
258; Graeber 2004; Rogers 2003). This is not to say that the innovations that
turned out to be successful were indeed generally valuable, albeit they seemed
that way to certain groups at the time. What is noteworthy is that a particular
set of technologies was employed in a systematic combination, at large scales,

and with impressive speed, creating what we now recognize as modernity. This includes the technology of the nation, which took the logic of small-scale communities and connected it to novel methods of production and organization.

## What Makes Nations Tick?

The technologies of the nation and its state are justified by a peculiar form of consciousness: nationalism. While it is generally agreed that nationalism is a kind of attachment or group loyalty to the nation, the concepts of nation and nationalism have been notoriously hard to define (see Anderson 2006: 3; Gellner 1983/2006: 6). This is, in part, because they encompass diverse cases, across time and space, each grounded in their own peculiar assumptions and claims. Some nationalisms stress cultural commonalities while others rely on a sense of shared civic institutions. Some seem comfortable uniting various ethnicities under their conceptual umbrella, while others rely on claims to ethnic homogeneity. In certain cases, nationalism seems to be leveraged by elite groups to establish the nation or maintain it; in other cases, nationalism appears to inform the activities of grass-roots movements, for instance in the case of popular nationalist protests.

To understand what the nation is and how it works, I would like to explore the ways in which national communities extend the logic of smaller groups, but also how they change this logic. For this purpose, I distinguish between four types of communities, each a sub-category of the previous type: human communities, imagined communities, patriotic communities, and national communities. Figure 2.1 represents how these four types of community are related.

Let me start with the outer circle of the diagram. We are all part of human communities that have their roots in face-to-face interactions. Whether we think of our high school classmates, our book clubs and sports clubs, our circles of closest friends, our network of co-workers, the local church, or our families, each is a community of people with whom we share a particular interest or purpose, as well as a culture and history. If you are part of an orchestra, you and your fellow musicians share a love for music, and you share the experience of practicing and performing together. Regardless of whether you are personally close to the member of that group (network analysts would say you share 'strong ties' with them) or whether you are merely acquaintances with occasional interactions (meaning you maintain 'weak ties'), you minimally know each group member personally. This is a crucial feature of small-scale communities: ties with other group members are traceable and they affect our lives in immediate ways, even if they vary in their strength and the frequency with which they are relevant to us.

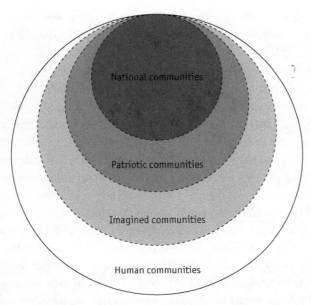

*Figure 2.1* Communities. Extending community logics from general human interactions to the nation. Florian Schneider

Granted, many of the interactions between members of such communities may not be strictly face to face. They are often mediated, for instance, when we write each other letters and e-mails, call each other on the phone or on Skype, or interact through social media. In some cases, members of such groups may have never actually met physically. A significant part of the research on digital media deals with what happens when personal interactions become increasingly mediated in this way, and a major realization that comes from this research is that the dynamics and pressures of social groups extend in often interesting ways to digital networks that work across distances.[7] If you interact with a high school acquaintance on Facebook, you may not agree with her idiosyncratic political views, but you are nevertheless unlikely to shower her with vitriol. After all, your relationship is at stake. It has a past, and you probably want it to have a future as well. Whether consciously or unconsciously, you are adjusting your mediated behaviour in the knowledge that the social interactions you are engaging in have personal consequences to you. The logic of sustained face-to-face interaction affects you in a way that would be quite different if you were dealing with a stranger you are unlikely to ever meet again, if you and your interlocutor remained anonymous, or if your social tie with the respective person meant very little to you. Our digital social networks are not 'virtual', as was often proclaimed during the early days of the web. They mirror the social relations we have 'on the ground', even if the mirror can, at times, have distorting effects.

Michael Stevenson aptly summed this up when he wrote that the idea of virtual space as 'an "elsewhere" falls apart when your mom friends you on Facebook' (Stevenson 2012).

Many of our interactions take place within such small-scale, face-to-face communities. They are, in a sense, an extension of tribal life, and I discuss later in this book how this tribal dynamic extends psychologically to the dynamics of nations. The difference with earlier tribal life, however, is that modern humans are part of numerous different 'tribes' simultaneously, and that many of these groups and their interactions are not at all small scale. If you are religious, for instance, you are part of a community that shares a particular faith, and that consequently also shares at least some similar experiences of how to make sense of the world. If you are Catholic, you share commonalities with all other Catholics on the planet, whether they live in South America, in Africa, or Asia. The same can be said, of course, if you are a Muslim, or a Buddhist, or an atheist. This logic extends to many kinds of groups: fans of specific sports franchises, large academic communities, members of political parties or movements, employees of multinational corporations, contributors to civic organizations or charitable causes, and so on. In each case, there is a 'tribe' of people out there who are linked through the belief that they have something in common.

What is interesting about these kinds of communities is that the members only know a small number of fellow tribe folk personally. If you are a Muslim, you do not personally know all other Muslims in the world, yet you may still feel a sense of community between yourself and other Muslims—a sentiment captured by the concept of the 'ummah' (see Shani 2008). For such larger communities, much of the social and psychological rationale that characterizes small-scale groups still holds, but something important has changed: the sense of commonality with the other group members is not based on actual social ties and direct experiences. It is based on potential ties, and these ties only work because they rely on a cognitive shift. Benedict Anderson argues that this shift constitutes an act of 'imagining' or 'creating' the community in our mind, since the members of such groups 'will never know most of their fellow-members, meet them, or even hear of them, yet in the minds of each lives the image of their communion' (1983/2006: 6). This is true as much for religious communities as it is for employees of large corporations or members of far-flung social and political movements.

The kind of imagined communities I have described so far are not tied to an immutable place. Religious communities, multinational corporations, worker movements, cricket fans, and so on may have churches and headquarters, meeting places and stadiums, and these sites may matter symbolically to the members, but overall the collective goals of the community do not rely on any single territory. However, if the members imagine their collective membership around a set of communalities *and* around a specific territorial expanse, we are confronted with a qualitatively different kind of imagined community. For example, if you are from a major metropolis, such as Berlin or New York, Shanghai or Mumbai, then you likely feel an attachment as much to the place as to fellow Berliners, New Yorkers, Shanghainese, or Mumbaikars. The same can often be said for people in particular boroughs of cities (Brooklyn or Queens, Puxi or Pudong), or of people in specific regions (Bavaria, Guangdong, South Holland, Yorkshire, etc.).

While these communities often coincide with administrative units like provincial states or municipalities, this is not a prerequisite. Territorially defined communities can also be constructed around geographical features such as rivers, mountains, or islands. The imagined ties that people maintain with communities from the Rocky Mountains, the Rheinland, the Peloponnese peninsula, or the Pearl River delta are all built around some notion of a 'homeland' and its people. In each case, the members of this community are connected through a belief in a collective history, shared culture, and common values. Quite often, this also includes a sense of common ancestry. References to a '*father*land' or '*mother*land' are indicative of this.[8] The core difference to other imagined communities is precisely this attachment to a place. I call the kinds of groups that attach a sense of common ancestry to a specific territory 'patriotic communities', and call the sentiment that leads members to affiliate with such communities 'patriotism'.

At this point, I should clarify that the categories I am drawing up here should not be understood in absolute terms, with clear-cut boundaries, but rather as a sliding scale that can help us establish which dynamics are in play in a specific community. It is entirely plausible for a non-territorial imagined community to justify group affiliation through kinship ties and attachment to certain places, for instance in the case of Maori communities (Moeke-Pickering 1996), Native American nations (Wilkinson 2005), or descendants of Scottish Highland clans (Chhabra, Healy, & Sills, 2003), but also in the seemingly innocuous case of sports clubs and fan groups.[9] Some of these cases may well sit at the intersection between community types, and such ambiguous group and place relations would warrant a closer empirical study of the community dynamic that are at work in each particular case. My point here is that there is a qualitative difference between imagined communities with or without an attachment to ancestral places, even where this distinction is contested or in transition.

If we accept that territorially defined imagined communities can be referred to as 'patriotic', then the next question is how patriotic communities and the sentiments that fuel them differ from nations and nationalism. There has been a long-lasting debate on how patriotism and nationalism relate. A major problem with distinguishing the two concepts is that attempts to do so have often been highly normative. In such understandings, patriotism—literally the 'love for one's country'—is believed to be a generally positive attachment to a group: a sentiment that brings people of a place together for the purpose of beneficial and altruistic collective action (e.g., Johnson 1997: 46). It is often believed to be an inclusive sentiment that does not discriminate against those who remain outside of the 'in-group'. Nationalism, on the other hand, is assumed to describe a sentiment that excludes, often violently, those who are not part of the community. In this view, patriotism is a 'rational' version of nationalism that focuses on civic issues and love for one's community, whereas ethno-nationalism or neo-nationalism describe an ostensibly darker 'emotive' type of nationalism that aggressively promotes ethnic ideas.

Such normative distinctions are highly problematic, since they obscure the underlying mechanisms that inform all group sentiments. The psychologist Michael Billig criticizes such practices, pointing out that patriotism often becomes synonymous for 'civic nationalism', but that, in order to function, such civic nationalisms require similar boundaries and mythologies as ethnic nationalism (2009: 48). To Billig, the term 'patriotism' is thus a misnomer, because 'even the most extreme of nationalists will claim the patriotic motivation for themselves. [ . . . ] The hatreds will be justified in the name of love' (2009: 57). Indeed, in the discourse of nationalism and patriotism, the two terms are often interchangeable. There may, nevertheless, be good reasons to distinguish these concepts analytically, but Billig is right to stress that, in much of the political rhetoric, patriotism tends to simply be what nationalists call their own nationalism, often with the intent to legitimate their identity claims and broaden or soften their appeal. This practice is particularly visible in China, where the authorities have indeed adopted a normative distinction that contrasts their own alleged 'patriotism', namely, the ideology of loving one's country/loving the state (*aiguo zhuyi* 爱国主义), with the 'nationalism' (*minzu zhuyi* 民族主义) of antagonists and ethnically divisive groups (Zhao 2004: 31), even though state-led 'patriotism' draws on strong ethnic distinctions and exploits often blatant prejudices.

The way in which group behaviour ties to the psychology of prejudice and exclusion raises serious concerns about a normative appraisal of sentiments like patriotism. The so-called intergroup attribution bias is a case in point (see Gries 2004: 100). All groups require 'others' who are not part of the in-group. As human beings, we are inclined to see the members of our in-groups positively, and when we encounter deplorable behaviour from group members, we write such behaviour off as the exceptional acts of a black sheep, or the acts of someone having a bad day. Yet, when we witness the actions of someone we perceive to be part of an out-group, we assume the worst of that person and draw the conclusion that this is typical behaviour from 'one of *them*'. Any evidence to the contrary—any positive behaviour on the part of our supposed antagonist—becomes the exception that proves the rule (Gries 2004: 100).

In many cases, these distinctions may not grow out of direct competition for resources or worries about personal safety, and they may not always lead to violent antagonisms: a book club may distinguish itself from non-members, or even from perceived antagonistic groups such as some local choir group, but it is unlikely that we will see book-club members involved in violent rows with music aficionados. Nevertheless, the antagonism is, in part, rooted in evolved psychological mechanisms that affect prejudice in intergroup dynamics. This is why it makes little sense to try and draw up 'good' versus 'bad' community sentiments. The two are intimately intertwined, and today's book club always carries inside it the seed to become tomorrow's 'Third Wave'.[10] In short, there can never be an in-group sentiment without some kind of out-group attribution, and it is part of our human evolutionary heritage that we draw up such self- and other distinctions wherever we find them. I return to such psychological mechanisms later.

In this context, it should be clear that Billig is right to criticize normative distinctions between patriotism and nationalism. The psychological underpinnings of these two sentiments are not as different as normative arguments claim. Both are forms of group loyalty; consequently, they are subject to similar social and psychological dynamics. Yet, even if we do not distinguish between different group loyalties based on normative criteria, there is an analytical distinction to be drawn between patriotic and national communities. Viewing oneself as American or Chinese is qualitatively different (though not mutually exclusive) from feeling strongly about being from New York or Shanghai, even though much of the underlying psychology remains the same.

Most analytical distinctions between patriotism and nationalism focus on the *object* of affiliation: in the case of patriotism this is believed to be the country, in the case of nationalism it is the ethnic group. However, as Anthony Smith (1991) has pointed out, this distinction is imprecise. Nationalism draws on both associations with a place (e.g., a 'homeland') *and* associations with ancestry.[11] Similarly, as I have discussed already, patriotism also evokes affiliation with a place (the city, the province, the river valley, etc.) while simultaneously suggesting kinship ties with the people who live in that place. In fact, such local patriotisms can create strong narratives of collective ancestry and collective purpose, for instance when New Yorkers trace their collective heritage back to a melting pot of earlier migrants, when Athenians view themselves as the bearers of democratic tradition, or when inhabitants of north-European coastal cities like Bergen or Hamburg evoke their 'Hanseatic' history. The distinction between a territorially bound group and an ethnically defined group is thus an extremely slippery one.

What, then, distinguishes a patriotic community from a national community? I believe it is the claim to political autonomy. As Smith argues, all national attachments demand 'autonomy, unity, and identity' (1993: 146). Whether we are looking at a long-established sovereign nation or a territorially defined group of people who aim to achieve a not-yet-realized independence, in each case we are confronted with a national community. A sense of pride in being Bavarian may be patriotic, but it contains within it the potential to become nationalist if Bavarian compatriots start to seek political independence. Such potential also exists in other territorially defined communities. If patriotic communities from cities like Hamburg, London, New York, or Shanghai claimed independence, their communities would become nations, much as the people of Singapore or Monaco consider their communities to be nations. Such a move of large cities towards nationhood is not as inconceivable as it may seem, as recent tongue-in-cheek debates in London demonstrate, where arguments for a 'Republic of London' have indeed gained popular traction in recent years (BBC 2011), especially in the wake of the Brexit vote. Claiming independence, in each of these cases, would mean claiming the right to maintain a set of political institutions for the purpose of autonomously governing the affairs of the territorially defined imagined community, and any movement in such a direction would consequently be nationalist.

In this sense, I agree with Smith's definition of nationalism as 'an ideological movement for attaining and maintaining autonomy, unity and identity on behalf of a population deemed by some of its members to constitute an actual or potential "nation"' (Smith 1993: 73). I will qualify below how nationalism's 'ideological' dimension connects with psychological mechanisms, but, in the present context, I want to highlight the claim to autonomy as a crucial element of national communities. All of the communities I have described so far are governed by organizational principles of some kind, whether it is the unwritten code of conduct of a book club or the highly sophisticated administrative mechanisms of a province or city. Patriotic communities like cities thus frequently have local polities of their own. However, my point is that the members of patriotic communities are not, and do not claim to be, politically sovereign in their own right. This claim is unique to nations and their specific polity: the nation state.

Much as there are liminal areas between what counts as an imagined or a patriotic community, the distinction between patriotic and national communities is also gradual. In fact, it is in the transition between patriotic and nationalist group attachments that many interesting political phenomena emerge. As my examples of Bavaria and London earlier suggest, patriotic sentiments can become the seed for nationalist movements. Allow me to illustrate this dynamic, along with the various conceptual distinctions I have been drawing up so far, by turning to a recent example: patriotism and nationalism in Hong Kong.

In 2015, a peculiar situation developed that had people in both Hong Kong and mainland China severely confused: student supporters of the democracy movement in Hong Kong had issued a statement in the run-up to the annual commemorations of the 1989 Tiananmen Massacre, stating that their student associations were not going to attend any of the vigils that take place annually in Hong Kong (see Iyengar 2015). Their justification was that the debates surrounding 4 July 1989 were a 'Chinese' matter, and, since they were 'Hong Kongers', the Tiananmen Protests and their violent break-up had nothing to do with them.

This statement caused strong condemnation from two unlikely bedfellows: liberal Hong Kong democrats who saw the PRC's communist government as their antagonist, and PRC citizens who saw Hong Kong as part of China. On both sides, the issue that caused confusion was how young students who spoke a Chinese dialect, wrote Chinese characters, looked Chinese, and lived by perceived Chinese cultural tenets could believe that they were anything other than ethnically Chinese. But herein lies the misunderstanding: people in Hong Kong—much like people in Shanghai or Beijing or Guangzhou—had long constructed a patriotic community around their local territory and their perceived collective heritage. What was now happening in Hong Kong was that part of the city's patriotic community had started claiming political autonomy, and this required the mental leap of turning this particular patriotic community into a national community, or, in Smith's words, claiming a Hong Kong 'ethnie' (1993: 21).

Nominally, Hong Kong is a special administrative region (SAR) within the PRC. It maintains its own state, but this local state is subordinated to the Chinese nation state. In mainland China, and in much of Hong Kong, the city is regarded as an inherent part of China, and Hong Kong's largest ethnic group is considered to be 'Chinese'. Indeed, the discourses in China and Hong Kong draw the same distinctions that I have criticized earlier, in which patriotism is an affiliation with a country and nationalism describes an affiliation with an ethnic group. With these concepts in mind, it is entirely plausible to many in China and Hong Kong that someone from the city could feel patriotism for the city, but it is generally considered politically incorrect to describe these sentiments as a form of nationalism, since this would suggest that Hong-Kong Chinese and mainland Chinese do not share the same ethnic ancestry.

However, the 2014 democracy movement in Hong Kong, and the social and political tensions that preceded it, demonstrate how such an understanding of patriotism and nationalism is based on a category error and is ultimately misleading. A major component of the movement has been the attempt to set the territory of Hong Kong and the people who inhabit it apart from the territory of the PRC, and this has been a decidedly nationalist activity in the framework I have outlined here. The consequence has been an odd rift between two groups from Hong Kong, both of which are, ironically, critical of PRC politics. To one group, Hong Kong is part of China, and criticism of PRC politics should be levied against the *state* of this specific nation, not against the perceived Chinese nation itself. In this view, commemorating the 1989 Tiananmen protests is a way to criticize the PRC government while hoping for a democratic future for the whole Chinese nation. To the second group, Hong Kong should be an independent entity; commemorating an event in mainland China indirectly signals membership in the national community of 'Chinese' and is consequently anathema to anyone claiming Hong Kong independence, whether implicitly or explicitly so.

Here, then, we have two groups of people, each feeling strongly about their homeland of Hong Kong, and consequently both acting patriotically. What sets them apart are fundamentally different nationalisms: one group felt nationalistic about Hong Kong, whereas the other group felt nationalistic about China. They each saw community autonomy located in a different place, and the objects of their nationalisms were separate imagined communities: one group wanted political sovereignty to lie with the city-state of Hong Kong, the other group wanted such sovereignty to lie with an overarching Chinese state. From this, it should be clear that patriotism and nationalism are indeed similar, since both describe sentiment that supports a particular territorially imagined community. However, there is an important difference. Nationalism is ultimately a particular type of patriotism. Whereas all patriotisms assert a common heritage in a territory (expressed, for instance, as a common idiom, a common history, common cultural and social practices, and so on), nationalism *additionally* makes claims regarding where political autonomy should be chiefly located. This brings me to the set of definitions that I employ throughout this book, and that I have compiled in Table 2.1.

I have drawn up these categories of communities and institutions to highlight two things: that communities are fundamentally similar, whether they are imagined or not; and that the way in which political institutions become attached to communities is a matter of social construction, power relations, and vested interests. In this sense, my definitions depart somewhat from the perspectives of previous scholarship.[12] Modernists rightly stress the ideological nature of nationalism, the social construction of nations and their states, and the role that elites play in creating and maintaining imagined communities. However, the modernist perspective tends to see these technologies as breaks with previous traditions that are not connected to general psychological predispositions but are established as part of a specific modern 'age'. Gellner, for instance, writes (1983/2006: 34):

> Contrary to popular and even scholarly belief, nationalism does not have any very deep roots in the human psyche. The human psyche

*Table 2.1* **Communities and Polities—Definitions**

| Community | Definition |
| --- | --- |
| Small-scale community | Any group of human beings with a common belief in a collective purpose, culture, history, or ancestry, in which the members maintain direct personal ties with each other. |
| Imagined community | Any group of human beings with a common belief in a collective purpose, culture, history, or ancestry, in which some members do not maintain direct personal ties with each other. |
| Patriotic community | Any imagined community whose members associate their common belief in a collective purpose, culture, history, or ancestry with a specific homeland. |
| National community | Any patriotic community that claims political autonomy. |
| **Institution** | **Definition** |
| Polity | Any formal set of political institutions that regulate human behaviour. |
| State | Any polity of a territorially defined community. |
| Nation state | Any polity of a territorially defined, imagined community that claims political autonomy. |

can be assumed to have persisted unchanged through the many many millennia of the existence of the human race, and not to have become either better or worse during the relatively brief and very recent age of nationalism.

As I outline in what follows, human psychology is critical to understanding how group attachments work, and bracketing this issue in the case of nationalism is unhelpful. On the other hand, primordialist and ethno-symbolist authors who indeed point towards psychological mechanisms to highlight the continuities between nations and earlier ethnic communities tend to de-emphasize how elites use power and resources to deploy the technics of the nation for their own ends. Such scholars frequently view nations as 'neutral' technologies that can be deployed for either good or bad (e.g., Smith 1993: 18)—a sentiment that clashes with the understanding of technology that I have presented here. This is ironic, considering how strongly ethno-symbolic approaches rightly make the argument that nations are constituted through communication technology.

# Mass Media and the Imagined Community

As I discussed previously, there are a variety of different imagined communities. Some predate the onset of modernity, as is the case with many religious communities and with what Smith calls 'ethnic categories'.[13] Other kinds of imagined communities, like the collective of people working for a transnational enterprise like Apple or Google, Chrysler or Toyota, Samsung or Xiaomi, emerged fairly recently, in conjunction with modern capitalism. In each case, however, the members of the community need a collective framework of meaning in order to recognize each other as members: a set of religious axioms and practices, a collection of corporate values and symbols, and so on. Imagined communities thus become 'imagined' because their members communicate a system of shared symbols through far-flung networks of interaction. As the media scholar John Thompson put it, 'we feel ourselves to belong to groups and communities which are constituted in part through the media' (1995: 35).

For example, what made Catholics an imagined community during medieval times was a system of religious symbols derived from a shared code of meanings, codified most notably in the bible, but traceable also throughout Christian art, literature, sermons, prayer songs, and so on. Anderson (2006: ch.2) makes this case in his discussion of religious communities and symbolic systems, and he goes on to outline how religious communities compare to other imagined entities like empires and nations. This is not to imply that the spread of religion did not also require an inordinate amount of physical violence, but simply to clarify that belief in a community has to be internalized by its members, and that symbolic interactions are crucial to that process.

The example of Catholic faith is further instructive in that it demonstrates that imagined communities are by no means fake or unreal—an argument that has frequently been made against Benedict Anderson's theory, and that could also be made against the concepts I present here. The critique is that talk of 'imagination' reduces the nation and other large communities to a set of immaterial, symbolic interactions and cognitive processes, thereby denying that the politics of nations are demonstrably grounded in real institutions, material production processes, and lived experiences. Who, for instance, would insist that a person held up at a nation-state border control is merely 'imagining' their plight?

However, this criticism is founded on two misperceptions. The first is based on a slippage between the idea of the nation and its nation state (see Guibernau 2004 for a discussion), which I hope my own definitions avoid. Border controls, military organizations, and so on are part of the nation state, not the nation; the nation is a community and not a polity. The second charge against Anderson is more serious, since it rightly points out how national communities rely on embodied ritual practices and material objects as much as on symbolic exchanges. However, this charge misrepresents Anderson's premise. Anderson (2006: 6) was specific about the idea that 'communities are to be distinguished, not by their falsity/genuineness, but by the style in which they are imagined'. His project has been to 'combine a kind of historical materialism with what later on came to be called discourse analysis' (Anderson 2006: 227), which brings him in close proximity with Foucault's attempts to show how conceptual frameworks and social practices ossify into real world institutions (e.g., Foucault 1978/ 1995).

As the example of Catholic institutions demonstrates, imagined communities are thus by no means illusions. Catholic faith allowed elites to connect a large number of believers, and real-world institutions played a major role in this process. The discourses of religion informed social interactions and rituals that reflected culturally and historically situated power relations, and these interactions, in turn, crystalized into organizations. The offices and hierarchies of the church, institutions like priestly celibacy, Sunday mass, annual holidays, and so forth, were powerful, premodern technologies for organizing a large community. Such a community could then be mobilized to act collectively, for instance to undertake large-scale construction projects such as cathedrals, or to go to war against outside groups, as was the case during the crusades. Imagined communities, like all communities, are always, at some level, enacted through rituals and social practices; they sediment into material objects, shape the use of other technologies, and have very real consequences.

Patriotic communities are also constructed through a common system of local symbols: a collective idiom, be it a language, dialect, accent, or individual 'native' phrases. While Gellner argues that non-national units like city-states 'seldom have a language of their own' (1983/2006: 14), and that this sets them apart from nations and their attempts to unify language, a collectively shared system of symbols does not have to be a unique language. Many imagined communities are multilingual. The main issue is that the community members think they share a mutual framework of *meanings*. A community's symbols and ceremonies are relevant because they 'embody its basic concepts, making them visible and distinct for every member, communicating the tenets of an abstract ideology in palpable, concrete terms that evoke instant emotional responses from all strata of the community' (Smith 1993: 77).

Nations are thus imagined through discursive and symbolic practices, which imbue members with a sense of community. Guibernau (2004: 134) has stressed that this sense of community relies heavily on the subjective feelings of its members that they share a common past. Control over the past is a fundamental cultural resource for building, maintaining, and legitimating nations and their polities. In Shapiro's words, 'the nation-state is scripted—in official documents, histories, and journalistic commentaries, among other texts—in ways that impose coherence on what is instead a series of fragmentary and arbitrary conditions of historical assemblage' (Shapiro 2004: 49). Nationalism, as a type of conscious-ness, draws from narratives of the past to present the fusion of nation and state as historically inevitable (Billig 2009: 17; see also Gellner 1983/2006: 121). It is thus in no small part the shared experience of mediated 'remembering' that lends the nation its cohesive power, and I return to this issue in chapter 5.

What sets nations apart from other communities, is that imagining a unity of people, culture, territory, and polity relies heavily on mass communication, and consequently on modern technologies that spread with the rise of capi-talism (Anderson 2006: 55). This includes print, which enabled the circulation of popular fiction and of national newspapers. Marshall McLuhan, for instance, believed that these technologies 'overlaid the complexities of ancient feudal and oral society' because of their 'typographic principles of uniformity, continuity, and lineality' (McLuhan 1964/2001: 15). Newspapers in particular contributed to a unified system of meanings among national elites, but they also created a sense of collective experience: the ceremony of reading the morning or evening paper. To Anderson (2006: 35), 'this ceremony is incessantly repeated at daily or half-daily intervals throughout the calendar', and this leads him to ask: 'what more vivid figure for the secular, historically clocked imagined community can be envisioned?' Anderson thus concludes that modern newspapers created a communal sense of 'empty time', meaning that individuals feel that events tran-spire simultaneously for all community members.

Yet, the written word is not the only medium that communicates nationhood. If this were so, the phenomenon of nationalism would be limited to literate elites alone. Granted, part of the national project has relied on elites to design edu-cational policies through the mechanisms of the state, partly to overcome the problem of illiteracy, partly to make sure that all citizens are indeed 'on the same page' of the national history and civic education curriculum (see Gellner 1983/2006: 33). However, nationalism is also communicated through statues and architecture, museums and exhibits, paintings and music, flags and currencies, celebrations and ceremonies, and much more (Smith 1998: 120). The symbols of the national community may seem banal, since they 'hardly register in the flow of daily attention, as citizens rush past on their daily business', but they have the profound effect of turning 'background space into homeland space' (Billig 2009: 38, 43).

Over the course of roughly the past century, the circulation of banal national symbols has increasingly been made possible through new media technologies such as radio, film, and television (Billig 2009: ch.5; Hardin 1995: 147). As Anderson writes, 'advances in communication technology, especially radio and television, give print allies unavailable a century ago' that enable elites 'to bypass print in propagating the imagined community, not merely to illiterate masses, but even to literate masses *reading* different languages' (Anderson 2006: 135, 140, emphasis in the original). Elites thus play a central role in creating as well as maintaining the imagined community of the nation, in part by producing a system of national symbols, in part by managing national mass communication systems. That said, the meanings of national symbols are not clear-cut, and they cannot be dictated top-down, even where elites labour under a different impression. In fact, the kind of propaganda that is visible in China is an example of specific national elites harbouring the idea that national symbols contain singular 'truths' that can and should be managed by a vanguard. The CCP's monopoly over the nation state and its mass communication system indeed assures that China's political elite remains without serious competition when it comes to the control of symbols, but much of the anxiety over digital technologies in China is rooted precisely in the idea that this monopoly might be challenged by new communication patterns. As Thompson points out, 'the political use of symbolic power' is a 'risk-laden and open-ended affair' (1995: 15). It takes the active co-operation of a wider population to create the sense of commonality that nations rely on, and how power works in such networked relations is a recurring issue throughout this book, particularly in chapters 4 and 8.

Nevertheless, control over communication technology places elites in very strong positions to relay and shape sentiments like nationalism. In my opinion, ethno-symbolists like Smith do not emphasize this relationship between power and communication technology enough, though they are right to be sceptical of approaches that view nationalism solely as a 'top-down' phenomenon. Nationalism is not simply indoctrination. The reason that communicating attachment to an imagined community like the nation is successful in the first place is that sentiments like nationalism are grounded in psychological and socio-behavioural patterns that are compelling to their members.

# The Psychology of Communities

As I have outlined so far, nationalism is the fundamental driver behind the nation state. It provides political actors with the ability to leverage the idiosyncrasies of human psychology and social interaction to create the cognitive foundation for a community that views itself as both culturally and politically cohesive. Nationalism, then, is a framework of thought, an ideology, and as such it 'comprises the habits of behaviour and belief which combine to make any social world appear to those, who inhabit it, as the natural world' (Billig 2009: 37). Russel Hardin has similarly argued that nationalism is a cognitive framework, and that it allows groups to acquire and manage scarce resources in the interest of the community (Hardin 1995: 14).

Understanding nationalism as a form of consciousness means that nationalism provides a cognitive map of the world, but also that it invites an emotional investment in that map. Feelings and emotions are crucial to how humans behave and how group dynamics work. The psychologist Dietrich Dörner writes (1996: 8):

> There is no thinking without emotion. We get angry, for example, when we can't solve a problem, and our anger influences our thinking. Thought is embedded in a context of feeling and affect, thought influences, and is in turn influenced by, that context.

Contrary to what rational choice approaches suggest, feelings and emotions are an intrinsic part of politics, even though this aspect has frequently been overlooked or ignored in political studies, at least until very recently.[14] This then is a departure from perspectives that view ideologies solely as 'text', or as sets of free-floating signifiers that are entirely arbitrary, and that avoid any connection with the human subconscious or the natural world. Indeed, as I have outlined earlier, ideational technologies artificially 'naturalize' power relations and social processes, but this is not to say that there are no natural processes to begin with. As Terry Eagleton (1991/2007: 38) has criticized, such a position would suggest that 'it is as though the machine runs itself'. Instead, it is important to acknowledge that ideologies rely to some extent on the idiosyncrasies of human nature, even if they cannot be reduced to this dimension. If this were not so, they would not be so successful (see Eagleton 1991/2007: 222–223).

Nationalism taps into human aspiration and needs, whether with regard to our social relations, our understanding of the complex worlds we inhabit, or our mastery of the tools and strategies that allow us to safely navigate our lives.[15] My argument is that any kind of group affiliation relies on such deep-seated psychological mechanisms, and I would suggest that we recognize four dimensions in which nationalism connects to human needs: existential needs, relational needs, a need for certainty, and a need for competence.

The first of these dimension deals with matters of subsistence and survival, that is, with the basic materialist or 'realist' concerns of being human. All humans seek to protect themselves from harm and want, and a need for food, water, shelter, sexual activity, and so on, is consequently a foundational driver of human existence. This need bleeds into group dynamics, in which the promise of protection is often a crucial element. Human beings are social animals not least because a social group potentially provides both safety from unpredictable risks and security from malicious outside threats. Group affiliation often draws energy from such risk and threat perceptions. This does not mean that we consciously join groups solely for safety and security reasons. It is also not to say that 'safety' and 'security' are entirely objective criteria on which we rationally base our decisions, even where they reflect very real, material needs; our sense of risk and threat is shaped by social processes.[16] An example is the frequent claim by nationalists that immigrants are taking away their jobs, their tax money, their housing opportunities, their potential sexual partners, and so forth. These claims may be demonstrably false, but they *feel* true to those who make them, and the reason for this lies in psychological dynamics that evolved in prehistoric times but that carry on to perniciously shape behaviours to this day.

The second psychological dimension that affects group affiliation is also closely related to issues of safety and security: the promise of social affirmation and group belonging. As Charles Tilly points out, groups provide a safe environment for 'high-risk, long-term activities such as reputation building, investment, trade in valuables, procreation, and entrance into a craft', and the 'networks thus formed and reinforced acquire strong claims over their members [ . . . ]. Since the very connections among members become crucial resources, external threats to any member become threats to the high-risk, long-term activities of all members' (2005: 57). Belonging to a group instils a sense of trust without which social interactions become extremely cumbersome, if not impossible. This trust may often be misplaced, but more often than not the general assumption that members of an in-group are trustworthy serves members of communities well. This is because groups create social pressures to not infringe upon group norms. As I have discussed already, offending someone in one's social network can damage the relationship and the offending party's reputation, and it can have long-term repercussions. However, social relations are not merely utilitarian: respect and trust feel rewarding, and all human beings have a need for social affirmation. Hugs are drugs, and a pat on the back—whether physically or metaphorically—provides important 'legitimacy signals' (Dörner 2001: 332).[17] On the other hand, disappointing someone's trust can elicit strong, negative emotions like shame and guilt.[18] These powerful emotions inform our quest for social affirmation, and they lead most people to not (or at least not visibly) frustrate the expectations of those with whom they maintain relationships. The wish for this kind of relational consistency provides strong glue for community cohesion.

The third kind of need that informs human behaviour is a need for certainty (Dörner 2001: 250). It can be profoundly unsettling and threatening to not know what is going on around us. In contrast, having a set of categories and theories available as to how the world works is comforting. Anthony Giddens has referred to this sense of certainty as 'ontological security' (see Giddens 1991: ch.2). What is interesting about communities is that they are constructed around shared 'world-views', and this, in turn, provides 'the hope of psychological wholeness', as Billig (2009: 137) writes. He goes on to explain that group ideologies like nationalism consequently offer 'the fragmented, disoriented person the promise of psychic security'. Similarly, to Smith (1993: 161), 'the primary function of national identity is to provide a strong "community of history and destiny" to save people from personal oblivion and restore collective faith'. Especially imagined communities and their ideologies have proven to be successful at providing precisely this sense of continuity and wholeness, for instance by promising to assuage fundamental anxieties about their members' mortality. This is equally true of religious frameworks as it is of nationalism, and the similarity between the two in terms of their rituals and ontological claims leads Marvin and Ingle (1999: 16) to conclude, 'the doctrines and ceremonies of nationalism clearly reference the sacred', making nationalism a kind of 'civic religion' (see also Anderson 2006: 10–11).

Whereas this need for certainty is a matter of making sense of the world (ontology), the fourth dimension I have in mind is a matter of *knowing* how to make sense of the world (epistemology). I have already explained how our need for certainty relies on an understanding of the world, how much of this understanding is socially generated in groups, and that this is achieved through a shared framework of symbols. Such a framework is not only useful because it creates certainty and order by clarifying what the world is like. It is also useful because knowing how to deal with the world creates confidence (Dörner 2001: 406). Equipped with an ideology, group members have the tools at their disposal to master the conceptual challenges of living in a complex environment, and this, in turn, yields a sense of competency; even where this sense of competency is actually deceptive (Dörner 1996: 187–189), it has the power to sustain group cohesion in the face of complex challenges.

What is more, there is comfort in knowing that the members of a group 'speak the same language'. This language can be German or English, Chinese or Spanish, but it can also be a more abstract set of shared background knowledge: for instance the collective understanding that flags and passports matter, or a shared knowledge of communal rituals and holidays. In any of these cases, being part of a community provides what Hardin calls 'the epistemological comforts of home' (Hardin 1995: 217). Being with one's 'tribe' obviates any cumbersome discussions of how we know what we know. As a group, we have already entered into an implicit agreement as to what principles of meaning-making we share.

Being part of communities then satisfies a number of profound human needs, and this is why community membership becomes such a fundamental part of our identity. This should by no means justify any specific kind of group. We are never just members of one group, and which of our many group affiliation matters is highly situational. We can get our psychological satisfactions from being part of a family, a circle of friends, a home town, a country, or even a group of people who hate being part of groups. However, while our sentiments for any such community are deeply natural and primordial, the communities themselves never are.

This is particularly important in the case of imagined communities, including the sub-categories of patriotic and national communities, which are qualitatively different from small-scale communities in that they have as their objects large, socially constructed entities. It is therefore indeed appropriate to call the ideas and sentiments on which such imagined communities are built 'ideologies' in the sense of false consciousness (Geuss 1981: 40–44). A sentiment like nationalism is parasitic of the psychological mechanisms that generally inform group association, such as the deep-seated human wish to feel a sense of 'belonging' or 'home' (see Guibernau 2013). This is why signalling membership in such an association, for instance by waving the flag or celebrating national holidays, is an existential matter for its members: it is a form of identity maintenance.

It is, then, precisely such needs for community that make us vulnerable to the deception that imagined communities are built on: that groups of people we will never know, and with whom we only share a small set of presumed commonalities, are, in fact, a direct extension of our small-scale kinship communities, for which they consequently deserve the same loyalty, love, and respect that we would award our closest family members. While the thoughts and feelings that people have for imagined communities like the nation are not false, the object that these sentiments attach to is falsely presented to members as a natural object for such sentiments. This is precisely the false attribution that Jackie Chan leverages in the song that started my discussion in this chapter: a song that suggests a seemingly natural continuity between the units of 'family' and 'nation state'.

Importantly, all who are involved in the collective deception of nationalism benefit from their involvement, albeit in different ways and to different degrees. Nationalists benefit psychologically and socially from being part of a national community. National elites, if they are, in fact, nationalists, benefit from the same mechanisms. At the same time, such elites also benefit from the opportunities afforded to them by advanced types of literacy, privileged access to communication technologies, and control over networks. These privileges allow elites to leverage community sentiments for their own ends, be they political (e.g., creating loyalty for certain people, institutions, or policies) or commercial (e.g., making money from selling nationalist culture). This interaction between elites and non-elites has strongly informed discussions of how nationalism works in China.

# Contemporary Chinese Nationalism

Chinese nationalism emerges as an influential ideological framework during the late imperial period, amidst complex attempts to make sense of the disruptive modernist developments that contemporaries saw themselves confronted with at the time and that were thrown into sharp relief as the last Chinese dynasty entered into disruptive conflicts with other empires, especially Britain and Japan. Debates during the late Qing (1644–1912) and the Republican period (1912–1949) were very much shaped by these experiences, generating struggles over what 'China' should mean and how this entity should modernize. As the historian Wang Hui (2014: 19) points out in the book-length introduction to his monumental intellectual history *The Rise of Modern Chinese Thought* (Wang 2008), 'China' (*Zhongguo* 中国) is 'an ancient concept that only in the modern era has been used to refer directly to a country', whereas 'over a long period of historical time, the population, geography, and the political communities referred to by this concept underwent continuous changes'.

Constructing the Chinese nation was indeed a conceptual challenge. The various dynasties had given their spheres of influence different names, which had covered rather different territorial expanses, not to mention peoples. Modern nationhood required, as Lydia Liu (2004: 77) puts it, 'the fabulation of a supersign *Zhongguo/China*', derived from earlier Chinese designations and foreign naming practices. Coming to grips with the diversity of peoples living within this new concept proved particularly challenging (see Leibold 2007). This was, in part, because the empire that served as the territorial template for the first nation state had been ruled by a dynasty of outsiders from Manchuria rather than by 'Han' Chinese; it was also, in part, because the terminology of 'ethnicity' still needed to be constructed.[19] From late Qing reformers like Liang Qichao through Republican figures like Sun Yat-sen to CCP leaders like Mao Zedong, the issue of how to govern a culturally and linguistically diverse entity such as the newly created China was at the core of the modernization efforts. For Sun Yat-sen, the Republic of China (ROC) would be a united 'Chinese nation' (*Zhonghua minzu* 中华民族), and he effectively viewed the Han majority as coterminous with 'Chinese' and assumed all other peoples of the newly founded country would eventually be assimilated (see Zarrow 2004: 215).

The CCP initially had a much more tolerant approach to ethnic unification, building on the idea of a 'multi-ethnic country' (*duoshu minzu guojia* 多数民族国家) to ultimately arrive at an idea of *Zhonghua* that incorporated 56 ethnic groups. This number was the result of a protracted process of categorizing ethnicities in the 1950s that was crucial to creating a unified, multi-ethnic PRC, and which Mullaney (2011: 543) has consequently called 'perhaps the largest social engineering project in human history'. Despite intentions to the contrary, CCP leaders would continuously struggle with the tension between multi-ethnic tolerance and ideas about assimilation throughout the PRC's history, and these struggles are today visible in unresolved and contradictory territorial as well as ethnic disputes (Hung 2016). Especially the popular idea of Chinese ethnicity, as a cultural category that unites diverse people around the shared Chinese script and an essence of ostensibly Chinese values such as peace and harmony, does not necessarily reflect the historical record (see Dirlik 2015; Lin 2009; Zhang 2001) and should be treated as primarily aspirational. In practice, debates over what counts as 'Chineseness' frequently make way for racial conceptions of ethnicity and nationhood (Friedman 1995; Leibold 2010), especially where 'Chineseness' then contrasts with 'the West' or 'Japan' (Gries 2004, 2005; Carrico & Gries 2016; Zhang 2017) or where perceptions of skin colour are involved (Frazier & Zhang 2014; Leung 2015). The idea of the 'Chinese nation' remains very much contested.

The complexities involved in constructing the modern Chinese nation, and particularly recent nationalist activities in the PRC, have led to recurring debates in Chinese studies over the question whether Chinese nationalism is a top-down or a bottom-up phenomenon, and over the role nationalism might play in Chinese policymaking. To understand these debates, it is important to recall that early nation-building attempts during the late 19th and early 20th centuries involved 'a relatively small elite who had access to books and ideas from the West and Japan, yet they sought to create a model for the nation that would enable them to mobilize all of China's vast population' (Mitter 2004: 118). The results were diverse, creative experiments, some designing the idea of a Chinese 'nation' along racial parameters, others using cultural rationales, yet others appealing to civic ideas to create China's 'New Citizens' (Mitter 2004: 118). These experiments were often intimately tied not just to anti-imperialist or anti-feudalist ideas but also to 'social issues like workers' rights, women's rights, and eventually peasants' rights' (Zarrow 2004: 364), and these issues, in turn, reverberated throughout PRC history, informing the often unapologetically paternalistic didactics of CCP attempts to educate 'the masses' and create patriotic citizens through state education and propaganda.

Contemporary Chinese nationalism is an excellent example of elite attempts to establish an imagined community through mass communication technology. It is, in many ways, a reaction to the PRC's accelerated modernity and rapid opening-up in the 1980s (Duara 2016: 421), and later to the traumatic break-up of the Soviet Union and the Tiananmen protests of 1989. This is not to say that nationalism did not play a role in uniting diverse segments of society under Mao, but the current discourse of a CCP-led Chinese nation overcoming a 'century of humiliation' at the hands of foreign forces is very much rooted in more recent patriotic education campaigns (Wang 2012). The CCP thus 'rediscovered' nationalism as 'pragmatic leaders began to wrap themselves in its banner, which, they found, remained the one bedrock of political belief shared by most Chinese people' (Zhao 2004: 213). To this day, the CCP strongly legitimates itself through its ability to guide China along its 'road to revival' (*fuxing zhi lu* 复兴之路, see Schneider & Hwang 2014b), drawing from past nationalist tropes in order to sell this dream of renewed national glory. This is evident in the state-led discourses of PRC mega-events like the Beijing Olympics with its opening ceremony (Barmé 2009), the Shanghai World Exposition with its towering China Pavilion (Schneider 2014b), but also more recently in the 2013 'China Dream' campaign (Callahan 2013) with its poster series, which creatively combines premodern concepts such as filial piety with Republican era aesthetics, Mao-era nostalgia, and contemporary symbols of progress (see Central Propaganda Department 2013).

Yet, as much as the CCP controls mass media in the PRC, it is by no means the case that Chinese citizens have simply been indoctrinated by elite discourses. The Party may have the ambition to define what nationalism means, and it deploys the power of the state to 'guide public opinion' along pragmatic lines, but the way these messages have been reworked by Chinese nationalists around the world challenges the idea that contemporary Chinese nationalism is purely an elite artifice established 'top-down'. Peter Gries has provided an important reality check to such conceptions, instead pointing out that 'both the Party elite and popular nationalists participate in nationalist politics, and both emotional and instrumental concerns drive their behavior' (Gries 2004: 87).

These controversies over the role of elite and popular nationalism in China are intimately tied to the question of how strongly and in what ways popular nationalism influences elite decision-making. Since the PRC lacks electoral mechanisms at the national level that might relay feedback from the governed to those who govern, how might public sentiment affect policymaking in China, particularly on issues of foreign affairs? One argument is that the CCP consists primarily of rational actors who largely remain in control of Chinese politics, and who are able to manipulate public sentiment to either improve their bargaining position in international affairs or to domestically signal their political alignments (see Weiss 2014; Wallace & Weiss 2015). In such interpretations, the Chinese state is adaptive and smart (Reilly 2012), and the leadership manages nationalism in a rational manner. In extreme cases, rationalist accounts make the argument that popular nationalist expressions such as online debates or street protests play no role in shaping the decisions of leaders, since such forms of expression wholly reflect 'the rational strategic calculations of the Chinese leadership' (Jie 2016: 160).

Much like the wider discussions about nationalism, these rationalist assessments of Chinese nationalism stand in stark contrast to accounts that highlight the importance of emotions in politics. Susan Shirk (2007: 63–63) stresses, 'for most Chinese, nationalism feels like a healthy act of self-assertion', and she argues these acts constrain how politicians can behave in the PRC, even threatening 'to unite disparate groups like laid-off workers, farmers, and students in a national movement' against the leadership. Gries and his colleagues (Gries, Steiger, & Tao 2016: 162) similarly question whether China's politicians are 'wise mandarins with the smarts to fully manage popular nationalism, perhaps even strategically manipulating it to improve their bargaining position'. Instead, they trace social media discussions about the East China Sea conflict in 2012 and show how military escalations on the part of the People's Liberation Army '*followed* popular nationalist protests against both Japan and the CCP party-state, suggesting—but not proving—that an autonomous public was one proximal cause of the Chinese government's escalation of the dispute' (Gries et al. 2016: 163, emphasis in the original). For Gries and his colleagues, it is the leadership's concern over political legitimacy that forces decision-makers to adjust their foreign policy choices to popular demands. To others, popular and state-led nationalism have largely converged 'as an increasing number of people in the state corridors of power find themselves sharing the views of popular nationalists' (Zhao 2016: 440). In either case, the dynamics between elites and citizens remain more complicated than rationalists argue.

As I show throughout this book, it is indeed problematic to view Chinese decision-makers (or any decision-makers) as principally rational actors who strategically manipulate nationalism to achieve desired effects. While I do not doubt that certain actors attempt to bargain and signal their way through politics, the manner in which nationalism influences political landscapes is not under any single actor's control. Some stakeholders are positioned more powerfully within the networks that generate and shape nationalist discourse, and some are directly responsible through technical and design choices for the forms that contemporary nationalism takes. That said, digital nationalism is ultimately an emergent property of complex interactions, not a coherent ideology that calculating actors create and then successfully deploy to indoctrinate the masses.

## Conclusion

In this chapter, I have argued that the nation and its nation state are technologies of modernity, and that they are sustained by the ideology of nationalism. This ideology is a particular type of patriotism that claims a homeland in the name of an ethnic group, and that insists this ethnic group should be politically autonomous. Like patriotism, nationalism is grounded in the same psychological processes that underlie all group affiliation, but it also shares the social and political dynamics that characterize other imagined communities. This includes the fact that the members do not know all other members, and that group cohesion therefore relies on a sense of communion that is built around shared symbols. These symbols are created and spread through mass media systems, in the form of discourse. They are deployed by elites to suggest a common culture and a common past, but they are also reworked through popular usage over time.

Contemporary nationalism in China is a useful example of these dynamics. Chinese nationalism has been promoted and to no small degree designed by elite actors, most notably political leaders, as part of their nation-building and nation-maintenance efforts. However, citizens rework, reinterpret, and redeploy the building blocks of this nationalism in their everyday personal quests for meaning and security, leading to highly diverse and idiosyncratic discourses of the Chinese nation that are not under anyone's full control. These discourses are powerful, since they push certain rationales onto politics that legitimacy-seeking political actors either internalize into their own belief systems or incorporate into their actions to make them acceptable to their constituencies.

If we are to understand contemporary nationalism, we need to ask what happens to these discourses when they are no longer merely transmitted through one-to-many mass communication channels, but also through many-to-many communication networks. As I have suggested here, we should not view technology as inherently good or bad, but we should ask how the use of technology is guided by three fundamentally important factors: design choices, the structural features of the political economy, and human psychology. These factors shape how suites of technologies like ICTs act upon other technologies, such as the nation and the state. A particularly illustrative example of this is the technology of the search engine, which provides the most common entryway into the digital networks of the web, and which is the focus of the next chapter.

# 3

# Filtering Digital China

If you Baidu it, you'll know it:

It is summer, and I am sitting in a cafe in a southern Chinese metropolis. Air-conditioned vapour is escaping through open windows and doors into the steamy heat outside, wafting away into sub-tropic vegetation. Young urbanites are lounging in spacious sofas and wicker chairs, iced lattes melting as they surf the web on laptops or text on their smartphones. I was originally meant to meet Lucy here, an editor at one of China's largest IT companies.[1] As it turned out, she had to fly to another part of China on urgent company business, so instead of seeing me in person she has agreed to discuss digital China via a popular chat app. At the moment, we are texting back and forth about Chinese search engines (*suosuo yinqing* 搜索引擎). 'Most recently', she writes, 'more and more people have started using Baidu's search engine to prepare for job applications, to answer questions they came across during the process. This is how widely accepted search engines now are: they solve 10,000 of your questions'.

What Lucy describes is a common phenomenon, not just in China. Search engines have become the 'switchboards of the internet generation', as the social media researcher and blogger Alexander Halavais (2009: 1160) puts it. They are one of the doorways through which we access information networks like the web. I have already discussed how nationalism relies on a trick of perception, a cognitive shift that prompts potential members of the nation who will never know each other to see themselves as part of a larger, imagined community (Anderson 2006). I have also pointed out that this cognitive feat is made possible through symbolic frameworks, and that these frameworks are shared through ICTs. As I show, search engines and their allied applications, such as digital maps and online encyclopaedias, play an important role in this regard.

This chapter turns to the entryways into digital China. I discuss China's search engine market, as well as the various products that the largest conglomerates offer to online users. I then take a look at the search interfaces and experiment with their search results, using queries about the Nanjing Massacre and the Diaoyu Islands to check how the different engines warp information on these topics. As it turns out, mainland China's search engines systematically reproduce the biases of the PRC's media ecology. Many of these biases are subtle, and some may even seem trivial, such as search engines returning results in a particular Chinese character script. The implication of these results, however, is that China's search engines largely filter topics through national frameworks of understanding. This outcome is informed by political decisions, economic rationales, and choices concerning the use of digital technology that form a particular 'media logic' (see Chadwick 2013), and in this case that logic sustains a predominantly national media ecology, conceived of by China's leadership as a 'sovereign' digital China.

## Filters of Knowledge

China's search engine environment is relevant in the context of national communities because search engines function as powerful knowledge filters. Community sentiment in imagined communities is always mediated. We know of the nation through national newspapers and television, and we interact with fellow compatriots in far-flung parts of the country through telephones and e-mail, video messages, and social media. While there are moments when we experience our nation-ness first-hand, for instance when we cross a border, we largely 'know' imagined communities through media. Our experiences with such communities are pre-filtered.

Of course, we never truly have unfettered access to the realities that we live in. All data in the outside world only makes sense to us once we transfer it to our inner world and attribute meaning to it. This can lead to interesting slippages in how we perceive the world around us (see Hoffman 1998), but for most purposes the process is ingeniously effective. Frith (2007: 134–135) sums this up as follows:

> Our brains build models of the world and continuously modify these models on the basis of the signals that reach our senses. So, what we actually perceive are our brain's models of the world. They are not the world itself, but, for us, they are as good as. You could say that our perceptions are fantasies that coincide with reality.

Every time we perceive anything at all, we are translating data into information, using sophisticated, albeit flawed sensory and cognitive organs to do so.

Communication technologies add an additional layer to the translation process. I am talking to you through the medium of text, which you translate into a conversation with me, an imagined person separated from you through time and space. In essence, this is true for any mediated information, including seemingly direct interactions such as phone conversations or Skype calls. Media technology provides a conduit for information, and the sum of all this information shapes how we make sense of the world.

This has both benefits and drawbacks. Most of our 'models of the world', to use Frith's words, are not based on our own first-hand experiences but on background knowledge, and this frees us from having to individually check and test every bit of information we come across for its validity. In most cases, we could, of course, check whether the knowledge we receive from a book page, a newspaper, or a conversation with a friend is indeed accurate, but most often it suffices to simply have that option and move on: if we trust the source enough, and if the information generally conforms with what we expect, we trade in constant fact-checking for the privilege of getting our information through convenient second-hand channels.

A sizeable amount of the knowledge that we possess of the outside world thus consists of what, in the introduction to this book, I have called discourse: communication practices that systematically construct our knowledge of reality and reinforce commonly accepted truths. We create such background knowledge by basing our 'models of the world' on a set of assumptions, and we receive these assumptions from other humans who have previously outsourced their knowledge, whether by transmitting it to us orally or in the form of anything from cave wall paintings or bamboo stripes to books and websites. We thus predominantly store and transmit knowledge in the form of cultural artefacts (Anderson 2006: 4; Sperber 1996: 82). This is also true for nationalism. In the previous chapter, I called nationalism an 'ideology', describing it as a set of assumptions that we internalize as background knowledge and that form a coherent cognitive framework for making sense of reality; in short, nationalism provides a model of the world. This model is communicated in the form of discourse, mediated through cultural artefacts. It is through discourse that nationalism 'travels' and that actors reconfigure knowledge of nations and nationhood.

Regardless of how effective specific kinds of artefacts may be at relaying knowledge, they require us to translate processes of the mind into other kinds of data and then back again to a human mind. Technological shifts that affect this translation process also affect societies more broadly, for instance if we are confronted with such vast amounts of information that we need to deploy selection mechanisms. Halavais (2009: 801) writes, 'we are essentially information-driven creatures, and when the primary way in which we navigate our informational world changes, it is fair to assume that those changes will pervade other parts of our culture'. ICTs thus serve as filters to what we know and how we know, or, in the words of Eli Pariser (2012: 237), 'when the technology's job is to show you the world, it ends up sitting between you and reality, like a camera lens'. Pariser goes on to stress, 'we tend to believe we have full command of the facts and that the patterns we see in them are facts as well' (2012: 1042), when really we are accessing the world around us through interfaces and, as discussed in the previous chapter, such technologies are not neutral.

The fact that modern humans are constantly receiving mediated information in this way has convinced some cultural critics that we have completely lost any connection to reality that we may have ostensibly once possessed, and that the symbolic systems through which we communicate are passing through so many layers of translation that they have become an inescapable machine of deception. The French philosopher Jean Baudrillard has referred to this machine as the  simulacrum, arguing that the symbols themselves have become the only reality we know, and that distinguishing between reality and ideology no longer makes sense. To Baudrillard (1983: 2), 'the territory no longer precedes the map, nor survives it. [ . . . ] it is the map that engenders the territory'.

Such interpretations provocatively draw attention to the level of mediation we live with today, but they also remain controversial. Personally, I am not convinced that they help us understand how perception, knowledge, and communication work. Contrary to Baudrillard's claims, reality is still very much 'out there' (Frith 2007: 182), and it is filtered and, at times, obscured by mediated background knowledge. Even if we can never have unfettered access to reality, we can analyse how this background knowledge is constructed, how it is used to legitimate certain politics, and who benefits from such activities.

Adherents to the idea that our world now only exists within information systems are, arguably, throwing out the baby with the bathwater (see Eagleton 1991/ 2007: 166), but the observation that ICTs shape the knowledge we rely on in our lives nevertheless remains important. Pariser (2012: 801) writes: 'Readers use Amazon. com. Searchers use Google. Friends use Facebook. And these platforms hold an immense amount of power—as much, in many ways, as the newspaper editors and record labels and other intermediaries that preceded them'. Halavais (2009: 2007) similarly comments, 'we rely on search engines to filter our results. It is important to understand that these filters, while they are generally not manipulable by individuals, remain subject to those who have traditionally wielded social power'.

This raises the question of how ICTs filter our perceptions. In his influential discussion of this issue, Pariser (2012) shows how a number of allied technologies interact to create 'filter bubbles' for users. This includes technologies like search engines, but, as I discuss in chapter 7, it also includes social media. A core force behind filter effects is the ambition of programmers and entrepreneurs to create ICTs that are as responsive as possible to users. This is today achieved algorithmically, through software products that track what individuals use them for and then extrapolate what future usages might look like. To a large extent, this involves our own consent. By logging into personal Google accounts, by explicitly allowing Amazon to place a cookie in our browser, by rating movies on Netflix, or by clicking the 'like' button on Facebook, we feed personal preferences and behavioural markers to the algorithms that then calculate what we might want to access next. In this sense, the idea of filtering information is not necessarily fuelled by sinister motivations to control users. In the face of an overwhelming amount of information, it is crucial to have mechanisms that can sort out the irrelevant while highlighting the useful. The promise of 'personalized' information access is attractive, and it is why most users are quite content to accept a certain degree of filtering: 'when personalized filters offer a hand, we're inclined to take it. In theory, anyway, they can help us find the information we need to know and see and hear, the stuff that really matters among the cat pictures and Viagra ads and treadmill-dancing music videos', writes Pariser (2012: 213).

In his view, our wish to retrieve salient information leads to three interrelated 'filter effects' that then act upon our perceptions (2012: 186–194). The first filter effect derives from the fact that personalization is, by default, about individual users and their preferences. Personalizing the experience of users is meant to help with individual media usage. If successful, it means that each user only experiences his or her own filters. What I see on my mobile phone, or on my personal computer, is different from what other users see on their devices. The second filter effect relies on the obscurity of the algorithms that govern our media usage. Personalization happens through mechanisms that are largely invisible to us, for instance when web trackers monitor our internet behavior without our knowledge. Even where we explicitly consent to inputting our preferences into filters, as is the case with music software that predicts which song a user might enjoy next, the exact workings of the algorithm are not visible. This can lead to the deceptive impression, as Pariser (2012: 186–194) writes, that 'the information that comes through a filter bubble is unbiased, objective, true. But it's not. In fact, from within the bubble, it's nearly impossible to see how biased it is'. Finally, the third filter effect is due to a 'shift in agency', as Pariser puts it. Whereas nonpersonalized media also frame our perception, audiences generally make a choice as to which media outlets will act as their filter (Pariser 2012: 186–194):

> When you turn on Fox News or read The Nation, you're making a decision about what kind of filter to use to make sense of the world. It's an active process, and like putting on a pair of tinted glasses, you can guess how the editors' leaning shapes your perception. You don't make the same kind of choice with personalized filters. They come to you—and because they drive up profits for the Web sites that use them, they'll become harder and harder to avoid.

While Pariser might be overestimating the degree with which media users actively and rationally choose their traditional news channels, he is right to point out that the ways in which algorithms 'push' certain information have a different quality than picking up a biased newspaper. This effect is especially influential in the case of search engines (see Becker & Stalder 2009), which suggest an objective ranking of relevance while actually stacking the deck according to invisible algorithms, undisclosed editorial choices, obscure corporate interests, and our own previous user behavior. The result is that these new 'gatekeepers' of information create subtle yet pervasive biases.

## The Digital Bias of Search Algorithms

A search engine, as Halavais defines it, is generally 'a system that indexes webpages', but more broadly it also includes 'a range of information environments and media forms, including multimedia and other content found on restricted intranets and individual computers' (Halavais 2009: 106). The purpose of such systems is to structure large amounts of digital content in ways that make it possible to retrieve information, and ideally to make such retrieval efficient. While there are numerous such systems in place today, the most famous and influential one is Google's search website. Google's search functionality is today allied to a number of other digital products and services, ranging from Google Maps to YouTube, which together form one of the world's largest IT corporations. In many societies, Google's market share 'is already a rounding error from 100%, and various sites report receiving an overwhelming share of both search and overall traffic from Google' (Edelman 2011: 32). Google has become a household appliance. In their introduction to a compendium of search engine research, König and Rasch (2014: 12) conclude, 'Googling is not only a word that made it to a number of dictionaries, it has become a social norm'.

What exactly counts as a 'bias' in search engines remains contested, and academics in legal studies or business economics tend to focus on intentional interventions by Google to favour Google services over those by competitors (Edelman 2011: 28–29). Unintentional effects receive consideration as well, but 'bias' tends to be understood largely in terms of choices that distort market competition, whether through human intervention or the way that algorithms are programmed to select data. Bias thus frequently refers only to own-content bias, suggesting that the problem is one of market distortions that disadvantage businesses and presumably 'rational' consumers. In the face of such criticism, it is easy to see how researchers at Google claim that 'only in instances when search engines abuse power to generate more revenue is there any risk of an information marketplace degrading' (Granka 2010: 369), and that since Google allegedly does not abuse its massive market monopoly, there is no problem of bias. Such statements remain highly contested, but whatever one might think of Google, the general premise of the discussion is here already faulty.

As I show, 'own-content bias' is indeed relevant, and market distortions are highly visible in Chinese cases as well, but focusing solely on issue of business competition ignores that media bias can have much more profound social and political implications. Search engines like Google are part of what Feuz and his colleagues have called 'semantic capitalism' (Feuz, Fuller, & Stalder, 2011)—an economic system that commodifies meanings—and this system relies on selling consumers the benefits of information biases. Bias should therefore not simply refer to negative bias, that is: a warped perspective or false truth that someone has intentionally manipulated for their personal gain. Bias is often unapologetically positive, in the sense of a warped perspective that confirms what I expected, or that provides what I was indeed looking for, and for which I consequently am willing to pay. Such a positive bias may even accurately reflect underlying social factors, such as the way that public opinion works in a networked society. However, it nevertheless remains a distorted perspective. I might, for instance, want to know more about an unpopular politician, and then receive only critical pieces of information. The critical perspectives may be correct, they may conform to what I personally think, and they may even reflect a larger consensus online. In short: the search engine may very well present me with a reasonable result in this case. However, if I am not seeing any divergent voices on the subject, my positive bias will provide me with only part of the story.

Moreover, if the nature of the bias is not transparent to me, I may labour under the false impression that the information I am receiving is indeed well balanced. As it turns out, most users are not aware that their search engine provides them with only part of the bigger picture. As far back as the early 2000s, users were 'not always clear about the concept of search engines, sometimes confusing them with Web browsers' (Hargittai 2007: 772); the fact that browsers and desktop software today often include search plug-ins, some of which install themselves without clear notification when users download services, is likely to have aggravated this problem of awareness. Even where users are aware of using search engines, they may be overestimating how knowledgeable they are about the underlying mechanisms of these applications. As Pariser (2012: 103) writes, 'In polls, a huge majority of us assume search engines are unbiased. But that may be just because they're increasingly biased to share our own views'. König and Rasch (2014: 13) make it clear why this is a problem:

> Search engines function as gatekeepers, channeling information by exclusion and inclusion as well as hierarchization. Their algorithms determine what part of the web we get to see and their omnipresence

fundamentally shapes our thinking and access to the world. Whatever their bias may look like, it is obvious that man-made decisions are inscribed into the algorithms, leading unavoidably to favoring certain types of information while discriminating against others.

It is therefore important to define 'bias' broadly, for instance as choices that 'systematically favor certain types of content over others' (Goldman 2006: 189; see also Jiang 2014: 217).[2] Such a broad understanding is useful, since it considers the discursive effects of information filters rather than only the much more narrow effects that filters have on the marketplace. Information bias distorts how we 'know' things, and I believe it does so in several ways (visualized in Figure 3.1). The first is through biases produced by our physical presence in the world and our interactions with the material structures that surround us. This 'material bias' is strongly related to the political economy and the capitalist logic that today governs it. The second path through which information bias works is social, reflecting our presence in human societies, our relations to others, the values that permeate the communities we inhabit, the rules and regulations that

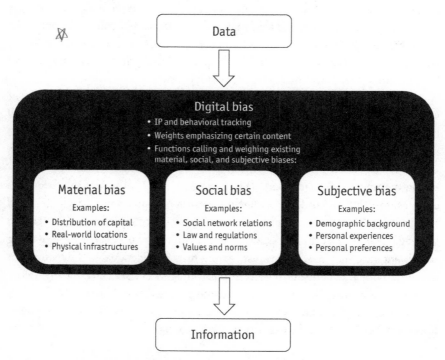

*Figure 3.1* Digital Bias. How data becomes information as it is filtered through algorithms that draw their variables and weights from material, social, and subjective biases. Florian Schneider.

govern them, and so forth. Finally, we are subject to our own subjective biases. These are the kind of biases that are introduced when we receive information vetted according to personal preferences. Subjective biases derive from demographic background, personal experiences, and psychological tendencies and aspirations.

These three types of biases—material, social, and subjective—are intertwined: our demographic background is intimately connected to the opportunities each of us received within the material world we were born into, for instance. Living a life of affluence shapes personal perspectives differently than living a destitute life. In a similar fashion, living in a rural environment is a very different experience than living in a city, and such differences affect the social and political patterns we are embedded in. None of this is new. What is novel, however, is that these different biases are today systematically mined for data points that may or may not reflect our actual life experiences, and that these data points are then weighted algorithmically to create obscure yet powerful mechanisms for filtering information. This is what I call 'digital bias': the provision of selective information by digital media technologies that systematically draw on and assess the salience of data, based on algorithmic interpretations of material, social, and subjective biases. Such digital bias results from the ways that the circuits of microchips are programmed to create specific logic gates, such as when the algorithm of a social media site or search engine returns one set of results rather than another. Like many types of biases, digital bias is not by default positive or negative. Bias is inherent to all algorithms, since any selection and manipulation of data requires choices. The question is how digital biases draw from and reshape the other three types of biases.

In this model, digital biases mediate material, social, and subjective biases. An algorithm thus draws from the variables that create these other distorting effects, and it then relates and weights them in ways that increase, decrease, recombine, or reshape their influence on the information we receive. If I am only able to see the world as consisting of nation states because I have experienced that world primarily as a series of border crossings, then I am subject to a material bias. If I believe that my nation is great because my family members and close friends say so, my high school textbook taught me so, or the evening news broadcast suggests this, then I am suffering from a social bias. If I hold this same belief because it provides me with comfort, then I am exhibiting a personal bias. In most cases, my bias will be informed by a combination of these factors. However, if my digital television repeatedly pushes a particular vision of the nation to my screen, based on programming that recognizes my past comfort zones or extrapolates what is popular in my social network, then a digital bias is at work; a bias that combines these other biases according to relations between variables and weights that are not visible to me.[3]

In short: the fact that the TV programming is biased is both a material and a social issue, the fact that I have a personal preference for that worldview is a subjective bias, and the way that technology relays these factors to me is a digital bias. These biases come together in search engines as well—with different intentions, at times as side-effects, but always in ways that shift what we can know.[4] In the Chinese case, such search engines draw heavily from national biases.

## China's Search Engine Environment

In most countries the online search process is dominated by Google. The Chinese situation differs markedly in this regard. The Chinese state carefully regulates market activity in core industries like ICT, and companies that deal in information and communication have to subject themselves to the CCP's overarching propaganda and censorship regime. I examine the governance of digital China in more detail in chapter 8. For the present discussion, it is important to note that the authorities' strategy for managing ICT is framed as an exercise in 'internet sovereignty' (*People's Daily* 2016), providing a decidedly national framework within which digital technologies are meant to be deployed. This includes measures that keep foreign services at bay while simultaneously promoting carefully monitored domestic alternatives. Clay Shirky (2015: 290), in his study of the Chinese IT company Xiaomi, has rightly stressed how the rationale behind this strategy to block foreign services is both political and economic: 'The blockade, in place since 2006, simultaneously prevents Chinese citizens from having access to communication tools that the government can't censor or shut down, and provides a competitive space for homegrown social media to flourish'.

In practice, this strategy has two implications: the first is that, with state encouragement, various Chinese firms have developed domestic alternatives to internationally successful media services. Instead of Facebook, Twitter, Wikipedia, or WhatsApp, Chinese users have Renren, Weibo, Hudong Baike, and Weixin at their disposal. This is not to say that these domestic services are mere clones. In fact, they address local demands and tastes in often ingenious ways, for instance by emphasizing features that are particularly popular among Chinese users, such as photo-sharing, casual games, or point systems that reward participation. Overall, however, the privileged starting position of these companies, as well as the collaborative relationship that they maintain with state agencies, creates high entry barriers to the Chinese market, especially for foreign competitors. Social media rely on social networks, and once users have established such a network on one service, it becomes impractical for most to reproduce their profile and their network on a redundant new service.

The second implication of current PRC media policy is that foreign ICT firms that indeed wish to take up the challenge and compete in China have to conform with often invasive government requirements, for instance by making user data available to the authorities. Otherwise, foreign companies face sanctions and can conceivably lose their license to operate in the PRC. Google pre-empted such consequences when it left the Chinese market in 2010, ostensibly as a reaction to Chinese hacking attempts on the Gmail accounts of human rights activists and as a form of protest against the Chinese government's position 'that self-censorship is a non-negotiable legal requirement' (Drummond 2010). Considering Google's willingness to conform to censorship requirements elsewhere (whether in Thailand or Zimbabwe, in Turkey or Germany; Goldman 2015), it is unlikely that the market exit was motivated by moral qualms over betraying the company motto to 'do no evil'. It is more likely that the Chinese market with its home-grown services proved harder to crack than the Californian company had anticipated, and that self-censorship in mainland China was simultaneously becoming a PR liability. Be that as it may, the company now offers Chinese-language services through its Hong Kong-based URL, but both the search engine and its related products (Gmail, the Google app store, etc.) were blocked within the PRC at the time of writing.

Chinese users can still access Google services by deploying virtual private networks (VPNs) and other techniques for circumventing internet barriers, but aside from such work-arounds China is effectively a Google-free zone, and users are confined by government policy and domestic economic dynamics to the national setting. Within this setting, users are offered a number of local search engine alternatives. First and foremost among these is Baidu 百度, which, according to one Chinese-based market research firm, attracted by far the most search traffic in 2014: of all queries made within China, 56.33% went through Baidu search (CNZZ 2014). In second place was Qihoo's engine '360 Search' (*360 sousuo*; 360 搜索, known throughout 2015 as 'Good Search', *Haosou* 好搜), with 29.01% of the queries, followed by Sohu's 'Search Dog' (*Sougou* 搜狗), with 12.75%. While there are numerous other search engines in China's market, including the state-run service 'ChinaSo' (or 'China Search': *Zhongguo sousuo* 中国搜索; see Jiang & Okamoto 2014), none of these attracted more than 1% of China's search traffic.

Chinese search-giant Baidu and its competitors follow a similar business strategy as foreign ICT firms like Apple or Google—a strategy generally referred to as 'lock in'. A lock-in approach aims to keep users 'locked' within the product range of a single company, for instance by linking hardware, a browser, or an app platform to other web-based and cloud-based services by the same proprietor. Since much of the profit in today's ICT industries comes from user-generated data, it is most lucrative when users never leave the confines of the home company's data-collecting product range. In this sense, as Pariser (2012: 564) writes, 'Gmail, Gchat, Google Voice, Google Docs, and a host of other products are part of an orchestrated campaign for Google lock-in'. Emulating this practice, Baidu, Sohu, and Qihoo each try to provide services ranging from digital maps to online encyclopaedias, from file-sharing to video hosting sites, all tailored to keep users committed to the respective company. For these enterprises, part of the strategy has been to use their search engines to promote their own services, and in the case of Baidu this has led to China's first anti-trust lawsuit in 2011, in which 'competitor Hudong Baike [a Chinese Wikipedia-like site], [ . . . ] sued Baidu for US\$124 million for demoting the site's ranking in favor of Baidu's own encyclopedia service' (Jiang 2014: 217). To what extent the discourses of these different encyclopaedia services differ when it comes to issues of the nation is a question I return to in chapter 5. With regard to the search engines, it is worth highlighting that their digital bias is often motivated to no small extent by commercial concerns.

The example thus already highlights how China's search engine industry produces substantial bias. The conflict between Baidu and Hudong is over a classic case of 'own-content bias', a largely material bias that stems from the way competition works in the political economy of digital China. I provide further concrete examples of this later. However, other types of bias are also programmed into China's search engines. A prominent practice has been for search services to promote the websites of paying clients in their rankings, but in ways that are not transparent to users. In her path-breaking work on search engines in China, Jiang Min (2014: 214) finds that whereas 'Google displays ads separate from organic results', Baidu 'continues to mix "promoted" results with organic ones in China', leaving users in the dark about the financial incentives that inform Baidu's search rankings.

Despite this strong prevalence of commercial imperatives, political intervention should not be underestimated as a source of bias. The authorities regularly communicate with commercial information gatekeepers like search engine companies about the topics that the CCP considers taboo, and the companies then work these guidelines into their search practices. The result is that certain sensitive keywords, for instance 'Taiwan', 'Tibet', or 'Tiananmen' produce decidedly warped results. To provide an example, I have reproduced below two searches for the Chinese word 'Tiananmen' (天安门), the 'Gate of Heavenly Peace' in Beijing. The first search used Baidu (left), the second used Google's service in Hong Kong (right). Since Google's service is blocked from within China, I used a Dutch IP address for these searches, but I also deleted the browser history before each search to limit the degree of personal bias. The results are represented in Figure 3.2.

*Figure 3.2* Searching for Tiananmen. Top search results for the Gate of Heavenly Peace in Baidu (left) and Google (right), using Chinese characters (天安门, top) and Pinyin transliteration (Tiananmen, bottom); screenshots taken on 20 October 2015. Florian Schneider.

What is striking about these results is how starkly they differ. Google's rankings provide generic information about the gate and the eponymous square, but they also offer links to additional information on the Tiananmen Protests of 1989. Pictures like the famous 'Tank Man' image appear in the prime real estate of the browser, in the visible part 'above the fold', where users do not need to scroll down to view information. Baidu, on the other hand, does not reference the events of 1989 at all. Instead, the Chinese search engine shows restaurant and travel trips, as well as sanitized historical information about the famous gate and square.

The contrast is even more pronounced when searching for 'Tiananmen' in Latin script. Google now presents information solely in English, and the protests are the predominant focus of the search results. Of the results above the fold, half deal with the events of 1989. Of the results below the fold (not represented in Figure 3.2), four out of the five remaining links provide information on the protests: one is an entry for 'Tiananmen Square Incident' in the Encyclopaedia

Britannica, one is a commemorative article for the 26th anniversary of the event that shows '25 photos from the bloody protests in Tiananmen Square', one is a *South China Morning Post* article titled 'Tiananmen Square Crackdown', and the final one is a *Time* article titled '5 Things You Should Know About the Tiananmen Square Massacre'. The remaining result provides a link with travel information. On Baidu, on the other hand, the word 'Tiananmen' again produces images of the gate as well as travel advice and historical information in simplified Chinese. In fact, only one entry is not in Chinese: the English entry for 'Gate of Heavenly Peace' in Wikipedia, which appears below the fold.

One could argue that the Baidu results are not too peculiar, considering that the search term was merely the name of the gate rather than a term more explicitly linked to the events of 1989. However, two additional searches demonstrate the degree to which the Tiananmen issue is sanitized by the Chinese search giant. A Chinese query for 'Tiananmen Incident' (*Tiananmen shijian* 天安门事件) produces links to the Tiananmen protests on 5 April 1976, at the end of the Cultural Revolution, but no information on 1989. A search for 'Tiananmen 1989', in turn, provides links to the parades commemorating the 40th anniversary of the PRC. Only a Chinese-language search for 'Tiananmen Incident 1989' produces any mention of the events, in this case two links to official CCP articles that present the protests as 'counter-revolutionary riots' (*fangeming baoluan* 反革命暴乱).

This bias on Baidu is stark indeed, particularly when compared to Google's results. Of course, Google's representation of the 1989 Tiananmen Protests is also biased: on the one hand, it introduces a political issue where more trivial information on the Gate of Heavenly Peace might be called for; on the other hand, the search engine provides predominantly information that sides with the accounts of dissidents and activists while eschewing the official PRC narrative entirely. Both of these effects may reflect the most common search-and-click behaviour of Google's users, but the result is nevertheless a one-sided representation of the issue. That said, and whatever one might think of the 1989 Tiananmen Protests and their representation in non-Chinese sources, there is a marked qualitative difference between providing a skewed version of the events and providing hardly any version at all. Deleting reference to public controversies impoverishes or even forecloses potential debate. If we were to take Baidu's query results at face value, then the 1989 protests never happened, or they merely represent a minor, misguided right-wing revolt against a benevolent ruling party. The same impression is created by the other prominent commercial search engines in China, Search Dog and 360 Search, with almost identical digital bias. In this fashion, mainland Chinese search engines provide highly specific and arguably impoverished windows onto political issues, and these windows clearly show a view that coincides with the one that China's leadership promotes as a national norm.

# How China's Search Engines Reproduce Systemic Information Biases

Chinese information gatekeepers carefully censor what users are able to access, particularly when it comes to controversial topics like the Tiananmen Protests of 1989. The question remains how companies like Baidu, Sohu, or Qihoo represent topics that are not taboo, such as China's conflict-laden history with Japan. More importantly, what role do Chinese search engines play when it comes to representing the imagined community of the Chinese nation?

To answer this question, I conducted a study in April 2015 that compared the search results for five different search engines. Throughout that month, once per week, I systematically queried Google.com.hk, Baidu.com, Sogou.com, and Haosou.com (i.e., today's 360 Search, then known as 'Good Search'), as well as the state-run engine ChinaSo.com, using two Chinese search terms related to disputes with Japan: 'Nanjing Massacre' (*Nanjing datusha* 南京大屠杀) and 'Diaoyu Islands' (*Diaoyu dao* 钓鱼岛). For each search, I deployed a research browser, in this case a version of Firefox cleaned of all personalized data. To simulate what these queries would look like from within China, the browser ran its queries through a proxy server that emulated searches from a Beijing-based IP address. Exceptions were the Google queries, for which I simulated the searches from a Hong-Kong–based computer. In each case, I logged the results and then examined each link on the results page. I also identified the IP address behind each listing, traced the geo-locations of the individual websites, and (where possible) logged their institutional affiliation.

Drawing inspiration from the visualization in Rogers (2013: 102), I have reproduced the search results in the chart in Figure 3.3 below. Looking at these results across search engines, it quickly becomes clear that 'own-content bias' is a major factor in how the various companies compile links (see also Jiang 2014: 224–226). Baidu consistently lists its own services among the top ranks of the page, but it is hardly the worst offender in this regard: Search Dog and 360's Good Search each reserve the prime real estate of their results page for in-house content (roughly, the first five links 'above the fold' of a standard browser window). This typically includes links to an affiliated encyclopaedia, to the provider's image and video archive, to the 'news' or 'new content' section of the respective search engine, and, occasionally, to allied social media. The results also contain content from other providers, especially links to video sharing sites like Douban or Youku Tudou and to official CCP or PRC sources, but these links are frequently listed at lower ranks.

To give a better impression of this bias in favour of in-house services, I have calculated how content from different sources was distributed across the various

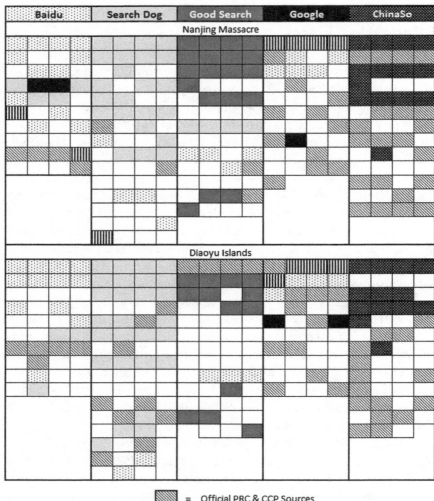

= Official PRC & CCP Sources

= Wikipedia

*Figure 3.3* How Different Search Engines in China Produce Results on Japan. Search results for two Chinese terms across five search engines. For each search engine, the columns represent different days (weekly queries throughout April 2015). The lines represent search ranks, and the cells' shading represent content associated with the respective company or institution as well as official CCP or state-media content. Florian Schneider.

queries, and I have visualized the results in Figure 3.4. For each source, I have aggregated all links that were either directly affiliated with the respective search engine company, or that directed users to an allied service (for instance, Sohu content includes all Search Dog services as well as content on Sohu's video sharing and social media services; Google content includes all Google services as well as content hosted by the subsidiary YouTube, etc.). I have also

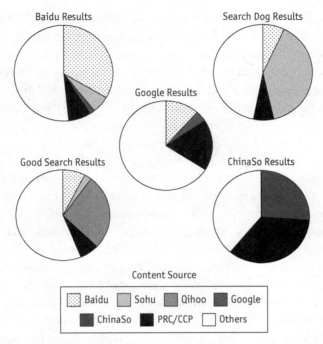

*Figure 3.4* Content Distribution and Own-Content Bias Across Five Chinese Search Engines. Percentages reflect the number of links affiliated with a particular source as a proportion of the total amount of links that the respective search engine returned on its first page across eight queries (total number of links: 80 for Baidu, 117 for Search Dog, 103 for Good Search, 81 for Google, and 103 for ChinaSo). Florian Schneider.

provided a measure for official content that was produced by either PRC or CCP institutions, for example, Xinhua News Agency, China Central Television, the *China Youth Daily*, and so forth. Included in this figure is also official content that appeared on commercial platforms like Sina News.

Of the four commercial search providers, Search Dog exhibited by far the largest own-content bias: 39% of the links directed users to in-house services. 360's Good Search and Baidu were roughly tied in second place, with, respectively, 31% and 30% of their content coming from their home company itself. The only true outlier is Google, which listed affiliated services only 4% of the time. All of these companies were eclipsed, however, by the state-run search engine ChinaSo, which pushed affiliated content 60% of the time (26% hosted on ChinaSo itself, and 34% coming from allied CCP and PRC sources). In fact, ChinaSo only once listed content hosted on one of the other four search providers, on Sohu News, and this was a Xinhua article.

In short, content from competing search providers takes a backseat on all search engines, with the exception of Google, which actually listed as much Baidu content as Google content. This is particularly noticeable when it comes to encyclopaedic entries. Baidu generally lists articles from its Wikipedia-like 'Encyclopaedia Baidu' (*Baike Baidu* 百科百度) among the first items. In fact, for the two queries, 'Nanjing Massacre' and 'Diaoyu Islands', Baidu always returned its in-house encyclopaedia entry first. This pattern is mirrored by Search Dog and 360's Good Search, which each privilege their respective Wikipedia-like services: 'Encyclopaedia Search Dog' (*Baike Sogou* 百科搜狗) and 'Encyclopaedia Good Search' (*Baike Haosou* 百科好搜; later renamed into '360 Encyclopaedia', *360 Baike*, 360 百科). Moreover, whereas Baidu lists competing knowledge archives like Wikipedia, Encyclopaedia Search Dog, or Hudong's encyclopaedia (*Hudong Baike* 互动百科) in its lower ranks, its competitors rarely do so. Search Dog listed the Baidu encyclopaedic entry for 'Nanjing Massacre' for all four searches, but, on average, placed the link at position 12 out of 15. For the Diaoyu Islands, the search engine returned entries in Encyclopaedia Baidu twice, at the bottom of its rankings. Only once did Search Dog return a Wikipedia entry (for the Nanjing Massacre, in the last slot of its result page), and it never listed a Hudong, Good Search, or ChinaSo encyclopaedia entry. As for 360's Good Search, across all eight queries, the search engine never once listed another encyclopaedic service. Its rare links to Search Dog and Baidu resources directed users to Sohu TV and to Baidu's web forum Tieba 贴吧. If the knowledge aggregator Hudong Baike felt that Baidu's rankings systematically discriminated against its encyclopaedia, one can only wonder what the company must think about its utter absence in the rankings of Baidu's competitors.

Aside from such own-content bias, all search engines reproduce the systemic biases of China's media system. Each carries an inordinate amount of official content, and in all cases materials from CCP or PRC sources appeared more frequently than materials from commercial competitors (the exception being 360's Good Search, for which official content and materials from Baidu where roughly tied as the second most relevant group of sources). Ironically, of all the commercial search engines, Google Hong Kong produced party and state materials most often (18% of the time), and often among the top results, skewing representations of Japan-related issues heavily towards the official position. The reasons for this likely lie in the fact that official resources are so prominently represented in digital China that Google's search algorithm returns them as the most appropriate (read: powerful) sources—an issue I return to in the next chapter. Be that as it may, the consequence is that with Google Hong Kong the Chinese authorities have blocked the search service that, in this case, was actually the strongest provider of official Chinese information, following the unpopular state-run search engine ChinaSo.

The question still remains what the relevance of the search engine biases is when it comes to mediating the idea of an imagined community like the nation. Considering the strong own-content biases, one might assume that, at the very least, the different search engines each provide their own unique perspective, and that those four perspectives contribute to a diversity of worldviews that may not collapse into a single national narrative. However, a closer content analysis reveals that, overall, the search engines privilege a particular kind of authoritative content that predominantly reiterates official positions on matters of political relevance. Outside of in-house content, the search engines may rank sources differently over time, but similar resources appear across all search engines, ultimately directing users to a consistent and relatively small range of actors. I examine these actors, their discourses, and their use of digital media technologies in the next three chapters to show how they construct and reproduce national frames of reference. Yet, one need not follow the links that search engines return to see how these digital filters relay a sense of national communion.

## Banal Biases and China's Imagined Community

What, then, do search engine biases imply about digital nationalism in China? An important part of the answer lies with the general characteristics of the search engine results and the way that these characteristics contribute to the construction of an imagined community. Many of these characteristics seem relatively banal at first sight, but recall from the previous chapter that banal factors can play a crucial role in creating a sense of community (Billig 2009). Seemingly trivial elements often make discourses appear natural, and they prime users to accept specific background knowledge as given.

Take, for instance, the role that geography plays throughout the searches. When searching for a key term like 'Diaoyu Island', the biases that search engines draw from create subtle nationalist effects. Two services that are repeatedly returned for such searches by mainland search providers are particularly instructive in this regard. The first is travel websites. Search Dog in particular tends to list the website 'where to?' (*qu nar* 去哪儿) as one of its top results, providing a specially embedded interface, or 'widget', so users can access the travel service from within the results page. Intriguingly, the search prompt for that service is already automatically completed to list the Diaoyu Islands as the travel destination. The search engines recognize the query term as a geographical place, prompting the display of the travel widget, which then fills in the corresponding location. This is a bizarre algorithmic outcome, considering that the islands are inaccessible. In fact, following the link of the travel website leads to an error. The information in the search results thus has no practical value.

Another similarly peculiar search result is the national weather service China Weather (*Zhongguo tianqi* 中国天气), which both Baidu and Search Dog return by default for all Diaoyu Island searches. Again, considering that the islands and

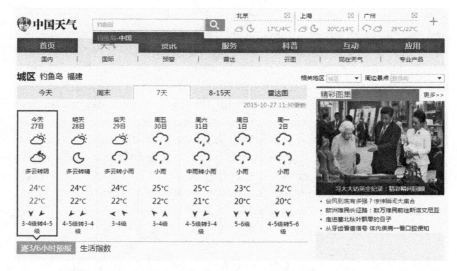

*Figure 3.5* National Weather for Contested Territories. 'China Weather' information for the Diaoyu Islands, screenshot October 2015. The header reads 'city area—Diaoyu Islands—Fujian Province', the automated search prompt provides the category 'Diaoyu Islands—China'.

their surrounding waters are off-limits, the information has little value. After all, China's navy or the regional fishing industry are unlikely to draw nautical advice from this weather widget, raising the question of why this service is listed at all. As it turns out, the weather service and the search engines here produce a peculiar digital bias, based on an algorithmic combination of geo-locative factors and pre-programmed national parameters. The result is a listing of the Diaoyu Island 'city area' (*chengqu* 城区) in Fujian Province, which is the mainland province that is geographically closest to the contested territories (Figure 3.5). The national weather service thus lists the islands alongside other domestic locations (Beijing, Shanghai, and Guangzhou), and it juxtaposes the weather forecast with national news items like Xi Jinping's diplomatic efforts, effectively normalizing the argument that the islands are a part of the PRC. In fact, entering the term 'Diaoyu Islands' in the search prompt of the weather service itself auto-completes the query to read 'Diaoyu Islands China'.

By embedding travel and weather information of this sort on the results page, search engines like Baidu or Search Dog suggest that these inaccessible, contested territories are a place like any other. More importantly, they are a place like any other *Chinese* place.

While this particular digital bias is relatively subtle, other aspects of the search results prime users more forcefully to view information through the lens of imagined communities. Most noticeable is the geographical and language bias in the results that the mainland search engines return. For both search queries, the results were exclusively in Chinese, and they came predominantly from mainland Chinese companies and institutions (Google's results were, again, an outlier). There are exceptions to the rule, for instance when searches for the Nanjing Massacre return resources at the Chinese University of Hong Kong, or when queries for the Diaoyu Islands provide news reports from Hong Kong–based Phoenix TV. However, none of these sources contradicts the official accounts in the PRC, and news providers like Phoenix in fact target the mainland specifically, conforming to PRC media regulations and using simplified character script to appeal to audiences there.

The issue of character scripts is particularly noteworthy: by default, all of the PRC search engines returned sources only in the simplified script that is dominant in mainland China. This is not merely the case for searches that used simplified characters. Even when queried in the traditional script favoured in Hong Kong, Taiwan, and many overseas Chinese communities (e.g., for 釣魚島, 南京大屠殺, or 釣魚台; the latter being the phrase for 'Diaoyu Islands' popularly used on Taiwan), the mainland Chinese search engines only return simplified script. The traditional character query is simply transposed into simplified script—a manipulation that Baidu and 360's Good Search each explicitly mark by printing the edited characters in bold script, but which remains implicit on Search Dog and ChinaSo. The only search engine that provides any traditional character results is Baidu, which lists a short compilation of 'news' links in traditional script in the bottom section of its search page. However, these links all point to mainland sources like the official *People's Daily* or *China Net*, which have simply been transposed into traditional script, likely to attract overseas audiences to these mainland offers. Media sources from Taiwan or Hong Kong hardly appear at all, and only if they are allied to official PRC media or are writing for a mainland audience.

This particular bias also extends to English-language searches, though not as prominently. While Baidu, Search Dog, and 360's Good Search each list English-language sources, the links direct overwhelmingly to materials authored in the PRC, for instance by Xinhua News Agency, *China Daily*, the *Global Times*, or the official Chinese broadcasting services China Radio International and China Network Television. That said, all three commercial search engines listed English Wikipedia entries, for instance the article on the island disputes, and these entries were accessible from within the PRC at the time of writing. Information that diverges from the PRC discourse is thus available, albeit in the lower sections of search results, sandwiched between mainstream sources from the mainland. The only search engine that did not list such links was ChinaSo. In fact, it did not list any English materials whatsoever, even when queried in English.

## Conclusion

Force of habit:

On an overcast summer day in 2015, I am meeting Kevin—a young, dynamic entrepreneur from a large Chinese coastal city, who successfully founded his own online company. Within only five years, he managed to turn a start-up that was worth less than 10,000 RMB (c. 1,000 euro) into a company that now generates ten million RMB in profits each year. Kevin's services have made it to the top of important online media aggregators like Youku, and his company has more than half a million followers on Weixin. We are sitting at a small bistro in the outskirts of his home city, near the site of his new office. Kevin, like many new media entrepreneurs in China, is expanding.

I ask him what he thinks of search giant Baidu, and of Google leaving China. 'Baidu is the most important search engine in China, but it seems they've fallen asleep. They're not doing anything new since Google left. I think Baidu is trying to copy Google on most services'. As it turns out, Baidu's competitors are expanding aggressively as well. '360 is trying to challenge Baidu', says Kevin, and he explains how Qihoo's 360 sales department recently approached him and encouraged him to place ads on their search engine. 'Their browser is popular with technologically less savvy people—with the older generation'. Does he think Baidu's competitors will catch up? He smiles wryly. 'What is needed for people to search on Baidu? They want to know something, and Baidu answers their needs. It's unlikely that people will go to a different search engine. They use Baidu because they're used to it'.

In this chapter, I have discussed how convenient digital technologies like China's search engine Baidu introduce subtle yet pervasive biases to how users look for and access information. Concretely, such technologies sit between us and the discourses we draw from to create knowledge of our world. They are powerful filters, and they skew our perception by creating what I have called a 'digital bias': a perspective that is created algorithmically, through programmes such as search engines that combine material factors, social parameters, and subjective criteria to selectively provide user with information. The results may not be 'negative', in the sense that the information we retrieve and share through ICT is false or unjust. Digital biases can often be 'positive', answering precisely our needs and providing us with a comfort zone that we are 'used to', as Kevin put it in the preceding anecdote.

In China, the search engines that are today available each produce strong digital biases. They push in-house content, promote paid links, and conform to restrictive government regulations. Halavais's arguments about search engines thus fit the Chinese case, where such services 'represent a largely conservative force' that increases 'the attention paid to those people, institutions, and ideas that have traditionally held sway' (2009: 1290). Indeed, Jiang Min, in her own comparison of Google and Baidu, writes (2014: 227):

> The not-so-small divergence between Baidu's and Google's search results alerts us to the arbitrariness with which search engines produce social realities, as well as the means and rules with which they determine presence and prominence, especially over controversial public issues. If search rankings cannot be perfect, they are, at their very best, simulated approximations of a constructed 'natural order' of things. However, user trust in search engines tends to turn algorithmically generated reality into truth in its own right. The programmable nature of search engines makes it possible for political authorities, search firms and other powerful interest groups to shape and control social realities via search.

Jiang's assessment is in line with the findings I have presented in this chapter. China's search engines select and rank sources in highly biased ways, and this is true not just for politically sensitive topics like queries for 'Tiananmen'. Topics related to the Chinese nation and its relation with neighbouring Japan are also substantially warped, pushing a national framework onto the issue and presenting that framework, as Jiang puts it, as the 'natural order of things'. That China's digital biases are not readily visible to users only contributes to these 'filter effects' (Pariser 2012). China's search engines relay information biases that are systemic throughout the Chinese media environment, and they simultaneously cater to the personal biases of users. The result is a set of seemingly diverse windows into digital China, all of which are heavily skewed by largely invisible commercial and political factors. Moreover, all of these windows guide perception in subtle, often banal ways towards a particular vision of Chineseness, for instance by privileging authoritative domestic sources, reproducing simplified character materials, or flagging the mainland Chinese context through national services like weather or travel applications. In this sense, China's search engines are complicit in creating the kind of 'sovereign' internet space that the PRC's authorities are envisioning as the standard version of digital China.

Yet, search engines are merely the entryways into digital networks. The networks themselves are similarly governed by power relations, and they relay specific discourses that are skewed in their own ways. These networks and the discourses they produce are the focus of the coming chapters.

# 4

# Digital China's Hyperlink Networks

Search engines provide a convenient entryway into digital networks; however, as I have argued in the previous chapter, their effectiveness comes at a price: the digital bias that these technologies rely on ranks and promotes information according to political, commercial, and demographic logics that are algorithmically relayed to users who for the most part remain in the dark about their functioning. In digital China, Chinese search engines routinely privilege in-house content and official sources, and they place political issues in seemingly banal but nevertheless pervasive national frames of reference. Yet, what happens when users access the digital networks to which these entryways lead? What kind of picture emerges as users click their way through the web to explore a specific topic?

In the early days of the web, the metaphor of 'cyberspace' suggested that the internet presented its own world of information, ready for users to travel or 'surf' across freely, like explorers venturing through a new realm. Concepts like 'virtual reality' became cornerstones of cultural imagination, especially in the 1980s and 1990s, when science-fiction authors such as William Gibson (1984/1995) or Neil Stevenson (1992) popularized the image of data jockeys riding the information highways of the web (see also Goto-Jones 2015: 31). In such visions of communication, the internet is often portrayed as a virtual cityscape that exists outside of, or parallel to, reality. Think only of the opening sequences of the 1996 Hollywood movie *Hackers*, which morphs computer switchboards onto aerial views of downtown Manhattan, or the now classic 1999 film *The Matrix*, with its bleak virtual urban spaces.

Such spatial metaphors draw attention to how the web links 'sites' of information, and how users might move from one site to another. Writing about encyclopaedic knowledge on the web, O'Sullivan (2011: 46) argues that the technical characteristics of digital media systems promise

> to enhance the user's navigation and understanding of knowledge. They free the reader from the straitjacket of fixed and hierarchical systems of information organization, allowing open-ended and nondetermined

navigation. Through these tools, users can organize relevant information following their own intuitive means, based not on imposed
structures or alphabetization but on their own habits of thinking—
following leads, making connections, building trails of thought.

Manuel Castells (2001: 202) makes a similar case when he argues that the web does
not consist of a single, unifying script that media producers generate to reach their
audiences. Instead, the hypertext that governs the web is 'produced by us, by using
the Internet to absorb cultural expression in the multimedia world and beyond';
what constitutes the web is thus 'not *the hypertext*, but my hypertext, your hypertext, and everybody else's hypertext' (Castells 2001: 203, emphasis in the original).

Arguments such as these provide an important reminder that navigating digital media content on the web is a creative process in its own right. However, is it
accurate to say that it is primarily the users who 'author' the content of the web?
What role do traditional stakeholders play in creating such content and providing
the guideposts for its usage and its understanding? Is the process of 'surfing' the
web really open-ended, unstructured, non-determined, and non-hierarchical?

The answers to these questions are intimately tied to how the infrastructure
of the internet and the architecture of the World Wide Web work in specific
contexts, for instance in China. In this chapter, I take a look at digital China's
web to explore how specific issues are embedded in online networks, particularly issues related to the nation. As I show, the Chinese web is not at all unstructured or non-hierarchical. Before going into the details of the Chinese case,
the first part of this chapter examines how the theoretical arguments I made
in chapter 2 relate to discussions of imagined communities such as the nation
and digital communication networks like the World Wide Web. Specifically,
I examine the role that power plays in such networks. The second section turns
to a major element that makes the web and its architecture special: the hyperlink. It outlines what methodological concerns inform the study of hyperlink
structures, and it discusses what might constitute an 'issue' or a 'community'
on the web. The chapter then explores empirically the networks surrounding
the Nanjing Massacre and the Diaoyu Islands on China's web, before providing
a check on these two cases by examining the web presence of Chinese higher-
education institutions in three different cities. It concludes with a discussion of
what hyperlink structures can tell us about digital nationalism in China.

## Power in Digital Networks

How a nation is imagined has much to do with communication. As I have
argued in chapter 2, imagined communities rely strongly on shared systems

of symbols, and actors who are able to take control of the media technologies that generate and circulate such symbols are in a position to shape their meanings. Constructing and maintaining imagined communities is a matter of power. Individuals imagine their nation in no small part by accessing information through communication networks, but not everyone has the same kind of power in these networks. In traditional Weberian understandings (Weber 1980: 28), power describes the capacity to achieve an end against potential opposition, and this capacity can rest on a number of 'resources', such as wealth, status, or the ability to inflict physical violence. This kind of power is still relevant today (see Lukes 2005: ch.1), but viewing power solely as a propensity to overcome resistance is insufficient for explaining how communication and power are connected. As Ulrich Beck (2007: 2) points out, in contemporary societies power no longer simply means winning at the game of politics. It means defining the rules of the game. Similarly, Castells (2009: 11) argues that we should examine power from the perspective of cognitive and communication processes. In this view, actors change the nature of the 'game' by 'switching' other actors in a network on or off, and by 'programming' networks with specific values (Castells 2009: 45).[1]

Castells's 'switching power' and 'programming power' illustrate how the nature of power changes in networked societies compared to the classic Weberian logic of the word. The two concepts also help redefine power in two important ways: first, they describe power not so much as a capacity but as a process. The power to switch or programme is not simply something that agents possess and use, it is something they do. Second, these concepts highlight how power does not have to be purely negative (meaning: coercive), and they suggest that it might be helpful to understand power not solely as a matter of domination versus resistance. Power is not necessarily exerted over others, against opposition, though such cases, of course, exist. Power can also create opportunities; it can connect different actors and enable certain interactions. Yet, despite these advantages of Castells's power concepts, they nevertheless still leave crucial questions unanswered. They do not yet tell us how power and technology are connected in practice. How exactly do actors 'switch' others into a network? How do they 'programme' a network with value?

The terminology of computer science promises a way forward. In networks, users have different kinds of permissions to access and handle data.[2] Some users possess read-only permissions, meaning they can access data but cannot produce, transform, move, or delete such data. Others possess write privileges, meaning that they are also able to produce and alter data. Finally, some agents have executive permissions: they can read and manipulate the data and they can execute scripts (operations that use and affect data); I also include here the ability to change the permissions of other users within the network. This is, quite literally, how access is handled in computer systems. However, it is also an apt analogy for information and communication networks more broadly.

Take traditional mass communication as an example. Mass media systems rely on a specific kind of network in which the vast number of users has been granted read-only permission. Readers of newspapers do not have the power to alter what is in the daily hard copy in front of them, and television audiences cannot edit the content they are watching. This mass-media logic is now changing or overlapping with new rationales, as digital distribution, 'narrowcasting', and personalization are re-shaping the relationship between media producers and consumers. Nevertheless, within the traditional mass-media logic, editorial powers are the prerogative of a small class of specially trained and accredited professionals, who have been allocated 'write permissions': journalists, editors, photographers, directors, and so forth. By assembling signs into statements, these actors produce discourse, and they spread that discourse by feeding their assemblage of signs into the network via their respective access nodes. To use Castells's terminology, these professionals 'programme' the network.

Then, there is a yet smaller class of privileged people, composed of capital owners, managers, state functionaries, and so on, who retain executive permission across certain parts of the network or, in the case of extremely powerful organizations and individuals, across the network as a whole. As I show throughout the book, and particularly in chapter 8, the CCP and its leading propaganda cadres deploy precisely such executive permissions to manage the PRC's media system. Agents with such executive powers have the ability to alter the write permissions of other agents in the mass communication network, for instance by accrediting journalists, hiring editors, firing photographers, and so on. They also have the power to add or remove entire nodes from this network, for instance by closing down an enterprise, arranging a merger, assigning a publishing licence, creating new distribution channels, and so on. This, I believe, is what Castells means when he writes about 'switching power' in networked societies.

Digital technologies are changing this traditional mass-media logic. As Andrew Chadwick (2013: 175) writes, contemporary media systems are becoming 'hybrid', and the assumptions and values that emerge from these hybrid systems then shape the constraints within which agents behave. In short, we live in a world in which mass communication networks are being systematically re-mapped, and this is happening in several ways. To return to the metaphor of network permissions, more people now have write permissions, causing the boundaries between established professionals and laypersons to break down (see chapter 7). Bloggers create their own WordPress sites, social media users send tweets, and file-sharing sites enable users to move and edit data. These processes are also visible in China, and they are, in part, responsible for the optimistic hyperbole that so frequently accompanies digital developments there. However, at the same time, as more and more users are granted write permissions, the global network is being revamped into a set of 'walled gardens': closed-off networks in which ultimate executive permissions rest with a small number of agents, and in which connections to other local networks are subject to substantial gate-keeping. As I have discussed in the previous chapter, companies like Facebook or Google, Baidu or Tencent, try to keep their users 'locked in', rather than seeing them 'bounce' to other real estate in the global network. In some parts of the world, Facebook has been so successful at this strategy that, paradoxically, to many of its users, the 'internet' as such no longer exists—there is only Facebook (see Mirani 2015). Finally, within local sub-networks, users are empowered with limited executive privileges. For instance, in many networks, users have some power to specify who should have access to their data. This is particularly true in social media networks, where users can make content available to only themselves, to a group of people in their sub-network, or to potentially anyone within the wider network. The nature of editorial privilege has likewise shifted, as users now influence what content the digital successors of the broadsheet or TV broadcast relay to them, either through conscious choices or through the digital biases of complex personalization algorithms.

Through advanced ICTs, today's elites have changed the access permissions to parts of our communication networks and have altered the 'rules of the game'. This has had transformative and often disruptive effects on the societies in which we live (see Owen 2015). However, the additional privileges are deceptive, since they may, at times, suggest that networked communication is, by default, non-hierarchical and, consequently, fundamentally different from mass communication. Just because mass communication networks are being transformed does not mean that privileged permissions no longer play a role. As I argued in chapter 2, and as other authors have also demonstrated (e.g., Chadwick 2013: 629), perceived new communication paradigms do not neatly replace the old, like successive 'ages' or 'periods' of development. Instead, different 'modes' of communication overlap.

In such complex media systems, power is still distributed unevenly, but this fact itself is becoming more obscure. For instance, elite users still have advanced permissions that can profoundly shape the nature of networks. A small number of people retain executive rights over crucial digital sub-nets like Facebook or Weixin, not to mention over the larger physical infrastructure of the network as a whole—the access points and cables that form the backbone of the internet (see Schiller 1999). In fact, expanding the write permissions and the locally bound executive permissions of users has been an intentional move by corporate actors like Facebook or Google, who profit financially from the allegedly 'free' flow of information within the sub-networks that they govern. Talk of ICTs as 'liberation technologies' (Diamond 2010) directly benefits these actors and their agenda, while saying little about who gets to enjoy which liberties under the access regimes that these actors enforce.

Those with the right privileges in a network are able to decide where symbols are going to circulate, and they are able to influence which symbols become conceived of as 'shared'. I show, throughout this book, what this means for the construction of imagined communities. Imagined communities like the nation are not built out of actual ties between their members, as is the case in small-scale networks. Nations consist of potential ties. It is due to media technologies like newspapers and radio transmitters, mobile phones and the internet, that these potential ties have meaning. Potential networks can even be mobilized into actual action, by making use of certain technologies. However, we should not be deceived into thinking these options are unconditional and limitless. As discussed in chapter 2, our options are made possible via technologies with specific designs, and they exist within social, political, and economic contexts. They are situated in broader networks, and these networks are governed by actors with advanced privileges.

When it comes to the communication networks that today shape the meaning of imagined communities like the nation, a diverse range of users are deploying the technological potentials of ICTs, but these users do not have unfettered access to the entire network, nor do they have the same levels of power. The way that such networks are structured by elites creates walled gardens in which people access and process information according to deceptively liberal privileges, but overall the global parameters of how these networks function are outside most users' control. The practical implications of this are visible in the way that specific networks are structured, for instance issue networks on the World Wide Web.

## Issue Networks and the Meaning of the Hyperlink

A cornerstone of the web's functionality is the hypertext, a mark-up language that signals to digital devices how to display media content. The use of hypertext changes the patterns of media production and consumption in a number of interesting ways, for instance by making it possible to combine various media types and by facilitating interactivity (see Bolter & Grusin 2000; Castells 2001; Jenkins 2008). What I am interested in here is a particular element of the hypertext: the hyperlink. Hyperlinks are digital objects that point to specific files on the internet, for example to web pages. In this sense, the hyperlink takes the scholarly concept of the reference and applies that concept to digital media. However, hyperlinks do not just provide a reference to media content, like a footnote or in-text reference in this book does. What sets hyperlinks apart from other kinds of references is that they make the content they reference immediately accessible to the user, regardless of whether that content is written text, an audio recording, a video or animation, or an interactive script. This enables what Yochai Benkler (2006: 218) has called 'see-for-yourself culture', which, in his view, represents 'a radically different and more participatory model of accreditation than typified the mass media'.

Lev Manovich goes even further, arguing that the technology of the hyperlink fundamentally disrupts the idea of hierarchy. He writes (2013: 76):

> We may be tempted to trace hyperlinking to earlier forms and practices of non-sequential text organization, such as the Torah's interpretations and footnotes, but it is actually fundamentally different from them. Both the Torah's interpretations and footnotes imply a master-slave relationship between one text and another. But in the case of hyperlinking as implemented by HTML and earlier by Hypercard, no such relationship of hierarchy is assumed. The two sources connected through a hyperlink have equal weight; neither one dominates the other. Thus the acceptance of hyperlinking in the 1980s can be correlated with contemporary culture's suspicion of all hierarchies, and preference for the aesthetics of collage in which radically different sources are brought together within a singular cultural object.

Manovich's arguments about the non-hierarchical nature of the hyperlink may be too optimistic, but they show that hyperlinks play more roles than merely being simple references. What, then, is the sociological and political meaning of a hyperlink? As I have discussed earlier, such linkages have traditionally been regarded as pathways through information sources, allowing users to seamlessly 'travel' or 'surf' from one web space to the next. Such analogies are indeed useful, as I discuss later, but they do not tell the whole story. Linking to a node in a network can reflect very different kinds of behaviour—for example, referencing an institutional affiliation, issuing a critique or an endorsement, deploying an aspirational marker, or merely referencing content. This plurality of linking behaviour in communication networks has led scholars to increasingly interpret hyperlinks as marks of acknowledgement (see Beaulieu 2005; Park & Thelwall 2003; Thelwall 2004).

An interesting question, then, is how different actors and institutions link to one another on the web. One method for exploring this question comes from the Digital Methods Initiative in Amsterdam, which has created a software program called the IssueCrawler. The IssueCrawler is a browser-based, open access program that allows researchers to input a number of webpages and map the linkages between them.[3] Various studies have deployed this method, for instance to explore how political blogs in Australia are connected (Bruns 2007), or how environmental issues are represented in European webspheres (Rogers 2013: ch.2). Since the software crawls websites for html code—the mark-up language that defines the web—it is not limited to sources in any specific language, and can consequently be used to map web networks that use non-Latin scripts like Chinese.

The mapping process looks for so-called co-links between source pages, meaning that the program collects all pages that a set of sources link to and then retains those that have received at least two links from those sources. To better understand the implications of this, imagine we wanted to create a network of people working together, based on the question of who has sent e-mails to whom over the course of recent months. We could map these relations by representing each person as a circle, and then drawing arrows to everyone who had received an e-mail from that source.

Now imagine a scenario in which the only interactions within this group were individual e-mail exchanges with one particular person, but no exchanges had taken place amongst the other group members. The resulting map would be a star, with one person at the centre and the other members each isolated at one of the star's points (see the image on the left in Figure 4.1). Such a scenario raises conceptual questions: to what extent is this really a 'group' of people? If we understand a network to be a system of *inter*connections, is it appropriate to view these linkages as such a system? After all, this structure of relations does not seem particularly 'web-like'. As Pariser (2012: 2042) explains, 'a community is a set of nodes that are densely interconnected—my friends form a community

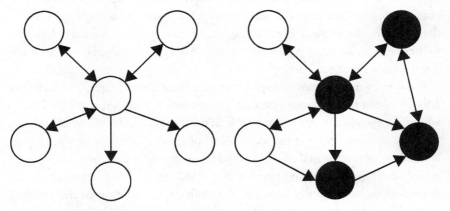

*Figure 4.1* What Constitutes a 'Community Network'? Left: single links between six actors, connected through the node at the centre. Right: 'co-links' between four networked actors (black). Florian Schneider.

if they all don't know just me but also have independent relationships with one another'.

The IssueCrawler incorporates this assessment by making a qualitative distinction between relations made up of such single links and those made up of several cross-links. In this view, simple star structures function differently than networks with wider interconnections. To return to the example, we would only consider a person to be part of a community network if he or she had received e-mails from at least two people in the group. The star-shaped formation on the left-hand side of Figure 4.1 would not constitute such a community, whereas the black nodes in the image on the right-hand side would.

Extending this logic to the World Wide Web, the IssueCrawler program thus retains only websites that have received at least two in-links from the sites that served as starting points for the search. The process can be refined in various ways, for instance by looking for links at different levels of remove, and by adjusting which of these levels of remove should be included as starting points for the co-link analysis. The different levels of remove (also called the 'degree') each have distinct implications. To return to the example of people sending e-mails to one another, let us assume we used a set of persons with a shared commonality as starting points (for instance, all employees at a university department) and collected all the contacts to which they had each written e-mails. The resulting map would be a 'first-degree' diagram, since it would include all connections at the first level of remove. This map would include a vast number of people, many of whom were not associated with each other. If we now retained only people who had received e-mails from at least two of the original starting points, that network would shrink. We might interpret it as representing communication on a particular project, for instance an undergraduate teaching programme or a research conference, though further analysis would have to confirm this by checking who the various actors were and what the content of their exchanges was. Regardless of the exact meaning we are later able to assign to these connections, what they make visible is a 'local' or 'neighbourhood' community network of our starting actors.

Now imagine we were to expand the 'crawl' of these correspondences not only by asking to whom our *first set of persons* sent e-mails but also by asking to whom the people *they got in touch with*, in turn, sent e-mails. We would now be mapping all connections at the second level of remove, or of the 'second degree'. If we, then, again retained everyone who had received at least two e-mails from any of the original group members *or* their contacts, we would arrive at a larger second-degree community network. A possible interpretation of the resulting network might be that it represents a set of people who are working more broadly on a shared theme, for instance researching issues in politics. Again, additional qualitative information would have to shed light on what the network represents, but the developers of the IssueCrawler refer to this sort of network as an 'issue network' (Rogers 2010, 2013): a system of connections between actors sharing similar concerns. The software applies this logic to the internet, making it possible to explore whether a particular set of websites is, in fact, linked into such an issue network through cross-references and acknowledgements of certain web resources.

## Networked Structures and Their Central Actors

If communication is indeed a matter of power, then it must leave traces of power in networks like these. But how can we detect such power? What would traces of power look like? In network analysis, exploring what is important in a network means asking who or what is particularly 'central' within that network's structure. There are several possible ways of answering this question. For example, imagine you regularly had to make your way across London, using the tube. In most cases, you will want to keep your commutes short and simple, meaning that you will try to find the shortest paths across London. Considering how London's underground network is structured, you will pass routinely through specific stations. If you are travelling through central London (see Figure 4.2), then your travels are likely to take you through stations like Baker Street, King's Cross, Liverpool Street, the Bank-Monument complex, and Embankment. These are nodes in the network where important underground lines cross, and these stations are, consequently, located between many places across London. Network analysts would say that these stations are especially central in terms of their 'betweenness', meaning that a large number of possible shortest paths across the network pass through them (see Goldbeck 2013: 982).

While awkwardly phrased, this 'betweenness centrality' of a node has important implications. For instance, if I were able to 'switch off' King's Cross station, it would profoundly affect transportation in London. As Scott (2012: 1891) writes, 'the betweenness of a point measures the extent to which an agent can play the part of "broker" or "gatekeeper" with a potential for control over others'. That this is by no means a hypothetical issue became tragically apparent in 2005, when terrorists attacked London's underground, apparently targeting the city's infrastructure based on such a rationale. At the time, the target stations King's Cross and Liverpool Street ranked high in terms of their betweenness centrality, prompting the network specialist Ferenc Jordán (2008) to conclude that the perpetrators may have calculated precisely this measure to locate the most vulnerable nodes in London's tube network. This is a somewhat bold conclusion to draw, since it is also possible the attackers chose their targets intuitively. After

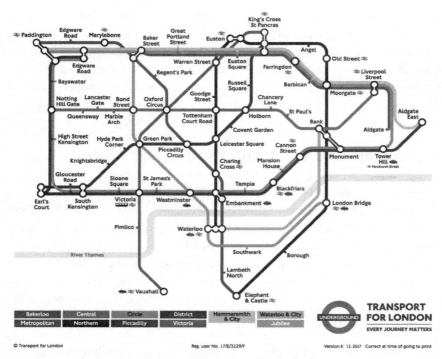

*Figure 4.2* Central London's Underground Network. Transport for London 2017.

all, most people who have some experience with London's transport system will be aware that King's Cross is important, even if they are not able to formally measure that importance. That said, the case illustrates *why* these nodes were important in the network. It also shows how the kind of switching power I have discussed earlier translates to the structural features of networks.

Networks like metro systems do not precisely resemble information and communication systems: a railway connection is not 'directed' at someone or something in the same way that an e-mail or a hyperlink is. The tube runs both ways between stops, whereas a message or a reference does not. Nevertheless, betweenness also matters in communication networks, for instance if data has to pass along isolated bridges in a network that connect important sub-networks. Such choke points can be used to monitor or control traffic, and this is one of the ways in which internet controls work, for example in China's extremely sophisticated system of internet governance (see Deibert et al. 2010: 449–487).

Betweenness centrality thus applies to both directed and non-directed flows across networks, and yet it is not the only measure of power. As I have indicated, in the case of hyperlink networks on the web, the question is not solely how users 'click' their way across this 'space' of information. Hyperlinks are forms of acknowledgement, which is why search engines like Google use them to map the reputation of websites. Halavais (2009: 998) explains:

> Google and others recognized that hyperlinks were more than just connections, they could be considered votes. When one page linked to another page, it was indicating that the content there was worth reading, worth discovering. After all, this is most likely how web surfers and the search engine's crawlers encountered the page: by following links on the web that led there. If a single hyperlink constituted an endorsement, a large number of links must suggest that a page was particularly interesting or worthy of attention.

The argument is that a website that receives many links must be particularly authoritative in a network: if thousands of people on the internet reference my website, then that might indeed single it out as more important than the website of a colleague who is only referenced a handful of times. However, such authority rests on more than just the *amount* of acknowledgement I receive. The *quality* of such acknowledgement also matters. If we treated all links equally, it would be 'a bit like treating all roads the same when some are driveways and others are multilane highways' (Halavais 2009: 1016). For instance, if the thousands of links to my website come primarily from obscure private bloggers with no other connections in the network, my website might not be so important after all. However, if the handful of links to my colleague's website comes from sites that receive a lot of attention themselves (e.g., the White House or China's State Council, CNN or the BBC, the United Nations or the World Bank), then that website is likely far more influential than mine.

The name for this measure of authority is 'eigenvector centrality', and it accounts for 'a node's importance while giving consideration to the importance of its neighbors' (Goldbeck 2013: 988). It is useful for assessing which actors are particularly authoritative within a network, which is why it features prominently in the algorithms of search engines that aim to assess the reputation and popularity of sources. What is relevant here is that eigenvector centrality connects to the idea of 'programming power': programming a network with a specific discourse is much easier from a node with a high level of authority than from a node that is of marginal importance. If my access point to a communication network like the World Wide Web is the prime real estate of the *Guardian*'s website, then the statements I make there are much more likely to filter through that network and shape discourses than similar statements hidden away in the sub-pages of a poorly connected academic blog.

What is interesting about networks is that they exhibit characteristics that influence how power works within their structure. Some of these characteristics are created and actively used by actors. This prominently includes traditional large-scale organizations like the state or multinational corporations that manage the material resources on which a network rests, for instance the physical server farms that create what internet users perceive as an immaterial 'cloud' (see Lanier 2011: 347; Pariser 2012: 1807–1812; Schiller 2014: 2463). Ownership of these resources allows such actors to conduct their activities with the highest of network privileges, giving them substantial switching power, and often putting them in positions of authority that enable the programming of networks or their sub-systems with specific discourse. At the same time, non-traditional actors now possess new levels of network access and permission, making it possible to exert programming power in sudden and at times unpredictable ways, for instance through a single tweet or blog post (see Shirky 2008: ch.1). Much of this relies on individual agents; yet, at the same time the characteristics of networks provide the boundaries of what is or is not feasible within their constraints. Once an interaction becomes networked, for instance once actors become linked into clusters, these linkages 'tend to reinforce themselves'; this tendency is called the 'power law', and it is visible in internet communication, where 'the natural tendency of the web (and of many similar networks) is to link very heavily to a small number of sites: the web picks winners' (Halavais 2009: 914–918).[4]

Power in communication and information networks thus plays out within structural constraints that are native to networked architectures and that actors leverage to achieve results. This leads to intriguing questions about what kinds of networks transport discourses about the nation in a country like China, which has been progressively expanding its digital network structures and has, consequently, witnessed profound changes in its information and communication environment. I have explored this issue by mapping the hyperlink networks for three different cases. This includes the Nanjing Massacre, the East China Sea dispute, and a case related not to Japan, but rather to what is sometimes referred to as 'Greater China': the academic websites of three major cities in the region.[5]

# Digital Networks of National Humiliation

As I have pointed out in the introduction to this book, the Nanjing Massacre is a long-standing topic that does not elicit much controversy within Chinese political discourse. The offer of websites that present this issue in digital China indeed reflect this, for instance by remaining relatively stable over time, and by presenting a narrow discourse—an issue I return to in detail in chapter 5. But what kind of websites deal with this topic, and how are they embedded in the broader infrastructure of China's web?

To find the major Chinese websites that deal with the Nanjing Massacre, I conducted keyword searches for the Chinese phrases 'Nanjing Massacre', 'Nanjing Incident', and 'Sino-Japanese War' on three prominent search engines: Baidu, Yahoo, and Google. I used the same research browser as the one used for the study I discussed in the previous chapter, that is, a browser that had been cleaned of personal data and that I reset after every query to limit personalization biases (see Rogers 2013: 111). To simulate searches from within China, the Baidu and Yahoo searches used a Beijing-based proxy server, and the Google searches used a server in Hong Kong. I then manually reviewed which results were relevant and checked them for links to other websites on the topics. At the time of the study (spring 2013), this process yielded 19 issue-related websites, all of which were accessible from within China at the time. I have listed these sites in Table 4.1.

Before exploring the 'online' dimension of the networks that these websites tie into, it helps to first examine the 'offline' institutional affiliations of the various sites. The 19 sites examined here consist of diverse actors, including Chinese companies; news organizations in the PRC; institutions of the Party, state, and military; academic institutions (including a university in Hong Kong); private persons or groups; and two American enterprises. A closer look at the websites and their affiliations, however, suggests that this diversity should not be overstated. First, three domains that deal with the Nanjing Massacre are run directly by the state news agency Xinhua, and many of the other domains are in one way or another associated with the state or the Party. This is the case for all PRC news organizations, academic institutions, and cultural organizations, including the state-run Nanjing Massacre Memorial Hall.[6] Second, it is not clear from the websites who exactly the actors behind the seemingly private web presences are. Consequently, it would be premature to rule out that the extensive issue website on Sina, the link collection on 163.com, or the materials on the (private) Leiting Military Affairs website were compiled by persons with affiliations to the propaganda system. For the case of Sina, the site strongly focuses on official news materials and information from the Nanjing Massacre Memorial Hall, suggesting a strong connection to scholars or administrators involved in maintaining this historical archive on the ground. Finally, aside from the two Hong Kong websites and US-based Wikipedia, all of the sites have IP addresses that are located in major mainland Chinese cities (Beijing, Chengdu, Guangzhou, Nanjing, Tianshui, Wenzhou, and Yangzhou), which means they have to adhere to local rules and regulations (see Wright 2014).[7]

How, then, are these different websites situated on China's web, and in what ways do they link to each other? To find out whether the sites create a network of issue-related pages, I have mapped out the part of China's web that contains the 19 issue websites. Methodologically, this process involved the use of two

*Table 4.1*  **Chinese Nanjing Massacre Issue Websites**

| Description | Starting Page URL | Institutional Affiliation |
|---|---|---|
| Action Committee for Defending the Diaoyu Islands | http://www.diaoyuislands.org/ | Hong-Kong-based activist group Action Committee for Defending the Diaoyu Islands |
| Baike Baidu full entry | http://baike.baidu.com/subview/2876/6475776.htm | Baidu Inc. |
| China.com | http://military.china.com/zh_cn/critical3/27/20090212/15321255.html | Global Broadcasting Media Group, a subsidiary of state-owned China Radio International |
| Chinese University of Hong Kong | http://humanum.arts.cuhk.edu.hk/NanjingMassacre/DD.html | Chinese University of Hong Kong |
| CIS issue site | http://diaoyudao.chinaiiss.com | China International Strategy Net, by the Hongzhi Tianxiang Network Technology Group Ltd. |
| Huanqiu issue site | http://www.huanqiu.com/zhuanti/world/diaoyudao | The *Global Times* (*People's Daily* affiliated Party tabloid) |
| iFeng issue site | http://v.ifeng.com/zt/diaoyudao/ | Phoenix Satellite Television Group |
| iFeng News history site | http://news.ifeng.com/history/zhongguojindaishi/special/diaoyudao/ | Phoenix Satellite Television Group |
| Leiting issue site | http://www.leiting001.com/zt/diaoyudaoyu | Leiting001.com Inc, affiliated with Shanghai Guangyu Net Science and Technology Company |
| Nanfang Net news article | http://www.southcn.com/news/international/gjkd/200406110497.htm | Nanfang Media Group (commercial state-owned media conglomerate) |

*Table 4.1* **Continued**

| Description | Starting Page URL | Institutional Affiliation |
|---|---|---|
| People's Net issue site | http://military.people. com.cn/GB/8221/72028/ 205795/ | People's Daily Group (Party News and Propaganda Outlet) |
| Qianyan001 issue site | http://www.qianyan001. com/zhuanti/bwdyd/ | Military Affairs portal. Affiliation unclear. |
| Sina issue site | http://news.sina.com.cn/z/ ourdydao | Sina Corp. |
| Tencent issue summary | http://news.qq.com/a/ 20080617/001801.htm | Tencent Holdings Ltd. |
| Xilu Military Website issue site | http://www.xilu.com/ diaoyudao/ | Subsidiary of privately run Guangdian Science and Technology Managing Group Ltd. (Engl.: CSNS) |
| Xinhua issue page | http://news.xinhuanet. com/ziliao/2003-08-25/ content_1044000.htm | Xinhua News Agency |

Retrieved Spring 2013.

digital tools: the first is the IssueCrawler software mentioned earlier, the second is the network visualization program Gephi, which I have used to represent the network data and highlight the most pertinent features.[8]

The analysis reveals that the separate web pages are not tied into anything that can legitimately be called an 'issue network'. Aside from the Sina.com commemoration site, which maintains eight links to the Nanjing Massacre Memorial Hall website, the various sites do not link to one another. This does not mean that the websites are not situated within larger networks, but simply that these larger networks have little to do with the Nanjing Massacre or with relations to Japan. In fact, thanks to the nature of the IssueCrawler, the programme is able to find networks and expand them beyond the original topical focus, depending on the parameters it is given at the outset of the process: a large number of (more general) initial starting sites, and a more extensive crawl (higher crawl-depth and more iterations), will generally produce large networks, regardless of whether the sites in the network actually deal with the relevant issue or not. The program will, at some stage, move away from any potential 'primary issue networks' and start mapping what Bruns (2007) calls 'secondary issue networks': sites that link to one another due to topical or institutional commonalities that are much broader than those between the initial starting pages.

The IssueCrawler can thus be deployed to map the immediate and extended neighbourhood of the Nanjing Massacre websites. What is noteworthy here is that the Nanjing Massacre websites produce a 'secondary issue network' very early on. The crawl that was meant to map the immediate neighbourhood of the starting pages (single iteration) already branches out to include a wide variety of pages that do not deal with the topic at hand.[9] This network consists of 80 nodes, but only five of the original issue pages are still present: the Chinese University of Hong Kong, the issue site on Sina.com (though not its commemoration forum, which is a different sub-domain), the Communist Youth League site, the issue site on China918.net, and the Nanjing Massacre Memorial Hall.

Processing the network data through Gephi renders additional features visible. For instance, two of the starting pages that are retained at this stage (the pages by the Chinese University of Hong Kong and the issue site on Sina.com) are not actually connected to the network, but remain outside the general structure as single 'isolates'. This means that they received at least two links from the original starting pages, but do not link to each other or the other nodes in the network. Another five starting points are indirectly represented, for instance through associated higher-level pages (such as homepages for general news sites), but the original issue pages are no longer part of the co-linked network at this level of analysis. I have visualized this network in Figure 4.3.

Once the analysis is expanded to include an additional iteration, the picture again changes dramatically. Only one issue page is still loosely included in this 100-node network (the news service China Economic Net). Other original starting points are only remotely associated with the network through their parent sites (e.g., Xinhua.org and Xinhua.net, or Sina.com). Yet others are missing entirely at this stage, including large sites like Encyclopaedia Baidu. The 'issue' has essentially disappeared. Recall that this result is produced by a crawl that uses the parameters that are designed for finding so-called issue networks (i.e., two iterations with the crawl depth of two pages), and that have proven effective at revealing issue networks in European, American, and Australian contexts (see Bruns 2007; Rogers 2010).

In this extended network, the majority of nodes represent large, institutionalized players. In the immediate neighbourhood of the original issue pages, this includes several websites that have dot-com extensions but are actually run by the state or Party, such as Xinhua, the *People's Daily*, or China News. If one were to surf this network by clicking one's way through the hyperlinks, then these nodes would be at the centre of the network's shortest connecting paths (they would rank high in terms of their 'betweenness').

In addition, the dot-com pages also include commercial sites like the IT service and retail site Zol.com or the internet portal Sina.com. Academic, military, or CCP actors are represented by Tiexue (or: 'Steel Blood', China's largest private

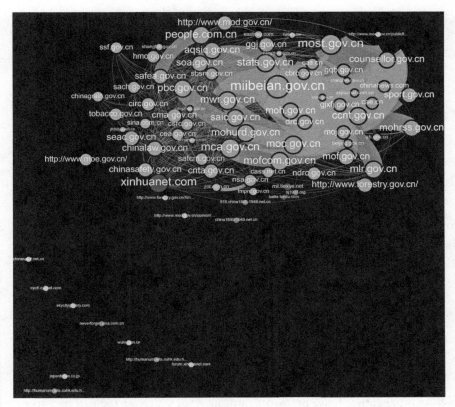

*Figure 4.3*  Immediate Neighbourhood of the Nanjing Massacre Issue Pages. Node size represents eigenvector centrality, thickness of lines (edges) represents the number of links (degree), shading represents starting points (crawl depth = 2, iterations = 1; algorithm: force atlas). The large cluster of light grey nodes in the north-eastern quadrant is not related to the issue. Network data collected on 3 May 2013. Florian Schneider.

military affairs website), the Chinese Academy of Social Sciences (CASS), and the Chinese Communist Youth League's history portal, each with either dot-net or dot-cn extensions, or, in the case of the CASS, with both. However, the over-whelming majority of nodes are clearly marked as government entities through their dot-gov-dot-cn extensions. I have visualized this network in Figure 4.4 by colour coding the different domain extensions and resizing the nodes according to their authority within the network, that is, according to their eigenvector centrality.

The graphical representation highlights an important feature: the fact that state actors dominate the network. This is surprising, considering how strongly theoretical assumptions of digital media scholars like Lev Manovich (2013: 76) emphasize the non-hierarchical potentials of hypertext, and how frequently discussions about China assume that digital networks challenge

*Figure 4.4* Extended Network of the Nanjing Massacre Issue Pages. Node size represents eigenvector centrality, thickness of lines (edges) represents the number of links (degree), shading represents domain types (crawl depth = 2, iterations = 2; algorithm: force atlas). Network data collected on 3 May 2013. Florian Schneider.

the power of established stakeholders like the state. Instead, the Chinese government—represented through numerous agencies and ministries, and centrally represented by the State Council's website www.gov.cn—is at the centre of this particular network. Looking at the authority that the different nodes possess, it becomes clear that government sites generally amass the most in-links from other authoritative network actors, many of which are themselves government sites. Based on this criterion, the two most relevant actors are the State Council and the Ministry of Industry and Information Technology (formerly the Ministry of Information Industry: miibeian.gov.cn), which is the institution responsible for managing the PRC's internet.

These findings suggest that when it comes to an established topic like the Nanjing Massacre, this section of the web adopts a traditional mass-media logic, where a few authoritative sources broadcast their information to a mass audience. Actors in this network use hyperlinks not to reference related content but to acknowledge affiliated organizations and, ultimately, Chinese government institutions. This raises the question of whether we see similar characteristics in the case of a more volatile, current affairs issue

## The Web Networks of China's Diaoyu Island Dispute

To answer this question, I conducted parallel studies of the East China Sea dispute on China's web, following the same work steps as for the Nanjing Massacre and using the Chinese search terms for 'East Sea' and 'Diaoyu Islands' to find websites that focused on this topic. An early study in the spring of 2013 yielded 16 websites (Table 4.2), all of which were accessible from within China at the time. Who were the main actors in the Diaoyu web network, and how were they connected? The web content is generally provided by large, authoritative websites, much as was the case with the Nanjing Massacre online. The issue webpages themselves do not link to each other; linking happens vertically within the hierarchies of a particular web domain, and then horizontally only between large information hubs. The effect is that the Diaoyu Island topic again does not generate a true 'issue network' in which information on the topic is shared, referenced through hyperlinks, or connected across different domains. Instead, the topic plugs into secondary issue networks that deal with general current affairs, military news, or tabloid-like popular information. The core players in this network are established news corporations and state information outlets.

*Table 4.2* **Chinese Diaoyu Island Issue Websites**

| Description | Starting Page URL | Institutional Affiliation |
| --- | --- | --- |
| Action Committee for Defending the Diaoyu Islands | http://www.diaoyuislands.org/ | Hong Kong–based activist group Action Committee for Defending the Diaoyu Islands |
| Baike Baidu full entry | http://baike.baidu.com/subview/2876/6475776.htm | Baidu Inc. |
| China.com | http://military.china.com/zh_cn/critical3/27/20090212/15321255.html | Global Broadcasting Media Group, a subsidiary of state-owned China Radio International |
| Chinese University of Hong Kong | http://humanum.arts.cuhk.edu.hk/NanjingMassacre/DD.html | Chinese University of Hong Kong |
| CIS issue site | http://diaoyudao.chinaiiss.com | China International Strategy Net, by the Hongzhi Tianxiang Network Technology Group Ltd. |
| Huanqiu issue site | http://www.huanqiu.com/zhuanti/world/diaoyudao | The *Global Times* (*People's Daily* affiliated Party tabloid) |

(*continued*)

*Table 4.2* **Continued**

| Description | Starting Page URL | Institutional Affiliation |
|---|---|---|
| iFeng issue site | http://v.ifeng.com/zt/diaoyudao/ | Phoenix Satellite Television Group |
| iFeng News history site | http://news.ifeng.com/history/zhongguojindaishi/special/diaoyudao/ | Phoenix Satellite Television Group |
| Leiting issue site | http://www.leiting001.com/zt/diaoyudaoyu | Leiting001.com Inc, affiliated with Shanghai Guangyu Net Science and Technology Company |
| Nanfang Net news article | http://www.southcn.com/news/international/gjkd/200406110497.htm | Nanfang Media Group (commercial state-owned media conglomerate) |
| People's Net issue site | http://military.people.com.cn/GB/8221/72028/205795/ | People's Daily Group (Party News and Propaganda Outlet) |
| Qianyan001 issue site | http://www.qianyan001.com/zhuanti/bwdyd/ | Military Affairs portal. Affiliation unclear. |
| Sina issue site | http://news.sina.com.cn/z/ourdydao | Sina Corp. |
| Tencent issue summary | http://news.qq.com/a/20080617/001801.htm | Tencent Holdings Ltd. |
| Xilu Military Website issue site | http://www.xilu.com/diaoyudao/ | Subsidiary of privately run Guangdian Science and Technology Managing Group Ltd. (Engl.: CSNS) |
| Xinhua issue page | http://news.xinhuanet.com/ziliao/2003-08/25/content_1044000.htm | Xinhua News Agency |

Retrieved Spring 2013.

Monitoring this network over the subsequent three years revealed the degree to which this part of China's web remains in flux. Power and authority shift frequently in this network, which, at times, sees certain webpages switched off and others switched on. Which of these shifts are due to linking practices, publishing and editorial choices, server outages, or other reasons is not visible from this angle onto China's web; research approaches such as close participant observations of web editors would have to shed light on the exact mechanics of such changes in digital China. The effect, however, is that the network remains much more dynamic than that of the historical Nanjing Massacre issue.

A pattern in these dynamics is that the network is generally highly commercialized. Official institutions interact with a complex set of private and commercial actors, which includes state-owned news conglomerates like the People's Daily Group or Southern Media Group, but also private content providers like Sina, Tencent, or China's search engine giant Baidu. As I have already discussed, these private companies are known to cooperate closely with state institutions, particularly when it comes to censoring users (see MacKinnon 2009), but the content they provide follows more than just political rationales: user 'clicks', 'likes', and reposts are bread and butter for these enterprises, which rely on advertising sales for their profits (Esarey & Qiang 2011).

I show in chapter 6 the extent to which the political discourses across these websites are indeed commodified. However, one need not look to the websites' content to see some degree of commodification. The fact that the issue is closely tied to commercial interests is also apparent from the link networks in which it is embedded. While there is significant turnover throughout the years in terms of websites that get linked, the majority of resources come from websites with dot-com extensions. Most of these sites are registered as companies with limited liability, suggesting that their websites are privately run. That said, it is not always clear to what extent these enterprises constitute independent commercial actors. Affiliations are often obscure. Considering the amount of military imagery and discussions of national interests on sites like Tiexue, Leiting, Chinaiiss, Qianyan, or Xilu, it is likely that the editors maintain connections to the Party's propaganda system that are not visible through information on the web—I provide examples of this in chapter 6.

Who, then, are the 'stars' of this network? I monitored these networks between 2013 and 2015, and there is considerable flux over time, which reflects the contemporary nature of the issue, but also the current affairs function of the news websites that host it. This section of China's web is subject to continuous change. Nevertheless, two features of the networks are worth noting (Figure 4.5): the first is the strong, recurring presence of media conglomerates like the state-run People's Daily Group or the private Phoenix Satellite Television Group with its online platform iFeng. The iFeng site hosts one of the most

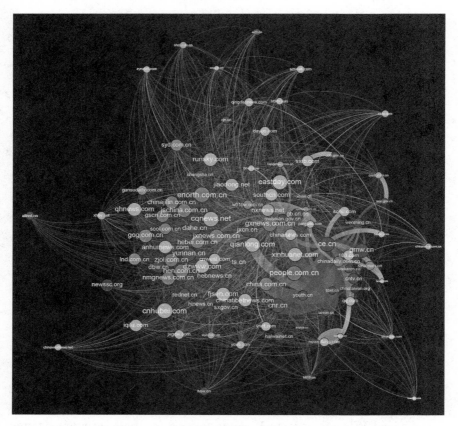

*Figure 4.5* Extended Network of the Diaoyu Island Issue Pages. Node size represents eigenvector centrality, thickness of lines (edges) represents the number of links (degree), shading represents domain types (crawl depth = 2, iterations = 2; algorithm: force atlas). Network data collected on 20 April 2014. Florian Schneider.

detailed web hubs for the East China Sea dispute, and the organization's news homepage is represented in the wider networks as an authoritative resource. Note that Phoenix is based in Hong Kong, but that iFeng presents its content in simplified Chinese characters and focuses on mainland news, which suggests the target audience consists of mainland internet users. The website also strongly features advertisements for PRC entities such as the People's Liberation Army (PLA), again hinting at some collaboration with the CCP's propaganda system.

Finally, Party and state institutions remain important. This includes a number of authoritative nodes in the network whose affiliation is obscured by the large amount of dot-com extensions represented in Figure 4.5. On China's web, not all such dot-com extensions represent privately owned enterprises. Many of China's state-owned enterprises and even some of its government's agencies also use such domain names for their web presence. Prominent examples are the *People's Daily*, Xinhua News Agency, or china.com.cn, which is a site run by the State Council Information Office and the State Internet Information Office. Overall, China's authorities retain a continuous presence through CCP propaganda department websites like wenming.cn or State Council outlets like Taiwan.cn—a website dedicated to Taiwan issues, but hosted by the mainland Chinese government. In a sense, the Diaoyu Island issue is located in a media ecology that is firmly rooted on the mainland and that resembles traditional, capitalist mass-media models with their strong focus on commerce and entertainment, and with their close links to the political establishment (see Herman & Chomsky 1988/2002).

While hyperlinks should not be mistaken for evidence of direct information exchange between commercial and public actors, they do hint at the level of acknowledgement that private actors feel they need to provide on the web in order to function in China's media environment. The same is true for occasional propaganda banners or official news content, which the private websites at times carry parallel to their more tabloid-like commercial contents. Being politically acceptable and commercially successful are not mutually exclusive endeavours on China's web.

## The Hyperlink Infrastructures of Imagined Community

The two cases I have examined so far present decidedly national online networks that are very much structured like traditional media systems, albeit to different degrees. Yet, one could legitimately ask whether this result is the outcome of a selection bias. After all, both topics deal with the Chinese side of a bilateral issue, and it might not be all that surprising to find that such topics are predominantly represented by online resources from mainland China.

There are several reasons why such scepticism may be unfounded. For instance, even a nationally relevant topic that was covered prominently by domestic institutions could acknowledge 'foreign' digital resources. In these cases, this could include Japanese or English websites. However, in neither network do such sources play a significant role. Even if we concede that the language barrier might make such acknowledgements impractical, it still stands to reason that websites from Hong Kong, Taiwan, or other overseas Chinese communities should appear prominently in these networks. Aside from a few exceptions, for instance the Chinese University of Hong Kong or Hong Kong-based media service iFeng with its target audience on the mainland, this is, on the whole, not the case.

Nevertheless, it is valid to ask whether the network structures I have described so far only appear in narrowly defined domestic settings. To check this, I have conducted another study that did not focus on a confrontational, bilateral international relations topic. Instead, it looked at the networks of higher education institutions in three major cities in so-called Greater China: Beijing, Hong Kong, and Taipei.

The rationale behind this study was that universities tend to present themselves as institutions with transnational linkages. This is apparent from university advertisements and the self-representations on their homepages, but it is not simply a promotional or mere aspirational claim: higher education institutions frequently collaborate on research projects or run international educational programmes. Moreover, scholars like Prasenjit Duara (2015) have made the case that many social processes no longer play out primarily within the confines of the nation state, and that the Asian region in particular consists of 'overlapping, intersecting networks, hubs and hinterland'. It stands to reason that a good place to look for such networks would be in the higher education environments of large, cosmopolitan centres. Even if such networks were not regionally or globally connected, they should at least acknowledge other actors within Chinese-language web spaces. Do such web spaces cut across traditional boundaries? Do they create networks of imagined communities that work through rationales like language or culture, rather than through infrastructural and institutional borders?

To answer these questions, I have first explored how the websites of higher education institutions within each city are connected to larger networks. Figure 4.6 shows how the six public higher education institutions in Hong Kong are connected online, first within a neighbourhood network, second within an issue network.

An analysis of the linking behaviour in this network reveals that the public higher education institutions do not normally link to each other. In fact, there is so little linkage between the original sources that most of them do not appear in a first-degree diagram. Much as in the case of the Nanjing Massacre and the Diaoyu Islands, we only arrive at something resembling a 'community network' at two levels of remove, when the software starts mapping how the sites that the universities link to in turn link to other sites.

These connections have very little to do with higher education. They are not 'issue' networks, in the sense that the original starting points of the analysis function as windows into scientific or educational concerns. Nevertheless, there is a rationale behind these connections: Figure 4.6 represents the links of education websites to media conglomerates, tech companies, and, most prominently, to government institutions. As it turns out, the university homepages are excellent at referencing information for anyone who wishes to learn more about the

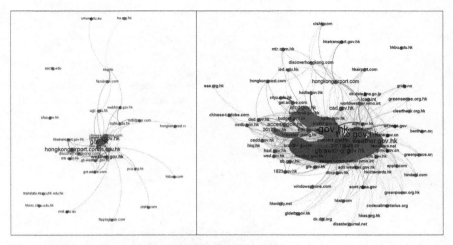

*Figure 4.6* Online Networks of Hong Kong's Higher Education. The 'neighbourhood networks' (left) and 'issue networks' (right) of Hong Kong's six public higher education institutions. Shading represents different domain types, thickness of lines (edges) represents the number of links (degree), and the size of the nodes and labels represents the centrality of the respective websites. Network data collected on 4 June 2014. Florian Schneider.

rules, regulations, and opportunities of living and travelling in Hong Kong. They do not, however, include much acknowledgement of other scientific institutions, whether in Hong Kong or elsewhere. The kind of pan-Chinese or even transnational collaboration that universities tend to celebrate on their homepages is not visible in the way that Hong Kong university websites link to other institutions. Regardless of the actual connections that Hong Kong academia might maintain, Hong Kong's universities are decidedly parochial on the web. The same is true for higher education institutions in Beijing and Taipei, respectively.

What happens if we change the starting points of the analysis by combining the public universities in Hong Kong, Beijing, and Taipei? If there is such a thing as a 'Greater China' on the web, then one would expect that the various institutions acknowledge actors across traditional territorial boundaries, particularly considering the cultural and linguistic similarities between these three locations. As it turns out, the institutions in all three cities again behave in much the same way. They are all tied into local government and business networks, but they do not normally link to each other (Figure 4.7).

I have shaded the nodes according to their URL extensions. Sites from Taiwan (e.g., dot-tw, gov-dot-tw, etc.) are clustered on the left, sites from Hong Kong in the lower left, and sites from mainland China on the right of the image. The map turns out to largely reproduce the territorial boundaries of the region. The 'domestic webs' of Taiwan and of China are clearly visible, with very few

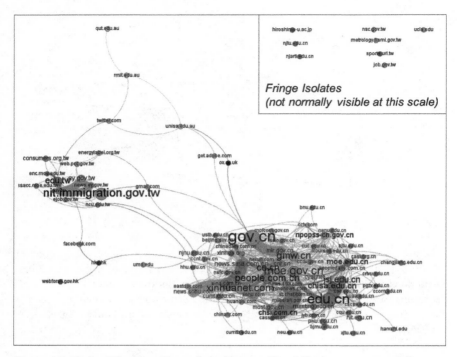

*Figure 4.7* Higher Education Networks in 'Greater China'. Shading represents different domain types, thickness of lines (edges) represents the number of links (degree), and the size of the nodes and labels represents the centrality of the respective websites. Network data collected on 4 June 2014. Florian Schneider.

connections between these two spheres. It is important to realize that the relational positions of the nodes to one another are crucial in network maps like the ones I am using in this chapter. However, the actual position of the nodes on the canvas is arbitrary. This means we could theoretically manipulate the network further without doing violence to its relational properties. We could, for instance, move the Taipei cluster to the right of the image, and could move the Hong Kong nodes to the lower edge, which would make the image increasingly look like a regional map of the East China Sea—a reminder that web spaces are not as disconnected from physical geographies as early pioneers of digital media were inclined to assume.

This level of analysis also highlights why it can be misleading to view web links as routes along which users 'travel' across the net. As I have discussed above, the links are unidirectional. In this case, it may look as though there are connections between the webspheres in mainland China, Hong Kong, and Taiwan, but in reality these connections only appear because certain actors reference the same sites, like Gmail, Adobe, Facebook, Twitter, or the University of South Australia and Oxford University, which are visualized here as sitting 'between' the main clusters (recall that both Twitter and Facebook are banned in the PRC—these are links emanating from sources in Hong Kong and Taiwan).

This demonstrates that even in a setting like academia, which is arguably relatively cosmopolitan (or at least tries to appear so), the online networks of major institutions are far more local than they are regional: they reference mostly domestic institutions, and hardly acknowledge sources across the Taiwan Straits and the Pearl River Delta. It is thus not merely conflict-laden bilateral issues that fall back on local and specifically national information networks, and it is not in mainland China alone that the web encourages parochial representations. The reasons for such an outcome have much to do with habits and conventions (an issue I discuss in chapters 5 and 6), and with policy choices and institutional setups (as I discuss in chapter 8). They also, however, follow from the way that networks function, for instance by encouraging behaviour that acknowledges sources that have been acknowledged in the past. Structural features like this 'power law' contribute to the construction of local, and frequently national, webs. This raises broader questions about politics and digital media, for instance to what extent we can expect truly 'transnational' cooperation across borders when the institutions that create and shape information networks fall back on local or national paradigms.

# Conclusion

The internet—a traditional medium:

I am sitting with two interviewees in a small room overlooking the traditional courtyard of a Hutong building in Beijing. In the central area, people are mingling with snacks and drinks. A party is underway; a launch event for a new, hip bar here in the old parts of China's capital city. Local musicians are providing live rock music.

I have been invited here by Judy, whose work is closely linked to China's cultural industry, and who knows her way around China's quickly transforming media environment. With us is James, a Chinese academic who studies digital China. We are watching the *'renau'* (or: joyful noise) beyond the window as we talk about the ways in which China's media ecology is changing. 'The traditional net is now an infrastructure', says James. 'It is not outdated, but it no longer plays the main role'. James explains how for most Chinese internet users, access to the internet now predominantly takes place via smartphones rather than via old-fashioned personal computers. The mobile web—that is where social interaction takes place. The web functions more like traditional media: ' . . . traditional media—their speed of creating content is of course much slower, but their content quality is much better. This is why traditional media are not becoming obsolete—they are becoming integrated into the larger media infrastructure'.

What James is describing is a hybrid media system that is in constant transition. Indeed, many of the media workers and academics I have talked to in China described China's media ecology in similar terms and, in particular, viewed the World Wide Web as a 'traditional' medium—a medium that works like newspapers or television. Intuitively, this may seem like an odd comparison, considering the degree to which digital technologies enable diverse actors to create and share information. The hypertext of the web is a powerful tool in this regard, particularly the hyperlink, which connects data and provides users with flexible ways to explore that data. Such hyperlinks can indeed be used to create serendipity, much as O'Sullivan (2011) has argued. However, serendipity does not occur naturally. To create it takes effort. It is an activity, an act of power.

Hyperlinks do not 'naturally' create non-hierarchical networks. Indeed, there may be physical properties to networks that encourage certain patterns rather than others. When such patterns are reinforced by political and economic incentives, networks can display extremely hierarchical features. The cases discussed in this chapter show what such alternative network structures can look like. The corners of digital China's web that deal with politically relevant issues are dominated by large corporate or state actors, and they behave very much like a mass communication environment. The parallels to 'traditional' media like broadcasting and printing are indeed striking. China's web behaves very much like an info-web.

This is the outcome of actors with different access privileges switching nodes into or out of digital networks, and programming the network with specific discourses, based on their understanding of what such networks should achieve. I return to such understandings and their political implications in chapter 8, and I discuss in chapter 7 whether similar processes are shaping the 'mobile web' and the social media that James mentioned in the preceding anecdote. What is important in this context is that there is no obvious default setting of what networks look like, and that the webs of digital China contain traces of the power that were used to customize them. In this instance, this included state actors and commercial corporations, which link to each other in highly parochial, hierarchical ways. The next question then is what discourses these actors construct within these networks.

# 5

# The Mediated Massacre

In the previous chapters, I have discussed how our access points into information networks are skewed by the digital biases of search engines, and how the web can create highly parochial networks. Both of these effects, I have argued, can facilitate the construction of imagined communities like the nation, for instance by creating national frames of reference or priming users with sets of national symbols. In China, for example, the web networks that present China in relation to Japan function like info-webs; they reproduce the mass communication logic of traditional media that broadcast professionally curated information to national audiences. So far, however, I have not discussed the content of these networks, or how actors make use of the digital features of web-based communication to relay such content. What does the discourse on Japan issues look like in digital China?

In this chapter, I turn to the Nanjing Massacre on China's web and discuss how digital resources allow national communities to collectively 'remember' their past. Of course, such 'digital remembering' does not exist in a vacuum. It is part of broader discussions that take place both 'online' and 'offline'.[1] This is readily apparent from the digital materials I examine in this chapter. Such materials reproduce the themes, general tone, and tropes that scholars have identified as part of the mainstream discourse in other contexts—a discourse that focuses heavily on the victimization of the Chinese nation at the hands of foreign aggressors (see Buruma 2002; Callahan 2010; Denton 2014).[2] This theme is at the heart of the state's patriotic education campaigns (Wang 2012; He 2007a & 2007b), and the CCP assures that this overarching narrative frames all official materials on modern Chinese history, ranging from textbooks to memorials, from museums to national celebrations. My argument is that the ways in which digital technologies and political prerogatives intersect with human psychology facilitates this victimization narrative, though these factors also introduce ruptures and ambiguities that make such a narrative less straightforward than it may at first sight seem.

My analysis of these processes starts with the online encyclopaedias (*baike* 百科) that China's major search companies maintain online. How do these information repositories present knowledge on the Nanjing Massacre? Next, I discuss the websites that make up the networks I examined in the previous chapter. What kind of discourse do these isolated beacons of information construct? This discussion also includes a closer look at the digital features that such websites deploy. Throughout that discussion, I draw primarily from two dedicated websites that deal with the Nanjing Massacre on China's web: the official website of the Nanjing Massacre Memorial Hall (available at www.nj1937.org), and the commemoration site 'Never Forget' on the influential web portal Sina.com (available at neverforget.sina.com.cn). An earlier analysis of these materials is also available in Schneider (2018). Before I turn to the empirical case of the Nanjing Massacre online, however, a note is in order regarding the idea that communities 'remember' the past. This is an issue that relates more broadly to knowledge, power, and the ways in which history can become a site of political activity.

## Collective Remembering and Outsourcing Historical Knowledge

Dangerous history:

After several weeks of interviews and meetings with digital media professionals in China, I am looking forward to exploring a slightly different topic. A colleague of mine has been busy arranging an interview for me with one of her mentors, an influential historian at a leading Chinese university. The plan was to receive a first-hand account on how modern Chinese history, and specifically the Sino-Japanese War, are today studied at a major research institute in the PRC—an issue that promises to connect my digital interests with more analogue processes. After all, what could be more analogue than 90-year-old archives, archaeological digs, and museum exhibits? One day, I indeed receive a reminder of how digital and non-digital knowledge practices relate, though this reminder does not come in the form of the interview I was looking forward to. An e-mail from my colleague informs me that there will be no interview: 'I am so sorry. I've not received any answers to my e-mails'. She goes on to explain: 'I'm afraid this is quite common. The professor's communications are under intense surveillance. E-mails are most certainly being read, and many messages never arrive'.

As I have outlined in the introduction, modern Chinese history is of paramount political importance to China's leadership. The CCP's legitimacy is closely tied to particular interpretations of history, and any scholarly debate that brings to light the nuances of the past or complicates the picture is unwelcome. This is also true under Xi Jinping's administration, which has issued numerous memos warning journalists from discussing political controversies with foreigners. I have been on the receiving end of these policy choices throughout my project, but as the snapshot above suggests, this imperative to stay in control of discourses also extends to domestic academic endeavours, and to questions of modern Chinese history. It is not clear whether the botched interview opportunity really was the outcome of direct censorship, whether it was the result of more subtle pressures to self-censor and avoid risks, or whether it was simply due to unfortunate technical problems or a personal oversight. It is telling, however, that my Chinese colleague considered it entirely plausible that a historian's e-mails would be tightly controlled by the state. Past censorship outcomes, obscure digital processes, and the strong state rhetoric of what constitutes appropriate political discourse powerfully combine in ways that make it seem risky to discuss issues like the 1937 Nanjing Massacre with a foreign scholar.

What this short anecdote further suggests is that there are two mutually exclusive ways in which to view the past.[3] The first is the ethos of the historian. This ethos treats the past as a forum, as an ongoing discussion between a multitude of understandings and interpretations. In this view, historical facts are resources that people draw from to make sense of and judge the past. History becomes a complex, multivocal, and open-ended process through which human beings make meanings. There is no single 'truth' that emerges from this process, and historical facts only have the meanings that we attribute to them in the present (see White 1987). This sentiment is reflected in the now-famous quote by philosopher Benedetto Croce that 'all history is contemporary history' (quoted in Allan 1972).

This idea of the past as a forum clashes with the view that it is a temple or shrine: something that is sacrosanct, that deserves to be honoured and venerated, and that is immutable. History, in its shrine form, is one grand narrative, a continuous movement 'forward' through time, in which historical facts tell us what is true and what is false. Such historical 'truth' is quite literally 'enshrined' in monuments and memorials, but it can also be promoted through history textbooks, through museums, through cultural products, and much more.

It is this view of the past as a shrine that informs the CCP's view towards history, but it is also at the heart of how nations more generally construct their past. As I discussed in chapter 2, narratives about the past are crucial in imagined communities; that is, communities of people who believe they share a collective purpose, culture, history, or ancestry. In the case of the nation, national elites and, in particular, institutions of the nation state deploy mediated symbolic and discursive resources to promote a sense of kinship ties. Historical narratives are central to this process, and a shrine-like treatment of the past serves this project. This shared construction of a seemingly immutable past is often referred to as 'collective remembering'. As Wertsch (2002: 1047) writes, 'in contrast to history, collective memory reflects a committed perspective, and belongs to one group, and not others'. When societies 'remember', they do so dogmatically, in a controlling way, and without tolerance towards ambiguities (Wertsch 2002: 667).[4]

To create this sense of collective remembering, imagined communities like nations rely on a double trick of perception, one that first retells the past as a coherent narrative, and that then convinces its members that this narrative is part of their own personal experience. Whether or not this narrative account is accurate is not the point. 'What matters', as Guibernau (2004: 135) explains, 'is not chronological or factual history but sentient or felt history'. Collective remembering 'feels' right. The reason such appeals to 'felt history' work as a community-building strategy is that our sense of the past is extraordinarily malleable. It may seem as though our capacity to recollect experiences and information provides direct, reliable access to the past, but human recollection is constructed in our mind, and it is strongly shaped by social relations and context. Recollection is, as Wertsch (2002: 497) writes, a mental effort 'grounded in traces from the past [ ... ] that actively reshapes them in the present'.

One example that illustrates the degree to which memory is constructed comes from the psychologist Kathryn Braun and her colleagues (Braun, Ellis, & Loftus 2002). To explore how personal recollection is affected by media frames, the team asked their adult research subjects to recount childhood experiences at Disneyland. By handing one set of research subjects a fake advertisement beforehand that prompted them to think about Bugs Bunny, the researchers were able to significantly increase some of their participants' confidence that they had met and shaken hands with the Bugs Bunny character at a visit to the resort when they were kids. This memory, however, was not based on actual experience: Bugs Bunny is a Warner Bros. character and would consequently not have made an appearance at a Disney theme park.[5] The sense of personal remembering was seeded by the advertisement, yet it 'felt' real.

Examples like this illustrate how we engage our imagination to construct our personal memories, and how this process can be facilitated by media scripts. Considering the degree to which societies outsource information to cultural products, it is not hard to see how similar mechanisms might be at play when communities imagine their *collective* past, and how traumatic events in living history may come to be seen as 'shared'. For those of us who have not personally witnessed events like terror attacks, natural catastrophes, national parades, or large-scale sporting victories, the valence of these events comes from media scripts that intimately connect them to our own, personal narratives.[6] Discussions of 'collective memory' extend this rationale to the non-lived past, and this is where the connection between the psychology of memory and the ubiquity of digital media becomes important: digital resources about the past are also resources for constructing our feelings of the past. They shape how members of a community appropriate and internalize shared narratives in ways that, at times, 'feel' like individual memory.

Nevertheless, 'memory' remains a metaphor. Nations are not persons, and they do not 'remember' as individuals do. What counts as national 'memory' is thus not so much a recollection, it is a discourse.[7] It is discursively constructed *knowledge* of the past, outsourced by different stakeholders to cultural products that then circulate through networks and invite those connected to the networks to embrace the idea of a shared past.

## The Wikiality of Digital China

How, then, is knowledge of the past outsourced to the web? A key activity in this regard is to archive such knowledge in user-generated online encyclopaedias, the most influential of which is the open access project Wikipedia. As discussed in chapter 3, Wikipedia entries also appear in the results of various Chinese search engines, and Chinese-language articles on the site are, at least at times, accessible from within China. More importantly, Wikipedia has inspired numerous Chinese companies to emulate and adapt the user-generated encyclopaedic model, and online searches for key issues in Chinese quickly bring up entries in the encyclopaedias of Baidu, Hudong, Search Dog, 360's Good Search, or ChinaSo.

It is not hard to see why the Wikipedia model has been emulated in this way. With its millions of entries in almost 300 languages, Wikipedia is a milestone achievement. The collaborative project has received numerous prizes, for instance the 2015 Erasmus Prize for its 'worldwide reach and social impact', and for promoting 'critical attention to text, sources and the expansion of knowledge' (Praemium Erasmianum 2015). At the same time, Wikipedia has also been the target of profound criticism, particularly due to the uneven quality of entries, the predominance of privileged men among the volunteer editors, and the frequently biased position of articles that claim a 'neutral point of view' (or: NPOV, in Wikipedia's own terminology).[8] The satirist Stephen Colbert famously encouraged the viewers of his comedy show *The Colbert Report* to edit Wikipedia articles in fallacious and partisan ways; he then lauded the results as evidence of how the online encyclopaedia 'democratized knowledge' (Colbert 2006) and coined the term 'wikiality' to describe this phenomenon, claiming that it allowed users to 'create a reality that we can all agree on—the reality we just agreed on' (Colbert 2006).

It is important to note that Wikimedia's user-generated online encyclopaedia does not aim to provide absolute 'truths', and that it explicitly invites discussion about the nature of knowledge. To the Wikimedia Foundation's credit, the online encyclopaedia itself provides an excellent article on the various shortcomings of the project in the entry 'Wikipedia'. Also, Wikimedia's collaborators tend to be much more self-reflective and modest about their work than many of the critics acknowledge (Reagle 2011: 23). What is important here is that Wikipedia is meant to be a forum, not a shrine. This is captured in its mantra for 'verifiability, not truth' (see the Wikipedia entry on that phrase), which has come to frame the lively discussions in Wikipedia's open editorial forums. Wikipedia is thus 'highly discursive, analyzing its own take on what constitutes relevant content and how to include it', making it an interesting successor to European enlightenment projects like the French *Encyclopédie* (O'Sullivan 2011: 47).

Today, Wikipedia is a household name, much like Google, and its social relevance is substantial. The open access platform has consequently received considerable academic attention since it was established in 2001.[9] A major issue of contention in this regard has been whether it is appropriate for such a project to aim for a 'neutral point of view'. As Lovink and Tkaz point out in their introduction to Wikipedia research, 'NPOV explicitly makes no claims to provide the truth, but it must nonetheless be based on a truth of what is neutral' (2011: 11).

This issue is aggravated by the fact that online encyclopaedias deploy digital features that change the nature of knowledge production and information sharing, compared to earlier times. In his historical overview of encyclopaedic works, O'Sullivan (2011: 46) stresses that Wikipedia presents a 'wholly new form' of dealing with knowledge, and that 'its digital nature means it is quite different from all pre-internet projects'. Using the metaphor of digital 'space' that I have discussed in the previous chapter, he writes (O'Sullivan 2011: 46):

> Take, for example, English Wikipedia's over 60 million hyperlinks, scattered among its three million articles. These links tend to ensure that any reader who browses for long gets to steer a pathway that few other readers will also traverse. As readers move through a web or network of texts, they continually shift the center—and hence the focus or organizing principle—of their investigation.

To O'Sullivan, Wikipedia has the potential to be radically progressive in ways that set it apart from more traditional, and in his view conservative, compendiums of knowledge like the Encyclopaedia Britannica. Wikipedia is, in many ways, caught between a modernist and postmodernist understanding of knowledge, on the one hand basing its entries on verifiability and facts, on the other hand allowing users to assemble and experience this knowledge in flexible ways. O'Sullivan goes as far as recommending that Wikipedia shed its modernist ambitions, that it abandon its pretence of a neutral point of view in favour of a wholly postmodern outlook that treats all knowledge as socially situated, that encourages critical reflection, and that explicitly showcases debates about knowledge (O'Sullivan 2011: 47).

However one might feel about Wikipedia, these popular and scholarly discussions illustrate that encyclopaedias are powerful filters of knowledge. They are highly political, for instance by serving implicit conservative or progressive goals through the information they create and the ways they present it. This raises interesting questions about how different Chinese online encyclopaedias function. What impression of knowledge do Encyclopaedia Baidu, Encyclopaedia Hudong, or Encyclopaedia Search Dog purvey, and how might they shape public discourse on a topic such as China's past relations with Japan? In short: what is China's 'wikiality' of Japan?

A comparison of the various Chinese encyclopaedic entries on the Nanjing Massacre promises to provide an answer.[10] To explore this issue, I have placed the entries of six Chinese-language encyclopaedias next to one another and compared their structure, style of representation, main arguments, and digital features. The differences are stark, at least between the Chinese-language Wikipedia entry and its PRC alternatives. I have compiled some of the key features that characterize the encyclopaedias and their Nanjing Massacre entries in Table 5.1.

Before going into the details of these entries, a few general features are worth highlighting. Of the six encyclopaedic entries, Wikipedia's article is by far the longest, followed by the Baidu and ChinaSo entries, and trailed by Hudong, Search Dog, and 360's Good Search with articles that are about two-thirds as long as the Wikipedia entry. Especially noteworthy across these entries is the amount of duplication. Large parts appear in all six encyclopaedias, and Baidu, Search Dog, Good Search, and ChinaSo share a particularly large amount of text. In fact, Search Dog's entry is essentially an abridged version of the Baidu article, and ChinaSo's state-owned offer is almost identical to Baidu's. Since these encyclopaedias do not offer information on the version history of their articles online, it is hard to say who has copied from whom, but considering how the articles on Search Dog, 360's Good Search, and ChinaSo conspicuously contain minor alterations to the Baidu entry (e.g., slightly different phrases at the start of paragraphs), it seems most likely that these articles were created after Baidu's, which is not a fully original entry either. It overlaps with the entries in Wikipedia (14%) and Hudong (20%). Considering Baidu's history of plagiarism, and especially of copying Wikipedia's Chinese-language articles (see

Table 5.1 **Encyclopaedic Knowledge about the Nanjing Massacre**

| | Wikipedia | Baidu | Hudong | Search Dog | Good Search | ChinaSo |
|---|---|---|---|---|---|---|
| **Editorial model** | user-generated content | user-generated content, editorial oversight | user-generated content, editorial oversight | user-generated content, editorial oversight | user-generated content, editorial oversight | officially verified (semi-) professional editors |
| **Core principles** | 1. neutral point of view | 1. authenticity | 1. objectivity | 1. accuracy | 1. objectivity | 1. based on authoritative sources |
| | 2. verifiability | 2. objectivity | 2. no original research | 2. objectivity | 2. verifiability | 2. created by certified professionals |
| | 3. no original research | 3. responsibility | 3. verifiability | 3. comprehensiveness | 3. relevance | |
| **Business model** | non-profit | commercial | commercial | commercial | commercial | state-owned |
| **Version history** | open to anyone | hidden | hidden | hidden | hidden | hidden |
| **Comment section** | on dedicated talk page | none | below entry | none | none | none |

| | Wikipedia | Baidu | Hudong | Search Dog | Good Search | ChinaSo |
|---|---|---|---|---|---|---|
| *Respective Nanjing Massacre Entries* | | | | | | |
| **Characters** | 24147 | 20485 | 14802 | 14554 | 18218 | 20301 |
| **Duplication** | 14% | 91% | 32% | 94% | 73% | 97% |
| **References Chinese** | 107 | 40 | 10 | 3 | 3 | 5 |
| **References English** | 7 | 0 | 0 | 0 | 0 | 0 |
| **References Japanese** | 18 | 1 | 0 | 0 | 0 | 0 |

Key features of six Chinese online encyclopaedias and their 'Nanjing Massacre' entries, as of 8 April 2015.

Nystedt 2006; Wikimedia 2015), a plausible scenario is that the editors at the commercial Encyclopaedia Baidu augmented their writing with segments lifted from these online sources, and that the other Chinese online encyclopaedias, in turn, duplicated Baidu's article.

Such a finding is striking, since it calls into question the self-proclaimed values of the Chinese corporations that produce such encyclopaedic entries (see Table 5.1). The sites frequently proclaim their commitment to non-plagiarism in the 'about' sections of their websites, yet they are comfortable claiming copyright for entries that are based on extensive plagiarism. It is further striking that this occurs on encyclopaedic sites that all opt for editorial models that combine user-generated content by registered writers with professional editorial oversight. These added layers of supervision do not appear to interfere with the degree of duplication that characterizes the content. In fact, it is not transparent to regular users who edited which part of which entry, or what editorial decisions informed the construction of an article. Contrary to Wikipedia's model, this information is only available to registered editors—a practice that, arguably, clashes with, for example, Baidu's core principle of acting 'responsibly' (*fuze* 负责) or Hudong and Qihoo's self-proclaimed goal of 'verifiability' (*you ju ke cha* 有据可查).

## The Nanjing Massacre on Wikipedia

How the various online encyclopaedias operate already suggests that the different editorial models might influence what kinds of discourses these sites produce. A careful look at the various encyclopaedic entries indeed shows how the Nanjing Massacre representation differs between Wikipedia and the mainland Chinese services. The Chinese Wikipedia entry on the Nanjing Massacre is a substantial piece of text, comprising 24,147 Chinese characters. At the time of the analysis, it consisted of 10 main sections, and it covered a range of different topics such as the wider context of the Sino-Japanese War, the siege of Nanjing, the various atrocities committed by Japanese soldiers, the role that European and American expatriates played in Nanjing's safety zone, the ways the events were reworked after the war, and their cultural and political relevance today. Throughout, the article references 122 sources, including academic materials, official documents, news reports, blogposts, and films, across three different languages: English, Chinese, and Japanese.

Wikipedia dedicates substantial space to presenting different positions and to complicating the issue, and the entry repeatedly suggests that knowledge on the Nanjing Massacre is no straightforward matter. For instance, the text discusses the various reasons why evidence for the actual course of events is hard to come by, what different kinds of source materials reveal about the atrocities, and how representations of the Nanjing Massacre in both China and Japan tend to be instrumentalized for political reasons. An example is the section that explicitly discusses the number 300,000, which is the official PRC victims count, but which is hard to corroborate with any certainty. The number has become politically sensitive due to its symbolic value, both to the PRC government with its patriotic education campaigns and to Japanese right-wing revisionists who hope to downplay the scope of the massacre. The Wikipedia entry attempts to provide a balanced view of such controversies. In a similar vein, the Wikipedia article explores what structural and historical factors may have prompted the Japanese forces to act as they did, and it reviews the attrition, frustration with the war effort, misleading orders, and other contributing factors that may have sparked or at least exacerbated the mayhem in late 1937 Nanjing.

Overall, the entry adds substantial nuance to the debate, not to mention a fair amount of Japanese materials. In this sense, it indeed attempts to live up to Wikipedia's ideals of 'NPOV' and 'verifiability', but it does so in a very uneven way. The style and quality vary for each section, or even for individual sentences, resulting in an ambiguous collage of user-generated ideas and arguments. This is very much evident in the language: the text switches between simplified and traditional characters, suggesting contributors from different Chinese language regions, for example, Taiwan, Hong Kong, or overseas communities alongside mainland Chinese users. The style, too, changes frequently, for instance from colloquial to highly scholarly language, from literary Chinese to official PRC rhetoric. Some contributors limit themselves to declarative, descriptive, and minimalist statements; others use colourful and metaphorical narrative styles reminiscent of diaries or novels, for example:

> From the riverbanks, the Japanese troops used heavy machine guns and high-speed mortars to fiercely fire upon the rooted [Chinese] troops drifting with the currents of the Yangtze, thus burying more than 2,000 people in the Yangtze in two hours.
>
> 在岸边用重机枪及高速炮向在江上漂流的溃兵猛烈射击，日军称两个小时就使2000多人葬身江中。

These shifts in tone create the impression of a patchwork, and this impression also extends to the quality of the research and the use of sources. While some passages are at pains to verify their claims and assure neutrality, others provide source materials that would be considered inappropriate in scholarly contexts. For example, the entry quotes orders by Japanese officers to rape and pillage through Nanjing at will, yet the source for this quote turns out to be a Chinese-language article by a Japanese historian (Tokushi Kasahara). That source indeed contains the same wording, but it does not explain where the quote originated and provides no further references to the official orders. It is, of course, possible, even plausible, that such orders went out at the time, but the Wikipedia entry depicts this piece of information as verified and factual, when it is actually an uncorroborated assertion.

There are other such instances, for instance on the infamous case of the two Japanese officers who allegedly competed for who could put the most Chinese civilians to the sword. The Wikipedia entry describes this 'killing competition' as a factual episode but fails to mention that the events remain highly contested (see Wakabayashi 2007a, for a detailed discussion of this case). Similarly, the text makes a fair attempt in some passages to stress that death counts often collapse various categories, such as rooted troops and refugees, yet other passages then take precisely such controversial numbers at face value. Indeed, fuzzy categories abound throughout the entry, and this is particularly noteworthy when the discussion turns to the unit of the nation. The aforementioned discussion of the number 300,000, for example, deploys concepts such as 'China' or 'the Chinese side' as self-evident collective actors. Other sections, such as the one describing the commemoration day that the PRC government introduced in 2014, juxtapose the PRC, Hong Kong, and Macau in a way that suggests a collective cause. Interestingly, that particular section on the commemoration day uses simplified character scripts and provides as verification official mainland sources, reproducing the style and language of such state-approved materials to a fault. This raises the question of who is actually speaking on behalf of the compatriots in Hong Kong and Macau.

Overall, the entry moves back and forth between scholarly and official discourse, between casual and high-brow language, and between simplification and nuance. It is very much an example of the messy knowledge construction that O'Sullivan (2011) commends, though it remains an open question what readers make of this messiness, and whether they attribute the same kind of disruptive, radical potential to it as O'Sullivan does. What is demonstrably the case, however, is that this patchwork approach contrasts markedly with the knowledge-making strategies of other Chinese online encyclopaedias.

## Baike-fying the Massacre

The mainland Chinese *baike* model of knowledge archiving is seemingly informed by the same tenets as Wikipedia, for example, verifiability and neutrality, but this similarity is deceptive. The Chinese services set very different priorities, tilting their encyclopaedic model from user-generated amateur content towards authoritative, professional writing. User-generated content is simply an input to the commercial endeavours of these corporations (or, in the case of ChinaSo, of the state), which use reward schemes to fuse play and labour on the part of their users into what is sometimes called 'playbour'.[11] Ultimately, it is the institutions behind the encyclopaedias that claim 'ownership' of the content for their own profit-oriented or political reasons. This alternative strategy to encyclopaedic knowledge is visible in the Nanjing Massacre discourse that Chinese online encyclopaedias relay.

Take the example of Encyclopaedia Baidu's entry on the subject, which is representative of the other Chinese encyclopaedias as well. Encyclopaedia Baidu presents history as factual, and it strongly emphasizes dates, numbers, and original quotes. Contrary to Wikipedia, Encyclopaedia Baidu does not reflect on the *nature* of historic knowledge. Its factual information is not accompanied by critical reflections on source materials and their value. Moreover, the article sidesteps any potential controversies and instead presents the massacre as a clearcut case with a singular truth. This becomes particularly clear when comparing how Baidu and Wikipedia each discuss the Nanjing Massacre's death toll. At a glance, both encyclopaedias seem to present a similar case. In April 2015, the two entries opened with almost identical introductory paragraphs, which I have reproduced and translated here in full, underlining the differences in the Baidu version (Table 5.2).

The degree of overlap is apparent here, though it is noteworthy that Baidu's entry differs in subtle ways, for instance in how Baidu uses only simplified characters whereas the Wikipedia introduction mixes simplified and traditional script in the messy way that I have described above. Some of the differences in the Baidu entry are conceptually significant: the main agent in the first sentence, for instance, is not 'Japanese troops' but 'Japanese militarism' more generally, and the context has shifted from 'China's War of Resistance against Japan' to 'Japan's War of Aggression against China'. These changes already hint at a different interpretive framework in which blame for the atrocities is placed with Japan more generally, rather than with the specific troops that committed the crimes. Another noteworthy difference is the lack of references in Baidu's version—a general feature across all of the mainland encyclopaedias that I return to presently. What is interesting with regard to the death toll is that both entries provide a potential range of victims, based on the assessments of other actors (the post-war military tribunals). In this way, the entries appear relatively neutral and balanced on the issue.[12] This first impression, however, has to be qualified by how the two encyclopaedias each go on to discuss these figures.

Both Wikipedia and Encyclopaedia Baidu include a section that lists the various approaches to calculating the death toll, followed by case-by-case figures for various individual atrocities. However, Wikipedia's entry also provides a section that explicitly discusses the controversies surrounding the death toll. This includes acknowledging how difficult it is to calculate exact numbers, discussing the political symbolism that informs the number 300,000 in the PRC, and carefully referencing different assessments by Japanese scholars that range from 'complete denial' to 'over 200,000' victims. Baidu does not include similar sections. It instead focuses only on approaches that yield victim numbers in excess of 300,000 and omits any mention of the political or scientific controversies that surround such numbers. Instead, its factual accounts are accompanied by

*Table 5.2* **Online Encyclopaedia Introductions to the Nanjing Massacre**

|  | *Wikipedia Introduction* | *Encyclopaedia Baidu Introduction* |
|---|---|---|
| **English translation** | The Nanjing Massacre [3][4] refers to the large-scale massacre, rape, arson, pillaging, and similar war crimes and criminal acts against humanity that Japanese troops committed in the Republic of China's capital of Nanjing during the early stages of China's War of Resistance against Japan. The atrocities of the Japanese troops chiefly took place from 13 December 1937, when Republican China's then-capital Nanjing was captured, until six weeks later, when order was re-established in Nanjing in February 1938. According to the relevant court verdicts and investigations of the Far Eastern International Military Tribunal and the Nanjing Military Tribunal after World War II, between 200,000 and 300,000 Chinese civilians and disarmed prisoners of war were murdered by Japanese troops during the massacre, roughly 20,000 Chinese women were raped by Japanese troops, and one third of Nanjing was burned down by Japanese troops. [5][6][7][8][9] | The Nanjing Massacre ( Japanese: Nanjing Massacre Incident; Nanjing Massacre) refers to the large-scale massacre, rape, arson, pillaging, and similar war crimes and criminal acts against humanity that Japanese militarism committed in the Republic of China's capital of Nanjing during the early stages of Japan's War of Aggression against China. The atrocities of the Japanese troops climaxed from 13 December 1937 onwards, when Republican China's then-capital Nanjing was captured, and they lasted for six weeks, until order was re-established in Nanjing in February 1938. According to the relevant court verdicts and investigations of the Far Eastern International Military Tribunal and the Nanjing Military Tribunal after World War II, between 200,000 and 300,000 Chinese civilians and prisoners of war were murdered by Japanese troops during the massacre and the city of Nanjing was wantonly set on fire by Japanese troops, destroying one third of the city of Nanjing and causing innumerable property damage. |

*Table 5.2* **Continued**

|  | Wikipedia Introduction | Encyclopaedia Baidu Introduction |
|---|---|---|
| **Chinese original** | 南京大屠杀[3][4]是中国抗日战争初期侵华日军在中华民国首都南京犯下的大规模屠殺、強姦以及纵火、抢劫等战争罪行与反人类罪行。日军暴行主要集中在1937年12月13日攻陷当时中华民国首都南京开始一直到之后的6周，直到1938年2月南京的秩序才开始好转。据第二次世界大战结束后远东国际军事法庭和南京军事法庭的有关判决和调查，在大屠杀中有20万以上乃至30万以上的中国平民和已经卸下武装的战俘被日军杀害，约2万中国妇女遭日军奸淫，南京的三分之一被日军纵火烧毁[5][6][7][8][9]。 | 南京大屠杀（日语：南京虐杀事件、南京大虐杀）是日本侵华战争初期日本军国主义在中华民国首都南京犯下的大规模屠杀、强奸以及纵火、抢劫等战争罪行与反人类罪行。日军暴行的高潮从1937年12月13日攻占南京开始持续了6周，直到1938年2月南京的秩序才开始好转。据第二次世界大战结束后远东国际军事法庭和南京军事法庭的有关判决和调查，在大屠杀中有20万以上乃至30万以上中国平民和战俘被日军杀害，南京城被日军大肆纵火和抢劫，致使南京城被毁三分之一，财产损失不计其数。 |

Taken from the Wikipedia and Baidu Baike articles titled 南京大屠杀 on 8 April 2015.

representations of Japan that are suggestive of how this antagonist should be viewed. A lengthy section that presents detailed victim arithmetic, for instance, concludes by presenting 'the Japanese side's defence' (*Rifang bianjie* 日方辩解). It reads: ' "The Nanjing Massacre absolutely does not exist, all of these were regular casualties of war"—this has for many years been the defence that Japan's rightists provide for the atrocities that the invading Japanese troops committed during the Nanjing Massacre'. Later sections go into greater detail about 'the Japanese side', yet these sections are similarly one-sided: controversies about Japan's war history are ignored or are presented in ways that leave readers with the impression that Japanese society must be dominated by rightists.

This is not to say that such egregious views of the Nanjing Massacre do not exist in Japan, or that they are irrelevant in wider social and political debates. A brief look at the Japanese Wikipedia entry on the Nanjing Massacre in 2015 provides an impression of how imbalanced some Japanese representations of the event can be: while acknowledging that Japanese troops raped and murdered Chinese civilians, the entry generally embeds these acts in an overarching narrative of Japanese soldiers trying to apprehend Chinese defectors in a city full of panicked civilians. The argument that the 'incident' remains controversial is highlighted again and again. The entry includes no images of the atrocities; instead, it contains a sole image of Japanese soldiers checking Chinese prisoners for weapons. An earlier version (spring 2013, no longer available) included an image of a hospital staffed with Japanese medical professionals, effectively suggesting that the Japanese presence in Nanjing was benevolent.

Such Japanese representations deserve more careful study than I can provide here. It would, nevertheless, be misleading to assume that all Japanese discourse on the Nanjing Massacre is this reductionist. It remains an open question how representative, for instance, the often extreme statements on Sino-Japanese history by individual right-wing politicians or intellectuals are. Ironically, the interplay between outlandish remarks by members of Japan's far-right interact seamlessly with public outrage in China. The result is an atmosphere in which 'China Threat' narratives may appear warranted in Japan, and in which historical revisionism may strike even moderate conservatives as sensible. In this sense, arguably, the Abe administration has been emboldened or even empowered by the radicalization of the issue as it attempts to move towards revising Japan's pacifist constitution (see the discussion in Wakefield & Martin 2014).

One-sided narratives about the event thus exist in both China and Japan, and yet Baidu's unwavering commitment to a single, clear-cut point of view remains an extreme example of how selected facts can be made to serve a shrine-like understanding of the past. The sense of factuality is strengthened by recurring sections that are explicitly dedicated to providing 'fact', 'evidence', and 'more irrefutable evidence'. Ironically, these sections then rarely provide verification for their factual claims. Encyclopaedia Baidu is not devoid of references, and the Nanjing Massacre entry specifically mentions a number of historical sources in the main article. It also includes an array of historical photos, some extremely explicit about the nature of the atrocities, others showing historic materials such as Japanese and Chinese newspaper reports from the late 1930s. However, the entry does not provide information that would allow readers to track down the source materials. None of the historic materials are fully referenced, which stands in stark contrast to Wikipedia's approach, which frequently provides full bibliographic information, down to the ISBN numbers of specific books.

Baidu's entry referenced 41 sources at the time of writing, which is still a prolific amount of referencing, compared to Baidu's competitors: Encyclopaedia Search Dog and Encyclopaedia Hudong each listed six references and three items for further reading, 360's Good Search Encyclopaedia provided three references, and ChinaSo listed five. On all encyclopaedias, however, these references point almost entirely to mainland materials in simplified Chinese (the exception being one reference on Baidu to Japanese diplomatic documents from World War II, provided by the website of Japan's Ministry of Foreign Affairs). The set of references includes some scholarly materials, but the general emphasis lies with recent state-media news reports or very broad sources like the Nanjing Massacre Memorial Hall's homepage.

Overall, the haphazard referencing practices clash with the self-proclaimed commitment of these sites to 'verifiability'. Surprisingly, the various encyclopaedias have demonstrably mined Wikipedia for text (or have copied from Encyclopaedia Baidu), yet they draw the line at incorporating the reference materials that are provided in the original template. The only exception is, again, Baidu, which makes use of the large fundus of digitized materials that mainland Chinese online archives provide. However, Baidu omits many references, even in instances where historic quotes are indeed verifiable, and where this verification is available online. For instance, the section of the Baidu entry that presents the 'killing match' concludes with the death sentence the two men received at the post-war tribunal in Nanjing. The entry quotes the verdict, which describes the men as 'real human vermin and public enemies of civilization' (*shi wei renlei maozei, wenming gongdi* 实为人类蟊贼，文明公敌). This is indeed a quote from the original 1947 court proceedings, yet the encyclopaedia does not provide the date of the ruling or the reference to this reproduction of the original source. Whatever one might think of Encyclopaedia Baidu's account of this event, its ambition to be factual and verifiable would have arguably been strengthened if it had emulated Wikipedia's approach to referencing.

It is hard to say why the editors at mainland Chinese online encyclopaedias make the editorial choices they do. The various Chinese media experts and media workers I have consulted on this suggest that such practices are the results of diverse factors, such as financial constraints, lack of personnel, or level of editorial skill. It is also possible that cost-benefit considerations make it seem unnecessary to provide meticulous verification on 'common-sense' issues like the Nanjing Massacre, which do not have strong counter-narratives in the PRC. Maybe adding a wider set of references, for example, in English or Japanese, would open the issue up to unwanted debate, or would bring users face-to-face with China's so-called Great Firewall as they click on 'foreign' content that is then not accessible. It is also conceivable that the referencing practices on Chinese online encyclopaedias are related to habits and conventions for instance in domestic academic circles, which apparently provide far fewer references than their international counterparts (see Zhou et al. 2010). I am not in a position, in this present study, to explore the causal factors behind these idiosyncratic referencing patterns, but the effect is that mainland China's online encyclopaedic entries largely eschew the kind of 'see-for-yourself' culture that web-based content could potentially facilitate. Instead of creating a forum for the past, the mainland encyclopaedias provide a coherent narrative that readers are encouraged to take at face value, based on the authority of professional editors.

## Assembling the Nanjing Massacre Discourse on China's Web

The 'collective remembering' that China's encyclopaedic services practice may not link much to other online sources on the Nanjing Massacre, but the discourse on the various *Baikes* nevertheless connects neatly with that of other websites. Where the encyclopaedias provide references, they predominantly mention or link to mainland resources. This includes a number of news corporations and military affairs sites that have either carried news items on the contemporary implications of the event or have dedicated part of their web resources to World War II history. It also prominently includes the Nanjing Massacre Memorial Hall website and the 'Never Forget' commemoration archive on Sina.com, which I examine in more detail in a moment.

Overall, the sites on China's web that deal with the Nanjing Massacre deploy highly emotive vocabulary and recognizable, emotionally charged visual and acoustic signs to evoke strong feelings of humiliation. In this, they emulate the patriotic education campaigns in the PRC, which set up 'a foil of Japanese evil' in order to construct 'a narrative of Chinese goodness', as Gries (2004: 77) writes. This discourse follows a number of patterns, which include reviving the Republican era trope of the Chinese nation as a raped woman (Gries 2004: 79), exhibiting artefacts and images of 'horror, death, and disaster' to show 'spectacular suffering' (Denton 2014: 138), and lending gravity to these accounts by quantifying and measuring the scope of events (Gries 2004: 80). As already discussed, the ever-present figure of the Nanjing Massacre's 300,000 deaths is a case in point, and, consequently, it appears prominently on websites that deal with the event (Figure 5.1).

Enumerations are generally part and parcel of how websites represent this issue. Aside from providing numerical figures, sites like 'Never Forget' leverage physical evidence, historical documentation, and eye-witness testimony to validate their accounts. Much like the encyclopaedic entries, the dedicated Nanjing Massacre websites go to great lengths to present historical materials as 'ironclad' (*tie zheng ru shan* 铁证如山) evidence that the atrocities are 'impossible to cover up' (*wufa yangai de zhenxiang* 无法掩盖的真相).[13] It is noteworthy that this insistence on factuality, and the commitment to a unique truth that it entails, becomes enshrined as a response to right-wing revisionists in Japan. Several of the sites, such as the ones at Sina.com or the Chinese University of Hong Kong, provide names, images, and key claims of revisionists, and then produce evidence to refute these claims. Sina (2005a), for instance, uses a section of its Nanjing Massacre web portal, titled 'history does not brook distortion' (*lishi burong cuangai* 历史不容篡改), to contrast 'righteous voices' (*zhengyi zhi sheng*

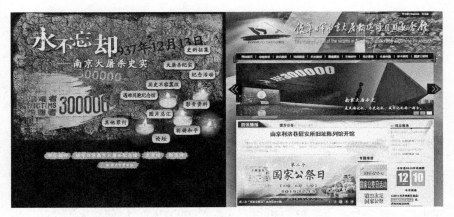

*Figure 5.1* The Symbolic Number 300,000 on China's Web. Homepages of the Sina.com 'Never Forget' portal (left) and the Nanjing Massacre Memorial Hall (right). Screenshots taken on 10 December 2015.

正义之声) with 'remarks that distort history' (*cuangai lishi yanlun* 篡改历史言论).

A particularly popular trope in this context is to compare the events of Nanjing to the Holocaust, and to draw parallels between the war crimes of the Japanese imperial forces and the genocide in Nazi Germany. Sina (2005b) reserves an entire subdomain of its portal to discussing the Holocaust and showing images of Auschwitz. As Denton (2014: 138) has pointed out, linking Japanese war crimes with the systematic genocide that the German Nazis committed, strengthens the official Chinese interpretation of the Nanjing Massacre while simultaneously delegitimizing historical revisionists: 'if it is not acceptable to deny the Holocaust, it is also not acceptable to deny the Nanjing Massacre'.

The effectiveness of such a discursive strategy remains questionable. On the one hand, Chinese attempts to liken the Nanjing Massacre to the Holocaust have elicited criticism for instrumentalizing Jewish history in the name of Han Chinese nationalism (see MacDonald 2005). On the other hand, as Michel Foucault has pointed out throughout his work, constructing such a discourse also opens it up to contestations by acknowledging and, to some extent, empowering the antagonistic position. The obsession with a reactionary Japanese minority discourse may give more credence to that discourse than is warranted. Be that as it may, the effect throughout these sites is not solely (or even primarily) that they inform users of actual events. Such sites draw up a clear and emotionally imbued distinction between the righteous Chinese nation and its historical antagonist Japan. In this, the hyperbolic use of holocaust tropes, misleading as they may be, are effective.

Like the encyclopaedic entries on the event, the web portals that depict the Nanjing Massacre at times also conflate Japanese right-wing arguments with Japanese public opinion in general. However, depending on the web resources, the online discourse is generally quite ambiguous in its depictions of Japan. This is not too surprising, considering the variety of source materials that such websites present, ranging from news articles in conservative state-media outlets such as the *Global Times* to more nuanced scholarly and journalistic articles. In particular, the Sina portal and the website of the Nanjing Massacre Memorial Hall include resources in their expansive archives that mention collaboration with Japanese institutions such as Kyoto's Ritsumeikan University or the Peace Museum in Nagazaki (see Memorial Hall 2005a), and they recount recent visits of Japanese delegations to Nanjing (e.g., Memorial Hall 2005b, 2005c).[14] In these sources, the framework for making sense of the past is the nation; yet, such accounts frequently attempt to draw a careful line between the Japanese state and its people. The call is still to 'never forget history', but this call is juxtaposed with reminders to 'also never forget the history of friendship between the people of these two nations' (*ye bu yao wangji liang guo renmin de na duan youyi* 也不要忘记两国人民的那段友谊; People's Net 2015a). Digital China's discourse on national remembrance thus also has a decidedly transnational dimension that emphasizes peace rather than belligerence.

It remains a matter of dispute how valuable conciliatory remarks or activities are in the overarching Chinese history discourse. Denton (2014: 147), for instance, is optimistic about cases of Sino-Japanese collaboration at the Nanjing Massacre Memorial Hall, which, to him, 'suggest that the site is more than just an empty shell embodying state-imposed memories'. In contrast, Buruma (2002) criticizes that such activities demand a specific level of piety on the part of Japanese participants, thereby effectively precluding any cultural exchange at eye-level. Buruma's point seems to be confirmed by the amount of online images showing Japanese delegations bowing in front of funeral wreaths in Nanjing and accounts of visitors from Japan 'squarely facing up to history' (*zhengshi lishi* 正视历史; Memorial Hall 2005d). Nevertheless, I would caution against focusing on such acts of piety alone. The web resources also tell stories of discussion and debate, of symposiums and conferences, leaving the impression that dialogue at eye-level is indeed possible on issues of past conflicts. An example of this is the 2015 conference that celebrated the 20-year anniversary of joint Chinese and Japanese efforts to rebuild Nanjing's city wall (People's Net 2015a). Where websites showcase such discussion and exchange, the past indeed becomes a forum rather than a shrine. But to what degree do such attempts extend to digital China? This is a question that has much to do with how the online discourse uses the digital elements that the web affords.

# The Digital Features of the Nanjing Massacre Discourse

The Chinese websites that focus on the Nanjing Massacre primarily take an archival approach to history: portals like Sina's 'Never Forget', the Nanjing Massacre Memorial Hall, or the *Global Times*'s web resources are designed as repositories for historical materials. Many of these materials are digitized versions of documents, testimonials, and pictorial evidence from the 1930s and 1940s, though these historical reproductions are accompanied by academic studies and contemporary news articles. The general editorial strategy is to digitize 'offline' materials from accredited sources and showcase these materials online.

It is noteworthy that the creators of the 'Never Forget' website decided against authoring and designing original online articles or blogposts specifically for the web, and the same is true for the other sites that cover the topic. When it comes to contemporary news coverage, for instance on Japanese right-wing politicians or on delegations visiting China, the sites overwhelmingly reproduce articles that have appeared in China's state media (Xinhua, *People's Daily*, etc.), thus largely copying verbatim the official discourse and its rhetorical patterns. In short, the Nanjing Massacre websites focus on digital reproduction, and they deploy the affordances of the web to achieve this end. Media types like text, image, video, and sound are made to converge on these sites, but at the same time the potential hypertextuality of the web is scaled back. The websites hardly ever include in-text links, opting instead to reproduce the non-interactive text blocks of traditional print media.

Where the sites do provide hyperlinks, these links rarely lead off-site. Source materials from other institutions include full references at the bottom, but these references do not point users to original digital templates, for instance the respective online Xinhua News articles. All sources are reproduced locally. The general practice is to provide a lengthy list of links on the homepage, often accompanied by images and teaser texts, and to have these links direct users to individual, full-text digitized articles at a local sub-domain. While these pages often still offer navigation menus for further browsing within the site, overall they seem designed as endpoints of the user's journey. In fact, navigating these resources does not feel much like 'journeying across' the web at all: the links are programmed to open in new browser tabs or windows, interrupting what could be a seamless transition through the materials. Accessing digital China's Nanjing Massacre websites is not so much like 'travelling' through an exhibit, moving through different rooms and sampling the information one comes across. Instead, the experience is more like opening the drawers of a huge file cabinet.

And huge it is indeed: at the time of this study, Sina's portal contained 1,765 posts, including 716 images and 65 video clips, making it the largest of the web portals. Other archives or link libraries, for instance the Nanjing Massacre Memorial Hall's homepage or the military affairs sites Leiting (literally 'thunderbolt') and Tiexue were much smaller, yet they each still offered hundreds of posts.[15] However, the scope of such information archives should not be overstated. The homepages, and often also the subpages, suggest a vast amount of diverse information across different categories; yet, despite often differing titles, many of the individual articles were duplicates, causing users to repeatedly cycle through the same materials. A closer look at the posts in the Never Forget archive, for instance, revealed that roughly one-third of the articles were redundant. Articles and images had often been uploaded twice or more, frequently to unique URL addresses. Sina suggests that its archive is vaster than it actually is.

It is not just the number of posts that leave such an impression. A particularly subtle way that Sina exaggerates its scope is visible on its commemoration site, which allows users to post a symbol of mourning together with a comment. According to the information at the bottom of the comment pages, the site had collected 768,601 individual comments at the time of this study. However, only the first 50 of the approximately 76,000 webpages contained original comments. From page 51 onwards, all pages were simply copies of page 50. Without speaking to the web editors, it is unclear what the rationale behind this duplication was (a technical reason, a strategic choice, or an oversight), but the effect is that users enter a seemingly huge interactive space that is actually quite small.

This leads me to another point: how the sites limit interactions and channel user content into recognizable scripts. Most of the sites have their comment function disabled so that users cannot post messages underneath the articles. The only voices on such sites are those of the authoritative authors. Where websites allow user comments, for instance on the Sina commemoration site or on the military portal Tiexue, the default mode of such commentary is righteous indignation and anger (see chapter 7). These comments frequently draw from racist tropes, and it is popular to demand that all Japanese be killed in retribution for the massacre. For ethical reasons, I do not single out individual users here; suffice to say that the comments frequently use nouns like 'dogs' (*gou* 狗) or 'foreign devils' (*guizi* 鬼子) to describe the perceived antagonists, and that sexual slurs are common.

Such user comments seamlessly tie in with the recognizable, highly emotive signs that the Nanjing Massacre websites regularly deploy. This includes animated Chinese flags, symbols of peace (in particular, white doves), and a host of symbols associated with mourning (e.g., white flowers or grave candles). However, it also includes icons or effects with violent connotations. The website China918.net, an amateur nationalist website on modern Chinese history, uses sniper crosshairs as bullet points for its section headers. An earlier version of the Nanjing Massacre Memorial Hall's website included a picture of the Nanjing city wall at the top of its homepage, animated in a way that would periodically drench the wall in rivers of blood. The Chinese University of Hong Kong used a similar visual trope, overlaying an image of the Nanjing Massacre Memorial's walls with red blotches. The sites make use of a recognizable fundus of emotive symbols, of 'pathos formulae' (Müller & Kappas 2011), which are then stacked to drive home one particular emotional interpretation in different modes.

The link collection on the Communist Youth League issue site is such an example: it juxtaposes a text full of national humiliation tropes with patriotic red colour, exclamation marks, animations of emotive slogans, and flashing red flames, all the while playing a score that combines monumental revolutionary music and melodramatic traditional themes with emotional renditions of movie quotes. The links to the sub-domains of the site are largely broken, but the posts that are accessible play fragments of the following text:

For a nation, for a country, some history can never be forgotten. Forgetting would be a betrayal. 13 December 1937—humanities day of mourning! Japanese troops occupy Nanjing, and Nanjing is reduced to hell on earth! 13 December—recalling this day makes one weep. The deepest suffering of this city is a scar in the hearts of its inhabitants that is difficult to heal; [it makes us] realize our humiliation in the deepest way.

National humiliation cannot be forgotten! We commemorate 300,000 ghosts so that their misfortunes may be engraved in our minds. We venerate 300,000 departed spirits so that all of humanity can experience everlasting peace.

The deepest, most painful grave is at the bottom of our hearts. The greatest efforts of today make it possible to grasp the most glorious future. Standing apart from savagery, standing apart from war, shouting out civilization, shouting out peace—this is how the departed comfort the living; this is how the living continue for the next generation.

对于一个民族，一个国家，有些历史是永远也不能被忘记的，忘记就意味着背叛。1937年12月13日——人类的忌日！日军占领了南京，南京沦为人间地狱!12月13日，一个让人想起就要落泪的日子；这个城市最深的痛，是市民心中难平的疤痕；我们更深地体会到落后之辱。

国耻不能忘记！我们纪念三十万冤魂，是为了铭记他们的不幸；我们祭奠三十万亡灵，是为了整个人类永久的安宁。

最深的痛埋在心底，最努力的现在把握最美好的未
来。远离野蛮，远离战争，呼唤文明，呼唤和平——
这是死者对生者的告慰，这是生者对后来者的承接。

This text also serves as the 'editor's note' for a 70-year commemoration site by
Xinhua (2007). Neither site discloses the source of the audio version, but the
text is extremely popular on China's web. An online search reveals that it is a
common source for emotive quotes with which commentators pepper their
digital contributions. It is, then, not too surprising that the web portals that allow
user interaction do not delete aggressively emotional remarks; after all, their own
representations of the event are often similarly pathos-laden, even where they
evoke tropes such as 'everlasting peace' and 'humanity'. The overarching theme is
that of a humiliated nation that will forever need to remember its suffering at the
hands of 'little Japan' (*xiao Riben* 小日本),[16] and this theme is circulated through
digital China in the form of recognizable symbols and recurring slogans.

## Conclusion

Venturing into digital China's web of Nanjing Massacre representations is an
ambiguous experience. Calls for friendship and peace sit awkwardly alongside
more aggressive, chauvinistic elements of the discourse. What ties this discourse
together is the use of highly emotional signs and tropes that are firmly rooted
in mainstream, official historiography. Overall, the websites that showcase the
atrocities that Japan's imperial forces committed in Nanjing relay their view of
what modern Chinese history should be by treating the issue as a shrine rather
than a forum. This is particularly apparent from the various mainland Chinese
online encyclopaedias, which scale back Wikipedia's model of user-generated
content and 'see-for-yourself' culture to provide the definitive word on the
event—even where that definitive word is heavily plagiarized. The singular dedication to one authoritative account of the past is also reflected on the large web
portals that represent the issue, and by suggestions that 'forgetting' these authoritative accounts would be tantamount to national betrayal.

A major concern across these accounts is to provide an 'ironclad' factual case
about the degree of suffering that Nanjingers had to endure in late 1937. This
strategy is heavily informed by the impression that such past suffering is being
ignored or denied by right-wing commentators in Japan. Much of the discourse
conflates such commentators with 'Japan' more broadly and arguably empowers
precisely the kinds of antagonists that it is claiming to challenge. Then again, the
actual ambiguities that shape debates in Japan would not work well with current

patriotic representation of Sino-Japanese history in the PRC, which relies on 'enshrining' the past in order to strengthen the imagined community of the nation.

This shrine-like logic of the discourse extends to the choices that web editors make to portray the event online. As far as the Nanjing Massacre is concerned, China's web is primarily an info-web. It serves as a repository for digitized historical documents and current affairs articles that users can access through relatively static web portals. The strategies that inform editorial practices for these portals enshrine historical facts on the web while keeping interactivity to a minimum. This is true of sites that were created and actively maintained in the 1990s or 2000s, so before the introduction of the social web ('Web 2.0') with its comment features, 'like' buttons, and sharing options (see chapter 7), but even recent sites that deploy such elements do so in carefully measured ways that do not allow much interaction. The use of digital technology on the Nanjing Massacre websites is clearly anchored in what Benkler (2006: 32) calls the classic mass-media logic of the 'industrial information economy'. Within such logic, websites are not spaces of interaction, nested in communication networks, but single authoritative information sources that broadcast content to a mass audience. This is also why this section of China's web creates the kind of hierarchical network structures I have examined in the previous chapter: the web content and its design follow a traditional logic of how to structure information, and this logic gives rise to an info-web network.

Despite the strong focus on factual, objective history, it is noteworthy that the sites frequently use pathos to frame their accounts of the past, disambiguating their message of humiliation by driving it home in overlapping modes of communication, namely, textually, visually, and acoustically. The Communist Youth League's site is a particularly extreme example, but the solemn visual design of the Never Forget web portal or the Nanjing Massacre Memorial Hall homepage similarly leave little question as to how particular elements of the historical accounts should correctly be interpreted and 'felt'. The default mode of understanding is a sense of deep-rooted humiliation that affects the entire nation. Humiliation at times makes way for conciliation, for instance when web resources depict Sino-Japanese collaborative efforts, and it is in moments like these that history starts to resemble a forum rather than a shrine. Yet, these conciliatory attempts rarely move beyond representations of China and Japan as two unitary actors, and even where websites describe transnational exchange at eye-level, they do so without making use of the web's potential to create actual forums. Comment sections are either disabled or they provide users with spaces to comment in ways that are shaped by the same emotive scripts that also inform patriotic discourse more generally.

What we are left with is the uncomfortable impression that an important piece of Chinese historiography is constructed online in ways that skew the constant appeal to historic 'truth' towards a particular vision of modern Chinese history. It would be tempting to explain such use of nationalist feelings with the CCP's wish to foster national unity and legitimate its rule. Considering how heavily this established topic is dominated by state and party actors, it may not be surprising that it reproduces so much of the discourse that informs patriotic education in China more broadly, but it is peculiar that conciliatory elements and attempts to showcase Sino-Japanese harmony are allowed to move into the background behind more antagonistic narrative scripts. The efforts of officials at the Nanjing Massacre Memorial Hall or at state media outlets like Xinhua suggest that chauvinism is not the preferred mode of understanding relations with Japan. Indeed, state and Party representations of the issue are not monolithic, even if the online representation of the topic largely suggests otherwise. What, then, drives such an outcome? In the Nanjing Massacre case, this has much to do with technical choices—with attempts to create an authoritative info-web and with design elements that privilege the more aggressive instantiations of the discourse, though not necessarily intentionally so. Is it then possible that chauvinism in China's web space is, to some extent, a side effect? As I show in the next chapter, the various interests that are negotiated through digital networks create externalities that, in the long term, may not benefit the actors involved.

# 6

# Selling Sovereignty on the Web

*There is no doubt that the Senkaku Islands are clearly an inherent part of the territory of Japan, in light of historical facts and based upon international law. Indeed, the Senkaku Islands are under the valid control of Japan. There exists no issue of territorial sovereignty to be resolved concerning the Senkaku Islands.*
—Ministry of Foreign Affairs of Japan

*Diaoyu Dao and its affiliated Islands (hereinafter referred to as Diaoyu Dao) are an inseparable part of the Chinese territory. Diaoyu Dao is China's inherent territory in all historical and legal terms, and China enjoys indisputable sovereignty over it.*
—People's Republic of China National Marine Data and Information Service

*In light of the latest controversies in the East China Sea and the Diaoyutai Islands, the government of the Republic of China (Taiwan) reiterates that the Diaoyutais are an island group that belongs to Taiwan and are therefore an inherent part of the territory of the Republic of China.*
—Republic of China (Taiwan) Ministry of Foreign Affairs

The above quotes illustrate how three separate governments frame their designs on a set of islands in the East China Sea. The statements, which were published in the wake of escalating territorial tensions in 2012, each appear on the official websites that the respective administrations have constructed to present their position on the issue: the Senkaku Island website by Japan's Ministry of Foreign Affairs (MOFA Japan 2014), the PRC's dedicated Diaoyu Island website (NMDIS 2014), and the website of the Republic of China's 'East China Sea Peace Initiative' (MOFA ROC 2012). Each presents its claims in various languages (Japan in 12 languages, the PRC in 8, the ROC in 3), and, in each case, the claims are laid out in historical, legal, and geographical terms, accompanied by maps and historical documentations that are meant to underscore their legitimacy.

It is not my intention here to assess the validity of such overlapping claims or their evolution over time. A sizeable set of academic literature already deals with the dispute.[1] My goal in this chapter is to explore how mainland Chinese web resources present the dispute, how they utilize the affordances of digital technology to do so, and how these communication practices contribute to nationalism in digital China. As I argue, there are two dimensions to this issue. The first is that the East China Sea dispute is not primarily about legitimating a claim to territory in the name of a national sovereign for the purpose of securing natural resources, even though it is frequently presented as such online. Instead, the online discourse uses the islands as a foil through which to make sense of Chinese nation-ness. This includes constructing the allegedly shared past that I have already discussed in the previous chapter, but also delimiting who belongs to the imagined community, asserting the moral status of this community, as well as naming and ordering its constitutive elements. The Diaoyu Island discourse is about constructing the very territory in the minds of the subjects who are meant to imagine national sovereignty in the first place.

The second dimension of the Diaoyu Island dispute that this chapter examines is the degree to which the issue is commodified, and the effects that this commodification has on discourses of the nation. As discussed in the previous chapter, the online discourse on the Nanjing Massacre is primarily programmed by authoritative institutions that take on the role of educators. The web archives of digitized materials provide templates for how to correctly make sense of this episode in national history. A noteworthy characteristic that I have so far sidestepped is that these digital activities take place largely outside of commercial spheres. Many of the players are state or Party agencies, and even commercial platforms like Sina have designed their information archives as public services. This stands in contrast to the case of the East China Sea dispute, which includes the kind of public service announcements I have quoted above alongside information from non-governmental organizations (NGOs) and private news enterprises. In particular, the commercial offers are swathed in advertising and click-bait, raising the question of what happens when discourses on sovereignty, territory, and the nation are designed in ways that are meant to sell.

To explore these issues, I first examine the main arguments that web resources in digital China make regarding the East China Sea dispute. This includes a closer look at the official government website that presents the issue, but also a tour through the relevant Chinese online encyclopaedias and the various news and NGO websites that are dedicated to the dispute. Most of the sites deploy visual and linguistic strategies to suggest their position is well balanced and objective; yet, at the same time, their representations strongly draw from the official discourse, avoid ambiguities, construct in-groups and out-groups, and ultimately relay very specific moral sentiments about imagined communities. Nongovernmental actors in particular provide a decidedly militant and frequently misogynist interpretation of national sovereignty. Finally, I turn to the degree of commodification that marks the East China Sea dispute online, and I discuss how the highly moralist framework that characterizes the discourse combines with commercial interests to create particular rationales of how to make sense of (inter)national affairs.

## Rectifying Chinese Territorial Claims

The PRC's official web resource on the East China Sea dispute is the website diaoyudao.org.cn. It was created in December 2014, initially in simplified Chinese only, then versions in English and Japanese were added (February 2015), and later it was expanded further with French, German, Russian, Spanish, and Arabic versions (September 2015).[2] Since I am interested here in how the discourse is constructed domestically, and how various actors appropriate the official Diaoyu Island discourse, I use the Chinese version of the website in what follows. Incidentally, the Chinese version was also the most complete and up-to-date at the time of this study (January 2016). The other language versions frequently did not include the same amount of historical documentation.

Peculiarly, diaoyudao.org.cn does not include any links to other websites, not even to the various state agencies that finance or supervise it. Institutionally, diaoyudao.org.cn is financed by the National Marine Data and Information Service (*Guojia haiyang xinxi zhongxin* 国家海洋信息中心) in Tianjin, which is a public agency under the central administration of the national State Oceanic Administration (*Guojia haiyang ju* 国家海洋局) and, by extension, the PRC's central Ministry of Land and Resources (*Guotu ziyuan bu* 国土资源部). The site is designed and maintained by the China Internet Information Centre (*Zhongguo hulianwang xinwen zhongxin* 中国互联网新闻中心), which is the agency responsible for providing official online information on China, and which is subordinate to the State Council Information Office (*Guowuyuan xinwen bangongshi* 国务院新闻办公室), that is, the central government's PR office. Diaoyudao.org receives links from its superiors, for example, from the State Oceanic Administration, but it does not link back.[3] It epitomizes the kind of isolated beacon of information I have examined in the previous chapters.

How is information on this official site presented? I have reproduced the top section of the homepage in Figure 6.1. Aside from the banner, with its Chinese and English title alongside the PRC flag, the page includes a navigation menu that leads users to different parts of the website, each designed to provide a

*Figure 6.1*  Homepage of the PRC's Official Diaoyu Island Website. Screenshot of diaoyudao.org.cn, taken on 26 January 2016.

particular kind of evidence in support of the PRC's territorial claims, such as geographic rationales, historical arguments and sources, legal documents, selected academic literature, news items, and videos. Most prominently, the page features a sliding image gallery with eight pictures of the islands, each accompanied by short blurbs. All of these images and blurbs follow the same pattern. The images show specific islands or rock formations, often with Chinese names added to the image, while the blurbs provide detailed factual information about the respective islet. This includes the specific longitude and latitude, length and width, surface area, the height of the highest elevation, and a short topographical description. Each paragraph ends with a statement, clarifying that the PRC government has standardized the names of the respective geographical locales. The blurb below, for instance, concludes: 'Our country has already promulgated the standard names for Beixiao Island, its two peaks, and its three surrounding islets.'

The practice of measuring, counting, and naming is prevalent throughout the website. I have already mentioned the discursive strategy of deploying numbers to create a sense of factuality in the context of the Nanjing Massacre discourse, but in the case of the East China Sea dispute this strategy takes on yet another quality. Providing this information is not simply about legitimating an argument by corroborating it with factoids. According to mainland media (China News 2014), the PRC naming practices followed an announcement in August 2012 by Japan's government to survey its maritime territories and disambiguate the official names of, reportedly, 158 islands in order to 'improve their administration.' The exact timeline of who started the naming competition is difficult to establish, but it seems the PRC Oceanic Administration already engaged in similar practices in March 2012, when it updated the PRC's 2010 'Island Protection Law' (*Zhonghua renmin gongheguo haidao baohu fa* 中华人民共和国海岛保护法).[4]

Be that as it may, the promulgation of Chinese names and their repetition in news reports from 2012 to 2014 needs to be seen in the context of a semantic arms race between two governments that each view the ability to standardize names as indicative of wider administrative rights and duties. Naming the contested islands is, in a sense, a way to construct sovereignty over these territories by rectifying names and ordering things—a strategy similar to the one that Foucault observed in his studies of territorial governance (Foucault 1978/ 2009: 20–23). This becomes clear on diaoyudao.org.cn, which contains a subsection on the geographical features of the islands. The section reiterates the measurements and names of the eight most relevant islets, followed by four lengthy tables with the specific nomenclature and coordinates of geological features associated with the Diaoyus, all framed by assertions that the PRC is the legitimate sovereign of these geological formations.

It is worth noting that the practice of standardizing names and measures has a long tradition in Chinese political thought, where the order of things in nature was frequently correlated with the order of society through cosmological rationales. Arguably, most influential in this line of thought has been the Confucian thinker Xunzi (see Hutton 2014), who reportedly argued that moral rectitude could only arise once things had been properly assigned their correct names. This theory of 'rectifying names' (*zhengming* 正名) drew from earlier attempts to agree on an inventory of philosophical concepts (frequently attributed to Confucius; see Steinkraus 1980, for a discussion) and to match signifiers with what they signified. Importantly, the relevance of these debates about language was political rather than semantic. Rectifying names provided 'the means of expressing a moral judgement' (Gernet 1972/2002: 96). As scholars of Chinese history have pointed out (e.g., Fairbank & Goldman 2006: 63–66), such premodern practices of conceptually placing everything in its right place were by no means restricted to the Chinese context. Similar attempts to order the world had also been made in Ancient Greece, for instance. Yet, they developed an inordinate amount of influence in early Chinese cultures, retaining that influence in various forms from pre-imperial periods through to PRC times.[5]

As Ori Tavor (2014: 325) argues, drawing from Foucault's work, the practice of rectifying names is part of a 'project of linguistic engineering' that 'can be understood as a technique of knowledge/power that shapes the way we perceive reality and engage with it. The rectification of names takes chronological and logical precedence since it sets the rules of the game. For these reasons, rectifying names is the ruler's number one priority.' It remains an open question to what degree contemporary CCP attempts to manage language should be assessed in this vein. Take, for example, a recent PRC directive to rein in the non-standard use of puns, slang, and loanwords in state media (SAPPRFT 2014), which has been interpreted as a 'crackdown' on language (Chen 2014), an outright 'ban' of puns (Silbert 2014), and ultimately as part of an Orwellian strategy to control political debate through language (e.g., Branigan 2014).

However one feels about state initiatives to standardize or purify language (whether in China or in other contexts such as France; see Meltzer 2013), such a depiction of recent language directives in China is misleading. This particular notice does not legally ban specific language uses, and most certainly not all puns, but instead instructs state and party media workers to act as role models by avoiding non-standard terminology. Rather than viewing such instructions as authoritarian attempts to assert dominance, it might be appropriate to see them in the context of the belief that the CCP 'vanguard' should empower China's population to become moral citizens, and that providing a commonly shared set of concepts and linguistic protocols is understood as part of this responsibility. It is this moral imperative that is also at work, I believe, in attempts to correctly name and number Chinese territory: by creating a standardized inventory of the nation, the state wills the objects of its sovereignty into being, clarifies the parameters of its politics, and establishes itself as the moral guarantor of national unity. It is an example of how a nation state creates and maintains the shared system of symbols that sustain its foundation: the imagined community of the nation.

Aside from such naming and numbering practices, the nation state also uses the issue of the contested territories to construct a linear narrative of a unified, national past. In the case of the official Diaoyu Island discourse, this means tracing territorial claims back through time to various dynasties. The site provides digitized versions of two dozen documents and maps, dated from 1403 to 1895, each marked up to show that the respective contemporaries had, in their time, already included these specific islands in their geographical and political understanding of the region. Particularly noteworthy is how these sources are integrated into a larger historical narrative, which is summarized on the website in a section titled 'Historical Evidence of China's Sovereignty over the Diaoyu Islands.'

The section provides three arguments in support of its territorial claims: that 'China was the first to discover, name, and utilize the Diaoyu Islands'; that 'China has long exercised jurisdiction over the Diaoyu Islands'; and that 'Chinese and foreign maps show the Diaoyu Islands as a part of China.' Take the first of these points as an example:

> While engaging in seafaring and fishing activities, ancient Chinese
> forebears were the first to discover the Diaoyu Islands and give them

their name. In classic Chinese documents, the Diaoyu Islands were known as the Diaoyu Islets, Diaoyutai, and Diaoyu Mountains. The currently known earliest reference to the Diaoyu Island, the Chiwei Island, and other place names was published in 1403 (the first year of Ming Emperor Yongle's reign), in the *Voyage with the Tailwind*. This shows that as early as the 14th or 15th century, China had already discovered and named the Diaoyu Islands.

中国古代先民在经营海洋和从事海上渔业的实践中，最早发现钓鱼岛并予以命名。在中国古代文献中，钓鱼岛又称钓鱼屿、钓鱼台、钓鱼山。目前所见最早记载钓鱼岛、赤尾屿等地名的史籍，是成书于1403年(明永乐元年)的《顺风相送》。这表明，早在十四、十五世纪中国就已经发现并命名了钓鱼岛。

Note here how the text treats the Ming Dynasty as synonymous with 'China' (*Zhongguo* 中国). This is a practice that elsewhere on the website also applies to the (Manchurian) Qing Dynasty and the Republican era. In this interpretation, the PRC is a direct extension of these earlier polities, all of which collapse into a single 'China,' despite the many ruptures, discontinuities, and diversities that marked each period, not to mention the often vastly different political institutions, cultural practices, and worldviews that set them apart from today's PRC (see Dirlik 2015). Premodern Chinese emperors, for instance, would have seen themselves as carriers of the heavenly mandate rather than as 'Chinese,' and they would have viewed their realm as everything under heaven rather than as 'China'; in this sense, projecting such modern terms into the past is an artificial, though often convenient, shorthand (Ter Haar 2010: 12–14) that is closely linked to nation-building efforts and attempts to create a seemingly primordial national conscience. In cases like the official Diaoyu Island discourse, this practice serves to unify a diverse past and turn it into a single, national narrative.

Moreover, we see here, again, the tendency to conceptualize territories as ancestral places that I discussed in chapter 2: the fishermen who worked these seas were not simply ancient, or Chinese—each term already loaded with assumptions—they were 'ancient Chinese *forebears*' (*Zhongguo gudai xianmin* 中国古代先民). Elsewhere, the website clarifies that 'the waters surrounding the Diaoyu Islands are China's traditional fishing grounds; *generation after generation* of Chinese fishermen have engaged in fishing activities in these waters' (my emphasis).[6] Evoking such kinship ties is necessary to turn a set of rocks into ancestral homelands. Parallel to constructing historical claims to certain territories, the writers at the China Internet Information Office also evoke a sense of national communion.

# Wiki Knowledge of the East China Sea

These communication practices on the official government website translate neatly into the assertive Diaoyu Islands entry on the state-run encyclopaedic service ChinaSo. The introduction to this other official account is worth quoting in full:

> The Diaoyu Island and its auxiliary islands are situated c. 92 nautical miles from our country's Jilong city in Taiwan Province, in the maritime waters of the East China Sea, and its principle islands include the Diaoyu Island, the Yellow Tail Island, the Red Tail Island, the Small Southern Island, the Small Northern Island, and several reefs. The Diaoyu Island and its auxiliary islands have been China's sacred territory since time immemorial; history is evidence and the law is proof.[7] The Diaoyu Island and its other islands were first discovered, named, and used by Chinese people; Chinese fishers have through all ages engaged in production activities at this island and in its coastal waters. As early as during the Ming Dynasty, the Diaoyu Island and its other islands had already been brought under the jurisdiction of China's coastal defences, as auxiliary islands of Chinese Taiwan. The Diaoyu Island has never been some sort of 'terra nullius'; China is the indisputable owner of the Diaoyu Island and its other islands.
>
> 钓鱼岛及其附属岛屿位于我国台湾省基隆市东北约92海里的东海海域，主要由钓鱼岛、黄尾屿、赤尾屿、南小岛和北小岛及一些礁石组成。钓鱼岛及其附属岛屿自古以来就是中国的神圣领土，有史为凭、有法为据。钓鱼岛等岛屿是中国人最早发现、命名和利用的，中国渔民历来在这些岛屿及其附近海域从事生产活动。早在明朝，钓鱼岛等岛屿就已经纳入中国海防管辖范围，是中国台湾的附属岛屿。钓鱼岛从来就不是什么"无主地"，中国是钓鱼岛等岛屿无可争辩的主人。

The passage again deploys the ideas of 'Chineseness' and ancestry that characterize the account on diaoyudao.org.cn, but it also reveals another noteworthy mechanism for constructing national sovereignty in this context. Note the use of Taiwan throughout the segment. The text makes it clear that territorial claims to the islands emanate from Taiwan while simultaneously suggesting that these claims are coterminous with PRC claims. The entry omits the official position of Taiwan's ROC, which holds that the islands 'constitute an integral part of the sovereign territory of the Republic of China (Taiwan)' (MOFA ROC 2013). This position would clash with the mainland Chinese interpretation of PRC territory, and would raise awkward questions about the One-China policy. The ROC's position is consequently reinterpreted here as that of a PRC province, and as an extension of PRC foreign policy. Phrases like 'our country's Jilong city in Taiwan Province' or 'Chinese Taiwan' co-opt Taiwanese territorial claims and reduce what is, in effect, a complicated triangular relationship between three states to a bilateral issue between the PRC and the State of Japan.[8]

How does this official presentation of territorial claims compare to the East China Sea discourse in other Chinese online encyclopaedias? Much of what is true for the Nanjing Massacre entries is also true for the entries on these islands: the lengthy and often repetitive entries plagiarize heavily and referencing practices remain haphazard, with Wikipedia providing 128 references, Baidu listing 49, and other services limiting themselves to about a dozen sources (Hudong and Search Dog; Good Search lists only two references). Links are often broken, and where mainland commercial encyclopaedias provide references, these lead exclusively to authoritative official sources, primarily produced by state institutions like Xinhua, the *People's Daily*, and the China Internet Information Centre.

I do not rehearse the arguments of the previous chapter here. What is interesting about the Diaoyu Island entries in the mainland encyclopaedias is how unapologetically they reproduce the one-sided political position of official media, despite proclaiming neutrality and objectivity. The introductory paragraphs of the various encyclopaedias are illustrative in this regard, and the contrast between the mainland services and Wikipedia is again instructive. Wikipedia's entry attempts to provide a balanced perspective, listing local naming practices from mainland China, Taiwan, and Japan. Its introduction also discusses explicitly how 'interpretations vary' between countries as to how the islands are described geographically: either as a part of north-eastern Taiwan or of south-western Okinawa, leading to different sovereignty claims. The overall impression is that the topic is a complex, multifaceted issue that needs to be viewed from various sides. The mainland encyclopaedias, on the other hand, are not as tolerant of ambivalence and position themselves clearly regarding the overlapping territorial claims in the region. Baidu's entry clarifies in the first sentence that the islands have 'since time immemorial been an inherent part of China's territory.' Hudong's article explains that 'the Diaoyu Island and its surrounding waters fall under the jurisdiction of the People's Republic of China,' adding that 'in reality Japan is illegally administrating the island.'

The various *baikes* thus disambiguate the issue to present what is, effectively, the official PRC position on the islands. The encyclopaedias achieve this end through a number of communicative choices. The first is to contextualize various actors within national units like 'China' and 'Japan.' The entries frequently mention specific agencies such as the PLA navy, groups like Japanese intellectuals, or individual politicians like Barack Obama or Abe Shinzo, and descriptions of their actions can at times be quite detailed. Yet, the actions of these agents are not presented in a way that complicates the overarching narrative, which is embedded firmly in a framework that makes sense of politics as conflicts between nations. Encyclopaedia Baidu, for instance, describes the actions of such diverse agents as 'Japan's approach' (*Riben taidu* 日本态度), 'America's position' (*Meiguo biaotai* 美国表态), 'England's approach' (*Yingguo taidu* 英国态度), and 'the Chinese side's response' (*Zhongfang huiying* 中方回应), making it seem as though individuals, nations, and their states should be understood as single, unified agents. This impression is strengthened by frequent statements that attribute particular actions to 'China' or 'Japan,' and by generalizations about what 'all Japanese people think,' and so on. The terminology of these encyclopaedias is thus already inherently nationalist, meaning that it relies on a frame of reference that sees politically autonomous, territorially bound imagined communities as the natural building blocks of politics.

It may, nevertheless, seem as though the entries are here acknowledging different political positions, but this impression also needs to be qualified. On China's *baikes*, the various national positions are not treated equally. In fact, the narrative is provided from a distinctly Chinese viewpoint, and this bias extends to the provision of factual information. Tables of rectified names and timelines of relevant events make frequent appearances across the various entries, but this factual information is selected in ways that anchor it to a Chinese perspective on the issue. An example is how the entries describe the location of the islands, as situated 'c. 358 kilometres from Zhejiang's Wenzhou city,' 'c. 385 kilometres from Fujian's Fuzhou city,' or 'c. 92 nautical miles from Jilong city in China's Taiwan Province,' thus connecting the readers' geographical orientation to places that are understood to be 'Chinese.'

In addition, the entries also deploy language and punctuation to provide a moral framework for how different positions should be judged, for instance by setting up a clear dichotomy between an antagonistic Japan and a morally superior China. The use of quotation marks is particularly interesting in this regard. Authors repeatedly place contentious terms in inverted commas, but only if the terms relate to foreign positions that are considered morally reprehensible within the Chinese discourse. For instance, the encyclopaedias of 360's Good Search and Search Dog each explain how the recent dispute with Japan started: 'In 1972, the "administrative jurisdiction" over this intrinsic territory was "given" to Japan by America, as part of the Ryukyus' (Good Search goes on to add, as an aside, that 'historically, the Ryukyus are not at all a part of Japan'). Importantly, phrases like 'administrative jurisdiction' are not marked when it is the PRC government that claims such jurisdiction. In fact, the official Chinese position is frequently presented without quotation marks, even where the entries are using direct quotes. In this way, the domestic position is naturalized while others are rendered artificial.

It is worth noting here that quotation marks in contemporary Chinese political discourse have frequently come not so much to mark direct speech but rather to signal counter-factuality, irony, or moral reprehension. This practice of using inverted commas to pass judgement is so widespread in China's media that it seems to at times eclipse the recognition of such marks as a potential means to *reserve* judgement. This became clear after knife attacks on Chinese commuters in Kunming's central train station in March 2014. When foreign media like CNN or the BBC quoted the Chinese government's assessment of the act as a 'terror attack,' Chinese internet commentators were outraged at these news companies for what they saw as a disrespectful dismissal of the tragedy and an attack on the Chinese government (for a discussion of this case, see Cole 2014). Inverted commas, in this view, were a device to question the moral foundations of a phrase or statement, not a device to mark a quote from a government press release.

## The Virtual News Room

The encyclopaedic entries already contain many of the discursive strategies that characterize the topic on China's web more broadly. As I discussed in chapter 4, the networks surrounding this issue are much more diverse than in the case of the Nanjing Massacre, but there are certain patterns with regard to who covers the issue and how. Aside from official government sites and the large online encyclopaedias, one set of Diaoyu Island websites belongs to non-governmental activist groups, and I return to their discourse in a moment. Another set of websites comes from media enterprises such as the nominally private military affairs services Leiting, Xilu, and China International Strategy Net (Chinaiiss), as well as established media conglomerates like Phoenix News' iFeng or state media's *Global Times* web service. This latter group of current affairs sites suggests through its linguistic and visual choices that users can expect a neutral, balanced, and comprehensive coverage of the Diaoyu Island dispute. Factuality again plays a major role in constructing this sense of fair reporting, even though the sites are hardly impartial. Through their use of numbers, maps, and factual information, these websites present the 'indisputable fact' that the Diaoyus are an inviolable part of the PRC's national territory (e.g., the website Xilu).

The factual elements are deployed in ways that create the impression of interactive newsrooms. The sites frequently visualize the conflict in the form of info-graphics. Visual elements like arrows, crosshairs, or comic explosions lend the topic an ostensible simplicity and clarity, for example in an info-graphic that depicts the 2010 confrontation between a Chinese fishing vessel and the Japanese coast guard (Sohu 2010). Other info-graphics depict the issue of air sovereignty in the region, Sino-Japanese standoffs in 2012 and 2013, and timelines of events. It is important to note, however, that while such graphics frequently create a dynamic impression through their use of arrows, shadings, blurry movement lines, and so forth, they do so entirely with the tools of classic print media. The graphics include no animations or digitally native elements such as hyperlinks or interactive pop-ups. In some cases, the info-graphics are indeed taken directly from print media. Leiting, for instance, features a text-heavy figure on the 'ambitions of an island nation' (*yi ge daoguo de yexin* 一个 岛国的野心), which turns out to be an uncredited low-resolution scan of a double-spread special report in Chengdu's *Tianfu Morning News* (2012). The same item also appears on Xilu, and the visual design with its samurai sword and rising sun has further been cropped to provide illustration for blog posts on iFeng and Sina. In a similar manner, Xilu (Bingdou Linglong 2013) recycles an annotated map that originally appeared in Taiwan's pan-blue newspaper *United Daily News* (*Lianhe bao* 联合报) before later being picked up by the *Global Times* (Liu 2013).[9]

In terms of media usage, such examples illustrate how heavily the Diaoyu Islands discourse relies on both the verbal and the visual vocabulary that users are familiar with from the established mainland print renditions of the topic. Chinese web outlets remain committed to traditional media scripts digitized for online consumption, and they closely follow the narratives that the CCP produced and approved.

In the case of the Diaoyu Island dispute, the overarching script is again one that focuses on the conflict between nations. News websites like iFeng, Leiting, or the *Global Times* predominantly showcase the issue as a stand-off between the two sides, using symbols such as national flags or images of military units to visually create a sense of antagonism. Much like the mainland encyclopaedias, these websites use punctuation marks to suggest that this antagonism is by no means one between equals. Articles place key terms on the Japanese side in quotation marks ('air defence identification zone,' 'island purchase,' etc.), but do not mark terms or claims on the Chinese side the same way. Figure 6.2 illustrates this practice. It shows a segment of an info-graphic on the Chinaiiss website that recounts a maritime dispute in July 2012, and that showcases the Chinese and Japanese perspectives on the issue. At first sight, the graphic seems to allocate the same amount of space and deploy the same visual style to each position, providing a fair contrast and even granting the last word on the matter to the Japanese argument. However, the representation is highly skewed. The Chinese side includes unmarked quotes and self-evident claims to national territory, whereas the lower

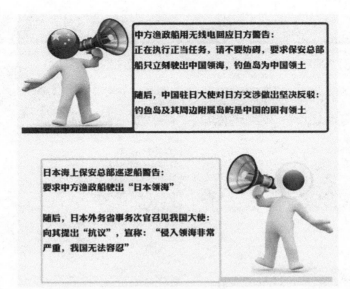

*Figure 6.2* Scripting Bilateral Antagonisms. Info-graphic presenting the Chinese and Japanese positions in a 2012 East China Sea confrontation. Screenshot of Chinaiiss.com, taken on 10 July 2015.

section that presents the Japanese position clearly marks direct speech as well as claims to 'Japanese territorial waters.' The info-graphic is careful to first provide a correct moral framework for the conflict and then contrast it with a depiction that leaves no doubt about the perceived irrationality and maliciousness of Japanese actions.

Assembling 'Japan' as a single antagonist is a crucial component of the discourse, but so is constructing 'China' as a unified actor. The various news websites draw heavily from a pool of national symbols to construct a sense of unity between otherwise disparate groups of people. Most notably, this means combining images of activists carrying flags from various parts of the Chinese-speaking world and then conflating these elements into a general sense of 'Chineseness.' Figure 6.3 shows a section of iFeng's issue website that illustrates this practice. The rather ostentatious title claims to cover 'the history of Chinese people around the whole world protecting the Diaoyus.' The choice of terminology is suggestive: the term for 'Chinese people' here is Huaren (华人), where *hua* evokes a historical imagination of Chineseness (*Zhonghua* 中华, see chapter 2) that connects the present with linearly conceived premodern ancestry, but without reducing this Chineseness to mainland inhabitants alone (see Chun 1996). The 'whole world' is here rendered as 'the two coasts (of the Straits), four territories, and the world' (*liang'an sidi shijie* 两岸四地世界), referring to mainland China, Hong Kong, Macau, Taiwan with its associated islands, and overseas

*Figure 6.3*   Pan-Chinese Unity on iFeng. Screenshot of the iFeng issue website section on non-governmental protest activities, taken on 16 February 2016.

Chinese communities. In the visual representation, this imagined community of *Huaren* is then 'flagged' through the symbols of three polities: the PRC, Taiwan's ROC, and the SAR Hong Kong.[10]

This section on iFeng exemplifies how websites emphasize a pan-Chinese 'non-governmental' element (*minjian* 民间) in the politics of the islands. Such practices have two discursive effects. Firstly, they legitimate Chinese territorial claims by presenting them as popularly supported. This assures that these claims do not appear motivated by any single state actor but instead as informed by the will of the nation as a whole. Secondly, this nation is presented as a community of people who are unified by a common cause: protecting ancestral homelands. Chinaiiss, for instance, features a banner with images of activist groups waving various flags, and the site juxtaposes this imagery with the statement: '1.3 billion Chinese will not hesitate to defend the inherent territory of the Diaoyu

Islands with their fresh blood!' (*13 yi Zhonguoren buxi yi xianxue hanwei lingtu Diaoyudao!* 13亿中国人不惜以鲜血捍卫领土钓鱼岛！). Seemingly banal nationalist symbolism serves to construct this community as united through shared ethnicity, with the territorial integrity of the homeland providing a major signifier for that ethnicity.

Importantly, on the news websites this representation of a diverse 'China' is almost exclusively constructed by actors from the PRC using mainland Chinese sources. Taiwanese and Hong Kong activists are repeatedly covered, but the websites do not normally provide a forum for the voices of these activists. The section on iFeng, for example, includes 26 links that are meant to provide further reading on this united national front. Closer inspection reveals that these links only point to five sources, published at different times over the span of seven years, but all uploaded onto the site on 16 and 17 July 2012, that is, 2 weeks after a stand-off between the Japanese and ROC coast guards near the islands. These sources include two articles from a 2010 *Life Week* special issue published by the China Publishing Group in Beijing (Yuan 2010a, 2010b), an article by the Shenzhen News Group (Jingbao 2012), a *Person's Weekly* report by the Guangzhou-based Southern Media Group (Wei 2011), and an abridged version of a 2005 master's thesis from Beijing Normal University's Department for Ideology and Political Education (Zhang 2005). Hong Kong-based iFeng constructs a sense of universal pan-Chinese ethnic identity solely through five mainland-Chinese mainstream texts.

This web discourse on Chinese identity is largely homogeneous, and yet there are aspects to this strategy of presenting ethnic unity that create inadvertent tensions. This is the case when the news websites attempt to report on complexities that do not easily fit into the overarching nationalist framework. An example is a case from 2013, during which non-governmental actors and individual administrators in Taiwan negotiated mutual fishing rights in the region with their counterparts in Japan. Such acts run contrary both to the relevant categories and the moral standards espoused in mainland Chinese media, and in such cases inverted commas again make an appearance to mark the illegitimacy of these actors and their statements (Taiwan's 'foreign minister,' Taiwan's 'coast guard chief,' etc.). Nevertheless, the idea that 'Taiwan officials' are 'selling out the country' sits uneasily with the idea that Taiwan and Hong Kong are part of a united endeavour to secure Chinese territory. Within the official online news texts (Liu 2013), this issue is downplayed by making the offending actors from Taiwan seem like exceptions to the rule, betraying the kind of group attribution biases that I discussed in chapter 2. However, this angle on the subject is demonstrably lost on the readers who make use of the comment section. The top five comments to the *Global Times* article (Liu 2013) are all belligerently chauvinistic, and they each struggle in their own way to fit the complex transnational processes described in the article into the nationalist frame of reference that the context demands. Most importantly, they do not treat the various actors as an exception to the rule. The following comment exemplifies the general conceptual struggle:

> Taiwan really is a loyal watchdog, saying it's an ethnically Chinese person, but really treating the enemy like a father. How did such a spendthrift get spawned? Now even the dirtiest words won't describe it. To be honest, Taiwan is even more despicable than Japan.
>
> 台湾其实就是一只忠实的看门狗，说是华夏民族的人，却干着认贼作父的事，怎么就出了这么个败家子，现在连最脏的话都无法形容了。说真的，台湾比日本还让人看不起。

Here, 'Taiwan' becomes conceptually comparable to 'Japan,' but at the same time possesses contradictory features, appearing at once dog-like and human-like, adult-like and child-like. Other statements blur the lines between 'Taiwan,' the ROC, its administration, and its president, making these elements appear interchangeable. This conceptual slippage creates serious ontological tensions in which the island of Taiwan both is and is not 'China,' moving the issue into uncomfortably ambiguous waters that are unlikely to be in the interests of the PRC's central government. Such ambiguities are common in digital China's more participatory spheres, for example, in blogs and microblogs, where individual users draw from the discursive resources that authoritative media provide, but then re-appropriate these resources in idiosyncratic ways. I return to this phenomenon in the following chapter. As far as the authoritative news sources that I have examined here are concerned, such contradictions are, nonetheless, the exception. Most news pieces do not shake the ontological foundations of the discourse in the way that this, arguably singular, news item on Taiwan–Japan relations does. Moreover, it remains debatable whether users of these authoritative web portals notice the subtle ruptures in the mainstream discourse. Overall, these sites overwhelmingly earmark the Diaoyu Island controversies as a conflict between nations, and their symbols and statements align neatly to drive this general understanding home.

# Non-Governmental Web Activism

While the issue websites by large news organizations frequently mention various NGOs, they do not provide space for these organizations to articulate their respective discourse on the island dispute. How do the activist groups present themselves and their endeavour?

On the Chinese-language web, three websites promote non-governmental, pan-Chinese interests in the Diaoyu/Senkaku Island dispute. All three are registered in Hong Kong but maintain close ties to mainland actors. The first is the Action Committee for Defending the Diaoyus (*Bao-Diao xingdong weiyuanhui* 保钓行动委员会), which at the time of writing showcased its activities at diaoyuislands.org. The second organization is the Chinese Federation for Defending the Diaoyus (*Zhongguo minjian bao-Diao lianhehui* 中国民间保钓联合会), or CFDD, which maintained the website cfdd.org.cn from 2004 to 2016, at which point it became defunct, for reasons unknown to me. The CFDD was formally established in Hong Kong in 2004 but unofficially continued the work of Beijing-based activists that started in 1996. The federation's financial accounts were also located in Beijing. The third organization, the World Chinese Alliance in Defence of the Diaoyus (*Shijie huaren bao-Diao lianmeng* 世界华人保钓联盟) or WCADDL, is headed by a former representative of the New Party (*Xindang* 新党) on Taiwan, a conservative party that promotes Chinese unification. The WCADDL maintains chapters across the Chinese-speaking world and has its website at wcaddl.org.

Of the three advocacy sites, only the first (diaoyuislands.org) is fully linked into the issue networks that I discussed in chapter 4. This is, in part, due to co-linkages with the prominent amateur history website china918.net, which is a well-connected nationalist site from the mainland.[11] It is, in part, due to the organizers' web activities, which include, on the one hand, frequent updates since the site was launched in 2006 and, on the other hand, references to a broad range of Chinese and international institutions. Of the other two organizations, only wcaddl.org appears in certain network constellations, but not prominently so. I was only able to isolate the site's connections in follow-up studies to my initial network analyses of early 2013. Web linkages to and from this site increase in the months and years after the territorial dispute that took place in late 2012. In the wake of that event, both diaoyudao.org and wcaddl.org gradually step up their activities, updating their sites and links, and, in the case of wcaddl.org, undergoing an overhaul in 2014. It is likely that these changes are responsible for more visible online linkages between these non-governmental actors in recent years.

Note that, in the broader scheme of Diaoyu Island networks, any linkages between such activist groups disappear behind the more powerful actors and their connections. Non-governmental activities are not central to the online discourse. Their presence and (lack of) interconnections on the web nevertheless reveal a number of patterns. Firstly, ties within this sub-network are primarily due to mutual acknowledgements between wcaddl.org, diaoyuislands.org, and china918.net. The CFDD website never appeared in any co-link analyses, whether of the first or second degree, regardless of which combinations of starting websites one used to map this part of the web. It did, however, receive references from diaoyuislands. org. Other actors that these sites frequently referenced were familiar web services like Baidu's online encyclopaedia, iFeng news, and the PRC's Ministry of Industry and Information Technology (MIIT). The reason the ministry is linked into this network is that wcaddl.org and china918.net run on mainland servers. Consequently, they have to feature the obligatory web registration number and MIIT link at the bottom of their homepage (see MIIT 2016). This is also true for the CFDD, which similarly had a Beijing-based IP address.

It is not just IP geo-location that the websites of the CFDD and WCADDL share with mainland web offers. Both websites largely follow the same design and communication choices as the large news hubs that I have discussed earlier, providing densely packed archives of images, videos, and articles. The WCADDL web service also provides official PRC information such as tables of rectified names and measures. The websites follow the familiar pattern of posting authoritative historical and current affairs information that falls within mainstream discourse. The WCADDL, for example, reproduces current affairs articles that have appeared in mainland state media, for example, the *Global Times*. There are, however, important differences between the non-governmental websites and the large commercial or state web offers from the mainland.

Take, for instance, the case of the Action Committee for the Defence of the Diaoyus and its website diaoyuislands.org, which presents itself in a somewhat amateurish way, with generally basic layout as well as somewhat haphazard colour choices and scripts that vary from page to page. It is small in scale, comprising mostly photos of rallies as well as old-fashioned link lists and message boards. The links include references to sources on the mainland, but also to a Canadian charitable organization and a web forum from Taiwan. The website's international dimension is also visible in the web resources that the site deploys, such as Facebook, Twitter, and YouTube. All of these services were inaccessible from within the PRC at the time of writing, but they remain popular in Hong Kong. This, then, is the main feature that sets diaoyuislands.org apart from the other sites: its local Hong Kong focus. In terms of the activities it covers, its language choices (traditional Chinese only), and its self-presentation, the site is strongly grounded in this particular city. The combination of local and global focus, of amateur content and dedicated maintenance, all lend the site an air of authenticity: here is a small group of activists from Hong Kong who promote their nationalist agenda through public protests and who present their activities on their own website.

This impression is markedly different from that of the other two non-governmental web presentations, that is, of the CFDD and the WCADDL, both

of which cater more strongly to a mainland audience and have a much more professional design, even though they at times use traditional Chinese characters
rather than the simplified scripts common on the mainland (see the petition text
below). That said, both websites also promote their individual causes, for example, attempts to sail to the disputed islands, and they each make use of participatory media such as web forums to allow broad discussion. Importantly, these
sites do not function here as 'forums' in the sense that I discussed in the previous
chapter. The activist discussions are still committed to singular perspectives.
Despite their interactive features, it makes more sense to view them as interactive shrines rather than forums of debate.

Finally, the sites also host original content. The CFDD, for instance, contained
mostly articles that were written and posted by organization members in 2007 or
2008. The presentation of these articles remained committed to traditional media
protocols, eschewing hyperlinks, and generally constructing the webpages as
endpoints of the user's engagement, but they nevertheless presented individual
voices on the issue, even if these voices reproduced primarily the accepted, dominant discourse on the islands.

The WCADDL, similarly, uses its web presence to advocate its own
agenda and activities. For instance, the alliance maintains its own, separate e-
commerce site. The organization has also published its own book, which deals
with the flora and fauna of the Diaoyu Islands (Li 2014). On its website, the
WCADDL sells this book for 50 RMB (c. 5 euro), and it ships the mail orders from its Xiamen chapter. To promote the book, the website has digitally
reproduced its preface, in which the alliance's president Huang Xilin (黄锡麟)
explains the relevance of the publication (WCADDL 2014). This introduction
starts by dating China's sovereignty claims over the islands back to the Ming
Dynasty, goes on to criticize the Japanese actions of 2012, and finally concludes
that knowledge of the island's wildlife will 'reduce the distance between us and
the Diaoyu Islands' (*lajin women he Diaoyudao de juli* 拉近我们和钓鱼岛的
距离). The organization here explicitly constructs knowledge on this territory
in a way that turns the island into a tangible, living and breathing place.

While this strategy neatly connects to the construction of territory in the official online discourse that I have outlined previously, the alliance also goes beyond
such practices, at times out-doing the central government agencies and mainland
news services in their nationalism. An example is how the WCADDL means to
lobby the PRC government to increase nationalism in mainland Chinese education. To promote this agenda, the alliance has set up an online petition that
calls on the central Ministry of Education to step up its patriotic education in all
textbooks and course curricula that might relate to issues of Chinese territorial
integrity. The call-to-action spells out the reasoning, which is worth translating
here in full, since it illustrates how certain actors in digital China challenge the

PRC government's highly nationalist educational policies, based on the perception that these measures are not nationalist *enough* (WCADDL n.d.):

> Japan's nationalization of the Diaoyu Islands is a scheme to implement the invasion and occupation of the Diaoyu Islands at the legal level!

> Japan's revisions of textbook content related to the Diaoyu Islands is a scheme to implement the invasion and occupation of the Diaoyu Islands at the level of education!

> Those outstanding descendants of the Chinese nation who have a sense of justice will never accept Japan distorting the facts about the Diaoyu Islands' history!

> We hope that everyone will participate and come together to push the Ministry of Education to augment and revise the content related to the Diaoyu Islands in China's textbooks. Actively participate in this petition by signing your name and leaving a message; use your strength for the Diaoyu Islands!!!

> Comparison of China's and Japan's Attitude towards Textbooks

> Subject focus of Japan's textbooks: ten subjects such as social studies, geography, history, civics, and more.

> Subject focus of China's textbooks: limited to geography.

> Japan's attitude: (1) unceasingly augment and revise textbook content related to the Diaoyu Islands; (2) from contested territories to inherent territory.

> China's attitude: (1) has never carried out any augmentation or revisions, touches on the subject with few words and only lightly.

> We demand:

> 1. China's Ministry of Education must augment and revise the textbook content related to the Diaoyu Islands.
> 2. China's government must fight back with concrete actions against Japan's provocative actions on the Diaoyu Islands.

日本國有化釣魚島是企圖通過法律層面對釣魚島實施侵占！
日本修改教科書釣魚島内容，是企圖通過教育層面對釣魚島實施侵占！
有正義的中華民族優秀子孫，是絕不會接受日本篡改釣魚島歷史的事實！
希望大家參與進來一起來推動教育部對中國教科書裏關于釣魚島内容的增補和修改。積極參與這個投票并寫下你的留言，爲釣魚島出一分力！！！

中日兩國關于教科書的态度對比

| 日本教科書科目 | 社會科、地理、曆史、公民科等十種 |
|---|---|
| 中國教科書科目 | 僅限于地理 |
| 日本的态度 | 1、　對教科書釣魚島內容不斷進行修改和增補。<br>2、從有爭議到成了固有領土。 |
| 中國的态度 | 1、從來沒有過進行過增補和修改，三言兩語，輕描淡寫。 |

我們要求：

1、中國教育部應該對教科書裏關于釣魚島內容方面進行增補和修改。

2、中國政府應該用實際行動回擊日本在釣魚島上的挑釁行爲。

It is, arguably, beside the point here that the petition misrepresents didactic practices both in China and Japan. What the petition exemplifies, however, is how a nationalist group constructs its own dualistic and highly nationalist perspective of regional history. It also exemplifies how this group envisions political actions in support of its perspective: as state-centric, authoritarian interventions into nation-based educational programmes. The perceived thought-work by 'Japan' is thus answered with a call to step up parallel activities at home.

The website uses the digital affordances of web-based communication to make this case, gather support, and lobby political actors. Aside from the petition itself, the site also includes a hovering pop-up that promotes the petition and an online poll that asks visitors whether they support or oppose the petition's sentiment. According to the poll, 96% of those who participated supported the petition's thrust. The total number of participants, however, was just slightly over 500 at the time of writing. In the context of China's internet, with its hundreds of millions of active users, this is hardly an impressive number. Without more detailed user data, it is not possible to assess how popular the site actually is, let alone who precisely is attracted to its activities. It is possible that many more names were submitted to the written petition than appear in this in-house poll. Regardless of the breadth of support, the WCADDL's activism did elicit a response from the respective ministry, which sent an official letter on 12 August 2015 thanking the alliance for its work and vaguely promising to promote territorial awareness further (WCADDL 2015). While this letter is hardly evidence that the organization and its activities affected Chinese politics, it is telling that a group with a potentially marginal position attracted attention from a ministerial-level state institution.

While it may not be possible to establish the exact online demographics that fuel the non-governmental activism on the Diaoyu Island issue, it is possible to explore who is most prominently represented within this discourse. I have collected all images from the NGO sites that depict the organizations and their activities offline. The WCADDL website shows almost 500 people in its images, protesting against Japan, sailing to the contested waters, attending meetings, burning flags, and so forth. Of the people in these images, 85% are male. Most are middle-aged or elderly men. On the website of the action committee, the gender imbalance is even more extreme. The site only depicts a total of 65 people engaged in activism, but, of these, only five are women (so: 8%).

The gender representation on the CFDD website appeared to be more even, but this was due to several factors: the majority of images that depicted the organization's activities were defunct; the remaining images mostly showed historical events, or they related to broader issues like the 2008 protests about foreign media reporting on China, or activism surrounding the legacy of forced sexual enslavement during the Sino-Japanese War. However, this should not distract from the skewed gender image that the site nevertheless presented. When it came to its nationalist narratives, the site's webmasters betrayed a deeply misogynist attitude. Take the case of a 2007 photo that made the news in the PRC. It depicted a girl holding a banner with the Chinese message 'remember like a child, study history like an adult' (*xiang haizi yiyang jizhu, xiang laoren yiyang du shi* 像孩子一样记住，向老人一样读史). The message, reportedly inspired by activities to commemorate the Nanjing Massacre (Xinhua 2007), is promoted on CFDD under the title 'On December 13th, she was China's most beautiful girl' (CFDD 2007). The accompanying post by a CFDD web editor lauds the woman for her patriotic sentiment, despite being 'delicate' (*xiuqi* 秀气) and 'frail' (*chanruo* 孱弱). The text then goes on to explain that her patriotic attitude makes her beautiful, even when it is not entirely clear from the photo itself 'whether or not she is also physically attractive' (*ta shifou wai zai zhenzheng meili* 她是否外在的真正美丽). Referencing a revolutionary song, the author presents his conclusions about the nation and about women. He writes:

> China's men should stand at the front, because 'the whole country's average folks' stand behind them, folk that are just like this beautiful girl. This must compel China's men to stand at the front, confronting the enemy without ever falling back a single step, resolutely and thoroughly exterminating the enemy, defending mothers, defending wives, defending daughters, and defending our beautiful sister.
>
> 中国的男人应该站在最前面，因为后面有"全国的老百姓"，他们就是像这位美丽的女孩一样的全国老百姓。这必须要求

中国的男人站在最前面，决不后退一步地挡住敌人并坚决彻
底地消灭敌人，保卫母亲，保卫妻子，保卫女儿，保卫我们
美丽的姐妹。

In the CFDD's martial discourse, Chinese women are best viewed as delicate wives, mothers, and daughters who are not capable of defending themselves without the strong men that sites like this envision as national heroes. On China's non-governmental websites, the Diaoyu Island issue is thus highly gendered and arguably betrays what Chinese feminists disparagingly call 'straight man cancer' (*zhinan'ai* 直男癌), meaning narrow-minded, highly self-righteous misogynist discourses (see Tang 2015). The NGO websites may not always delve into such explicitly sexist sentiments, but they generally exhibit a lack of female perspectives, opting instead to speak on behalf of women from the perspective of men. This is symptomatic of the nationalism discourse more generally, which frequently evokes metaphors that turn China's sovereign territory into a woman in danger of being raped by antagonistic forces.

## Commodifying the Nation

This proximity of nationalism and misogyny is particularly visible in the commercial parts of digital China's Diaoyu Island networks. In general, the Diaoyu Island discourse is heavily commodified. This is especially the case for the various commercial news websites I have discussed above, for example, the numerous private military affairs sites like Xilu or Leiting. These websites rely on web advertising to make a profit, and this introduces dynamics to the topic that both draw from and reinforce a perniciously gendered perspective of international affairs. On these sites, content leans heavily towards tabloid-like features, interspersing information on military issues with images of scantily clad girls. Some of these women wear uniforms or playfully fondle guns (exclaiming, for instance, 'oh it's so loud!'), most are stripped to their underwear and shown in compromising positions. Pop-ups are ubiquitous, as is click-bait that leads to conspiracy theories, gambling sites, pornography, or snuff content. Figure 6.4 provides a comparatively harmless example from the homepage of the military website Xilu. Surfing through the content on territorial sovereignty quickly yields much crasser images and videos, including pictures of raped and murdered women.

Such content choices are suggestive as to who the perceived target audience of the issue might be. The site managers seem to have a predominantly male audience in mind, and they assume that these readers will have a fetish for phallus-shaped military equipment and masculine power fantasies, while simultaneously

*Figure 6.4*  Guns, Games, and Girls. Click-bait on a military affairs website. Screenshot of the section 'military history picture archive' on Xilu.com, taken on 10 July 2015.

being in need of pharmaceuticals that promise to counter hair loss or lack of sexual virility. The amount of computer-game advertising further suggests that content creators and advertisers are hoping to attract the kinds of users who are frequently (though not necessarily accurately) associated with China's vibrant PC computer gaming scene: lonely, frustrated, and possibly unemployed men who have lost out during China's rapid economic transformation and have few prospects to attract a partner from across China's highly uneven gender divide. This group of men has become known as the 'diaosi' (屌丝), or China's 'loser' generation (for a nuanced discussion, see Szablewicz 2014).

Two points are worth noting here. The first is that the offers on commercial military affairs websites are the result of digital capitalist rationales. Web editors and content creators derive their income from advertising profits, and these profits are, in turn, accrued when users access web content with online ads. A similar dynamic holds sway in other parts of China's media system, for instance in broadcasting, where misleading assumptions about audience behaviour create incentives to produce conservative content (see my own work in Schneider 2012: ch.6). In the case of web content, such dynamics are compounded algorithmically. Success or failure on the commercial web relies on computer-generated feedback that sheds light on 'site traffic,' that is, on the frequency with which certain content was accessed. This feedback is created by web analytics software that measures clicks, or 'page views,' and this produces incentives to create specific forms of content. In the case of the Diaoyu Island discourse on China's web, the consequence of these dynamics is that assumptions about an algorithmically constructed target audience define how the issue is structured, presented, and promoted.

Ultimately, the content on these sites says little about who actually visits them, or whether the visitors indeed read, understand, let alone internalize the discourse presented there. Popular Chinese nationalism is frequently associated with young men, both domestically and in foreign accounts; much of the discussions over who drives contemporary nationalism assumes that it is 'angry youths' (*fenqing* 愤青) who continue the tradition of politically radical student movements of the past (Rosen 2009). Judging by the amount of videogame, military, and pornographic content, it seems that the websites also assume that such 'angry youths' are accessing their web offers. And yet, the caricature of sexually frustrated male users with gaming addictions that the sites take for granted as their prime audience may not actually exist as a coherent demographic.[12] With regard to the online discourse, this hardly matters. The discourse is very much shaped by a self-fulfilling prophecy: from the perspective of website optimization, it makes no difference whether the hits that a page receives represent approval by the assumed target audience or disapproval by users who clicked the content for whatever other reason. It does not matter whether visitors are young men or a completely different demographic. What matters is that this representation of China's territorial sovereignty generates clicks, which, in turn, provides the incentive to continue framing the issue in the simplistic chauvinistic terms that ostensibly generated the clicks. It is conceivable, at least theoretically, that neither the creators of the web content, nor most of the users that access it support the underlying sentiment, but that their interactions within the logic of digital capitalism nevertheless create incentives to frame the issue thusly.

The second point worth noting about the degree of commodified, pornographic offers in this part of China's web is that the racy content is not blocked by the censors. As I have discussed elsewhere (Schneider 2012: 172–173), the CCP's censorship regime is built around the self-proclaimed goal to weed out four types of content: porn, violence, drugs, and gambling. All four types are available in abundance here. Considering the degree of sophistication with which China's censors monitor the web, I find it highly unlikely that this is an oversight. Considering the staggering amounts of revenues that web advertising generates in digital China, and particularly the way in which the porn industry is often at the forefront of digital commerce, it seems plausible that the censors turn a blind eye to the ways in which the discourse becomes sexualized and radicalized for commercial consumption.

Regardless of the reasons behind this tacit acceptance, the effect is that political actors, commercial enterprises, NGOs, and internet users alike are all locked into a rationale that makes digital nationalism a viable commodity. The results can be quite bizarre, for instance when the links on the non-governmental website cfdd.org do not take users to nationalist content as promised but instead to a digital casino from Macau. The non-profit organization WCADDL similarly opts to bolsters its budget through capitalist practices, though in this case the method to generate income is tied to the cause: at its sister-site gouwu.wcaddl. org, a member of the alliance has set up his own nationalist web store. Through the site, users can purchase a variety of Diaoyu Island–themed commodities, ranging from beer to tea, from towels to suitcases (Figure 6.5).

*Figure 6.5* Commodified Nationalism. Diaoyu Island-themed consumer products, as sold on gouwu.wcaddl.org on 20 February 2016.

The owner of the store, who runs his business from the city of Baoding in Hebei province, describes his enterprise as an experiment in generating funding while simultaneously creating territorial awareness in China:

> This is an attempt. For the longest time, the private Chinese folks defending the Diaoyus have made extraordinary efforts to return the Diaoyu Islands to China's territory as soon as possible. From each of their by no means comfortable lives have they squeezed massive amounts of time and energy, and yet they were unable to raise funds. I know, none of the colleagues defending the Diaoyus have complained or have any regrets!
>
> Every time we see Japan's rightists, with their vast and mighty motorcades, convene anti-Chinese activities, we can't help but feel indignation at how weak China's popular patriotism is.
>
> We should be much more formidable than the enemy! Only that way will we be able to effectively take a stand and defeat them!
>
> The Defend the Diaoyus online store is precisely such an attempt. We are attempting to create a sustainable source of capital for the popular patriotic protection of the Diaoyus. Thus we will fundamentally grow in strength and we will be able to continue our mighty and sacred patriotic undertaking.
>
> If we succeed! China's popular patriotic movement to protect the Diaoyus will enter a new period of expansion.
>
> Should we fail! Please draw lessons from my experience.
>
> In any case, the patriotism of China's popular Diaoyu-protection will take a step forward! It will continuously move forward!
>
> Come! My beloved compatriots!
>
> Come on! My beloved Diaoyu-protection brothers!
>
> On the patriotic road we shall always remain!
>
> Until the Diaoyu Islands are returned we vow to stay our chosen course!
>
> The Protect the Diaoyus shopping centre is now online! It fervently expects your patronage!

> 这是一个尝试。长期以来，中国民间保钓人士为了中国领土钓鱼岛早日回归中国，做出了艰苦卓绝的努力。在各自并不宽裕的生活中挤出了大量的时间和精力、还有无法计算的金钱。我知道，所有保钓同仁都无怨无悔！
>
> 每次看到日本右翼的车队浩浩荡荡的举行反华活动。不由得感慨中国民间爱国力量的薄弱。

我们应该比敌人更强大才是！这样，才能做有效的抗争，并打败他们！

保钓实 体店，就是这样一个尝试 。我们尝试用商业的形式，创造一个持 续民间爱国保钓资金来源。从而从根本上壮 大并可持续伟大而神 圣的爱国事业。

如果成功！中国民间爱国保钓运动将进入一个新的发展时期。

假如失败！请汲取我的经验教训。

无论如何，中国民间保钓爱国的脚步，将会一起向前！一直向前走下去!

来！我亲爱的同胞！

来吧！我亲爱的保钓兄弟！

爱国路上，我们一如既往！

钓鱼岛回归，我们矢志不渝！

现在，保钓商城也在网上上线了！热切期待您的光顾！

Fusing nationalist activism with the logic of capitalism, the online store promises to donate half of its proceeds to the WCADDL. The aim is to aid the alliance in maintaining its boat, the 'Protect the Diaoyus' (*Bao-Diao hao* 保钓号), and to organize activist cruises to the contested territorial waters. Each sold bottle of Diaoyu Island beer will contribute the equivalent of 30 cents to that cause.

## Conclusion

On China's web, diverse actors shape the discourse on the contested Diaoyu Islands and their relevance to the Chinese nation. The state uses its official web resources to construct these abstract territories into tangible places, anchoring them in space and time to a linear narrative of Chineseness. This discourse is reproduced by mainland Chinese encyclopaedias and large current affairs news websites, which rely heavily on nationalist categories to reduce the complexity of the issue and pass moral judgement about the righteousness of PRC claims. Antagonistic Japanese actors are conflated into the unitary agent 'Japan,' which is then framed as sinister, belligerent, and generally morally inferior to the Chinese nation. China, in this discourse, becomes the repository for various diverse groups from across the Chinese-speaking world, including compatriots from Hong Kong and Taiwan, who are imagined as a single force with a common goal: securing the territorial foundation of the PRC.

Among the websites that contribute to this discourse are organizations that present themselves as bottom-up, popular initiatives. These NGOs frequently reproduce the mainstream discourse, and they tie into efforts that portray the protection of Chinese territory as a unifying pan-Chinese endeavour. The discourse of amateur groups frequently draws from the content that authoritative mainstream actors have created, but it also re-appropriates that content to make militant and, at times, radically authoritarian claims that effortlessly outshine even the most orthodox positions in official sources. Most noticeable across this discourse is its general degree of misogyny. The actors that are engaged in the issue are, overwhelmingly, older men who present a militaristic and highly gendered view on the subject. These actors claim to speak for all of China, and they construct a vision of the Chinese nation in which women play the role of beautiful yet frail national treasures that require the protection of self-styled righteous men.

Such sexist sentiments connect neatly with the commercial content that frames the articles and info-graphics on territorial issues. This section of China's web confronts users with swathes of pop-ups and advertisings that peddle gambling opportunities, pharmaceuticals, and pornographic representations of women. Is it the misogyny of the nationalist discourse that makes such advertising viable, or is it such advertising that inspires the misogynist discourse? It is hard to say in which direction the causalities run, but it may well be that nationalism in this part of the web is governed by a self-reinforcing cycle between commercial content and nationalist statements. Importantly, this dynamic is owed in large parts to the logic of digital capitalism. Especially on commercial websites, nationalist content is juxtaposed with revenue-generating click-bait that assumes a very specific target audience. This audience is imagined as masculine and aggressive, and as possessing arguably singular tastes in fringe entertainment. It is these assumptions, reinforced by algorithmic mechanisms such as web analytics, that create incentives for highly idiosyncratic discursive practices. The resulting discourse on gender and the nation does not offer a prominent voice to alternative interpretations. Instead, it makes a particular chauvinistic position salient. This position is fostered by various stakeholders to increase their political clout or make money in these highly commodified segments of digital China. The result is a pernicious view of nations and their politics, which emerges largely as an externality to how various actors make use of digital technologies as they pursue their own political and commercial ends, but which says little about who actually supports popular nationalism in China, and to what degree.

It is not my aim in this chapter to provide a firm connection between online discourse and the political developments in the East China Sea. My goal has been to show how the symbolic and discursive resources on China's web frame the issue, and how they consequently provide the context within which different domestic actors need to position themselves. As other authors have noted, such background structures are crucial for understanding politics, whether in China (Reilly 2012; Wang 2012) or in other countries such as the United States (Gries

2014) or Russia (Wertsch 2002). In the case of the Diaoyu Island discourse on China's web, these background structures combine official state-centric narratives of international politics with commercial incentives to produce racy nationalist representations. Ironically, the largely militant and chauvinistic outcome may not represent popular sentiments in China, and it may not be in the long-term interest of the stakeholders who created it, and yet it provides the discursive resources and sets the conceptual parameters through which public debates over national territory and sovereignty can take place.

# 7

# The User-Generated Nation

From traditional to social medium:

I am meeting my next interviewee in the heart of China's growing digital industry. Here, in a borough of a major Chinese metropolis, slick steel-glass edifices sit among manicured lawns, providing office spaces for China's IT giants and their ongoing digital conquest. My interviewee, Sarah, greets me in the lobby of one such IT firm, then guides me through the digital security check. We pass the large company logo, which beams at us in friendly letters, and enter one of the building's common rooms with its comfortable seating area. Everything seems designed to facilitate maximum creativity. If it were not for the thick smog outside, the scene could very well be set in California's Palo Alto.

Sarah and I find ourselves a table, and she tells me about her work as a web editor for her company's blog service. I ask her about China's 'traditional' internet, the web with its authoritative information sources, and in particularly their dearth of Web 2.0 functionalities. 'Yes, interactive elements are rare. This is mostly because of lacking new media knowledge among older content creators and editors. They moved to digital media from traditional news media, but they don't necessarily understand the potential of digital media. Interaction is regarded with suspicion, because it's hard to monitor and censor. That's why comment sections are viewed with scepticism'.

She goes on to tell me about the blogging boom that started in 2005, and that had its height at the time of the 2008 Olympic Games. 'Once microblogging was introduced, blogging decreased', Sarah explains. Blogs still provide a personal tool for users who want to express themselves and develop their own persona online, usually over extended periods of time. Every tenth Chinese user still has their own blog. However, social media with their focus on brevity, simplicity, and speed are 'making the traditional web less important', as Sarah puts it. 'Social media are the future, and this is where developments in China are the fastest'.

In the previous chapters, I have discussed how China's web spaces adopt a 'traditional' mass-media logic when relaying political discourses, and how this logic rewards nationalist outlooks on issues related to foreign affairs. When it comes to the PRC's relation with Japan, the web is largely a conservative force. Yet, while the web may be dominated by large news corporations, NGOs, and institutions of the state and the Party, it also includes outlets for individual expression. In 2014, according to official survey data (CNNIC 2015: 43–44), roughly 110 million Chinese internet users were blogging and about 130 million were active on messaging boards. Moreover, the traditional web is by no means digital China's only realm. The mobile internet with its many social functionalities is quickly becoming the core digital experience. Roughly 242 million internet users were microblogging in 2015, and more than 600 million communicated through instant messaging services on their smartphones (CNNIC 2016: 30, 36).

As Sarah describes in the encounter that opens this chapter, social media are rapidly changing the functionalities and dynamics of the PRC's media system. Indeed, the evolution of digital media technologies in China is so rapid that it has led to a sense of constant disruption. Throughout my interviews in China, I was regularly scolded for my interest in some technology or application that struck my interlocutors as passé. At first, it was the web that seemed outdated; instead, blogs, internet forums, and Tencent's QQ messenger created significant amounts of hype throughout the 2000s. Then, these sites and applications ostensibly gave way to social media services like Renren, which, in turn, seemed outmoded by the end of the decade when microblogging became fashionable. By 2013, many of my interviewees were convinced that the biggest microblogging site Sina Weibo would quickly die out, considering recent government regulations and the popularity of the short messaging service Weixin, which had been introduced by Tencent in 2011. At the time of writing, interest was growing in the community platform Zhihu (知乎), which enhances the question-and-answer interactions between its registered users with gamic elements. Considering the rapid changes, it can be tempting to follow the hype or even dismiss earlier media dynamics in digital China as entirely fleeting. However, as Chadwick (2013: 989) rightly points out, and as I have also discussed in chapter 2, seemingly revolutionary new technologies do not neatly replace previous technologies; they are integrated in complicated ways into existing social and technological systems. They do not necessarily make older technologies obsolete, though they can at times shift existing media logics in interesting new directions.

What then happens in such a media system when interactive technologies are introduced to the media mix? More importantly: how do mediated community sentiments like nationalism change when media become participatory and social? This chapter examines these developments and explores how they affect discourse about Japan in digital China. It discusses how commenting, tweeting, texting, and 'liking' might shape the imagined community of the nation, and where the power to influence these processes may lie. As I have pointed out in the introduction to this book and in chapter 4, a frequently held expectation is that participatory media technologies facilitate diversity, that they empower users against established media stakeholders, and that these dynamics consequently constitute a progressive force. There are good reasons to take these expectations seriously, and the first part of this chapter reviews the various ways in which participatory digital media indeed disrupt and re-shape communication dynamics more generally. These changes in communication empower new actors, but they do so within certain boundaries, and not always in ways that are progressive. This becomes clear from various examples of how discourses on Japan work. For reasons of scope, I limit these discussions to online contents that were visible in China since 2012, when the anti-Japanese protests took place, and when Xi Jinping's administration came into office (note, however, that some of the resources I analyse may include online content such as comments that were posted at earlier times but that remained part of later discussions). This period of time coincides with the perceived rise and fall of microblogging in the wake of increased political restrictions on social media, as well as with the increased popularity of smartphone messaging services. My analysis covers three different digital contexts, examining first how discourses work on message boards and in web comments. Next, I turn to the microblogging platform Sina Weibo (hereafter 'Weibo'), and I conclude by discussing the community chat spheres of Tencent's popular mobile app Weixin (微信), which is available outside of China in slightly altered guise as WeChat, and which was receiving increased attention at the time of writing as it continued its success story in China.

I am bracketing here the question of how personal blogs fit into this mix of interactive media.[1] For most users, blogs serve as places for personal expression (Hollenbaugh 2010), creating not so much a coherent 'blogosphere' but rather what Dean (2010: 35) calls a fragmented 'blogipelago'. While these outlets can amass substantial followings, the most influential users tend to be famous celebrities who also shape public discussion in other forums, for example, trendsetters like the Chinese race car driver and writer Han Han, whose social commentaries strategically balance audience demands for shrill publicity with state and party demands for conservative discourses and nationalism (Strafella & Berg 2015). As the analyses in chapter 4 showed, most personal blogs remain 'switched off' within networks of digital China (see also Leibold 2011). This should not detract from the importance that personal, diary-like narratives can develop for specific individuals or groups. Annika Pissin (2015), for instance, has shown how so-called mommy blogs can be a wellspring of community sentiment in China. However, the role that such personal everyday practices play in shaping Chinese nationalism will have to remain a question for future study. My focus here is on social technologies such as comment functions and social media platforms, which are frequently described as 'game changers' that alter how media work.

## The Power of Participatory Media

Throughout this book, I have remained sceptical of views that portray digital media and their social technologies as radically transformative of every aspect of society and as heralds of a new age. Too many continuities characterize how ICTs work today to envision, for example, social computing as a drastic break with the past. That said, innovations in participatory, interactive media have changed the dynamics of contemporary media systems. The digital features that are frequently associated with the Web 2.0 have added a new rationale to media. 'Web 2.0' refers to a set of technical functionalities and design choices that increase the interactivity and flexibility already inherent in the World Wide Web. The term was first coined by Darcy DiNucci (1999) to capture how diverse digital devices, ranging from mobile phones to televisions, would create 'fragmented' webs and would challenge designers to create content and interfaces for different delivery systems. To DiNucci (1999: 32), 'the relationship of Web 1.0 to the Web of tomorrow is roughly the equivalence of Pong to *The Matrix*'.

O'Reilly Media later popularized the term 'Web 2.0' to emphasize that the web idea remained relevant in the wake of the 2000 dot-com crash in America. According to the company's founder Tim O'Reilly (2005), the Web 2.0 allows corporations to capitalize on data management, turning software into 'free' infoware services that attract users while relying on large-scale user participation, rather than individual professional publishers, to create and spread content (see Jenkins, Ford, & Green, 2013). The outcome is meant to be a kind of scalable crowd wisdom (Surowiecki 2005) that makes any web service 'better the more people use it' (O'Reilly 2005), which is, arguably, the logic that drives the business model of social networking services from Instagram to Weixin.[2]

What is important here is that the features of Web 2.0 also affect how nationalism works. We need to ask what happens politically when media become user-generated and social. Three aspects are particularly relevant: how digital media today rely on recalibrated network permissions, how they encourage specific network architectures, and how they invite users to personalize their media experience.

I argued in chapter 4 that the power dynamics between actors in networked societies are driven by varying levels of access permission. The Web 2.0 paradigm illustrates this practice: privileged elites expand read and write permissions to a broad range of users, introducing a participatory element to media that far exceeds audience involvement in traditional media production and broadcasting. People who had previously only been granted partial read-only rights in mass-media systems can now access, produce, reproduce, and distribute information more liberally. Blogs are an early example of this, as they promise to provide 'the people formerly known as the audience' (Rosen 2006) with access to 'the button marked "publish"' (Shirky 2010: 488, 603–613). However, such extended permissions are not limited to traditional publishing activities; they also affect how data is categorized and structured, with users now 'tagging' or 'bookmarking' media to create a collective, systematic, and searchable 'tagosphere' (see Rogers 2013: 32), or what Vander Wal (2007) has called a 'folksonomy' of annotated digital media objects.

Directly related to these strategically expanded permissions are the network architectures that accompany the new usage patterns. O'Reilly (2005) envisions an 'architecture of participation' that consists of news feeds, linking practices, and asynchronous scripts, and that creates a highly interactive and flexible 'live web': a vast sphere of discussion that is updated and accessed by millions of users in real time. At their core, the novelties associated with the Web 2.0 idea are social in nature, allowing users to connect with each other and with media objects in ways that are not possible with analogue technologies. The new networked patterns rely on users to 'architect' linkages between people and objects, for instance by using social media buttons, by sharing content through cloud services, and by spreading media through social networks. Importantly, the digital services encourage users to talk back at content, for instance in the comment sections of online posts and articles, or by discussing media and links in social networks. Through these new practices, media are meant to become a conversation.

Finally, the business models that are built around the Web 2.0 idea are monetizing user data, and this means that they rely on users to disclose as much as possible of their personal information in exchange for convenient services that are seemingly free. The effect is that users carry their life worlds, and specifically their social life, into digital spheres. The updated web leverages personal characteristics and social relations to facilitate the flow of data. To fully benefit from the affordances that such flows offer, users have to collaborate with the service providers by submitting their social graphs, geo-location, and user-generated content. An anonymous social media account, for instance, may allow a user to access some of the network content; yet, by avoiding the personalized social dynamics of that network the user foregoes many of the conveniences that a personal account provides. To fully make use of social media, users are prompted to embrace the kinds of digital biases I have described in chapter 3, for better or worse. This also means that, through the many data points that are required to make personalized media work, users' online activities remain firmly tethered to the real world. This can have profound implications for how users behave within social networks, for instance in Weixin communities where members know each other and consequently have a strong incentive to only produce discourse that seems appropriate in the respective setting.

In short, the kinds of ICT developments that have taken place roughly during the past two decades have promoted a media rationale in which users receive network privileges to create media of their own, enter into novel network architectures that encourage them to spread such media, and carry their everyday social life into these digital interactions. Each of these novelties creates strains on existing media regimes and ultimately encourages established stakeholders like news conglomerates to adapt, for instance by integrating the various digital functionalities into their existing media system. In today's digitally upgraded media ecologies, two sets of motivations and interests exist side by side: The first is the legacy of mass media's professionalism, which promotes an elitist model of information and communication built around the idea that knowledge should be wielded by trained specialists. The second is the amateurism engrained in social media's logic, which advocates a populist model for ICT in which knowledge should be accessed and wielded by as many people as possible.

Professionalism is, arguably, a core feature of modernity. In its progressive guise, professionalism aims to inform or educate those who are non-specialists; in its most conservative guise, it aims to preserve knowledge and prevent its potential contamination by non-specialists. In either case, it is a paternalistic approach that promotes elitist assumptions about the intrinsic value of specialist knowledge. It is also an approach that relies on the division of labour and the economies of scale that form the basis for modern industrial production. In capitalist societies, professionalism, ironically, downplays the personal viewpoints of media professionals and instead incorporates these individuals into large-scale hierarchical networks like state agencies, news corporations, or academic institutions, where their behaviour is guided by the respective network's institutional values.

Professionalism is not limited to media systems. It also plays a major role in education, in economic production and trade, in administration and political decision-making, and anywhere else where the work of elites is channelled into scripts that emphasize the quality and perceived objectivity of specialist labour. This is why the ideology of Web 2.0 is so 'disruptive' (Owen 2015) to contemporary societies and politics: the paradigm that fuels the expansion of social and participatory media promotes (and monetizes) precisely the kind of amateur activities that are anathema to professionalism, and it does so in many more settings than just the traditional mass-media system.

In contrast to professionalism, the logic of amateurism remains sceptical of the idea that knowledge should be concentrated in the hands of a few. Amateur reasoning eschews hierarchies and celebrates egalitarian media usage, challenging elitist understandings of information and communication. The amateur approach to media introduces a decidedly personal element, emphasizing individual viewpoints and emotions rather than the dispassionate position of experts. Amateur media rely on individuals voicing their personal views, regardless of whether these views lead to insightful and creative information exchanges or to the kinds of entrenched uncivility that is frequently visible in online comment sections. More importantly, amateur media users are switched into networks that are structured differently compared to traditional institutional systems of state and social organizations. This does not mean that the networks these users populate are entirely without hierarchies and governing values; it means that such hierarchies and values are created collaboratively within a framework that a different set of elites has provided: the designers, programmers, and administrators who make up the institutional actors of the digital movement, such as Facebook, Sina, or Tencent.

The celebration of amateur media is originally a cornerstone of the Silicon Valley utopianism that has been driving much of past ICT innovation (Turner 2008). This ideology is not entirely new—it accompanied the rise of the internet from its very inception—but it has powerfully come to the fore as technical and social changes placed easy-to-use digital devices in the hands of more and more people. As Benkler (2006: 219) points out, having the power of a supercomputer in one's pocket, and being able to direct that power at anything one encounters, promises to change society:

> In a complex modern society, where things that matter can happen anywhere and at any time, the capacity of people armed with means of recording, rendering, and communicating their observations change their relationship to the events that surround them. Whatever one sees and hears can be treated as input into public debate in ways that were impossible when capturing, rendering, and communicating were facilities reserved to a handful of organizations and a few thousands of their employees.

Indeed, it is important to realize that 'the internet is no longer a computer-based medium' (Chadwick 2013: 1148), and that a range of devices now enables amateur media production and networked information exchange. These new devices change what is visible to people and this, in turn, has the potential to alter political discourse. In China, smartphone users have repeatedly challenged the discourses of the authorities in ways that have unhinged established political practices. Examples include popular collective actions against environmentally questionable industrial plans (Liu 2014) as well as 'online mass incidents' that criticize government failures (Bondes & Schucher 2014). Such activities frequently shift policy outcomes, end political careers, and change the parameters of public debate, and the features of social and participatory media play a major role in making these shifts possible.

## Digital Commentary and the Nation

How, then, do the new social features of digital media affect the imagined community of the nation? The major novelty in digital communication is that media become social, participatory, and personal. This is most evident in the social network services that are specifically designed to leverage the personal relations of their customers, but it is also apparent from the various Web 2.0 features on the traditional web. One such feature is the online forum that encompasses dedicated messaging boards; it also, more broadly, includes the comment sections that today accompany many online articles. How is the discourse on the Chinese nation and its relationship with Japan constructed in such forums?

As Herold (2012: 2) points out, it is today a truism that digital China's many forums create diversity. The vast number of popular message boards provides room for users to articulate viewpoints that span the entire spectrum of political positions. Indeed, as Ye, Sarrica, and Fortunati (2014: 10) found in their quantitative study of the popular forums Tianya (*tianya luntan* 天涯论坛) and Phoenix (*fenghuang luntan* 凤凰论坛), online message boards contain contradictory individualist and social dynamics that are, in their view, 'redefining the social representation of selfhood' in contemporary China. Despite these contradictions and the general fragmentation of discussion on Tianya, Medaglia and Yang (2017: 745)'s large-scale study of four forums on the platform finds that the discussions, overall, tend towards homophily, meaning that commentators 'tend to prefer interactions with similar-minded individuals', raising questions about the degree to which such digital forums might provide walled gardens and echo chambers, rather than spaces for exchanging diverse views. On issues related to Japan, An and Yang (2010) found that discourses vary dramatically, but that this variation depends on the specific forums in question. The nationalist message board Strong Country (*qiangguo luntan* 强国论坛), for instance, overwhelmingly hosts anti-Japanese debates, whereas the more liberal forum Keyhole (*maoyan kanren* 猫眼看人) predominantly contains discussions that are supportive of Japanese perspectives, suggesting again a certain degree of homophily. The authors conducted their study before the 2012 outbreak of anti-Japanese sentiments, but even in the face of shifting Chinese public opinion their work is a reminder that, even though the lively realm of message boards provides room for internet users to develop a large range of political perspectives, these perspectives are frequently developed among like-minded users.

The question remains how particular patterns emerge in discourses that relate to Japan, and what role digital and social factors play in reinforcing such patterns? Wu Yanfang's study (2015) of Diaoyu Island comments on Tianya suggests that forums without dedicated gatekeepers may breed 'incivility', and that users often reacted positively to rude comments rather than challenging them. Closed forums like Zhihu might work differently in this regard, since they include gamic elements that specifically encourage civility. I have not been able to explore these dynamics on Zhihu, since accessing this members-only forum requires a local Chinese account (linked to a Chinese mobile phone number). Additional research is needed to fully assess how digital game mechanisms such as 'points', 'levels', and 'medals' work in such contexts to shape discourse. I find it highly plausible that such features indeed dampen emotional discussions, for example, on nationalism, though I also suspect that the gamic pressures might encourage users to conform to expectations in ways that could further facilitate homophily. Be that as it may, nuanced discussion in such closed forums is largely hidden from view in digital China, whereas public forums like Tianya with their crude commentary remain highly visible. These public discursive spaces ultimately shape public discourse more than their closed-off counterparts.

My own study of such discursive dynamics has focused on three smaller discussion spaces: Sina's Nanjing Massacre forum, the comment sections of the military affairs website Tiexue, and the discussion sections that accompany Encyclopaedia Hudong's Nanjing Massacre and Diaoyu Island entries. The Sina forum is explicitly designed as a space of solemn commemoration, the Tiexue comment sections are part of a commercial news enterprise, and the Hudong discussion spaces are meant to provide comments on encyclopaedic knowledge. To check whether these forums contain specific discursive patterns, I have collected the various comments and have analysed them both quantitatively and qualitatively. As I have discussed in chapters 5 and 6, discussion on the Nanjing Massacre and the Diaoyu Islands largely follow established media scripts, and this is visible in all three of these cases.

Take the example of Sina's Never Forget forum: across the 510 unique comments that users left in the commemoration section of the website, a large number of users simply reproduced the standard slogans associated with the Massacre. It is common practice in the forum to reiterate mantras like 'never forget' (*yong bu wangque* 永不忘却), 'don't forget national humiliation' (*wuwang guochi* 勿忘国耻), or variations on these themes. In fact, calls to 'not forget' appeared in 45% of the individual posts, and 23% of the individual posts used the term 'national humiliation', often more than once. Moreover, the point of reference across the comments was not so much the city of Nanjing, or humanity more generally, but 'China', the 'Chinese nation', or 'the Chinese people'—terms that every fourth post used to clarify who should be remembering these atrocities.

While many comments in Sina's commemoration forum were satisfied calling for collective remembering, and often for peace, a total of 120 posts were targeted directly at the antagonist 'Japan'. The following is a relatively mild example:

> Where is the conscience? Where is the humanity? True, this is all in the past, it has already become history, but we will never be able to forget what the Japanese once did. I will forever hate Japan, forever hate everything about Japan.
>
> 良心何在?人性何在?  是的,都过去了,已经成为历史了,但是我们永远都不能忘记日本人曾经做过的事情.我永远恨日本,  恨日本的一切.

This sentiment is reproduced in other forums as well, where it serves as the default framework for making sense of modern China's past. Whether in Sina's forums, in dedicated messaging boards like Tianya, or in the comment sections of military affairs websites and state news organizations, hatred against 'the Japanese devils' (*Riben guizi* 日本鬼子) is ubiquitous. It would be premature to associate these statements with a particular demographic, for example, with the 'angry youths' or the recently fashionable term 'little pinks', that is presumably female millennials (see Fang & Repnikova 2017 for a reality-check on that gendered term). It is equally conceivable that such comments are either left by entirely different types of internet users, as I have also suggested in chapter 6, or even that they are deliberately planted by propaganda workers. Such propagandists are commonly referred to as the 'fifty cent army', based on the perception that they consist of CCP loyalists who receive 0.5 RMB each time they leave a comment that is in line with party propaganda guidelines (see Han 2013; King, Pan, & Roberts, 2017)—a condition that extreme chauvinistic and misogynistic comments are unlikely to meet.

Regardless of the user identities, it is noteworthy that inflammatory remarks and racial defamations are not deleted by the authorities or the website providers. Moreover, aggressive comments dominate many of the discussion spaces because of the logic that interactive, participatory technologies introduce to web spaces. The case of the website Tiexue is instructive in this regard. Many of the most aggressive statements are sanctioned by a virtual red 'stamp' that marks the comment as a particularly 'popular reply' (*remen huifu* 热门回复), based on the number of 'likes' they received from other users. I have reproduced one such instance in Figure 7.1.

This comment to a post on Tiexue about rape during the Nanjing occupation suggests that anyone killing a Japanese person should be paid 1,000 RMB, and it concludes with the words 'kill kill kill . . . .' While this is an exceptionally crude comment, it is ranked highest in terms of 'likes'. The 'popular response' stamp is visible in the top right corner. Such interactive mechanisms create the impression that nationalist outrage is indeed an appropriate or even praiseworthy response to the event. As discussed in chapter 5, there are also website sections that promote mutual respect between China and Japan, and, likewise, the comment sections also contain conciliatory remarks; yet, such sentiments are comparatively rare, and they become further marginalized by the way in which social dynamics and algorithmic mechanisms combine to promote chauvinistic statements.

Another interesting example of such dynamics is the online encyclopaedia Hudong Baike. Contrary to its competitor Baidu, the popular knowledge archive from Hudong allows users to comment on the encyclopaedia articles, and

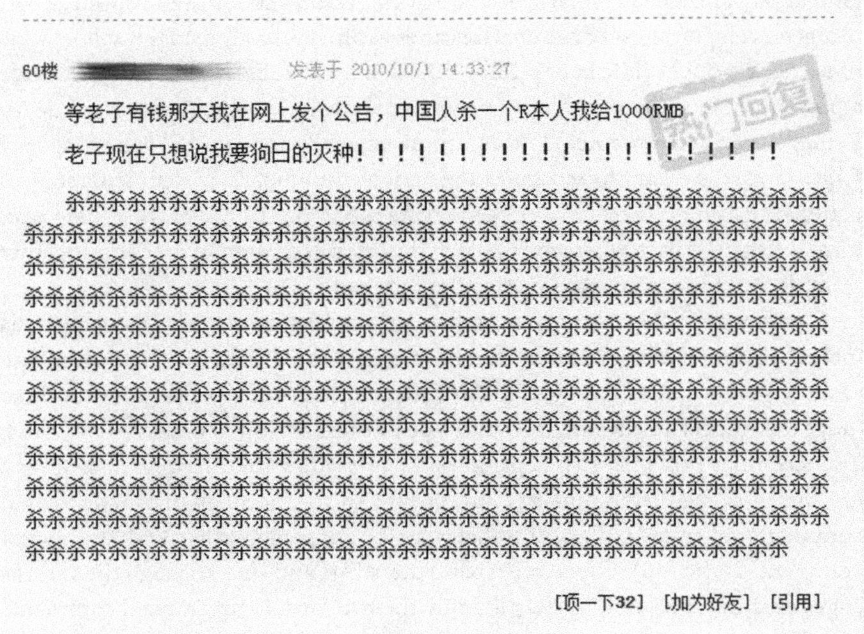

60楼 ▓▓▓▓▓▓▓        发表于 2010/10/1 14:33:27

等老子有钱那天我在网上发个公告，中国人杀一个R本人我给1000RMB

老子现在只想说我要狗日的灭种！！！！！！！！！！！！！！！！！！！！！！！

杀杀杀杀杀杀杀杀杀杀杀杀杀杀杀杀杀杀杀杀杀杀杀杀杀杀杀杀杀杀杀
杀杀杀杀杀杀杀杀杀杀杀杀杀杀杀杀杀杀杀杀杀杀杀杀杀杀杀杀杀杀杀
杀杀杀杀杀杀杀杀杀杀杀杀杀杀杀杀杀杀杀杀杀杀杀杀杀杀杀杀杀杀杀
杀杀杀杀杀杀杀杀杀杀杀杀杀杀杀杀杀杀杀杀杀杀杀杀杀杀杀杀杀杀杀
杀杀杀杀杀杀杀杀杀杀杀杀杀杀杀杀杀杀杀杀杀杀杀杀杀杀杀杀杀杀杀
杀杀杀杀杀杀杀杀杀杀杀杀杀杀杀杀杀杀杀杀杀杀杀杀杀杀杀杀杀杀杀
杀杀杀杀杀杀杀杀杀杀杀杀杀杀杀杀杀杀杀杀杀杀杀杀杀杀杀杀杀杀杀
杀杀杀杀杀杀杀杀杀杀杀杀杀杀杀杀杀杀杀杀杀杀杀杀杀杀杀杀杀杀杀
杀杀杀杀杀杀杀杀杀杀杀杀杀杀杀杀杀杀杀杀杀杀杀杀杀杀杀杀杀杀杀
杀杀杀杀杀杀杀杀杀杀杀杀杀杀杀杀杀杀杀杀杀杀杀杀杀杀杀杀杀杀杀
杀杀杀杀杀杀杀杀杀杀杀杀杀杀杀杀杀杀杀杀杀杀杀杀杀杀杀杀杀

[顶一下32]  [加为好友]  [引用]

*Figure 7.1* Sanctioning Anti-Japanese Anger on China's Web. User comment on the message board Tiexue.net. Screenshot taken on 15 May 2013 (user name obscured for ethical reasons).

the Hudong entries for 'Nanjing Massacre' and 'Diaoyu Islands' had respectively generated 202 and 537 user comments at the time of writing. Commentators have the option to use an individual handle and display a portrait of their choosing as they leave comments, but a more commonly used feature of the site is to represent users with a generic name and picture. Most commentators make use of this option, and the encyclopaedia then assigns each user a name and image that represents their real-world location. Commentators thus become identifiable as voices from specific Chinese provinces and municipalities, that is, as a 'Hudong Encyclopaedia Beijing netizen', a 'Hudong Encyclopaedia Sichuan netizen', and so on.[3] Such domestic users are additionally assigned a pre-selected visual representation of their locality, for example the Leshan Buddha for Sichuan, the Yellow Mountain for Anhui, the Pearl Tower for Shanghai, or the Heavenly Temple for Beijing. Meanwhile, commentators whose locations do not map onto this framework of provinces are instead represented as 'overseas netizens' (*haiwai wangyou* 海外网友), represented by a thumbnail that looks out across an ocean.

The design of the comment section thus already creates a national setting with a clear 'inside' and 'outside', framing local identities within the boundaries of 'China'. The choice of local landmarks also means that the comment section circulates the kind of recognizable national symbols that Anderson (2006: 182) viewed as part of a 'general logoization' of national treasures to provide easily recognizable sources of patriotic pride. While banal (Billig 2009), these symbols nevertheless provide a powerful visual shorthand, not only for local patriotic belonging (e.g., pride for Beijing or Sichuan Province) but also, more generally, for national belonging: any Chinese user is meant to recognize the various thumbnails as representations of national treasures. These images then create the impression that the online platform is a shared space where members of the imagined community come together from all over the nation, even visiting from abroad.

Aside from this identity-management mechanism, the encyclopaedia includes another design feature that frames how the discourse in the comment section works: a three-pronged suite of social media buttons that allow users to judge the respective comment (thumbs up or thumbs down) or leave a response. The site then provides two separate entryways into these comments: first, a list that is sorted by popularity (according to the number of reactions that comments generated); then, a list that is sorted chronologically (with the newest comments at the top). Users can expand these lists and click through the various pages of comments, but, by default, only the five most highly ranked comments and the ten most recent comments are visible on the website. This mechanism provides an intriguing window into the discussion: how do users comment on the Nanjing Massacre and the Diaoyu Island dispute entries, and how does the social approval system structure these comments?

Overall, the comments range from emotional outrage to sarcastic trolling, from meaningless chatter to spam, from chauvinistic statements to comments that downplay or even question nationalist narratives. For example, when it comes to the Nanjing Massacre entry, representative nationalist comments in March 2016 included sentiments such as these:

> Our China is starting to become formidable!!!!!!! Let's be proud of our homeland!!!!!!!!!!!!
>
> 我们中国开始强大起来了 ！！！！！！！ 为我们的祖国自豪吧！！！！！！！！！！！！！

> Let's have a 'Tokyo Massacre'.
>
> 来个'东京大屠杀´

> As long as there's a single person left in China, they will have to kill those Japanese swine.
>
> 只要中国还有一个人，都必须杀掉日本这些畜生

Both with regard to the Nanjing Massacre and the Diaoyu Islands, nationalist comments frequently used derogatory slurs when referring to Japan, and it is common to call for 'Japan' or 'all Japanese' to be summarily executed, eradicated with nuclear bombs, or raped to death. In contrast to this uncivil narrative, the comment sections also included remarks that either rejected such understandings or otherwise complicated the picture. These are three examples from the Nanjing Massacre entry:

> I'm fed up with these senseless studies of what one thing did or what some other thing meant. Human nature has always been like this.
>
> 吃饱了无聊研究那些干什么 有什么意义 人性本来就是这个样子的啊

> Don't get deceived by those old folks; these things have absolutely nothing to do with today's young people.
>
> 别被那些老人家骗了 那些事情跟现在的年轻人一点关系也没有

> 300,000 people really is a lot, but how many more died during the civil war?
>
> 三十万人确实多，但内战又死了多少人？

The comment section for the Diaoyu Islands was similar in this regard: hateful remarks and more ambiguous comments co-existed side by side. However, the discourse was generally imbalanced. Chauvinistic comments by far outnumber critical remarks. Of the 202 comments that users had left on the Nanjing Massacre entry by March 2016, 145 were aggressively nationalist, meaning that more than 70% included derogatory, racist slurs or calls for various aggressive actions against the neighbouring country (economic boycotts, use of military force, individual violence, etc.). For the Diaoyu Island entry, 380 of the 537 comments were aggressively chauvinistic, so a similar percentage to the Nanjing Massacre entry. The remaining comments includes a few nonsensical posts and a handful of thoughtful remarks, but most of the non-aggressive statements were still nationalistic, for example, calling on compatriots to love the Chinese home-land or to never forget national humiliation.

In Hudong's encyclopaedia, this plethora of nationalist statements is then filtered through social media mechanisms such as likes and dislikes. Overall, ag-gressively nationalist statements receive the most positive responses, sensible statements tend to get ignored, and any pro-Japanese sentiments are strongly disliked and showered with derogatory vitriol. The web service aggregates these dynamics, creating a social ranking of what is the most popular (and by exten-sion: appropriate) response to issues that relate to Japan. I have reproduced this top-five ranking in Table 7.1.

Worth noting here are the comments that other users left to these posts, which, in this case, included two users who challenged the nationalist discourse explicitly. The first user commented twice on aggressive Nanjing Massacre remarks, first arguing that 'Japan may be at fault but the Japanese people are in-nocent', then responding to a user's call for violence by asking, 'does that not make you the same as the Japanese invaders?' The second user commented on Diaoyu Island remarks, responding to a call to 'eradicate Japan' by writing: 'If we want peace, we should start by eradicating brainless idiots like yourself'. These comments show how the discourse does not remain unchallenged, but the fact that the users did not post their responses in the main comment section has repercussions for how visible this counter-discourse is. The challenges to the aggressive comments only become visible once users click on the small 're-sponse' link that accompanies the respective main post, and then only in much smaller script and framed by further chauvinistic comments. The result is that the critical, more reflective discourse remains hidden away in the comments to the comments, rather than becoming a central feature on the website.

Through its design choices, Hudong creates communication dynamics that privilege aggressive nationalist commentary. A similar combination of algorithmic processes and social interactions also shapes the discourse on other websites, for instance those of NGOs or of military affairs websites. Where web forums allow interactive comment sections, they reproduce the same pattern: comments are predominantly aggressive and racist, alternative

**Table 7.1  Encyclopaedia Hudong's User Comments**

*Top Five Comments: Nanjing Massacre*

| Rank | Chinese | English Translation | # Likes | # Dislikes | # Comments |
|---|---|---|---|---|---|
| 1 | 如果我要当了兵，就该给他们来一场东京大屠杀 | If I ever join the army, I'll give them a 'Tokyo Massacre'. | 80 | 21 | 5 |
| 2 | 用原子弹消灭日本 | Exterminate Japan with nuclear weapons. | 59 | 13 | 1 |
| 3 | 俺们都是中国人，狗日的太可恨了，别让我碰见你，干死你！女的就日死你！！！ | We are all Chinese, and you despicable sons of bitches, don't let me run into you, I'll kill you! If you're a woman, I'll rape you to death!!! | 47 | 16 | 1 |
| 4 | 扔几颗原子弹炸死他们，还便宜了他们。 | Killing them by throwing a couple of nuclear weapons is still too good for them. | 51 | 10 | 0 |
| 5 | TAT太恐怖了 | *weep* really horrible | 31 | 14 | 0 |

*Top Five Comments: Diaoyu Islands*

| Rank | Chinese | English Translation | # Likes | # Dislikes | # Comments |
|---|---|---|---|---|---|
| 1 | 日本，我亲爱的祖国 | Japan, my beloved homeland | 13 | 89 | 1 |
| 2 | 甲午恨，何时灭；卢沟耻，何时雪！ | The hatred of 1894 [i.e., of the First Sino-Japanese War], when will it be extinguished? The humiliation of the Marco Polo Bridge [i.e., the start of the Second Sino-Japanese War] when will it be wiped clean? | 41 | 0 | 0 |

*(continued)*

*Table 7.1* **Continued**

*Top Five Comments: Nanjing Massacre*

| Rank | Chinese | English Translation | # Likes | # Dislikes | # Comments |
|---|---|---|---|---|---|
| 3 | 钓鱼岛是中国的固有领土，所以中国政府有权保卫它！不管其他国家对钓鱼岛怎么做都是非法的！人不犯我，我不犯人，人若犯我，我必犯人！ | The Diaoyu Island is China's inherent territory, so China's government has the right to protect it! Regardless of how other countries behave towards the Diaoyu Island, it's all illegal! If someone doesn't attack me, I don't attack them, but if someone does attack me, then I have to attack them! | 32 | 1 | 0 |
| 4 | 我们要向保钓爱国人士致敬学习！我忠心希望国人团结一心学习韩国不要忘了国耻家仇，不接受日货！不与仇人小日本人合作！也希望政府不要忘记历史的国耻永远不要与小日本人一切合作！孤立小日本！钓鱼岛是我们的！！！如果想灭小日本，就从不买日货开始 | To protect the Diaoyus, we have to respectfully learn from other great patriots! I strongly hope that my fellow compatriots will wholeheartedly unite and study how South Korea is not forgetting its national humiliation and isn't accepting Japanese goods! Don't collaborate with personal enemies like the little Japanese! I also hope the government will not forget that due to history's national humiliation we can never ever collaborate with the little Japanese! Isolate little Japan! The Diaoyu Islands belong to us!!! If we want to extinguish little Japan, we have to start by not buying Japanese goods | 26 | 3 | 1 |

*Table 7.1* **Continued**

Top Five Comments: Nanjing Massacre

| Rank | Chinese | English Translation | # Likes | # Dislikes | # Comments |
|------|---------|---------------------|---------|------------|------------|
| 5 | 如果想灭小日本，就从不买日货开始 | If we want to extinguish little Japan, we have to start by not buying Japanese goods | 20 | 3 | 2 |

Most popular comments on Encyclopaedia Hudong's entries for the Nanjing Massacre and the Diaoyu Islands, retrieved April 2016.

statements are few and far between, and the most nationalist comments are ranked most prominently. The overall outcome is that the discourse on Japan is forced into a framework that relies on simplistic stereotypes and chauvinistic viewpoints, but that, nevertheless, becomes sanctioned as the appropriate way to understand modern Chinese history. Despite providing forums for discussion, these spaces still function as shrines to national assumptions; the novelty that Web 2.0 introduces is merely that these shrines are now interactive.

## Micro Announcements, Micro Debates: Nationalism on Weibo

Whereas web forums allow users to engage in a localized discussion, often creating incentives to post a single, anonymous statement, the medium of the microblog promotes a stream of short messages that are meant to be rapidly shared, and that often include media objects and links. What do debates on issues like the East China Sea dispute look like in such an environment? What kind of exchanges about the Chinese nation does a popular service like Weibo facilitate?

To answer this question, Feng Miao and Elaine Yuan have examined a large corpus of Weibo tweets that were published in 2012, at the height of anti-Japanese tensions.[4] They found that the discussion contained many aggressive statements about Japan, but it did not collapse into a single, dominant narrative (Feng & Yuan 2014). Instead, commentators made sense of the issue in idiosyncratic ways, often negotiating with each other what 'Chineseness' should mean in the face of this particular challenge to national territorial sovereignty. This included calls for restraint and 'civilized' behaviour, alongside reminders of how important Sino-Japanese trade was for the Chinese nation. Feng and Yuan call these sentiments 'rational patriotism' (*lixing aiguo* 理性爱国); a term used throughout digital China to refer to the kind of liberal views of the nation that reflect 'both the material position of an emerging middle stratum as conscious property owners and sensitive consumers and their subjective disposition in broad contemporary Chinese society' (Feng & Yuan 2014). Moreover, the online discourse also includes voices that highlight domestic injustices, such as forced demolitions or the bureaucratic fiat of so-called city inspectors, and it is noteworthy that many users repurpose the nationalist framework of interstate conflict to emphasize their own interpersonal struggles with the Chinese state. The following is a Weibo comment from Feng and Yuan's study that illustrates such practices (Feng & Yuan 2014):

> When it comes to land use, the party has always dealt with us little guys by tabling the dispute and siding with the developers. Now in the dispute over the Diaoyu Islands, the party was shocked to realize that it had become the little guy itself, Japan was tabling the dispute and going right ahead with the development. . . . Summon the city inspectors to destroy Japan by force.

It remains controversial whether such 'feelings of injustice and distrust' really 'act as a fundamental brake on the nationalist patriotic emotions', as the authors of the study conclude (Feng & Yuan 2014). I find it interesting that, despite the diversity of arguments that coexist within the Weibo debates, comments generally remain committed to making their case *within* the us versus them frameworks of Chinese nationalism. The comment quoted above does not challenge the underlying assumption that the world is divided into nation states that behave like persons. Comments of the 'rationally patriotic' kind similarly reproduce the logic of national interest that legitimates nation states as guarantors of a nation's prosperity. One comment thus reads (Feng & Yuan 2014):

> People have been so excited about expressing our strong patriotism because of the Diaoyu islands. It is great. But today I saw the gathering, slogan, and demonstration in front of Heiwado [a Japanese store in Changsha, China]. It only hurts our people more if we vent our anger by boycotting Japanese goods and smashing Chinese stores carrying Japanese goods. Maybe we need to be more sober.

Discursively, such statements reinforce the impression that the imagined community of the nation is indeed the correct framework for making sense of politics and economics. The idea that there are antagonists to the nations is not fundamentally challenged; it is simply the measures for fighting this antagonist that are questioned here.

I have discussed in chapter 2 how problematic it can be to distinguish patriotism and nationalism, since the two sentiments rely on the same underlying
psychological mechanisms to construct in-groups and out-groups. This is also
the case for the comments just quoted, which remain nationalistic, despite their
very different arguments. In fact, the basic background categories that nationalism provides are a common feature of the discussion and are not noticeably
subverted. Nevertheless, what Feng and Yuan's study vividly demonstrates is
that this nationalist discourse is indeed fragmented; it does not become coterminous with a single state-approved position, and, at times, it turns the nationalist rhetoric against the leadership itself. The island dispute, as a discursive
event, becomes an excuse to air a range of grievances that are not directly related
to territory or sovereignty. We are witnessing in such instances the attempt of
specific actors to re-programme nationalist discourse for their own purposes.
This kind of behaviour is specific to social media contexts. In traditional web
spheres, where accredited sources frame the issue in terms of national sovereignty, such manoeuvres do not play the kind of discursive role that they do on
Sina's microblogging site.

Large corpora of Weibo tweets are useful because they can provide insights
into how the microblogging discourse is structured, on what issues it touches,
and how specific statements are legitimated. They do not, however, tell us anything about the Weibo networks and who asserts power over social media
discussions online. On Weibo, as much as in other networks, not all contributors
are equal. The vast majority of microblog users maintain relatively small social
networks, and they use their accounts to follow important institutions like
news corporations or prominent private accounts like those of celebrity users.[5]
This latter group is particular important on Weibo, where the large accounts of
verified users (or: 'Big-V' accounts) form central nodes in the network. As Han
and Wang (2015: 77) show in their study of user networks on Weibo, 'V-users
occupy the core or gatekeeping positions and thus have more control over the
information flow through the channels from one node to the other'.

Big-V microblogging can mean big business, with advertisers paying hefty
sums for perceived opinion leaders to plug products and services to their millions
of followers. In my conversations with media practitioners and scholars in China,
an issue that frequently came up was the degree to which Chinese internet users
perceive many Big-V celebrities to be acting dishonestly or even fraudulently online in order to make money through their followers. It is this financial dynamic
that the authorities claim to be targeting with their clampdowns on Big-V users,
and it is not surprising that such moves receive support from a Chinese public that
is increasingly weary of fraudulent online behaviour (for examples, see Koetse
2015). That the hunt for 'rumour-mongers' has also ensnared a number of vocal
activists who had been challenging the authorities on protracted social and legal

issues is bound to be viewed as a positive side effect by China's leaders, though it is unclear how much of a motivation this provided for originally rolling out new Weibo restrictions in 2013 (see Chin 2013; *Economist* 2013). In any case, the effects on celebrity microbloggers have been chilling (Bai 2015). For the present discussion, the outcome of the clampdown matters little, since these measures only took effect in the year after the 2012 island controversy. Nevertheless, the concern that informs these measures illustrates that the authorities are apprehensive about the influence that users might wield if they are positioned powerfully within social media networks.

Yet, despite the massive number of followers that 'Big-V' celebrities frequently accrue on Weibo, it is not at all self-evident who is most influential. Recent IT studies have made inroads into the network structure of Weibo (e.g., Bao, Shen, Huang, & Cheng 2013; Liu & Li 2015; Xiong, Zhou, Huang, Chen, & Xu 2013), but such studies are often mathematically involved, and they only rarely disclose how the researchers gained access to Sina's data. While intriguing, such studies thus offer social science and area studies researchers few chances to reproduce the methodological procedures in other contexts. This is a missed opportunity, since the medium would allow for extremely interesting 'small data' research, for instance by systematically tracking a particular post or by mapping the follower networks of various institutional or 'Big-V' accounts. There is a very real need to create accessible research tools for the systematic study of Weibo networks. To my knowledge, such tools were not freely available at the time of writing, and future attempts to create open-source software solutions of this kind remain confronted with serious challenges, considering the commercial interests of the Sina Corporation, the Chinese state's concerns about foreign access to domestic data, and the consequently unclear and frequently shifting rules according to which Sina allows selective access to its data through its application programming interface (API).[6]

For this present study, I have chosen a workaround to these methodological challenges. Sina itself calculates rankings of top users, which it calls 'star power charts' (*mingxing shili bang* 明星势力榜). The index from which these charts are calculated is not visible for all users, but Sina provides a real-time top-50 ranking on its website that also lists the elements that shape the index.[7] According to the corporation, the charts are based on four variables: number of mentions (*tiji liang* 提及量), number of interactions (*hudong liang* 互动量), number of searches (*sousuo liang* 搜索量), and an obscure 'admiration value' (*aimuzhi* 爱慕值). Based on such figures, the *South China Morning Post* released a top-10 list for the year 2012 (Zhou 2013), which I have reproduced in Table 7.2, with additional information from the time of writing.

While such calculations can only serve as an approximation of 'power' or 'influence' on Weibo, they nevertheless demonstrate who the Sina Corporation

*Table 7.2* **Top-10 Weibo Users in 2012**

| Rank 2012 | Name | Chinese | Gender | Location | Occupation | Followers (Jan 2016) | Posts (Jan 2016) |
|---|---|---|---|---|---|---|---|
| 1 | Lee Kai-Fu | 李开复 | m | PRC | venture capitalist | 49,991,639 | 14,521 |
| 2 | He Jiong | 何炅 | m | PRC | TV presenter | 74,519,727 | 7,361 |
| 3 | Xie Na | 谢娜 | f | PRC | TV presenter | 79,352,452 | 8,456 |
| 4 | Ren Zhiqiang | 任志强 | m | PRC | real estate mogul | 36,828,824 | 89,667 |
| 5 | Charles Xue | 薛蛮子 | m | PRC | angel investor | 10,939,141 | 99,248 |
| 6 | Yao Chen | 姚晨 | f | PRC | actress | 78,876,891 | 8,356 |
| 7 | Amy Cheung | 張小嫻 | f | Hong Kong | novelist | 63,716,607 | 3,177 |
| 8 | Yang Mi | 杨幂 | f | PRC | actress | 58,389,582 | 3,255 |
| 9 | Pan Shiyi | 潘石屹 | m | PRC | real estate mogul | 17,840,048 | 22,733 |
| 10 | Ashin | 阿信 | m | Taiwan | singer | 19,452,960 | 1,402 |

Data reproduced and expanded from Zhou (2013).

itself considers to be most influential in its network. On Weibo, I have examined more closely how the ten users who were categorized as most influential in 2012 behaved during the month of September, when the PRC witnessed the height of its mass protests and riots over the East China Sea issue (see also my short discussion in Schneider 2017). For the technical reasons just discussed, I am limiting this study to a qualitative assessment of relevant tweets at the time.

What characterizes the way that different Big-V microbloggers reacted to the dispute with Japan in September 2012? Firstly, several of the celebrities listed in Table 7.2 did not post information on the developments in their blog feed at all. The TV hostess Xie Na and the starlet Yang Mi, for instance, posted pictures of cute animals or animation characters alongside updates on China's pop scene or their own careers, but they side-stepped any political controversies. Likewise, the author Amy Cheung posted pictures of the moon or of flower bouquets, accompanied by her cryptic musings about love and life: 'you only need to love a person and there will always be a moment when you lose hope', contemplates the romance novelist. Three of the four female celebrities thus stay apolitical in the face of events that turned out to be PR minefields for some. Jamie Coates (2014) discusses how treacherous the debates quickly became for the Japanese adult film actress Sola Aoi, who originally intervened in the discussion with a call for peace and understanding. While her tweet garnered much support from her fans, it also generated vicious backlashes online and generally politicized her cultural activities. The star later refrained from further politically charged comments, probably to avoid fallout for her growing pop business in China.

It is likely that such business considerations loomed large for many celebrities, for example, for the Taiwanese singer Ashin, the only other celebrity from outside the mainland in my sample, who did not mention the territorial dispute in his feed. For the other users, reactions were mixed. Many tweets are simple observations or re-tweets that the respective celebrities did not discuss further. One example is the TV host He Jiong (@何炅), who re-tweeted a news item on September 17 that showed more than 1,000 Chinese fishing boats ostensibly preparing to challenge Japanese maritime claims in the East China Sea. His comment to his followers simply reads 'pay close attention' (*miqie guanzhu* 密切关注, at 16:59 hrs), leaving it unclear what his personal views on this form of activism were. Another example comes from real estate tycoon Pan Shiyi (@潘石屹, September 18, 2018, 18:10), who posted a picture of a boarded-up Japanese restaurant draped in Chinese flags, commenting only: 'Beijing's Japanese restaurants all have the same decoration'.[8] While it is likely that Pan's comment was meant cynically, such ambiguous posts ultimately leave it to users to attribute meanings and debate the issue, which hundreds of followers did, in often nuanced ways, in the comment sections. Posting a simple photo or re-tweeting official media thus served as a safe way to remain visibly involved in current affairs discussions without the risk of offending any followers.

However, not all posts played it safe. Yao Chen (@姚晨), the only female celebrity in my sample to get involved in the issue, complicated the picture on September 18, China's commemoration day for the start of the Sino-Japanese War. One of her posts recalled the story of a war veteran who was later mistreated during the Cultural Revolution, which is arguably an unusual theme to highlight within the overarching East China Sea discourse. The star accompanied her news tweets with comments like 'patriotism—please start by loving every single person' and 'this is actual national humiliation'.[9] This sentiment, in combination with the reference to the violent fervour of the Cultural Revolution, thus subtly linked the collective actions on display in China's streets to one of the PRC's most harrowing examples of political mobilization gone wrong.

Several of the celebrities also took a stand on the anti-Japanese protests, and, in particular, the outbreak of violence seems to have served as a catalyst for Big-V commentary. An event that received special attention from the microbloggers was the riot in Xi'an on 15 September, which I recounted in the introduction to this book, and which saw the 51-year-old car dealer Li Jianli nearly bludgeoned to death for driving a Nissan (Chubb 2012). He Jiong posted twice on the rioting, in neither case relaying any specific news item, but instead referencing the events indirectly:

> Post #1: Patriotism is a very noble word. Those people who smash the cars of our compatriots, or who eat their fill at a Japanese restaurant and then skip out on the bill, all foul-mouthed, or randomly beating up foreigners at their door step—don't insult patriotism! The islands are of course ours, but our actual dignity is also in your and my hands!
>
> 爱国这个词很高尚，那些砸同胞车，在日料店吃饱了骂骂咧咧逃单，在自家门口无缘无故打老外的，别侮辱爱国这词！岛一定是我们的，可是实实在在的尊严，也在你和我的手里！(05:56)

> Post #2: Some vile persons have emerged from the water, it makes the back of your neck crawl! Patriotic compatriots, don't forget your original intentions. Don't get taken in by all the beating, smashing, and looting. Smashing the cars and restaurants outside your door won't get us back our islands!
>
> 一些恶人浮出水面，更加让人脊背发凉！爱国同胞勿忘初衷，别被打砸抢恶行利用了，砸遍家门口的车和店，也砸不回咱的岛来！(16:59)

On the same issue, the actress Yao Chen re-tweeted several news pieces (including a video that was later deleted, probably due to its graphic content), and she commented a week later: 'Scum! Something not even the devils [i.e., the Japanese imperial soldiers during World War II] would have done. Those swine!'[10] Meanwhile, Charles Xue, also known as Xue Manzi (@薛必群), used the opportunity to debate with his followers where responsibility for the events should lie, taking the strong view that the local authorities escalated the situation and should be blamed (he would later be arrested on charges of solicitation; his Weibo account has since been deleted).

Much like the comments that Feng and Yuan examined in their study, these interventions never abandon the established categories of us versus them that characterize the nationalist discourse. He Jiong's comments, for instance, remain firmly anchored in a 'patriotic' narrative that sees Japan as the antagonist. However, such comments are much more nuanced than the angry nationalist remarks that feature strongly in other parts of digital China, for example, in online comment sections. Overall, the Big-V celebrities repeatedly urged their followers to critically reflect on their own behaviour. The venture capitalist Lee Kai-fu (@李开复), for instance, provided such a self-reflective note in the following post on September 16 (08:44):

> Xi'an, I'm sorry. Today, your virtuous spirit of 13 dynasties was trampled underfoot. The great breadth of mind of your Tang dynasty was sullied. Your ancient allies and beautiful streets were altogether crushed by thugs. Please pardon my incompetence. It's like being crushed by an oncoming vehicle. I am like all these other people who grieve for you. Today we failed to defend your 1,000-year-old honour, but in the process we have come to understand ourselves. We have awoken to new life and will wash the stinking blood stain from your scars. I want to say: Xi'an, I'm sorry.
>
> 西安，对不起。今天，你十三朝的德魂被践踏，你大唐的胸襟被玷污，你被暴徒碾过一条条古巷美街，请原谅我的无能，就像拦不住拉土车碾过一样。我和大多数为你伤心的人一样，今天我们捍守不了你千年的尊严，但我们会觉悟自省，唤醒新生，清洗你伤痕里腥臭的血渍。我要说：西安，对不起。

Note how the post still deploys the discourse of popular nationalism to create a sense of a shared, continuous past, but how this past then becomes the basis for an ethical judgement of what membership in the imagined community should mean, namely, that association with this ancient civilization implies peaceful, civilized behaviour.

These microblogging practices show that the Diaoyu Island discourse takes on nuanced political contours as it is reworked by Weibo celebrities. Judging by the comment sections (usually with thousands of remarks), the fans generally shared the concerns and interpretations of their idols. During the 2012 dispute, there was thus room on the platform for political interventions that emphasized restraint, and these interventions were inserted into the discourse by users who occupied powerful nodes within the social media network. In such celebrity networks, nationalist discourse may have indeed been subject to the dampening influence of these highly influential users. While arguably leaving the underlying national parameters of the discourse unchallenged, Big-V celebrities nevertheless made use of their 'write permissions' to programme the discourse with their comparatively liberal values.

Much has changed on Weibo since 2012, especially following the anti-rumours campaign that Xi Jinping's administration launched against social media users in 2013 and that engulfed many outspoken Big-V bloggers. Nevertheless, three years after the campaign, Weibo still had 242 million users (CNNIC 2016: 36) and many of the trending topics that generate heated debate on the platform were still sparked by issues relating to Japan and its history of war. Weibo commentators continue to engage in discussions over the meanings of Chineseness, for example, following the publication of Japanese posters in Kyoto that promoted national pride by featuring a model who turned out to be Chinese rather than Japanese (BBC 2017). Microbloggers have debated what forms of patriotic behaviour should take, for instance in discussions over a real estate tycoon's confession that he always leaves the water tap running when staying in Japanese hotels in order to get back at 'little Japan' (Koetse 2016a).

The ensuing discussions again do not easily collapse into simple grand narratives of the Chinese nation. Take the example of a video that went viral in late February 2017, depicting a recital at a privately run kindergarten in Osaka, Japan. The video shows a group of young students at a sports event, proclaiming that 'Japan will not be outdone by other countries, we will protect the Senkaku Islands' (see Koetse 2017). On Weibo, the hashtag 'Japanese right-wing kindergarten takes oath' (*Riben youyi you'eryuan xuanshi* 日本右翼幼儿园宣誓) became top trending, and by May 2017 nearly 400,000 users had viewed the topic or reacted to posts. Manya Koetse (2017) recounts how the discussion overwhelmingly condemns the school and the people financing it, but also how Weibo provides an opportunity for users to raise questions about China's patriotic education, for instance asking 'isn't China exactly the same?'

These examples already demonstrate that Japan remains an important template for making sense of the nation on Weibo, and that cases like the East China Sea dispute resurface regularly as hot-button issues. It may, at times, seem as though a topic like the Nanjing Massacre is outdated, and that Chinese social media discussions about Japan have moved on from such historical topics, but this is by no means the case, as a controversy illustrates that started trending on Weibo in early 2017. At the time, two bloggers posted a Weibo video showing that the rooms in the Japanese Apa hotel chain featured revisionist history books in English and Japanese (the video was posted by @KatAndSid on 15 January 2017, at 17:15). The book, written by the Apa Group's CEO Toshio Motoya, depicts the Nanjing Massacre as a fabrication and generally attempts to revise the history of Japanese imperialism to present 'The Real History of Japan' (see *The Japan Times* 2017). By May 2017, the video had been re-posted over 700,000 times, generating more than 40,000 comments on Weibo, each of which, in turn, received tens of thousands of online interactions.

While I am not in a position here to provide a detailed analysis of the Apa controversy and its various Weibo hashtags, the scope of the affair demonstrates how relevant the Nanjing Massacre remains in digital China's social media spheres and how much Japan still provides the raw material for discourses on the Chinese nation. On Weibo, such discourses visibly contain attempts by diverse microbloggers to 'programme' the values of the networked interactions, often leading to contestations over symbols and their meanings. These interactions may privilege certain prominent users over others, but they are, on the whole, a messy affair: nationalism on Weibo is very much under construction.

## Weixin and Its Messaging Communities

Weibo's messiness is the outcome of specific design choices. It may be a social medium, but it combines radically revised access privileges to the 'button called publish' with many features that characterize traditional one-to-many broadcasting: individual users post public statements that go out to a potentially vast audience. While the medium allows other users to react to the statement in a similarly public way, and while social networks shape how these interactions then play themselves out online, Weibo relies on a broadcasting mentality. In this, it differs somewhat from the booming messaging service Weixin, which also contains a microblogging feature on its public accounts platform (*Weixin gongzhong pingtai* 微信公众平台; see Ng 2015), but which overall relies heavily on its ability to enable smaller, more personalized group interactions.

At the time of writing, Weixin discourse remained extremely difficult to study empirically. Like other such chat services (e.g., Line, Kakao, or WhatsApp), the service is built on top of mobile phone texting practices, though it also incorporates a large range of other multimedia functions. Weixin combines text messaging, microblogging, social networking, voice mailing, video chat, e-commerce, online banking, and much more (Chao 2016; Millward 2015). In all of this, it relies on the user's personal connections to small-scale communities. It is possible to follow specific public accounts on Weixin, but the app unfolds its full potential through its many overlapping private groups. Pieces of information like personal statements, media objects, or links to objects elsewhere on the web circulate within individual groups and are passed on by users to other groups to which they are connected.

Weixin communication thus crosses the unstable borders between different private groups, and this makes it largely unfeasible to track communication patterns across the service, both for ethical and practical reasons. A number of studies have nevertheless tried to come to grips with this complicated medium, and these studies allow us to draw several conceptual inferences about how Weixin dynamics work, what digital and social mechanisms Weixin interactions rely on, and how the platform compared to services like Weibo.

The work of Yu Guoming is instructive in this regard. Yu (2014: 4–5) points out how Weixin leverages the strong ties of its users to create overlapping 'friend circles' (*pengyouquan* 朋友圈) for 'narrowcasting' (*zhaibo* 窄播). Since these online friend circles represent actual social connections, for instance with family members, co-workers, fellow students, and other acquaintances, users have an incentive to discipline themselves as they interact and spread media content. To Yu, this implies that Weixin has a civilizing influence on discourse. Examining the perceived decline of Weibo and the success of Weixin, he writes (2014: 7):

It is a character flaw for someone to not take responsibility for their actions and to stealthily hurl abuse at others. A platform that condones and encourages such an environment for quick success and instant profit is bound to destroy itself. The sudden rise of Weixin is grounded in trust, responsibility, and the right to choose an alternative where people can promote their good taste and social upbringing.

一个人对自己没有责任的担当，鬼鬼祟祟地谩骂他人是人格的缺陷，容忍鼓励这个环境安排的平台则是急功近利自我毁灭。微信的崛起在于信任、负责和选择的权利，人们会提升优雅与社会教养。

Indeed, Yu likens Weibo to a 'frontstage' and Weixin to a 'backstage' of the information system—a sentiment very similar to Goffman's (1959) famous categories of front and back regions of social interactions: agents act differently when their behaviour is under public scrutiny than if they are acting in more private settings. Social media behaviour seems to confirm such dynamics (see also Bullingham & Vasconcelos 2013), and it seems plausible that users would present different aspects of their identity on Weixin than on Weibo or in anonymous web forums. The kind of sociality that Weixin promotes apparently increases users' trust in one another, especially when social ties are already fairly strong, which then, in turn, increases the likelihood that users will engage in positive 'electronic word-of-mouth' communication (Lien & Cao 2014).[11] My own interviews in China suggest that many Weixin users assume that their small-group interactions are fairly private and that Weixin offers a place for opinion expression that many perceive as genuine. Wang and Gu (2015) argue that Weixin's design features indeed enhance privacy and security, and they conclude that this is likely to benefit free speech and grass-roots activism on the platform. Similar observations about a perceived lack of censorship and the strong potential for personal bonding on Weixin lead Tu (2016: 348) to argue that the platform potentially serves as 'an online public sphere' and consequently 'contributes to the development of civil society in China'.

I have no doubt that many users believe their Weixin interactions to be private, personal, and meaningful. I also find it convincing that users would perceive their exchanges as empowering in ways that may at times drive political engagement (see Chen 2017), but I remain sceptical on a number of issues related to this platform. For one thing, interactions on Weixin may not be as private as many users believe. Ng (2015) and Ruan, Knockel, Ng, and Crete-Nishihata (2016), for instance, have studied censorship practices on Weixin, showing that the company Tencent is heavily involved in managing public opinion on its Chinese platform, an issue I return to in the next chapter. These censorship practices raise questions about the degree of privacy and security that Tencent can actually guarantee its users and about the amount of trust that interactions on the platform should inspire; clearly the authorities are still capable of monitoring and, at times, intervening in discourse on this seemingly private chat app (see also Harwit 2017: 10–12).

I also remain sceptical about Weixin's potential to function as a public sphere for civil and potentially progressive political discussion. This is partly because of the challenges to such public sphere narratives that I have discussed in chapter 1 of this book. It is partly because I do not share the optimism about Weixin's design choices that proponents of the platform often express. Whereas issues related to privacy may not be of much concern if users do not take them seriously (and if they do not cross any politically sensitive lines), arguments that Weixin's design enables more honest and equal discussion than other social media platforms may be premature. Yu, for example, argues that 'what is presented on Weibo is a fake self, whereas what is represented on Weixin is the true self' (Yu 2014: 7). But is this assessment convincing? As social agents, we continuously assemble the aspects of ourselves that we want others to see, making the idea of a 'true self' (*zhenxingqing de ziwo* 真性情的自我) controversial. It also remains an issue of contention whether the broadcasting approach of a service like Weibo is really as odious to public discourse as Yu seems to imply. The examples of Big-V discourse that I have discussed earlier seem to suggest otherwise.

To me, assessments by scholars like Yu (2014), Tu (2016), or Wang and Gu (2015) are instructive because they highlight how digital designs amplify specific social and psychological tendencies. Whereas posting on Weibo is a bit like voicing an opinion in a public square, posting on Weixin is like voicing an opinion at a private dinner party. Each is governed by its own social logic, and this makes certain discursive statements and strategies more appropriate than others, depending on the respective setting. However, this does not have to mean that the design of Weixin's familiar friend circles indeed promotes discourse that is responsible, civilized, and in good taste. It also does not mean that Weixin is inherently more egalitarian than Weibo or freer of corporate manipulation. Both services seem to reproduce social inequalities by empowering those who are already privileged (Fang 2015), and Weixin's digital features (see Harwit 2017: 5–6) frequently limit usages and encourage specific communication patterns. For instance, as Peng (2017: 8) argues, Weixin's 'moments' allows users to develop a personal online profile full of 'everyday life episodes' that is specifically 'designed to address and even encourage their desire to maintain their relationships with friends and family'. At times, these functionalities can take on an almost Foucauldian surveillance dynamics, for instance when interactions between parents and their children prompt young adults to self-censor their presentations of the self and 'to construct a positive image as an independent and mature adult in front of their parents' (Zhou, Wen, Tang, & DiSalvo, 2017: 6).

In short, it may well be that Weixin's digital design features promote group conformity over serendipitous, conflict-prone interactions. Gan (2017), for instance, suggests that the 'liking' behaviour of Weixin users frequently reflects the wish to provide or seek social support, and Chen (2017: 13) finds that concerns over interpersonal relations on Weixin reduce the willingness of users to voice controversial opinions in their friend circles. Such concerns can increase civility, but group conformity also implies adhering to the values that are programmed into the community network. If the dominant value of a community network is a sentiment like nationalism, then group pressures are likely to exacerbate such sentiments rather than providing spaces to critically question them. Future research will have to confirm whether small-scale groups on digital services like Weixin still provide room to voice and debate opinions that have become framed as inappropriate within such groups.

Another issue with Weixin discourse is that the small-scale, real-world networks of the service are likely to facilitate the same kind of group biases and polarizations of opinion that scholars have observed in other digital social networks (see Conover et al. 2011). Users tend to seek out people and ideas that confirm their personal views, leading to the kind of homophily that Pariser has criticized (2012: 1126):

> Consuming information that conforms to our ideas of the world is easy and pleasurable; consuming information that challenges us to think in new ways or question our assumptions is frustrating and difficult. This is why partisans of one political stripe tend not to consume the media of another. As a result, an information environment built on click signals will favor content that supports our existing notions about the world over content that challenges them.

As I have discussed earlier, such dynamics have indeed been observed for Tianya forums (Medaglia & Yang 2017), but also for internet use in China more broadly

(Wu 2014), and I see no reason to assume that the digital walled gardens of Weixin's friend circles would create different dynamics. In fact, the degree to which the service relies on social conformity suggests that it might be even more prone to create echo chambers for its users than public platforms like Weibo. Where such echo chambers become the home of nationalist discourse, that discourse could potentially reverberate largely unchallenged. It will be one of the major challenges for coming scholarship on digital China to develop methodologically and ethically sound ways to study how topics related to the Chinese nation travel through Weixin's public and private forums.

## Conclusion

It is correct that Chinese social media contain diverse discourses (Ye, Sarrica, & Fortunati 2014), and this is also true for nationalist discussions (Feng & Yuan 2014). On issues related to Japan, online forums and microblogging networks contain both chauvinistic sentiments and more nuanced reasoning, and there is frequently space for individual users to explore the multitude of meanings inherent in the concept of the Chinese nation. However, the design choices in digital China pre-structure this diversity and relay a particular impression of what is appropriate discourse on national issues. Through the dynamics of Web 2.0 features, aggressively chauvinistic statements become privileged on China's web, drowning out more thoughtful arguments. Even where the discourse is not aggressive, it relies on fundamental assumptions of how the world works today, and this includes a firm commitment to the idea of the imagined community: users may disagree on how to make sense of China and its relation with Japan, but they implicitly agree that concepts such as 'China' and 'Japan' matter. When it comes to microblogs, nationalist discourse is far less mainstream than on the traditional web. Weibo users frequently re-appropriate the nationalist discussion to highlight their own personal struggles, and this includes frequent criticism of the CCP. While discussions on Weibo can be heated, and at times uncivil, it is noteworthy that celebrity microbloggers do not necessarily have the kind of detrimental influence on public discourse that Chinese critics in government and academia usually associate with these influential actors. The 2012 East China Sea dispute on Weibo demonstrated how such celebrities attempted to de-escalate popular sentiments. While the discourse remained within the confines of established nationalist categories, the most influential Big-V users deployed these categories as a means for political intervention into perniciously chauvinistic protests. It is ironic that only one year later the Chinese state would target such users as part of its campaign to civilize microblogging practices.

With Weibo seemingly in decline in the wake of the new policy measures, the novel must-have social media service in China is Weixin. Indeed, social media are evolving so quickly in China that one might wonder whether research on any single media technology will rapidly be obsolete. I have made the argument here that such concerns may be exaggerated: media technologies exist alongside each other in hybrid media systems, and it is by no means the case that new, popular technologies make previous ones redundant. This is also true for Weixin, which has benefitted from government crackdowns on Sina Weibo, but which promotes somewhat different usages through its designs, ultimately augmenting rather than replacing Sina's microblogging offers.

The Weixin platform provides a suite of digital media services that leverage users' social networks to facilitate narrowcasting. This is a major departure from microblogging services like Sina's Weibo, which also relies on networks, but not on the kinds of friend circles that Weixin promotes. On Weixin, users engage overwhelmingly with people they actually know as real-life acquaintances. This means that it makes little sense to have an anonymous Weixin account: the benefits of Weixin only materialize if the user reveals who they are so that their digital media usage can connect with their social network (and their bank account). Broadcasting and sharing information then become fundamentally more personal and social endeavours than in other media. The psychology of small groups affects what people are willing to say and do, leading to more group-conforming behaviour. While such conformity may improve social responsibility, it does so through extrinsic pressures rather than through intrinsic motivations. I find it unlikely that such dynamics will actually improve the 'quality' (*suzhi* 素质) of citizens that China's leadership is so concerned about. Instead, Weixin's walled gardens also hold the potential to function as echo chambers in which users can eschew serendipity in favour of homophily (McPherson, Smith-Lovin, & Cook, 2001). Nationalism, which is essentially an extreme form of homophily, is likely to thrive in such environments.

In short, the technical affordances that social media provide within the PRC's political and economic setting indeed empower users to shape discourse about the nation, but this process remains uneven. Not all users are empowered equally, and discourses are still situated within overarching dominant frameworks that privilege parochial understandings of politics. This is largely the result of the PRC's current media logic, especially of the government's attempts to promote professionalism and centralize political information through an often paternalistic approach to information and communication management. It is this management strategy and its effects on digital nationalism that I turn to in the next chapter.

# 8

# The Cultural Governance
# of Digital China

In this world, a hundred streams faithfully return to the ocean,

Serving as a measure for Chinese civilization.

The sediments of 5,000 years settle and give rise to the light of new thinking.

Incorruptibility is the nation's clear ripples.

We unite at the centre of heaven and earth,

Our faith and devotion course the great distances of the Yellow and Yangtze Rivers.

Internet superpower! The net is where glorious dreams are.

Internet superpower! From the distant cosmos to the home that we long for.

Internet superpower! Tell the world the China Dream is lifting up the great China.

Internet superpower! Each of us represents our country to the world.

在这个世界百川忠诚寻归海洋
担当中华文明的丈量
五千年沉淀点亮创新思想
廉洁就是一个民族清澈荡漾
我们团结在天地中央
信仰奉献流淌万里黄河长江
网络强国　网在哪光荣梦想在哪
网络强国　从遥远的宇宙到思念的家
网络强国　告诉世界中国梦在崛起大中华
网络强国　一个我在世界代表着国家

These lyrics are part of a song that the Cyberspace Administration of China (CAC, *Zhongguo renmin gongheguo guojia hulianwang xinxi bangongshi* 中华人民共和国国家互联网信息办公室) wrote to illustrate its understanding of digital media.[1] The CAC was established in 2014 and constitutes the state arm of the CCP's central leading group of cyberspace affairs. It is one of the core institutions that govern digital China under the leadership of Xi Jinping. The CAC website, cac.gov.cn, welcomes visitors with a Xi-quote that also doubles as an institutional mantra: 'Without internet safety there can be no national safety; without informationalization there can be no modernization; work hard to turn our country into an internet superpower'.[2]

Under Xi Jinping's leadership, the CCP has indeed worked hard to expand its governance over digital China and define the parameters of ICT usage. Throughout this book, I have pointed out what kind of nationalist discourse emerges from within such parameters, and I have made the case that this is the outcome of a particular media logic that grounds technological design and usage in the capitalist structures and political institutions of the PRC. This chapter now moves away from Japan discourses in digital China and turns to the political institutions that govern this complex media ecology, exploring what managerial strategies inform digital China's media rationale. In short, this chapter examines how the authorities govern digital China in ways that encourage particular forms of user engagement. This issue is crucial to understanding what it takes to calibrate networks for the spread of digital nationalism.

Foreign media tend to interpret Chinese media governance as the workings of a monolithic authoritarian apparatus that is trying to win a 'cat and mouse' game (*Economist* 2013) with the 'forces of freedom of expression' (Sudworth 2013). Such assessments can also be found in academic accounts, where Chinese media workers and government officials are, at times, seen as 'unapologetic spouters of lies' (He 2008: 38) who exert their dominance over China's population (for an important reality-check, see Repnikova 2017). There is, of course, much to criticize about censorship and propaganda in the PRC today; however, it would be misleading to view such communication and information politics solely as top-down acts by the state, enforced against a contentious public. The reality of cultural regulations is far more complex, and without a careful look at the intricacies of governance strategies in the PRC, there is a risk to view such management techniques as unique to 'authoritarian' political systems, or to understand the kind of digital nationalism I have explored throughout this book as exceptionally 'Chinese'. Instead, it is more helpful to see digital nationalism as a consequence of technological affordances, economic incentives, and policy choices that play a role in the politics of all modern nation states, albeit to varying degrees and with varying effects. Ignoring these parallels means misunderstanding how and why nationalism is resurfacing as a major political force around the world, including places like North America or Europe.

The purpose of this chapter is to capture some of this complexity. The first section examines what it might mean to govern in a 'democratic' or 'authoritarian' manner, and it makes the case that we should understand politics not so much as the processes of either democratic or authoritarian *systems*, but rather as processes of combining egalitarian and hierarchical governing *technologies*. The following section takes a look at the rationale behind such governing choices in China, and it explains how mechanisms of democratic centralism have shaped Chinese media and communication politics over the past decades. The subsequent sections then examine how this outcome is achieved through both hard and soft governing techniques, and how it relies on the collaboration of media workers and the self-regulation of China's internet users. The final section discusses what consequences such politics have. My argument is that the Chinese authorities are centralizing political communication, and that this includes arranging the networks of digital China into hierarchical structures. As I show, the resulting network architecture benefits China's political and commercial elites while at the same time satisfying certain user demands, but it also creates a media ecology that encourages nationalism.

## The Technics of Political Communication

It is tempting to view the political and economic choices that China's elites make primarily as a function of authoritarianism, and as fundamentally different from politics in democratic systems. Party leaders have repeatedly reiterated their scepticism towards liberal democracy, which they criticize as inefficient and biased in favour of property-owning classes (Xinhua 2009). The former PRC president Hu Jintao, for instance, made it clear during his term in office that the PRC 'will never copy a Western political system' (see Meng & Mou 2012). His successor, Xi Jinping, similarly argued that the political systems of other countries 'would not fit' and 'might even lead to catastrophic consequences' (Xinhua 2014). This is a sentiment echoed by parts of China's entrepreneurial elite (e.g., Li 2013), which relies on close collaboration with the political establishment and the guarantee of 'social stability' to conduct business.

The Chinese political establishment consequently remains suspicious of political mechanisms that might disrupt 'stability' (see Sandby-Thomas 2011), such as competing political parties, universal suffrage, individual rights, the rule of law, a press that is independent of the ruling party, or a separation of legislative, judiciary, and executive power. Instead of such liberal mechanisms, PRC politics creatively combine hierarchical governing strategies with what Howland (2012: 3) calls 'managed participation', creating a contemporary form of 'democratic centralism' that is meant to assure popular sovereignty in China.[3]

In its ideal form, democratic centralism implies that political decision-making is centralized in a way that first passes relevant information upwards through political organizations, then entrusts a meritocratically selected vanguard to debate and decide policies in a consensual fashion, and, finally, deploys all relevant state institutions to powerfully implement these policies. The process characteristically includes moments of popular consultation and deliberation during its input phase, but it does not suffer dissent lightly once a decision has been reached at the top of the political pyramid and needs to be implemented as a policy output.

The study of Chinese politics frequently focuses on this political pyramid, its authoritarian outputs, and its ability to adjust its Marxist-Leninist premise to a rapidly changing social and economic environment. The Chinese case has alternatively been analysed as a case of 'authoritarian resilience' (Nathan 2003), 'authoritarian consolidation' (Göbel 2011), 'consultative authoritarianism' (Teets 2013), 'authoritarian deliberation' (He & Warren 2011, Jiang 2010b), 'responsive authoritarianism' (Weller 2008), 'fragmented authoritarianism' (Lieberthal 1992), and 'fragmented authoritarianism 2.0' (Mertha 2009). Much of this discussion has been guided by questions of why and how China's political system has defied the pattern of 'democratic waves' that Samuel Huntington (1991) proposed. Once non-liberal political systems are exposed to liberal forces like the market or the free exchange of ideas, should the benefits of liberal governance not become so eminently apparent to citizens that they increasingly demand liberal reforms from their authoritarian leaders?[4] Considering how the political systems of South Korea or Taiwan transitioned to embrace liberal-democratic principles, it seems puzzling that market dynamics and rapidly expanding regional and global integration have not led to a similar democratic transition in the PRC. It is this apparent puzzle about the various ways in which the 'regime' has managed to 'reconsolidate itself' (Nathan 2003) that occupies much of the non-Chinese literature on China's authoritarian politics. Most recently, the debates have been updated to incorporate the increasing ubiquity of ICT usage, leading to new labels for Chinese politics, such as 'authoritarian informationalism' (Jiang 2010a) or 'authoritarianism 2.0' (Stockmann 2014).

These discussions of authoritarian politics draw attention to the many ways in which the PRC's leadership and its managerial approach are successfully adapting to the challenges of governing a networked society. There is nevertheless a risk in seeing 'authoritarianism' primarily as a characteristic of specific political systems, and to then distinguish 'authoritarian regimes' from liberal democratic systems. The word 'regime' already implies that such systems are inherently illegitimate, and it is rare to see perceived democratic alternatives similarly described as 'regimes' (for an exception, see Göbel 2011). What is more, such a distinction between democratic and authoritarian systems potentially reinforces

Orientalist dichotomies of 'Eastern' versus 'Western' politics, making it seem as though authoritarianism is today primarily a legacy of 'Oriental' traditions with their ostensible propensities for order and hierarchy (Zheng 2010).

Such assumptions obscure the degree to which politics in so-called authoritarian regimes also include meaningful consultation and participation (Salmenkari 2006; Teets 2013). Political systems, regardless of their make-up, can only be effective if they are able to justify themselves to their subjects; that is, if they are able to legitimate themselves. This is also true for the Chinese case (see Holbig 2009; Holbig & Gilley 2010; Sandby-Thomas 2014; Schubert 2008, 2014; and Zeng 2014). It makes sense to ask whether there are elements to China's political system that do indeed convince many of its citizens that the system is effective and fair, much as elements in North American or European politics are able to convince citizens that the political systems they live under are worthy of popular support. As it turns out, legitimacy in China is not simply generated by economic performance, that is, the ability to buy citizens off with increased incomes generated through economic growth. The promise of increased wealth plays a role, but legitimacy is also generated by the many ways in which the street-level bureaucracy successfully satisfies popular demands (Ahlers, Heberer, & Schubert 2015; Schubert 2008), the degree to which citizens feel they are involved in political consultation and decision-making at the lower levels of urban and rural politics (Heberer & Schubert 2008; Schubert & Heberer 2009), and the ways in which media and education policies inspire nationalist support for the Chinese developmental approach (Schneider & Hwang 2014a; Shue 2004; Wang 2012).

Moreover, the idea that authoritarian and democratic systems are fundamentally different overlooks the many similarities between such systems. Christian Göbel (2011: 177, 181) makes this clear when he writes:

> many of the challenges democratic and authoritarian rulers face are actually quite similar: both must aim at establishing and upholding universal rules of the game to prevent splits in leadership, secure society's compliance and gain support if the regime is to become sustainable. [ ... ] Just like their democratic counterparts, authoritarian regimes are faced with the task of preventing breakdown, deepening and organising the regime and generating legitimacy among elites and the population.

Indeed, much like their authoritarian counterparts, democratic polities also rely on mechanisms that are decidedly coercive. If we consider 'democracy' to mean 'rule of the people', and, in that sense, to describe political processes in which the individuals who ultimately suffer the consequences of a political decision were involved in making that decision, then any form of political delegation or representation is potentially undemocratic. This, I believe, is what Noam Chomsky (2013: 121) means when he criticizes 'power that isn't really justified by the will of the governed'. In a similar vein, it would be a mistake to down-play how hierarchical, non-participatory, and forceful the political institutions of representative democracy can be. As David Graeber points out, modern liberal democracies also possess 'nightsticks' that they can deploy, however they hide those sticks very effectively (2011a: 657):

> The rarity with which the nightsticks actually appear just helps to make the violence harder to see. This in turn makes the effects of all these regulations—regulations that almost always assume that normal rela-tions between individuals are mediated by the market, and that normal groups are organized by relations of hierarchy and command—seem to emanate not from the government's monopoly of the use of force, but from the largeness, solidity, and heaviness of the objects themselves.

What we are then left with is that modern nation states, in general, draw from a variety of governing technologies, or what Mumford (1964) has called dem-ocratic and authoritarian technics. Democratic technics are those mechanisms that emphasize egalitarian participation and ensure consensus-building, whereas authoritarian technics emphasize centralization of power and compliance with decisions. In Mumford's view, democratic technics include 'communal self-government, free communication as between equals, unimpeded access to the common store of knowledge, protection against arbitrary external controls, and a sense of individual moral responsibility for behavior that affects the whole com-munity' (Mumford 1964: 1). To Mumford, such 'scattered, diversified' technics of organization that are 'cut to the human measure' are the norm in small-scale communities; however, once communities become imagined as larger entities, small-scale democratic practices become 'supplemented by a more abstract, depersonalized form' that draws from 'a new configuration of technical inven-tion, scientific observation, and centralized political control' to create 'the pecu-liar mode of life we may now identify, without eulogy, as civilization' (Mumford 1964: 2–3).

Following this reasoning, I believe we need to assess, on a case-by-case basis, in what form and to what degree a particular political process draws from each of these sets of technics, and how digital technologies act upon and contribute to the efficacy of different technics. If we want to establish whether a political decision or measure is democratic, we should not presume that the answer lies in the nominal setup of the overarching political system, that is, that systems qualify as liberal democracies if they fulfil a list of conceptual criteria (universal suffrage, elected representatives, etc.), and that 'regimes' that fail to meet these criteria are, per definition, authoritarian. This would be begging the question. We should also avoid assumptions about how digital technology in general facilitates 'democracy' or 'authoritarianism'. Instead, to assess whether digital politics are democratic or not, it is important to analyse who makes which decision, deploys what tools, and to what effect. Democratic politics then consist of decisions made by those who are ultimately affected by their consequences, whereas authoritarian politics consist of centralized decisions by proxy. In that sense, much of China's digital politics is indeed undemocratic, but so is much of digital politics in European or American societies.

## The Logic Behind Media Controls in Digital China

Chinese media governance incorporates both democratic and authoritarian technics, but it arguably places a particularly high premium on mechanisms that reinforce hierarchies, relegate discussion to carefully circumscribed spaces, and concentrate power in the hands of elite actors such as professional media workers, state administrators, and party cadres. Throughout the tenure of Xi Jinping as party secretary and president of the PRC, commentators have pointed out how his administration has tightened control over China's media system. Censorship and propaganda measures that the authorities introduced in early 2016 had commentators speculating as to what the reasons behind Xi's media policies were (ChinaFile 2016): a bid for more power amidst factional struggles, a way to silence concerns about the PRC's economic slowdown, or an attempt to unify the party? Other news outlets were less nuanced about the motives. The *Wall Street Journal* called these developments a 'publicity blitz' and compared Xi Jinping with Mao Zedong (Wong 2016), while *Quartz* argued that the authorities were 'stepping up an increasingly brutal, unabashedly public global campaign against critics of the Communist party' that demonstrated how China's leaders were 'growing increasingly desperate' to control public discourse (Timmons 2016). Meanwhile, the *Guardian* interpreted such policies as 'a "no holds barred" battle to wrestle absolute control of all media' and, referencing an editorial in the *China Daily*, made the case that this 'battle' was fought 'in order to maintain control' (Phillips 2016).

Interestingly, such talk of a desperate media battle fails to account for the often careful reasoning behind China's media controls, let alone the degree of collaboration and negotiation that these controls entail. For example, the *Guardian's* summary of the *China Daily* (2016) discourse focuses on state-enforced control, whereas the *China Daily* itself presents a much more nuanced perspective that is primarily concerned with generating public support for party politics. The editorial argues that mass media are 'essential to political stability' and to the 'legitimacy' of the Party, which is an argument that has informed media politics in China for decades. The editorial then goes on to shed light on an important element of these media politics, which is the Party's goal to 'guide public opinion'. Interestingly, the state outlet argues that such guidance can only be effective if it moves away precisely from the kind of heavy-handed tactics that foreign journalists tend to criticize. According to the editorial, 'sermons only make people tired', and 'while the media needs to report the positive aspects of the society, it must also cover the negative side, too, so that social progress is possible' (*China Daily* 2016).

Such calls in official Chinese media for debate and for balanced reporting tend to be omitted in foreign news assessments (e.g., Phillips 2016; Wong 2016), which are overwhelmingly one-sided when it comes to PRC politics. Yet, dismissing the nuances in the official position can lead to simplistic conclusions, for instance 'that China's leaders and political system are simultaneously both child-like and evil' (see Timmons 2016), which are unhelpful for explaining how and why media governance in China works the way it does. Moreover, such journalistic accounts also do little to assuage the concerns of Chinese government officials and entrepreneurs alike that foreign media do not provide fair coverage of China, making it seem ever more imperative for Chinese media professionals to promote national interests and, by extension, nationalism. Ironically, reductionist foreign reporting thus feeds back into the Chinese discourse on national sovereignty, providing yet another incentive to expand nationalism and deploy authoritarian technics to govern digital China.

Another controversial interpretation of recent developments in China is that media governance under Xi Jinping is decidedly different from the practices of his predecessors. While Xi Jinping's administration has indeed introduced a number of innovations to Chinese propaganda and censorship, these innovations are no radical departure from well-established patterns in CCP policy. Media governance in the PRC has always been subject to cycles of press freedom and control, depending on how CCP leaders assessed the 'stability' of Chinese society at any given point in time. Overall, Xi's policies are consistent with the longstanding tradition of how the Party views mass media and their role in modern society: for political leaders in China, it has long been imperative to take charge of political communication and exert interpretive sovereignty over systems of meaning.[5] Mao Zedong was a particularly ardent defender of what he called 'thought reform' (*sixiang gaizao* 思想改造), as is evident from his famous programmatic speech at Yan'an (Mao 1942) and its radical interpretations during the early years of the Cultural Revolution (see Mitter 2004: 210; MacFarquar & Schonhals 2006: 17, 93). However, comparisons between Xi and Mao serve largely rhetorical purposes while omitting the important continuities that characterize Chinese political communication more generally.

Despite later apprehension about Mao's drastic revolutionary politics, the legacy of Maoist cultural understandings has remained influential throughout the subsequent decades (Brady 2008: 35–39). The leader generations after Mao held fast to the idea that the Party needed to reform China through 'ideological work': Deng Xiaoping famously argued that propaganda was 'imperative for all revolutionary work'; his successor, Jiang Zemin, stressed that the media should function as 'the mouthpiece of the Party'; and Hu Jintao was unambiguous about the idea that 'correct guidance of public opinion' was 'beneficial to the Party, the country, and the people' (quoted in Zhang 2011: 31). Recent campaigns under Xi Jinping to promote the 'China Dream' or to sanction media workers and citizen journalists who report critically about contemporary affairs need to be seen in this historical context.

Media politics in China continue to be informed by a Leninist understanding of what culture is, what role it is meant to play in society, and what negative effects it might exert if left unattended by the vanguard of the ruling party. Importantly, the contemporary view of media governance continues a tradition of cultural politics that reaches as far back as pre-imperial times, when political thinkers of various ideological persuasions debated how to 'cultivate' the morally correct behaviour of rulers and subjects. Confucian thinkers, for instance, believed that individuals generally emulated the actions of others, and that the sage ruler consequently needed to set a positive example through superior moral conduct (Munro 1969: 190). This is emphatically not to say that Chinese politics are intrinsically and immutably 'Confucian' throughout the ages, but it serves as a reminder that contemporary ideas about political communication cleverly combine past and present experiences. As Zhao (1998: 26) points out, the fundamentally elitist 'Confucian belief' in morally cultivating rule later connected seamlessly 'with the Leninist concept of a vanguard whose task is to enlighten the people and help them to see their own interests'.

Such a Leninist view of culture has inspired several important assumptions, each of which informs media management in the PRC today. One such element is the Marxist belief that culture is part of a superstructure, sitting on top of material processes like economic production and distribution, and that cultural products will consequently either promote fair and equitable socio-economic conditions or reproduce exploitation and alienation. At the heart of this belief lies an arguably reductionist understanding of culture and human cognition, or what Pinker (2002) has called the 'blank slate' view of the mind, in which the human psyche is easily moulded by external influences, for better or worse. As anachronistic as such a view may be, it strongly informs the CCP's cultural politics and its concerns for citizen's 'quality' (*suzhi* 素质) to this day, and this leads to an unapologetically moralist stance in which it is a core part of the party's mandate to educate, cultivate, and ultimately emancipate 'the masses'.[6]

Such paternalism provides a powerful incentive to adopt authoritarian technics in the name of the greater good. Information control in China has a tradition that reaches back to antiquity, and connotations of censorship (*shencha* 审查) and propaganda (*xuanchuan* 宣传) are by no means automatically negative.[7] Indeed, they are frequently morally and pragmatically positive, particularly with regard to discourse that could constitute an ideological challenge to Chinese sovereignty or cultural identity.

Another aspect of the CCP's Leninist legacy that reflects a commitment to authoritarian technics is the belief that state institutions should be tools that the leadership deploys to manage China's progress along the socialist road. The state and its system of state-owned media enterprises have always been subordinate to the Party's democratic centralism, providing practical means to implement decisions throughout China's various issue-related political systems, or *xitong* (系统; see Lieberthal 2004: 233). One such *xitong* is the CCP's propaganda system (see Shambaugh 2007; Brady 2008), which is headed by the Central Leadership Small Group on Propaganda and Ideological Work and managed administratively by the CCP's Propaganda Department. The CCP retains influence over state institutions through its personnel politics and the party core groups it maintains in all social and political organizations, and this includes the state's centres of cultural production and dissemination. The Party connects diverse actors with the Party's propaganda network and defines the values according to which these actors are meant to behave.

A frequently overlooked dimension of Leninist organizational strategies is that the leadership does not use media solely to disseminate politically correct views, but that it also relies on media organizations to monitor public opinion and consult citizens (Tsang 2009). This, at times, includes authoritarian surveillance technics, but it is in this context that the CCP also deploys democratic technics, for instance policy consultations with local citizens, hotlines for feedback on policy implementation, cadre assessments that include the opinions of local citizens, online polls about future policy choices, and so forth. Throughout its history, the CCP has concerned itself with the question of how to remain 'close to the masses'—a concern that once informed Mao's politics of sending CCP cadres 'down to the countryside' to study the life of average Chinese citizens (see Lee 1978: 937). Today, the CCP uses media, and increasingly digital technologies, to assess the needs and wishes of the much-evoked 'average folks' (*putong laobaixing* 普通老百姓). This is evident in the State Council's programmatic 2010 White Paper on the role that the internet should play in China. According to the document (Information Office 2010), the purpose of the internet is to spread 'China's splendid national culture' and 'publicize government information', but it is also meant to help 'the government get to know the people's wishes'. The 2010 roadmap for China's internet management is very much an extension of the CCP's existing Leninist ideology of how to think about information.

# The Soft Communication Controls of Digital China's Neoliberal Governance

The PRC's authorities have long realized that governing a networked nation state requires a flexible toolbox of authoritarian and democratic technics. Today, the party and the state deploy a vast, sophisticated system of hard and soft controls to manage political discourse (Brady 2008; Schneider 2012: ch. 7; Shambaugh 2007), and this system has progressively been expanded to also cover digital China. The CCP's model of digital information management includes a range of coercive mechanisms, such as preventing access to webpages, blocking search results, removing online posts, or arresting contentious internet users (see Deibert, Palfrey, Rohozinski, & Zittrain 2010: 449-487; MacKinnon 2009; Ng 2013 & 2015; Ruan, Knockel, Ng, & Crete-Nishihata 2016). These hard controls are deployed inconsistently by local authorities (Wright 2014) and with some trepidation: a forceful intervention highlights weaknesses in the Party's ability to generate compliance, and it draws attention to politically sensitive issues. The Party's preferred approach is to align citizens' interests with its own, rather than having to resort to coercion. This is the reason why the CCP takes a pro-active approach when it comes to manipulating online discussion, for instance by paying cadres to 'astroturf' across digital China's forums (Han 2013; King, Pan, & Roberts, 2017), that is, to promote the Party's interests but mask such commentary as genuine 'grass-roots' behaviour.

Of similar importance as such pro-active interventions into public discourse are governing technics that transfer the responsibility to regulate digital China to private companies and individual internet users. One set of such soft controls that the authorities have successfully used in the past makes use of economic dynamics. By manipulating the framework in which economic interactions take place in China, the Chinese state attempts to align the interests of diverse actors with the interests of the ruling elites. This approach has served the CCP well, for instance in the mass-media sector (see Schneider 2012: 164–171), and the authorities consequently attempt to reproduce this successful cultural governance strategy in digital contexts. A cornerstone of this strategy is to use a system of production permits, distribution permits, import controls, and content regulations to create incentives for private actors to generally conform to Party politics. The PRC's licencing system for web content, for instance, assures that only approved institutions can maintain websites. State agencies like the State Internet Information Office (SIIO) and CAC additionally define to what degree and on which topics domestic websites can publish original content and on which topics they are required to relay copies of official news materials.

To improve its governance, the state has long relied on strategies that encourage conglomeration in the media sector (Zhao 2000). As I have discussed in chapter 4, the major sources of information on China's web are either established state news sites like those of the People's Daily Group, the Xinhua News Agency, and the Southern Media Group, or websites of large, accredited private enterprises like iFeng, Sina, Sohu, or 163. A particularly interesting case is the popular independent news service Caixin, which is known for its investigative journalism. In late 2013, state-backed China Media Capital bought a major stake in the company, bringing it officially under the leadership of the same manager who also heads the state-run Shanghai Media Group (Frater 2013). To what extent this affects Caixin's independence will have to remain a matter for detailed future research, but such financial manoeuvres at the very least suggest that the authorities continue to experiment with ownership structures to manage China's media.

The state encourages conglomeration in the private sector, and this also affects social media. As I have already pointed out, the PRC's censorship system, commonly called 'the Great Firewall of China', blocks domestic users from accessing foreign social networking and media sharing services such as Facebook, YouTube, or Twitter. Meanwhile, the state nurtures private Chinese enterprises that develop local alternatives. The social media platform Renren, the web forum Tianya, the video-hosting service Youku Tudou, Sina's microblogging service Weibo, and Tencent's mobile messaging service Weixin are all children of this policy. While these various services provide spaces for diverse cultural exchange and political dissent (see chapter 7), they nevertheless depend on the state for their licencing and are, consequently, subject to PRC media controls.

This arrangement is doubly advantageous for the Chinese state, since, on the one hand, it creates strong, internationally competitive champions of industry that generate employment, tax revenues, and international prestige, while, on the other hand, it allows domestic discussions to take place in walled gardens that can be monitored and censored for unwanted content. That the authorities remain innovative and adaptive when it comes to managing digital culture is apparent from the campaigns against 'online rumours' that have characterized cultural governance under Xi Jinping's leadership (see Kaiman 2013): the authorities have been experimenting with various techniques to curb the spread of content through China's digital networks, and this has included mechanisms such as real name registrations and sanctions for inappropriate tweets, especially for users with large networks of followers.

A particularly ingenious element of the PRC's neoliberal governance approach is that it outsources the responsibility for web monitoring and content management to private companies and their users (see also Creemers 2016b: 94–95). Since companies rely on their licences and their contacts to state officials to remain competitive in China's capitalist economy, they have a strong incentive to demonstrate their commitment to the overarching governance framework, for instance by signing voluntary 'public pledges' to manage the internet 'in an ethical way' (ISC 2002; see also Ng 2013: xxiv). Such self-imposed ethical guidelines then make it possible for the authorities to transmit broad (and often vague) policy preferences indirectly to private actors, who enforce them throughout the market economy. On a case-by-case basis, private companies interpret what it means to 'jeopardize state security and disrupt social stability, contravene laws and regulations and spread superstition and obscenity' (ISC 2002). The private enterprises then use their technical know-how and resources to turn these guideposts into practical measures within their respective network.

The vagueness of these guideposts is important: the uncertainty of media controls in China prompts private companies like Sina or Tencent to err on the side of caution and apply the overarching policy framework conservatively (Ng 2013: xxiv; MacKinnon 2012). What is more, the profit-driven companies transmit their uncertainties to the users, who have to stay within the confines of acceptable terms of usage if they want to benefit from the companies' services. As Jason Ng (2013: xx) explains, the transparency with which an enterprise like Sina communicates its censorship practices to Weibo users serves as a powerful reminder that the company constantly scrutinizes the discussions on its servers:

> In a way, the search blocks [on Sina Weibo] condition users to recognize the limits of acceptable discourse, and even when the limitations are taken away later, the residual effect of the censorship can remain. Such 'transparency' serves as an effective training mechanism, thus furthering the goal of decentralizing the censorship and moving the onus for it from the government to the media companies and, finally, to the individual.

To put it another way, the authorities are creating a high-tech, capitalist version of Jeremy Bentham's panopticon (see Foucault 1978/1995: 200–209) in which private actors discipline themselves and others, in this case in order to reap the fruits of digital communication.

## Collaboration and Self-Regulation

China's 'Three-Ws':

When I ask Kevin, the young entrepreneur who runs his own online company, what he thinks of Chinese internet users, he becomes pensive. Then he describes how disturbed he was when his work first confronted him with the low digital literacy of many of his clients. 'When we started the company, we had problems with what I call the "Three-Ws". When our system asked our clients for their e-mail contact, a large number of people—probably 5 percent—kept putting "www-dot" in front of their address, and then they complained that the system was broken. It would never have occurred to any of us that so many internet users don't know how e-mail addresses work. I've had to realize that citizens' quality isn't what I thought it was. Most people are not like my acquaintances here in the city. There are a lot of Three-Ws out there.'

The neoliberal governance framework that the authorities use to manage digital China can, ultimately, only be effective if users accept this framework as legitimate and conform to its rules. This is not always the case. Scholarship into online activism and sub-cultures in digital China has demonstrated repeatedly how specific groups or individuals creatively circumvent internet controls and adapt their contentious exchanges to shifting regulatory structures (Yang 2009). An interesting phenomenon has been the degree to which internet users deploy wordplay and irony within the state-imposed constraints (for examples, see Henochowicz 2015). It is common, for instance, to discuss controversial phrases using homophone or metaphorical alternative Chinese characters in order to prevent the censorship system from filtering out the discussion. In this fashion, the date of the Tiananmen Massacre turns from '4th of June' into '35th of May', the political agenda to create 'harmony' (*hexie* 和谐) becomes 'river crab' (*hexie* 河蟹), or the expletive 'fuck your mom' (*cao ni ma* 肏你妈) becomes 'grass mud horse' (*cao ni ma* 草泥马).

These practices have given rise to a rich culture of often crude parody (or *egao* 恶搞) that mocks official discourse (see Esarey & Qiang 2008; Gong & Yang 2010; Li 2011; Meng 2011; Nordin 2014). A particular point of debate in the literature has been whether such parody constitutes a form of substantial political resistance or merely banal and inconsequential apolitical banter; whether it functions as part of carnivalesque processes of mass-distraction or as subtle disruptions to the official stability narrative (see Nordin & Richaud 2014; Poell, de Kloet, & Zeng, 2014).

It is such creative censorship circumvention that, at times, creates the impression that internet users are playing 'cat and mouse' with the authorities (*Economist* 2013). Yet, as attractive as this metaphor may be to highlight the frequent back-and-forth between state censors and contentious internet users, it does not capture all the intricacies of such interactions. Two issues are worth keeping in mind: the fundamental power and information asymmetries between state actors and contentious users, and the degree to which China's media ecology generally inspires users to cooperate with the authorities' governance approach for digital China.

In capitalist societies where people are highly networked, digital ICTs can slant the power relations in ways that benefit authoritative collective actors while marginalizing individual users. Contrary to individual users, IT companies and state agencies have preferential access to information and communication networks, and this includes private information on citizens. The advanced surveillance and data analysis methods that the authorities and their commercial allies have at their disposal make it possible to monitor the various fringe activities of individual citizens in ways that are opaque to the potential offenders. This is true in any networked society, for instance the United States (see Halavais 2009: 2261), but it has powerful implications in the Chinese context with its combination of political uncertainties and socio-economic scarcities. In the PRC, the cut-throat capitalist environment strongly encourages citizens to try and manipulate social, political, and economic systems to their advantage, for instance by finding loopholes in the tax system, writing off personal expenses, and cashing in on gift-giving practices and systems of mutual favours. While such practices are by no means exclusive to the Chinese context, they are ubiquitous in China, where commercial and financial activities frequently take place within the grey areas of a legal system that can be murky. The vast majority of Chinese are likely to have 'gamed' China's constantly evolving system of rules at one point or another.

This provides the authorities with the bureaucratic fiat to charge any unwelcome behaviour with tax evasion or corruption, safe in the knowledge that such a charge is likely to have some substance. Being the subject of such a charge is a risk that constantly hangs over anyone who has ever transgressed a norm in China, which is pretty much everyone. This means that anyone in China may at some point find themselves at the receiving end of a future political campaign against corruption or moral indecency. This risk may even extend to past actions that either did not constitute transgressions or were merely acceptable minor norm infringements at the time, but that are now etched into elusive digital records. The result is that anyone with a contentious agenda is at a structural disadvantage vis-à-vis the Chinese authorities.

Yet, not every internet user has a contentious agenda. Most internet users are perfectly willing to submit to digital China's governance system. There are three interlocking reasons for this. The first is that in China's strongly connected society digital connectivity has become highly convenient, if not indispensable, and the cost of non-compliance is prohibitive. The second reason is that cyber-governance is frequently invisible to users, who either do not come up against the boundaries of what the censors find permissible or do not recognize interventions when they occur. Finally, the third reason is that the authorities can rely on powerful public concerns over social stability, which are aggravated by fraudulent behaviours online, and which make digital governance seem vital to many users.

Discussing the issue of digital convenience in China, De Seta (2015: 99) points out that digital technologies have become so strongly engrained in everyday life that it may be appropriate to think of China as a 'post-digital' society. Indeed, the degree to which daily practices are today amalgamated with digital tools means that non-participation in digital China would strike most users as a noticeable reduction in quality of life. Tencent's powerful smartphone chat service Weixin, for instance, is increasingly crucial for keeping in touch with professional and social contacts. As I mentioned in the previous chapter, this is not just because Weixin combines text-messaging, microblogging, social networking, and video chat. The service is also a fully fledged e-commerce platform with integrated e-banking, a real-time geo-location tracker, an organizer for appointments (including arrangements for public transport), a casual gaming platform, and a way to hook up (Millward 2015). Combined with various other Chinese digital services, for instance Baidu's online maps or Taobao's online marketplace, the PRC now features a sophisticated and integrated lifestyle maintenance system for those who are digitally switched on. As one US-based commentator notes, when the PRC government walled off digital China, it 'was also buying itself time to build inside those walls a thriving, parallel ecosystem that could enthral a giant, quickly digitizing audience—an ecosystem that by a number of measures easily surpasses that of the U.S.' (Chao 2016).

During my interviews and conversations in China, the general sentiment was that the level of convenience that digital China offered made it worthwhile to forego anonymity and privacy. As one academic told me, 'Chinese users are of course also concerned about privacy issues on the net, but users here are very pragmatic. They understand that if you block geo-location and social data, then you are no longer able to profit from the commercial advantages of the mobile internet'. Bruce Schneier (2012) calls this kind of rationale 'internet feudalism', arguing that in order to benefit from increasingly essential digital services, users have to 'pledge allegiance to the United States of convenience'. This is true for anyone with a Facebook, Google, or Apple account, and it is a logic that China's authorities are relying on for their governance strategy.

The second issue is that these governance strategies are frequently invisible: within the carefully circumscribed walled gardens of digital China, most users remain unaware of the degree of control that takes place at the backend of the media services they are using. In a study of how university students talk about their digital media use, Jin Xuelian (2015) shows how her research subjects were largely convinced that the state's information controls did not affect them personally. Interestingly, this belief still held even in the face of blatant content filtering. One student, for instance, recounted her struggle to find online information on student protests or political controversies; confronted with the lack of information, she 'gave up' and later 'forgot to search for information' again (Jin 2015: 142). Another student, who had accessed foreign news content, voiced his frustration with the multitude of diverging opinions outside of digital China. In his understanding, this cacophony of views was far less trustworthy than the simple, homogeneous narratives that dominated the domestic online news environment; after all, if domestic news sources all report 'roughly the same', then this must mean that the reporting is accurate (Jin 2015: 290). While such examples are anecdotal, they nevertheless demonstrate how successful digital China's governance mechanisms are at concealing their workings and convincing users that they are inconsequential in everyday life.

Finally, where the governance strategies become visible, for instance when high-profile bloggers are arrested or popular websites like Instagram are blocked, the state can rely on its paternalistic discourses of 'social stability' and lacking 'citizen quality' to shore up support for its policies. As I have discussed earlier, not all interventions into communication practices in China are informed by the motive to retain power. In many cases, attempts to regulate China's digital networks are grounded in the perception that unfettered usage of information networks lends itself to abuse, that much of what happens online does not serve social justice, and that many internet users do not have the digital literacy to make responsible choices online. Kevin's experience with the 'Three-Ws' that I recounted at the start of this section shows how such arguments connect with the everyday experiences of many middle-class and wealthy Chinese. The fact that Chinese society is plagued by substantial social and economic inequalities, not to mention often egregious antisocial and exploitative behaviour, further makes these discourses an easy sell.

Considering the many well-publicized instances of digital vigilantism (Cheung 2009; Herold 2011; Lagerkvist 2010: 61), online extortions and scams (Koetse 2015), and disturbing viral 'body-shaming' challenges (Westcott & Ge 2016), such concerns are by no means fallacious. Impressions about the risk of 'fake news' in the wake of political transitions in especially the United States and United Kingdom have only added to the powerful discourse that information needs to be carefully vetted by authorities (see, for instance, the arguments by Ran 2017). It remains controversial whether the kind of paternalistic approach that the authorities have opted for is the best response to these risks and problems (personally I have strong doubts), but acknowledging that the response grows out of socially shared concerns goes a long way to understanding how this response works and why it is so widely accepted—and in some cases explicitly demanded—by the users themselves. The metaphor of the 'cat-and-mouse' game seems inadequate to capture these dynamics.

# Centralizing Digital China

Chinese politics today exist in an uneasy balance between democratic and authoritarian technics. This is very much apparent for the case of digital media governance, which relies heavily on the participation of private actors within a larger hierarchical network. Politically, the network is built around the CCP's central leading group of cyberspace affairs that I mentioned at the start of this chapter. This institution sets the programmatic parameters within which digital governance then takes place. On the state side of China's political system, various administrative bodies at the ministerial level have the authority to enforce these parameters; this includes state departments that might have a stake in a particular digital affair (e.g., the Ministry of Education when it comes to the media usage of minors; the State Ethnic Affairs Commission when ethnic groups are involved, and so on). Importantly, however, it includes the SIIO and its Cyberspace Administration.

Within the parameters that the authorities provide, the Party and the state try to solicit the support of media professionals to implement media governance. In many cases, digital services are created collaboratively between public and private actors, or such services are 'outsourced' entirely to private enterprises like Baidu, Alibaba, or Tencent. For the Party, such collaborations are beneficial in several ways. They bring together expertise that CCP propaganda workers and censors do not necessarily possess, they legitimate digital politics by involving a wide range of actors, and they promise to turn a profit. Most importantly, they create spaces for seemingly free interactions that appeal to audiences while still assuring that the state retains a degree of control over these spaces.

Yet these collaborative attempts at governance are not merely beneficial to the authorities but are also beneficial to the various private actors that are involved. This is a point that Rogier Creemers makes when he calls the collaboration between industry giants and political agencies a 'strategic nexus'. As Creemers (2016a) explains, 'born out of a recognition of mutual dependence, this nexus is increasingly enabling both sides to pursue their own strategic interests through ensuring the other side can do so as well'.

This idea of the 'nexus' serves as a reminder that the communities that political and commercial actors form in China are ultimately networks in their own right, and that the choices these actors make determine how such networks are structured. Networks can generally resemble three basic patterns, which I have illustrated in Figure 8.1. The figure shows different forms that a network with ten actors can take.[8] The top diagram depicts the network with all its possible connections. The bottom diagrams show versions of this network, each with different potential connections realized. The network on the left concentrates

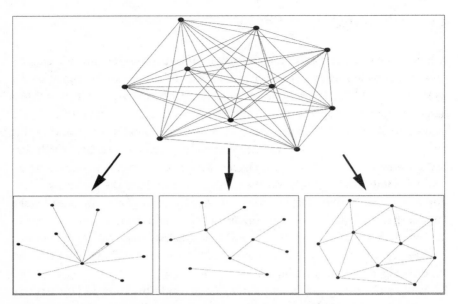

*Figure 8.1* Network Formations. A network with ten actors (top) and three possible instantiations (bottom), from left to right: centralized, decentralized, and distributed. Florian Schneider.

the linkages on a single actor at the centre. This star-like formation represents a fully centralized network. The middle diagram establishes connections in a way that creates several hubs rather than a single centre. Such a formation represents a decentralized network. On the right, the connections no longer privilege any specific nodes in the network, creating a distributed network.

The dynamics of networked systems, in particular the so-called power law, generally create more centralized patterns, but constructing any particular network architecture in a networked society still leaves room for agency. Networking is a kind of work (Latour 2005: 132). As I have argued in chapters 4 and 7, agents with privileged network rights are in a position to connect nodes in ways that create certain patterns, and the degree of centralization that a network ultimately exhibits is a matter of political activity and of power. This is evident not just in China: as scholars in peace and conflict studies have shown, some types of ICT generate hierarchical networks whereas others make it possible to create horizontal, distributed networks, and each configuration has different implications for how groups coordinate their collective actions, for example, during ethnic conflicts.[9]

China's leaders may not use the terminology of network analysis, but their policy choices are nevertheless aimed at structuring digital China according to patterns that are more easily governed by traditional elites. This is evident from the official documents, speeches, and policy guidelines that lay out how the PRC is meant to become an 'internet superpower' (*wangluo qiangguo* 网络强国). The Chinese authorities conceptualize, update, and promote their cyber vision at the annual 'World Internet Conference', an event organized by the PRC and attended by international tech companies and political representatives from like-minded states such as Kazakhstan, Kyrgyzstan, Russia, and Pakistan (Beech 2015). At the 2015 conference, PRC president Xi Jinping outlined his principles of internet governance. In typical CCP fashion, they include 'one goal', 'two major points', 'three grand strategies', 'four principles', and 'five propositions'. The Beijing News (Xinjingbao 2015) has compiled the original wording in an infographic, and I have provided a translation of the core principles in Figure 8.2.

This conceptual framework provides a foundation for the PRC's three new cyber policy plans: the 'internet superpower' strategy with its focus on governance, the 'national big data' strategy with its emphasis on surveillance and

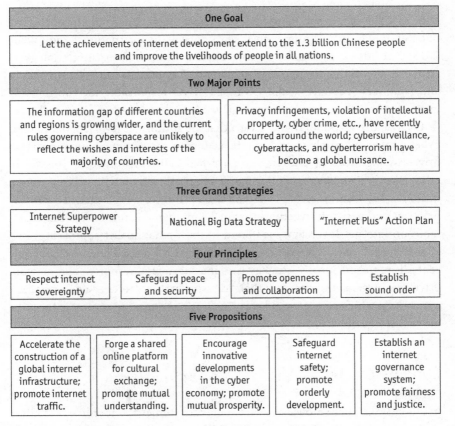

**One Goal**

Let the achievements of internet development extend to the 1.3 billion Chinese people and improve the livelihoods of people in all nations.

**Two Major Points**

| | |
|---|---|
| The information gap of different countries and regions is growing wider, and the current rules governing cyberspace are unlikely to reflect the wishes and interests of the majority of countries. | Privacy infringements, violation of intellectual property, cyber crime, etc., have recently occurred around the world; cybersurveillance, cyberattacks, and cyberterrorism have become a global nuisance. |

**Three Grand Strategies**

| | | |
|---|---|---|
| Internet Superpower Strategy | National Big Data Strategy | "Internet Plus" Action Plan |

**Four Principles**

| | | | |
|---|---|---|---|
| Respect internet sovereignty | Safeguard peace and security | Promote openness and collaboration | Establish sound order |

**Five Propositions**

| | | | | |
|---|---|---|---|---|
| Accelerate the construction of a global internet infrastructure; promote internet traffic. | Forge a shared online platform for cultural exchange; promote mutual understanding. | Encourage innovative developments in the cyber economy; promote mutual prosperity. | Safeguard internet safety; promote orderly development. | Establish an internet governance system; promote fairness and justice. |

*Figure 8.2* China's Cyber-Policy Framework. The principles of internet governance under Xi Jinping. Florian Schneider, adapted and translated from Xinjingbao (2015).

analysis, and the 'Internet Plus' plan with its focus on innovation, commerce, and logistics.[10] More importantly, it recalibrates digital politics to fit into the setting of the nation state. A cornerstone of this strategy is the idea of 'national internet sovereignty' (*guojia wangluo zhuquan* 国家网络主权), which translates the PRC's traditional emphasis on sovereignty and non-intervention into digital contexts. In his speech at the 'World Internet Conference', Xi Jinping justified this focus as follows (Xinhua 2015):

> The principle of sovereign equality enshrined in the Charter of the United Nations is one of the basic norms in contemporary international relations. It covers all aspects of state-to-state relations, which also includes cyberspace. . . . We should respect the right of individual countries to independently choose their own path of cyber development and model of cyber regulation and participate in international cyberspace governance on an equal footing.

Various CCP cadres and Chinese legal scholars have since attempted to flesh out this framework, legitimating it with appeals to international law (Wang 2015; Zhi 2016), and explicitly constructing China's governance strategy as an alternative to the practices of the Internet Corporation for Assigned Names and Numbers (ICANN)—the US-based NGO responsible for coordinating internet protocols and domain names (Lu 2016).

Overall, the vision for digital China that the authorities have laid out in their cyber framework emphasizes domestic economic development and innovation driven by high-tech IT clusters and governed by the nation state. This vision relies on expert knowledge, authoritative agents, hierarchical lines of communication, and concentration of power, and these priorities are reflected in the media practices and network structures that make up digital China today. The CCP's focus on internet sovereignty is in and of itself a nationalist approach geared at creating national networks. In line with the CCP's principle of democratic centralism, this nationalist strategy uses the substantial resources and network privileges of the authorities and their industry partners to create decentralized networks in which core state and party institutions remain in control of the most important nodes.

## Conclusion

In this chapter, I have moved away from the case studies about online discourses on Japan to discuss how China's political elites attempt to govern digital China; a highly networked media ecology that is confronted with a range of challenges that affect both the production and the dissemination of culture. Digital media make it possible to quickly copy content and spread it almost instantaneously through non-hierarchical, diffuse communication networks. Chinese internet users are adept at using these networks for their personal purposes, and by manipulating cultural templates and creating user-generated content they come to pose a real competition to professional media workers. Since internet users are neither tied into the CCP's propaganda system nor motivated by the same commercial incentives that govern China's professional cultural industries, their activities do not necessarily lend themselves to the regulatory mechanisms that traditionally govern the cultural sectors. To nevertheless assure the leadership's sovereignty over communication processes, the Party today combines a series of soft and hard governance mechanisms to create a contemporary version of democratic centralism. This approach legitimizes itself by generating spaces of deliberation, often through digital media, and by providing internet users with the opportunity to relay their concerns and wishes to leaders.

It would be a mistake to dismiss such attempts to 'get to know the people's wishes' solely as lip service to appease potentially unruly citizens; they are also meant to add a participatory element to the policy-making process and assure that those who are affected by policy choices have a say in how those choices come about. It remains questionable whether these democratic technics can be successful in a political environment that remains fundamentally committed to hierarchical structures. Recent research suggests that a range of externalities emerges from the combination of popular feedback mechanisms with stringent party and state hierarchies, and that these externalities may be detrimental to the political process as a whole: many local cadres are now frequently caught between the diverging demands of their superiors and their constituency, and these target conflicts can lead to shifts in political priorities.[11] Göbel recounts a case of local cadres feeling forced to personally help the farmers in their county with menial tasks, such as fixing private homes, in fear of negative work assessments. In cases like this, the focus of politics moves towards areas that are not traditionally part of state administration while simultaneously making administrators more responsive to popular demands and increasing the sense of citizens' political efficacy.

Importantly, such shifts in political dynamics are not the result of an authoritarian state intentionally colonizing the affairs of its citizens; they are the result of citizens demanding that the state legitimate itself by serving their particularist interests. This has important implications for politics in the PRC, as the party's cadres become ever more committed to serving public opinion, for better or worse.

It is for this reason that guiding public opinion is such a crucial aspect of Chinese politics. The degree to which the CCP and the Chinese state have been able to rein in discussions in digital China demonstrates that views of the internet as a motor of political change may be overly optimistic. The Chinese authorities are constantly refining their technical, economic, and legal toolset to reshape digital China in the image of the PRC's mass-media system, and contrary to John Gilmore's argument that 'the Net interprets censorship as damage and routes around it' (see Gilmore 2013), China's censorship regime has been fairly effective at managing Chinese digital spheres. The leadership has adapted its strategy for managing cultural expression to China's changing social, economic, and political environment, and this has had two major effects: The first is that the role of state and Party has changed from institutions that govern cultural content in a straight-forward fashion to agencies that now mainly use soft controls and market mechanisms to influence the wider framework in which cultural production takes place. The second is that cultural production involves a wide range of actors in collaborative efforts to produce and disseminate culture. Borrowing from the work of Michael Shapiro (2004) and William Callahan (2006), I have elsewhere referred to this strategy as 'cultural governance' to describe these collaborative attempts to regulate society by regulating its cultural parameters (Schneider 2016b).

Importantly, the CCP has established its cultural hegemony across China's media system through negotiations with and tacit consent from Chinese media workers and internet users (Zhang 2011). The many risks and threats that online users are regularly confronted with across digital China provide a powerful resource for the authorities to legitimate their approach to media governance, prompting users to voluntarily submit themselves to the overarching governance framework and self-regulate their behaviour in line with state and Party norms. Even in the absence of risks and threats, users have a strong incentive to conform to the governing premises of digital China, for instance by giving up parts of their privacy. Without such concessions, China's increasingly advanced digital ecology simply would not yield its enticing benefits. Like elsewhere in the world (see Schneier 2015), many of these benefits today seem indispensable to everyday life.

Overall, the CCP's cultural governance approach is very much tailored to a world of mass media, where a small number of professional media outlets manage vast audiences through delivery technologies that can be monitored by the state. The authorities have adapted to changes in this media environment, but these adaptations are informed by an understanding of media and culture that reflects the realities of 20th-century mass communication. China's cultural governance is built around a paradigm of one-to-many communication, and it is built around the paradigm of national sovereignty. Outdated as these conceptions may seem, China's state and party are committed to extending them forcefully into the 21st century. Through its centralizing politics and its decades of patriotic education, the leadership has programmed China's political and social networks with the value of nationalism to assure support for its governance framework. This has stacked the deck in favour of nationalist interpretations of politics, and it stands to reason that, in an environment that is heavily committed to serving public opinion, the often highly visible rhetoric of nationalists will provide a strong incentive for administrators to produce further nationalist politics.

# 9

# Conclusion

## *The Future of Nationalism in the Digital Age*

We live at a time when affordable multi-media computers, broadband internet access, and advanced mobile communication tools are changing political, social, and economic practices around the globe. These developments have also swept the PRC, a new geopolitical superpower and now the second-largest economy in the world, with a population of nearly 1.4 billion. At the time of writing, the PRC already had more internet users than Europe had citizens, and the country was expanding its digital coverage as part of its 13th Five-Year-Plan. What are new ICTs doing to China—and what is China doing with such new ICTs?

Communication scholars often interpret ICTs as harbingers of a cosmopolitan age where the flow of diverse information will educate and empower users. The Chinese case defies these expectations. While communication in digital China is certainly diversifying, the much-evoked digital age has not ended one-party rule, nor has it led to the peaceful, pluralist digital public sphere that liberal scholars have envisioned. Two observations in particular challenge what we may call the liberal, cosmopolitan vision of ICTs. First, the CCP and the government successfully cooperate with stakeholders from the private sector and with users to steer public opinion towards officially sanctioned discourse. This strategy appears to strengthen rather than weaken the Chinese state. Second, online political discourse in digital China turns out to be clustered around a small number of recurring themes, and the most notable of these is nationalism.

This prevalence of nationalism in digital China constitutes a challenge to scholars who believe that ICT will reduce nationalism and the efficacy of nation states. Writing at the height of such cyber-optimism, Smith (1993: 155) argued, there has been a rapid growth in the range of power and mass telecommunication systems and a vast expansion of computerized information networks. The scope and sophistication of such systems make it impossible to limit information networks to even the largest of national units; at the same time they provide the material basis for an amalgamation of national into regional cultures and even for the formation of a global culture. It is now possible to put out and package global information and imagery that can swamp more local information networks and the national messages they emit.

More than two decades on, such assessments seem anachronistic.[1] Nationalism has proven to thrive in networked societies. As I have argued, advanced digital communication reproduces the group dynamics that are at the heart of communities like the nation, and contemporary ICTs lend themselves to the kind of elite politics that scholars like Gellner (1983/2006, 1997) and Breuilly (1993) have observed for the modern construction of nation states more generally. At the same time, the nature of these politics changes once advanced ICTs are involved, and this in turn makes it necessary to update our understanding of nations and nationalism. Throughout this book, I have treated the nation as a technology that interacts with other technologies, based on design choices, political and economic incentives, and the idiosyncrasies of human usage. I have also argued that we should view the nation as a networked community: a complex system in which power works according to the logic of networks, generating nationalism as an emergent property. The example of digital China, itself a vast laboratory for social, cultural, and political change, illustrates why our understanding of nations and nationalism is in need of such an update.

## Tracing Nationalism Across Digital China

Throughout this book, I have traced nationalist discourses across various digital spheres in China, using the modern history between China and Japan as a case. While this analysis has not been about Japan itself—a society that faces its own complex and often worrying discourses about modern history and the nation—the spectre of China's wars with Japan still strongly shapes how nationalism works in the PRC, providing one of the most important building-blocks for Chinese nation-building and nation-maintenance projects. My argument has been that taking the medium seriously and following the infrastructures and contents of digital media can provide insights into how such crucial political projects work in an emerging great power. More importantly, I have made the case that the Chinese situation can shed light on what generally makes nation-alism 'tick' today.

In digital China, three factors come together to shape the networked com-munity of the nation: design choices, the political economy, and human psy-chology. This is apparent from the role that Chinese search engines play in structuring knowledge. Despite the competitive search engine market, the var-ious companies that rank and sort the Chinese web for users do so on the basis of digital biases that privilege the national context. Search services by enterprises like Baidu, Good Search, or Search Dog rely on algorithms that draw variables and weights from the material, social, and subjective biases that characterize China's national media ecology more broadly, and a consequence is that these services largely filter topics through national frameworks of understanding. In short, China's search engines are complicit in creating the kind of 'sovereign' internet space that the PRC's authorities are envisioning as the standard version of digital China.

Indeed, entering the web networks of digital China reveals the degree to which such spaces resemble the kind of authoritative, hierarchical information networks that the authorities encourage across China's more traditional broad-casting sectors. On issues related to China's history with Japan, for instance, China's web is structured in a highly parochial way, reflecting a traditional mass-media logic of how information and communication should work. In such digital networks, information is presented on a range of isolated web beacons, which are not directly connected online, almost exclusively digitize and repro-duce party-approved materials, and allow only a modicum of discussion within the confines of sanctioned parameters. The outcome of this media approach is a PRC internet that has ossified into a highly regulated yet profitable info-web, and which the media workers I spoke to in China rightly describe as a traditional medium.

The effects of this traditional mass-media logic are visible in the way the in-famous Nanjing Massacre is presented online. China's web constructs such his-torical events largely as part of a single, monolithic national narrative, and the authoritative actors that create this discourse use the medium of the web pri-marily as an archive for historical facts. This leads to a fairly narrow nationalist discourse regarding neighbouring Japan, replete with the recognizable rhetor-ical, visual, and emotional tropes that other scholars have identified for cultural artefacts on the topic, for example, in museums, exhibits, or textbooks. On China's web, the Nanjing Massacre remains anchored in the mainstream, though in seemingly interactive ways: websites strategically deploy comment functions and social media buttons to sanction a discourse that is predominantly framed by righteous indignation. There are exceptions to this practice, for instance when Chinese websites call for friendship and peace with Japan, or when online articles present collaborative commemoration activities between Chinese and Japanese groups. Overall, however, the default for engaging with such historical events remains highly aggressive and chauvinistic anger. Sources such as the various Chinese online encyclopaedias leave no doubt about the moral justifications for such anger, and they present the complexity of the massacre as a clear-cut case of national humiliation. Despite the potential of digital media to facilitate a 'see-for-yourself' culture and to provide spaces for communication, national history does not become a forum for discussion and critical reflection. Instead, it functions as an interactive shrine that deserves to be venerated. In this sense, the Nanjing Massacre discourse in digital China is part of a larger project of 'collective remembering', which to this day provides the building blocks of national identity maintenance in the PRC.

The contemporary affairs issue of territorial disputes in the East China Sea provides another example of how China's info-web contributes to nationalist discourse. When it comes to the Diaoyu/Senkaku islands, digital China presents a united front of state and non-state actors across mainland China, Hong Kong, and Taiwan, all of whom oppose a belligerent and highly irrational Japan to secure inviolable territories of the nation. Aside from reproducing a sense of 'we-ness' through this discourse, the Chinese web resources also help construct the sense of national territory in the first place, turning a set of uninhabited rocks into part of the 'homeland', and into an existential concern. Yet while this concern is presented as a unifying narrative, the discourse is overall dominated by actors with highly chauvinistic views. What is more, the representation of the issue is skewed towards mainland Chinese positions, silencing the often-complex meanings that the island dispute has in places like Taiwan. Even where non-mainland actors are involved in constructing the island discourse, these actors are overwhelmingly older men, raising the question of how representative their aggressive and often misogynistic views about national sovereignty actually are. Overall, such views nevertheless remain most visible in this part of digital China's web, which is highly commodified and sells the nationalist discourse alongside guns, girls, and games as part of a largely chauvinist package. This outcome is owed to the signals that web editors receive from users via the software that mediates their interactions, and it is owed to the logic of digital capitalism that informs how politics can be presented online. These factors create a digital, networked complexity, giving rise to a nationalist discourse that is ultimately more than the sum of its parts. This discourse emerges from digital China's networks without any specific actor being in full control of the process.

The internet is not just the web, it encompasses various spheres. What happens, for instance, to political discourse in the parts of digital China that embrace Web 2.0 technology? In online forums, social and participatory technologies frequently reward aggressive media scripts while marginalizing more careful, nuanced perspectives. This phenomenon is particularly noticeable where users are able to rank each other's comments. When such popularity mechanisms interact with the accepted parameters of nationalist discourse, the outcome is frequently crude and uncivil. Yet the situation seems to be somewhat different on the popular microblogging service Weibo. Scholarship on this service has shown that Weibo provides spaces for diverse discourses, and this diversity extends to nationalist issues. User comments can diverge substantially from the mainstream discourse on China's web. On Weibo, the nuanced meanings of Chinese nationalism are not under the unambiguous, top-down control of China's authorities, despite their extensive censorship activities on the platform. This important finding is in line with research on history and memory, which demonstrates that no single actor 'owns' a discourse (Evans 2003: 12): 'Historians may be hard at work redesigning the past, however, but so too are politicians, painters, novelists, sculptors, movie-makers, television producers, textbook writers, teachers, museum directors and a whole host of other people, and what comes out as the end result may not be quite what any of them intended'. In a similar vein, work on political discourses in digital China reveals that meanings are ultimately far more fragmented than the official position—sometimes to the point of opposing it (Huang & Sun 2014, Tong & Zuo 2014, Qiu 2009, Zheng 2008).[2]

Nevertheless, I remain sceptical about the potential for diverse, critical, and egalitarian debate online. Sina Weibo, for instance, may be populated by hundreds of millions of users, but the power to programme online discourse is distributed unevenly in this medium, and influential celebrities have significantly more power to infuse large networks with ideas. It is interesting that China's most influential microbloggers, the 'Big-V' users who are often accused of irresponsible self-promotion and egregious rumour-mongering, complicated the 2012 anti-Japanese events in China through nuanced and socially aware commentary. This commentary seems to have resonated with their followers, who received the messages of their idols in the tens of millions, with thousands sending support and feedback. It seems that at least on Weibo, the discourse surrounding China's relation with Japan was not 'hijacked' for nefarious purposes by online users, but was instead used by the most powerful actors to inspire debate about the nature of patriotism and the responsibilities of modern citizens. Nevertheless, the discourse in which these communicative moves take place remains committed to the overarching symbolic framework of the imagined community, and it remains dominated by elite actors. The fact that social media, in their current guise, tend to reproduce comfort zones also does not inspire confidence that the seeming diversity and nuance of online discussion aggregates into some larger civic consciousness. In fact, it may very well be by design that these diverse discussions remain fragmented and contained within manageable social media bubbles, for instance on the popular smartphone service Weixin.

# Managing Digital Discourse

Digital China is indeed diverse, to the extent that pointing out this diversity is becoming a cliché in journalism and academia. What is worth keeping in mind is that such diversity is an outcome of the cultural governance model that the Chinese authorities have adopted: a model that restricts direct control over meanings to sensitive political issues and otherwise promotes collaboration and participation in processes of meaning-making. In this approach, party and state agents limit themselves to the role of public opinion 'guides', setting the parameters of discourse but allowing diverse actors to negotiate the exact meanings. This process ultimately generates far more legitimacy than direct, top-down intervention. It would be a mistake, however, to interpret this outcome as empowering contentious citizens against the state. The state collaborates with diverse actors to create a governance framework in which users are presented with strong incentives to regulate their behaviour in line with the moral values that the authorities have defined for digital China, often drawing directly on the input of conservative internet users who are concerned about trust, stability, and maintaining the status quo (Hawkins 2017).

As Gang and Bandurski (2011: 71) have pointed out, digital technologies have been a game changer for political communication, in China as much as elsewhere. However, the game has not changed solely to the benefit of the much-evoked contentious 'civil society'. In contemporary China, the ruling CCP is trying to harness what Castells (2009) has called 'communication power': the power to shape political decisions by influencing the discursive contexts and symbolic resources in which events take place. This strategy extends to internet networks, where power no longer simply works according to the traditional Weberian logic of one actor asserting their will over another, against opposition. That logic continues to play a role, but more important are moves that either 'switch' actors into or out of the networked infrastructures, or that 'programme' the discourses that flow through these network in ways that align the interests of actors (Castells 2009: 52). As far as the parts of the web are concerned that have been the focus of this book, the CCP's governance strategies are visible in the hierarchical configurations and carefully circumscribed interactions that characterize these networks.

The online discourses on the nation, and the wider digital infrastructures that give rise to them, provide a look behind the scenes of the Chinese authorities' cultural governance approach and their understanding of political communication. Rather than follow the 'Silicon Valley model' of communication (see Turner 2008) that informs digital politics in many foreign contexts (for the United States, see the programmatic speech by Clinton 2010), the Chinese

authorities have developed a different framework for making sense of digital politics. Institutions like the State Council Information Office and its Internet News
Coordination Bureau are using a Leninist, authoritarian understanding of mass
communication (see Shambaugh 2007; Tsang 2009; Zhang 2011; Zhao 2008) to
devise and implement their own model of communication. This approach aligns
capitalist interests and political imperatives: it allows diversity on entertainment
and life-style issues while simultaneously promoting a relatively narrow range of
political discourses that are meant to strengthen the nation state and legitimate
one-Party rule.

The policies that govern digital China are designed to centralize communication power, creating a framework built upon, and conducive to, national sovereignty. The authorities have been working hard to integrate the web into their
existing mass-media model of communication. Online interactions largely take
place within authoritative, sanctioned media networks: information is presented
on a range of isolated beacons on the web, which are not directly connected online, almost exclusively digitize and reproduce party-approved materials, and
allow only a modicum of discussion within the confines of sanctioned scripts.
Contention is channelled into proprietary online services where capitalist
enterprises regulate and surveille them on behalf of the state, providing useful
popular input into and legitimating signals for elite politics. In that sense, digital China uses the affordances of digital communication in a very specific way
that betrays an underlying consensus on how ICTs should work. At the heart
of this understanding lies a mass-media approach to communication, revamped
to suit a society where digital technologies have become ubiquitous. Through
market mechanisms, ideological guidelines, legal coercive tools, technological
innovations, and a good deal of persuasion, China's ruling party and state are
updating political communication for the digital age (see Esarey & Qiang 2011,
Han 2013, King, Pan, & Roberts, 2017, Schlæger 2013, Sullivan 2014).

## Performing Sino-Japanese Relations on Digital Stages

The Chinese state and its ruling party retain the highest managerial privileges in
digital China, unapologetically intervening into public discourse by switching
actors in the network on or off, and by programming the discourse in line
with Party policy. The aim of these interventions is to avoid non-sanctioned
discourses to spread—an aim that must seem paramount to China's leaders,
considering the speed and scale at which digital technologies are now believed
to shape public perceptions. The result of these paternalistic interventions is that
digital China's networks remain decidedly parochial, and that the discourses that

spread through them, at least in the case of high-profile political issues such as Sino-Japanese relations, place politics within a simplistic, nationalist framework of understanding.

This does not mean that the audiences of this framework buy into it wholesale. Mass communication is not brainwashing, despite the persistence of such metaphors. It is entirely possible for actors in such communication networks to reject the main discourses and assess the issue in idiosyncratic ways, as they indeed do. However, such media users at the very least have the deck stacked against them. As Halavais (2009: 1243) writes, the logic of specific networks encourages certain uses: 'While the internet provides a platform for self-expression, that expression is constrained by the values of the network'. Indeed, the symbolic resources that are predominantly available in digital China on issues related to international politics emphasize values such as sovereignty, authority, national community, and righteous indignation rather than transnational understanding, nuanced debate, and multi-faceted meaning making.

While I have largely side-stepped questions of international relations throughout this book, debates both in area studies and international politics strongly revolve around assumptions about China's so-called rise, about presumed 'power-shifts' in East Asia, and about nationalism's role in the PRC's relations with its neighbours; it is worth asking what the findings of this book might say about such assumptions, and what they might mean for relations between China and Japan. As Gustafsson (2014) has shown, the leaderships of modern nation states like the PRC or the State of Japan are today deeply concerned about the integrity of their respective worldviews, or 'ontological security'. Nationalism forces politics into a framework of understanding in which such psychological concerns become the urgent matter of state affairs. The human need to feel safe about material and social needs, and to feel certain about the world and confident in knowledge about it, are each 'securitized' in the name of national sovereignty, prompting political actions to try and assure the community's material, relational, ontological, and epistemological security. In China, and especially under the leadership of Xi Jinping, the authorities are increasingly trying to 'securitize' virtually all aspects of social life, as the recent national security law demonstrates (see Huang & Horwitz 2016). What this means in the case of specific bilateral relations can be a matter of heated debate, as the discussions on Chinese social media demonstrate. Nevertheless, with these overarching security concerns in place, political actors need to position themselves vis-à-vis nationalist discourse wherever they appear in public. In a world shaped by digital media, the relational, communicative dimensions of politics matter more than ever.

My point is not that military might, or economic interactions, do not significantly shape international relations. My point is that the understanding that actors have of such factors relies strongly on the discursive frameworks within which they operate, and that communication practices configure and reconfigure these frameworks. This makes it all the more pressing to explore how a framework like nationalism shapes the discursive resources available to actors in international relations.

As I have argued elsewhere (Schneider 2014a), the case of Sino-Japanese territorial disputes is an excellent example of how various actors such as politicians and administrators play different roles on different stages (see Shih 2012), in each case adjusting their discursive contribution to a particular target audience (see also Sullivan & Sapir 2013). In contexts that are perceived to be dominated by particularly aggressive nationalist expectations, political actors have a strong incentive to cater to nationalist discourse. In a world that is interconnected and in which public performances are predominantly mediated, the stages on which actors play their roles are closely linked. What is said in one context can have ramifications in another. In the case of Sino-Japanese relations, the domestically popular discourse of nationalism provides the constraints within which actors can behave on other stages that deal with Sino-Japanese relations.

Ironically, aggressively chauvinistic nationalism may not be the dominant attitude towards Japan in China, just as right-wing reactionary views are not the dominant view on China in Japan. In fact, recent research suggests that nationalism may not be on the 'rise' in China, as is usually assumed, and that preconceptions about young people driving nationalist sentiments in the PRC may be in error (Johnston 2016). However, in terms of the discourses that travel through digital China's networks, the actual beliefs of actors may matter fairly little. The dynamics of digital media today bring strong views to the fore, and the CCP's ideas of democratic centralism and popular legitimacy lead to the misconception that these views need to be heeded. This is largely a side-effect of the CCP's own making. Decades of patriotic education policy have primed citizens and elites alike with the parameters of nationalism, and media politics geared at centralizing a capitalist digital China have created incentives to emphasize these parameters even further. As Halavais (2009: 2083) points out, 'sometimes structural inequities and technocratic decisions that may be perfectly rational and lacking any harmful intent can nonetheless lead to problems in the human systems that make up the web', and the case of Chinese nationalism today is a prime example of how the self-styled benevolent activities of administrators can produce malicious externalities.

Nevertheless, the fact that today's politics are often the unanticipated side-effects of trying to regulate complex networked societies does not acquit regulators of having brought those side-effects about. In China, for instance, the PRC's state continues to push its nationalist agenda, despite evidence that such an agenda is detrimental to peace and prosperity in the region. In 2014, the central government designated 13 December as the official national day of remembrance for the Nanjing Massacre (BBC 2014); in 2016, the Ministry of Education released additional policy guidelines that spell out how patriotic education needs to be deepened and extended even further (MOE PRC 2016). The victory over imperial Japan is quickly becoming the new 'national day', prompting the authorities to organize the kind of military parades for the occasion that are normally reserved for the day of the PRC's founding on 1 October. The lesson that China's administrators have taken away from their own past politics is not that Chinese citizens have been primed with too much anti-Japanese nationalist discourse; it is that they have not been primed with such discourse *enough*.

The state's emphasis on nationalism has implications beyond the bilateral relations between China and Japan, as important as that relation is. Chinese nationalism also targets other 'out-groups', notably the 'West', a term that provides a vehicle for anti-American and often antiliberal sentiments (see Callahan 2010). Notorious cases were the anti-CNN and anti-Carrefour protests in 2008, driven by the impression of many Chinese nationalists that foreign media were systematically misrepresenting China in the run-up to the Beijing Olympics (see Gries 2009, for an analysis of the various perceptions and misperceptions that fuelled the disputes). Popular nationalism in China has also connected with perceptions of African 'others' in ways that are often blatantly racist (Sautman 1994), as is exemplified by anxieties over immigrants from sub-Saharan countries to cities like Guangzhou, or by debates about 'racial purity' following a reality TV show that featured a Chinese contestant whose father was black.[3] It is difficult to see how such in-group and out-group biases will fit into ambitions of the Xi administration to contribute to 'peaceful development' in foreign settings, for instance through involvement in African economies or through collaborations with central-Asian countries through the 'One Belt, One Road' initiative. While CCP leaders may believe that promoting 'rational patriotism' will allow them to re-programme nationalist discourses in their favour, they may be underestimating how strongly their own emphasis of categories like sovereignty traps them in nationalist discourses that create all manners of domestic and international contradictions.

Take the example of the South China Sea dispute.[4] Domestically, long-standing commitments to the importance of sacred 'homelands' combine with activities within China's controversial 'nine-dash line' demarcation of territorial waters to frame relations with neighbouring countries as realist zero-sum interactions, creating expectations at home about how to protect Chinese 'national interests' in the region. Internationally, perceptions about the 'rise' of Chinese nationalism and a supposedly more 'assertive' PRC foreign policy in turn inform China-threat perceptions, potentially facilitating precisely the kind of 'containment' and 'power-balancing' strategies that fuelled Chinese nationalist anxieties in the first place. Antagonisms in the South China Sea then become a self-fulfilling prophesy for all parties involved, even if the original assumptions that informed these interactions were deeply flawed.[5]

## Digitally Imagined Communities

Such circular logics highlight both how artificial and how detrimental the ideology of nationalism is. As a framework of thought, it frequently informs bad decisions, and yet we should be careful not to reduce nationalism solely to false consciousness, in the sense of the Frankfurt School's understanding of ideology (see Geuss 1981). Nationalist ideology does have that dimension, but nationalism also has social and psychological value to those who buy into the ideology. Dismantling nationalist narratives is not simply a matter of explaining to nationalists, in rational terms, how nationalism is not actually in their own interest. It sadly often is in their interest, though not in the sense in which rational-choice proponents would necessarily define the term 'interest'. Nationalism, like all group affiliations, is deeply rooted in our human psychology and our somatic feelings, and adopting it as a default worldview comes with many benefits, such as a sense of belonging, of safety, and of security. This is why the nation is such a clever modern technology: it has allowed elites to unite disparate smaller groups into a larger community that can be set to work on new forms of production and conquest.

It is important to keep in mind the insight of the philosopher Melvin Kranzberg that 'technology is neither good nor bad, nor is it neutral'. Like all technologies, the modern nation is emphatically not neutral. It is not a technology that can at times be deployed positively, for instance to fuel democratic revolutions or fight pernicious colonial oppressions, and that can at other times have negative consequences, such as ethnic violence or international conflict. Imagined communities do not simply become 'good' or 'bad' depending on how people use them. The 'design choices' that went into creating nations, the political and economic conditions that shape their usage, and the psychological predisposition of their members to think in terms of in-groups and out-groups all affect how nations ultimately work. An imagined group association like the nation always requires a degree of violence, both conceptually and physically. Imagined communities do violence to their members through a cognitive trick that misrepresents what the object of human psychological and emotional attachments should be. They do violence to the potential diversity of social life, which must submit itself to the homogenizing premise of the group. They also do violence to non-members, through exclusion and often very explicit forms of aggression. None of these outcomes are 'neutral'.

Some scholars of nationalism ultimately find this degree of violence justifi-able, at least where it gives rise to 'civic nationalisms' that are assumed to provide the only practical foundation for democratic political organization. Smith (1993: 176) thus claims:

> Nationalism (is) a source of pride for down-trodden peoples and the recognized mode for joining or rejoining 'democracy' and 'civiliza-tion'. It also provides the sole vision and rationale of political solidarity today, one that commands popular assent and elicits popular enthu-siasm. All other visions, all other rationales, appear wan and shadowy by comparison.

Importantly, Smith reiterates the common perception that the system of nation states is without alternatives. However, if alternatives to nations and nationalism 'appear wan and shadowy', then the question should be: Who benefits from this appearance, and what acts of power were involved in bringing this appearance about? I believe that the answers to these questions lie in the structures and dy-namics of networked politics.

In a way, nationalism has always been about networks. It has always been about realizing and mobilizing the imagined ties between people for political purposes. What has changed with the spread of digital technologies is that more network configurations are now potentially available, and that more actors par-ticipate in constructing the network and programming it with discourse. This is not to say that digital media herald the end of nations or nationalism. In fact, the networks of imagined communities still lend themselves to the kind of hierar-chical structures that defined nationalism in previous centuries. How precisely such networks are ultimately configured depends on political will and active la-bour: networking is a kind of political work.

In the 1960s, Marshall McLuhan observed how new technologies where connecting people in ways that had previously seemed impossible. To McLuhan (1964/2000: 5), the globe has become 'electrically contracted' and is conse-quently 'no more than a village' (McLuhan 1964/2001: 5). However, contrary to popular interpretations of McLuhan's 'global village', his point was not that the world was becoming 'flat' and that we were witnessing the rise of a cosmopolitan age.[6] McLuhan's emphasis on the 'village' was pejorative. It was a reference to parochial communities full of what he saw as myopic people who busied them-selves with petty judgements about their neighbours. It was a reference to the dark side of human tribalism, amplified through technological innovation.

The paltry and rude commentaries that accompany so much of the web's content seem to confirm this understanding of advanced communication networks as villages (see Halavais 2009: 1962–2360). Liberal, cosmopolitan visions of technological progress have been slow to fully come to grips with the implications, which have forcefully come to the fore as serious impediments to humane interactions and as easy levers for manipulation. Recall the shock expressed across mainstream media as new far-right movements were winning one success after another in the mid-2010s. In Europe, viciously anti-Islamic movements gained seemingly sudden popular support, orchestrating 'sophisticated event-based, highly modern post-democratic "New Politics 2.0"' through social media (Druxes 2016: 30; see also Vossen 2017). In England, dissatisfaction about health-care standards, work/life balances, and education costs exploded spectacularly into anti-foreign, anti-European sentiments, as the 'leave' campaigners ushered in the British Exit, or Brexit, from the European Union (see Farrell & Newman 2017; Freeden 2017).[7] In the United States, both liberal democrats and moderate conservative republicans where stupefied by Donald Trump's meteoric rise to president and the significant popular support his misogynist and racist tribal rantings on social media have been generating.[8]

While these developments are indeed harrowing, even terrifying, they should not strike anyone as surprising. They have been long in the making. They are a direct consequence of what happens when the inherent contradictions of advanced capitalist societies rob people of their sense of personal agency and meaning, and when poorly designed communication technologies invite the losers of modernity into the comforting and safe spaces of imagined community. Importantly, the characteristics of contemporary digital technologies, combined with power and knowledge asymmetries, create opportunities for some digitally enabled media users to manipulate the concerns of others, fostering and guiding resentment for political or financial gain. According to Engesser, Ernst, Esser, and Büchel (2017), social media like Facebook and Twitter have enabled politicians to spread populist views and promote their agenda. In other cases, it might be less clear who benefits from networked interactions, for instance in cases involving 'fake news', that is, pieces of factually incorrect yet plausible information that are targeted specifically at certain user-groups, leveraging their biases to encourage a viral spread of false information (see Derczynski 2017a, 2017b; Lipton 2017).[9] No internet user is entirely immune to these manipulation techniques, which rely on the ubiquitous vulnerabilities that networked communication creates as it interacts with human psychology. Unravelling such manipulations requires no small amount of digital literacy, critical thinking, and energy.

Parochialism works against our ability to critically question background knowledge. Structural and technological factors aid and abet our human propensity to adopt insular mind-sets. Ultimately, we are witnessing a synergy between different technologies, in this case of digital ICTs and the modern technology of the nation, brought about by specific elite actors. This is why I have argued that digital technologies should not be interpreted as challenges to established institutions like the nation state, even where ICTs like social media seem to flatten the power asymmetries inherent in the traditional one-to-many communication patterns that characterize national mass-media systems (see Benkler 2006). It would be a mistake, for instance, to interpret diverse discursive statements on nationalism as acts that reconfigure the discourse and construct a rational, liberal nationalism through social media: a nationalism that provides the foundation of a political community based on civic values. Such an interpretation is ultimately problematic, since it is grounded in three misperceptions of how digital communication facilitates open discussion.

The first is the idea that diverse meaning-making through digital media constitutes a public sphere. As authors like Dean (2003) have argued, the internet is a domain that reproduces the power relations of capitalist modernity, privileging elite (largely male) actors according to rules negotiated between nation states and capitalist tech companies (see Hindman 2010, Morozov 2011). Resulting social media 'services' like Sina or Tencent (or Facebook, Google, or Twitter, for that matter) may indeed seem to facilitate diverse discussion, but that is only because these enterprises have commodified certain kinds of interactions and now stand to profit from seemingly open debate.

It is not my intention to deny that digital technology could create interactions that resemble public spaces of discussion, although a careful revision of Habermas's assumptions about rational discourse would probably have to accompany our understanding of such interactions before we call them 'public spheres'. My point is that the conditions of contemporary digital capitalism and the current sets of digital technologies should engender careful reality-checks whenever digital networks are presented as part of a larger public sphere, whether in China or in other societies. Personally, I find Chen Xiaojin's (2016) argument about the concept of the public sphere convincing: that it provides various actors with a discursive category that is repeatedly invoked, contested, and rejected. In this view, we should explore arguments about the 'public sphere' on a case-to-case basis, rather than buying wholesale into the misperception that such spheres actually exist at the aggregated level of national internets or proprietary social media platforms.

The second misunderstanding is that social media empower users and their 'bottom-up' discourse against political and economic elites. Such a view is informed by an interpretation of power that sees state and society as oppositional actors, each trying to enforce their interests against the other. However, power works in more complex ways than this, relying more strongly on persuasion rather than coercion, and involving many more actors than fit into a state versus society dichotomy. In China, the authorities assure their sovereignty over public discourse by collaborating with private actors, and they frequently regulate overarching network configurations and interaction parameters rather than enforcing their will coercively against opposition. A cornerstone of this strategy has precisely been to bring many-to-many communication channels like the web into the fold of the traditional media system with its capitalist conglomerates and its tendency to privilege the voices of authoritative, vetted actors. Recent studies demonstrate that the state is increasingly successful in extending this mass-media logic to the more socially interactive sphere of microblogging, to e-mailing services, and to virtual private networks that allow users to circumvent China's censorship system (for discussions, see Gao 2015; Ng 2014; Sullivan 2014; Svensson 2014).

Finally, the belief that a differentiated online discussion about national identity, Chinese or otherwise, might translate into a 'positive' form of nationalism misunderstands what nationalism is: a form of consciousness that lends meaning to the world by seeing it through the lens of a politically and culturally cohesive community. Despite wishful thinking to the contrary, nationalism does not separate into distinct positive 'civic' versus negative 'ethnic' components. As Billig (2009: 55) has argued, such distinctions are themselves ideological. The core idea of nationalism is not about exact meanings, it is about an imagined sense of group attachment, and such in-groups are always built around 'some features that make them special and, in a certain way, "superior" to the rest' (Guibernau 2004: 137).

It is with these considerations in mind that we should re-evaluate the potential of digital media to redefine or even unhinge feelings of nation-ness. Digital technologies are not a challenge to the rationale of traditional media, but an extension of them, which means that, if configured in specific ways, they reproduce nationalism very much as those traditional media do. Gellner writes (1983/2006: 122):

> The most important and persistent message is generated by the medium itself, by the role which such media have acquired in modern life. That core message is that the language and style of the transmissions is important, that only he [sic] who can understand them, or can acquire such comprehension, is included in a moral and economic community, and that he [sic] who does not and cannot, is excluded. All this is crystal clear, and follows from the pervasiveness and crucial role of mass communication in this kind of society. What is actually said matters little.

Social media, with their rationale of serving users like-minded ideas while muting challenges to their worldview (Pierson 2014), are ideal allies to established mass communication channels, particularly in countries where political elites try to unify media under the banner of national sovereignty. Digital media are well suited for the kind of comfort-zone maintenance on which nationalism relies. Through such media, we can warm ourselves at the hearths of our 'epistemological comforts of home' (Hardin 1995: ch.7). In the end, however, the in-built propensity of such digital spheres to inspire myopic views and feelings does not bode well for disputes such as those that are today common in modern societies. As long as such disputes are framed through nationalism, they remain anchored in false dichotomies (e.g., us vs. them), attribution errors (e.g., what exactly feelings like loyalty and scepticism, love or hatred should be attached to), and dogmatic commitment to specific narrative protocols (e.g., victimization or glorification of the group). These dimensions of imagined communities raise serious concerns about the prospect of meaningful reconciliation between diverse peoples. Historical narratives in East Asia are an excellent example of this, but they are by no means unique.

I have argued throughout this book that the construction of discourse, whether digital or analogue, is a collaborative process, shaped by negotiation and compromise. It is not always a struggle. That said, in the case of nationalist discourse, it probably should be a struggle. Not a struggle over who has the 'correct' narrative, but a constant struggle to challenge the idea that there can ever be a coherent, simple, 'correct' narrative in the first place. This is a struggle to assure our discourses reflect the multifarious and messy nature of human interaction, rather than simplifying them to the level of digestible but misleading 'common sense' truths. The complex problems that humanity faces today deserve better solutions than the reductionist thinking of a time gone by. The 17th-century technologies of the nation and its modern state are awkward tools to address today's issues. Imagine we were to use medical equipment from the Renaissance to conduct complicated surgical procedures. Most of us would feel ill-at-ease at such a prospect, and yet we are content to live, on a day-to-day basis, with the design flaws of anachronistic political technologies. What is more, we allow these technologies of early modernity to serve as solutions to advanced modernity's problems, ignoring that it was these very technologies that helped bring about our contemporary predicaments in the first place.

These predicaments extend far beyond conflicts over how to make sense of history. Problems like global poverty, exploitative labour practices, demographic changes, environmental degradations, or diseases with near global reach all pose challenges that need to be understood and addressed in their full complexity. It is understandable that many feel reluctant to lean into such complexities; it is not comforting to relinquish hard-earned 'common sense'. We need to treat ourselves and our fellow humans with compassion wherever we fail to spot and challenge our epistemological blind spots. After all, we are only human. That said, it is unlikely that such a willingness to live with complexity can co-exist with the shrine-like veneration that imagined communities like the nation frequently demand. Nations, like the people who populate them, do not suffer ambiguities lightly, and they interface with communication technologies in ways that strengthen rather than weaken their resolve to promote inside-of-the-box thinking.

The need for community cohesion that nationalism relies upon indeed connects seamlessly with the kind of group dynamics that many digital technologies today promote, especially where such technologies are forced into national governance frameworks and political economies. In this way, pernicious ideologies become natural, and behaviour informed by these ideologies becomes habit. As the English poet John Dryden famously warned, we first make our habits, then our habits make us, and this is also true for the habitual reproduction of national narratives. As users of ICTs, we each need to get out of our bubbles and challenge the beliefs and habits that we have internalized as common sense. Many of course do so, challenging existing ideologies through their own discourses, and demonstrating that discursive interactions can bring about meaningful change. However, we should be careful not to lay responsibility for such change at the feet of individual users, stylizing them as neoliberal 'netizens' and expecting them to be ever vigilant and active (see the critique by Hoofd 2012). In the end, it is up to designers and innovators to help users form better habits, by creating digital technologies that connect people in ways that bring out the positive potential of social dynamics, and that provide opportunities for interactions beyond nations. It is also up to policy-makers and administrators to facilitate innovations that make it possible to imagine diverse, overlapping communities outside of national frameworks.

However, as long as political and commercial stake-holders view the capitalist nation state as the primary guarantor for safety and prosperity, and as the only conceivable locus of political activity, we are bound to remain locked into parochial worlds. This is largely a side-effect of how technological, psychological, and social factors interact, and it may indeed seem that such externalities are outside of anyone's control, that they are an inevitable tragedy of our continuing modernity. However, the realization that nationalism and other pernicious ideologies are the emergent properties of complex networks should not obscure that real people created the default parameters that enable such emergence. The politicians, designers, entrepreneurs, journalists, academics, technicians, and activists who refuse to change these default parameters and who continue to allow anachronistic technologies like nationalism to emerge as acceptable frameworks of contemporary interaction are identifiable. Some may benefit directly from creating or perpetuating the default. Others may simply accept the default as common sense. In neither case do such actors deserve to be surprised when hateful politics arise from the structures they themselves helped create. We have tried nationalism as the default setting for imagining our politically most influential communities. It has brought us a modern world full of segregation, isolation, and anger. It is time to imagine community differently and to deploy digital technology to that end.

# Notes

Chapter 1

1. The QQ quote provided here is one of the many comments that Barefoot (2012) has collected on the website *chinaSMACK*. A selection of images from the various protests and riots is available in *The Atlantic* (Taylor 2012), including photos of Japanese restaurants draped in Chinese flags. The summary of the Xi'an riots is based on a detailed reconstruction of the events in *The Beijing Youth Daily* (Li 2012); Chubb (2012) has provided an English translation. The renewed online discussion in 2016 as well as the statement by Li Jianli's wife have been reported by Koetse (2016b).

2. There is no single moment in history that marks the advent of nations, nationalism, and the nation state. Tracing these concepts and institutions back to their origins has remained fraught with controversies in historical research, with many scholars associating them roughly with the French Revolution and the start of industrialization in 18th-century Europe (e.g., Gellner 1983/2006; Hobsbawm 1990). An earlier watershed moment was the Peace of Westphalia in 1648, which established sovereign nation states in Europe. National narratives of 'chosen people', however, can be traced to the time of the Protestant Reformation, which began in 1517 and saw the Bible translated into many regional vernaculars that would later become national languages (Burke 2013: 26). Regardless of the exact point of origin, nations and nationalism are intricately linked to the rise of the modern world, particularly to novel technologies in government, commerce, and warfare, with innovations in transportation and communication playing a particularly important role. I return to these dynamics in the subsequent chapter. On the complicated history of nationalisms around the world, see the various contributions in Breuilly (2013).

3. For similar assessments, see Callahan (2010), Gries (2005), Nyíri et al. (2010), Rosen (2009), and the contributions in Shen and Breslin (2010).

4. See Wang (2012: ch.4) for a detailed introduction to China's patriotic education campaign and Hughes (2006) on the evolution of contemporary Chinese nationalism since the late 1970s.

5. On the controversies that surround Japan's history textbooks, see Saaler (2005) and Cave (2012). Kingston (2007) analyses one of Japan's most controversial war memorials, the Yasukuni Shrine in Tokyo. Zhang (2014) and Suzuki and Murai (2014) have analysed the news coverage of recent territorial disputes in China and Japan, respectively.

6. See Li, Xuan, and Kluver (2003) for a similar argument regarding the case of US–Chinese international relations.

7. On Japan's relief efforts in Sichuan, and on the confusion over the role that Japan's military should play in this case, see Wang and Okano-Heijmans (2011: 137–138). The online

comment was reported in *The Times* (MacArtney 2008); the quotes by Japan's foreign ministry and the unnamed air force official are taken from *The Guardian* (McCurry 2008).

8. The World Bank estimates that the average Chinese income per year was around 300 US dollars at the time (see World Bank n.d.).

9. The impacts and usages of digital technologies in rural China are still sorely understudied. Most research has focused on urban developments, and while more Chinese today live in cities than in the countryside, this bias can nevertheless be misleading. For an assessment, see the discussion in Oreglia et al. (2015). Recent inroads into the topic of digital technology in rural China have been made by Tom McDonald (2015, 2016).

10. Each of these Chinese IT giants is producing significant income each year: for 2014, the data portal *Statistica* reported 10.16 billion US dollars in revenue for Baidu, 15.69 billion for Alibaba, and 21.9 for Tencents (http://www.statista.com/, accessed 15 May 2017). Nevertheless, together, the three companies still only earned roughly half of Google's revenue and less than a quarter of Apple's income that year.

11. Yang Guobin has updated his earlier arguments in Yang (2014); Bondes and Schucher (2014), Volland (2011), Zhang (2011: 96–105), and Zheng (2008: 98–101) each provide additional discussions of collective action and ICTs in China. Qiu (2009) examines how mobile phones have changed the lives of working-class people in the PRC. Lindtner and Szablewicz (2011) analyse the interactions surrounding digital gaming, and Li (2011) discusses how irony and parody function as forms of resistance in digital China.

12. For a general critique of Habermas's concept of the public sphere, see Thompson (1995: 70–75).

13. See Hoofd (2012: 70–74) for a discussion and critique of the 'multitude' idea, which is particularly popular in radical Italian political thought. As for who is ultimately empowered by digital technology, Morozov goes as far as claiming that the internet 'empowers the strong and disempowers the weak' (2011: 295), a position that turns optimistic claims on their head, but that does little to move beyond dichotomies of power versus resistance. As Hoofd writes, Morozov's 'simplistic division' ultimately 'still conceptualises the Internet as at base a volatile "empty" space to be filled by the strongest force' (2012: 11–12). Much like the narratives that Morozov challenges, his own account remains firmly rooted in the idea that digital interactions are a cat-and-mouse game between forces of freedom and forces of oppression. It is merely that, to Morozov, the power relations in this 'battle' are shifted in favour of 'the secret police, the censors, and the propaganda offices' (2011: 307, 737).

14. The quote was first reported in *Time Magazine* by Elmer-DeWitt (1993). Two decades later, Gilmore remained convinced that the statement is generally accurate, writing, 'Internet users have proven it time after time, by personally and publicly replicating information that is threatened with destruction or censorship. If you now consider the Net to be not only the wires and machines, but the people and their social structures who use the machines, it is more true than ever' (Gilmore 2013).

15. This incident took place in 2003. Li and Shooshtari (2007) have covered it in detail; the online comments quoted here are taken from their study. See also O'Barr (2007) for additional information on advertising faux pas in China. The *Beijing Time* (2003) has reproduced the ad and its digitally altered version as well as quotes from Toyota's apology.

16. I thank Mari Nakamura for drawing my attention to the overlap between these historical developments.

17. On the Nanjing Massacre's relevance today, see Buruma (2002), Denton (2014: ch.6), and Mitter (2003). Fogel (2000) and Wakabayashi (2007b) provide collections of nuanced, historical studies on the topic, and Yoshida (2006) analyses how Nanjing Massacre narratives have been instrumentalized in China, Japan, and the United States.

18. The phrase 'rape of Nanking' was popularized by Iris Chang (1997/2012) in her bestseller of the same name. For a discussion of this popular yet controversial account of the event, see MacDonald (2005).

19. Hagström (2012) has provided a recent analysis. See also my own work on how Chinese international relations theorizing holds up in the face of this complex conflict (Schneider 2014a: 695–701).

20. This definition of discourse follows the work of Michel Foucault (e.g., 1978/1995). Howarth (2000) has provided an insightful introduction to discourse theory.

21. My own approach follows the methods of Chilton (2004), Jäger (2004), and Van Leeuwen (2008). For two excellent collections that introduce different methods and source materials in discourse analysis, specifically in the field of 'critical discourse analysis' (CDA), see Wodak and Krzyzanowski (2008) and Wodak and Meyer (2009). A foundational text in CDA is Fairclough (1995).

22. Jack Qiu similarly stresses how important the visual dimension of discourse is, arguing that Chinese online nationalism has undergone a 'transformation into an image-driven form in recent years' (2015: 162).

23. See Rogers (2013) on 'digitally native' elements, and Knox (2009) and Pauwels (2005) on website analysis.

24. Available at https://www.issuecrawler.net. For an introduction, see http://wiki.digitalmethods.net (both last accessed 18 March 2018). Additional discussions of the programme and its analytical implications are available from Bruns (2007) and myself (Schneider 2015).

25. Gephi is available online, along with tutorials, at: https://gephi.org/users/ (last accessed 18 March 2018).

26. I use the phrase 'media ecologies' frequently throughout this book to describe media environments and to highlight that in digital contexts such environments are complex, interacting systems that retain their material qualities and are 'inhabited' by both software and human actors (see Fuller 2005). The organic metaphor of the 'ecology' also provides a useful reminder that such environments are 'grown' in specific contexts, and that they provide material restraints within which things are 'born' and 'spread', as is the case with 'digitally native' elements that go 'viral' in certain media spheres, for instance.

## Chapter 2

1. Chan is a staunch promoter of Chinese nationalism in his home city of Hong Kong (*China Daily* 2005) and an ardent critic of foreign countries like the United States (Fisher 2013). On Chinese social media, he has repeatedly caused controversy, for instance by admonishing his Chinese compatriots for speaking ill of the PRC to foreigners, by belittling the environmental concerns of Beijing citizens, and by claiming that Chinese people are not capable of dealing with liberal-democratic rights such as freedom of speech. For a collection of such statements and subsequent online reactions in China, see Tang (2013).

2. While Habermas includes digital networks in his discussion, his scope extends to globalization processes more broadly, asking what the nature of community can be in a world of prolific transnational interactions. On globalization and its interaction with nation states, see Strange (1996) and Mann (1997), as well as the various contributions in Held and McGrew (2000). Frost (2006) provides a discussion of 'post-national constellations' specifically in the context of ICT.

3. On the problems of applying modernist European biases about innovation specifically to China, see Keane (2013).

4. Scholars from various disciplines have drawn similar conclusions, and discussing all of the different angles would exceed the scope of this book. Instructive arguments have come from psychologists (e.g., Damasio 2010: ch.11; Frith 2007: ch.7; Llinás 2001: ch.11), historians (e.g., Diamond 1999: ch.13), anthropologists (e.g., Sperber 1996: ch.2; Tomasello 2008), and other social science and communication scholars (e.g., Carroll 1998; Chilton 2004; Eco 1979; Turner 2001). Listing these sources here should not imply that they are without frictions or controversies—several issues remain highly contested, for instance how innate

human capacities and external environmental factors balance out in human communication, or how the psychological processes in the human mind relate to the biological processes in the brain. On this last issue, I agree with the cognitive psychologist Chris Frith (2007: 23), who argues, 'everything that happens in the mind (mental activity) is caused by, or at least depends upon, brain activity'. What happens in the human mind is an emergent property of the underlying brain functions; it cannot be reduced to those functions in a deterministic way, but it is bounded by them nonetheless.

5. Mizuko Ito and her colleagues, in their comprehensive study of how digital youth cultures are anything but shallow, write that 'contrary to adult perceptions, while hanging out online, youth are picking up basic social and technical skills they need to fully participate in contemporary society' (Ito et al. 2008: 2). Henry Jenkins has similarly provided a nuanced antidote to reductionist views of ICT in his work on how digital technologies encourage social sharing and creative 'remixing' (Jenkins 2008; Jenkins et al. 2013).

6. Ceruzzi (2012) and Liang (2011) have each provided concise introductions to computation and its history. For a complex and mathematically involved treatment that traces algorithms to Babylonian, Egyptian, and premodern Chinese precursors, see the various contributions in Chabert (2013). Insightful fictionalized treatments are Neal Stephenson's *Cryptonomicon* (1999) and *The Baroque Cycle* (2014).

7. A now classic study is Miller and Slater's (2000) analysis of digital media usage in Trinidad. More recent studies have examined how social capital works on Facebook (Ellison et al. 2014), how online and offline activities such as dating or group coordination intersect (Ramirez et al. 2015; Lai 2014), and how location-based technologies affect social media use (Hjorth 2014; Schwartz & Halegoua 2015).

8. The attribution of gender to the nation may well have important implications. As the psychologist George Lakoff (2002) has argued for the case of US politics, references to strict father figures are often deployed in conservative politics, whereas references to nurturing mothers tend to inform liberal politics. Whether such dynamics extend to different national metaphors, especially across time and space, remains an open question. I suspect that mother figures are more readily mobilized in victimization narratives (the 'raped' nation, etc.), but future research will have to explore how gendered metaphors of the nation compare in different settings.

9. The literature on the social dynamics of sports fans is too vast to discuss here in full. For an introduction to the complex dynamics of football fandom, see the various contributions in Armstrong and Giulianotti (1999). Quiroga (2013) has provided an in-depth study of how football contributes to the construction of Spanish, Catalan, and Basque national mythologies. For similar studies of baseball, see for example, Guthrie-Shimizu (2012) and Morris (2011).

10. The Third Wave refers to the 1967 high school experiment by Ron Jones (1976) that aimed to showcase how community sentiments could turn into fascism. The famous fictional account of this experiment is Todd Strasser's *The Wave* (1981/2013).

11. Interestingly, Smith himself remains highly ambiguous about whether patriotism and nationalism should be distinguished on analytical grounds. In parts of his discussion, he treats patriotism as synonymous with nationalism, for instance, when examining the nationalist activities of French revolutionary 'patriots' (Smith 1991: 76). Elsewhere, he provides an alternative meaning for patriotism: analysing the rise of nationalism in colonial societies like India, Kenya, or Indonesia, he argues that nationalism became a tangible ideology once the colonial powers unified territorial spaces into coherent administrative units that had not existed before, eventually ushering in a 'growth of a *territorial patriotism* based on this space and limited by its boundaries' (ibid.: 107, emphasis in the original). In this context, Smith's patriotism seems to describe primarily a 'civic and territorial model' of nationalism, setting it apart from 'ethnic and genealogical models' (ibid.: 82).

12. For an excellent discussion of 'primordial', 'modernist', and 'ethno-symbolic' theories of nations and nationalism, see Zubrzycki (2009).

13. To Smith (1991: 20–21), 'ethnic categories' are groups that share a sense of cultural, linguistic, or historic commonality but that do not link that sense to territorial sovereignty. Smith contrasts these 'ethnic categories' with what he calls 'ethnies', which are ethnic communities that mobilize to claim an autonomous homeland. Smith's 'ethnies' consequently share some resemblance with what I call national communities in this book. In contrast, 'ethnic categories' might include examples like Hispanic communities in North America or Chinese communities in South East Asia. They are imagined communities in their own right, but they are not nations.

14. See the various contributions in Thompson and Hoggett (2012) for discussions of the recent 'affective turn' in politics. Peter Gries (2004: 88) has discussed the relevance of emotions for the case of Chinese nationalism.

15. I use the word 'need' with some trepidation and primarily to keep the terminology simple. From a psychological perspective, using the word 'need' in this context is a simplification, since needs imply innate urges, whereas what I describe overlaps to some extent with socially formed drivers of human behaviour, namely, aspirations and wishes. In addition, discussions of needs usually turn to the classic arguments by Abraham Maslow (1943), which are highly controversial. One point of criticism has been the idea that needs should be understood hierarchically (see the critique by Wahba & Bridwell 1976; for a discussion in German, see Dörner 2001: 310–313), an argument that has had a lasting influence on modernist understandings of human progress and social development. That said, what I have in mind here is a series of psychological mechanisms that motivate humans to satisfy perceived requirements in their lives, and for this the notion of 'need' shall suffice.

16. For a thorough discussion of realist claims about groups and the criticism that such claims have elicited from symbolic-interactionists, see Huddy (2003). On the social construction of risk in modernity, and the illusion of rationality in risk perceptions, see Ulrich Beck's influential work on the 'risk society' (1992).

17. Chilton (2004: 127–128) provides an insightful discussion of how in-group speech acts can relate to self-legitimation processes.

18. A discussion of 'social emotions' such as shame, embarrassment, guilt, and so on, is available in Damasio (2010: 125–129). For a discussion of shame in sociological accounts of human behaviour, see Barbalet (2001: ch.5).

19. James Leibold (2016b) has discussed the complexities of this terminology and the difficulties of translating the Chinese term *minzu* (民族) that has come to mean both ethnicity and nation.

## Chapter 3

1. Her name is not actually Lucy. For ethical reasons, I have changed the names of all the people I interviewed for this project. The reason for this is that the political climate in China can change suddenly, and what may seem like a politically correct conversation today may be inappropriate tomorrow. This is especially true for professionals dealing with foreign interlocutors, who are always at least implicitly at risk of divulging information that could conceivably become a 'state secret' at a later point in time.

2. Note that Goldman uses this definition to defend search bias as crucial to the workings of search engines; he goes on to argue that concerns over search bias mainly reflect the 'disappointed expectations' of 'search engine utopianism', and that technological progress and market dynamics will fix the problem 'naturally' and 'organically' as long as these processes are allowed to proceed 'without regulatory distortion' (2006: 199–200). Ten years on, such libertarian claims seem at the very least anachronistic.

3. Note that this is also why 'bias' is not synonymous with 'world-view': all world-views are biased, whether due to personal, social, or material factors, but not all biases are world-views. A data selection bias, for instance, is not itself a world-view, even though it skews what information a person receives and thus potentially shapes that person's perspective.

4. Simon Knight (2014: 232) makes a similar case in his insightful discussion of search engine use in education, though he uses a different terminology.

## Chapter 4

1. To some extent, Castells's view of power overlaps with the concepts that Steven Lukes (2005) has developed in his seminal work. Aside from the classic decision-making power that Max Weber focused on, Lukes introduces two additional 'faces' of power: non-decision-making power, that is, the ability to include or exclude agents in politics and set political agendas (see also McCombs 2004), and ideological power, that is, the ability to persuade actors and re-align their interests. On this latter type of power, see also Raymond Guess's (1981) discussion of ideology and interests in critical theory and Foucault's work on discourse, power, and sovereignty (e.g., Foucault 1978/2009, particularly pp. 63–66).
2. The distinction between 'data' and 'information' is subtle, but it is relevant. Data here refers to a set of signifiers that have been selected and combined in a way that potentially carries meaning. Information is what becomes of such data once the meanings are decoded. Data are raw packages that agents turn into information. To give an example, a sound wave is data, which turns into information once someone listens to it, processes it cognitively, and understands and feels it to be music. In semiotics, this relationship is traditionally described as a triangle between three entities: the sign, the object, and the interpretant. In such an understanding, signs are data, objects are what the signs point to, and interpretants are the information: the meaning that an observer arrives at by attributing the sign to its object. For a detailed discussion, see the work of Umberto Eco (1979) and Charles Sander Pearce (in Hoopes 1991, especially ch.8 and ch.16).
3. The tool is available upon registration at the following URL: https://www.issuecrawler.net/index.php (last accessed 18 March 2018).
4. For detailed discussion of the power law in communication and information networks, see Benkler (2006: 243–246), Shirky (2003, 2008: 122–130), and Walker Rettberg (2014: 1147).
5. I have previously discussed these studies in three journal articles, and the figures and arguments presented here are largely taken from these publications: see Schneider (2015) on the academic networks and (2016a, 2018) on the Japan-related networks.
6. An interesting outlier is the issue website of the Chinese University of Hong Kong, which was set up in the 1990s, and which does not fall under the purview of mainland legislation. As I discuss in chapter 5, the website nevertheless seamlessly ties in with the discourse of the mainland sites, hinting at a degree of shared 'pan-Chinese' nationalism that may not be confined to the PRC.
7. To geo-locate the websites, I cross-referenced the results from two digital tools: the Digital Methods Initiative's URL/IP-to-Geo tool (https://tools.digitalmethods.net/beta/geoIP/) and Webroot's BrightCloud URL/IP lookup tool (http://www.brightcloud.com/tools/url-ip-lookup.php). The only websites that these tools could not properly locate were the three Xinhua domains, but BrightCloud's IP results suggest that the server that hosts news.xinhuanet.com may be located outside of China, in eastern Los Angeles (IP: 65.255.44.6). Be that as it may, Xinhua is a ministry-level organization under the PRC's State Council (China's cabinet), which means the agency works firmly within the framework of official legislation (Xin 2006).
8. The Gephi software is freely available online, along with useful tutorials, at: https://gephi.org/users/ (last accessed 18 March 2018).
9. To further examine at which point this diffusion sets in, I ran two additional sets of exploratory crawls, for which I progressively lowered the number of iterations and removed starting pages that were not part of a website dealing exclusively with Sino-Japanese history. These crawls revealed that paths between the issue pages only become visible when pages on larger web hubs are included (i.e., sites such as Baidu, Sina, 163.com, or the military

portals Tiexue and Leiting). It is these generic sites that function as portals to the Chinese web at large, and that consequently switch the Nanjing Massacre discourse into the wider infrastructure of China's web.

## Chapter 5

1. Such dichotomies should be treated with care. In contemporary societies, digital/analogue as well as online/offline processes are deeply intertwined and frequently bleed into one another. For a discussion, see Van Dijk and Poell (2013).
2. For a discussion of victimization narratives and their function in the context of collective remembering, see Wertsch (2002: 1502).
3. Brian Wallis (1997) discusses these two approaches with regard to American museums in the wake of what is often called the 'culture wars'. I am basing my discussion primarily on Wertsch (2002: 667–715), who is influenced on this issue by the works of Edward Linenthal (1996) and Peter Novick (1999).
4. Young (2000) provides a similar discussion for the case of Holocaust memorials. See also Linenthal (1995) and Novick (1999) for provocative analyses of Holocaust remembering in America. The seminal treatment on how communities construct a liveable past is arguably Halbwachs (1992). See also Cruz (2000) on national remembering.
5. For earlier studies in a similar vein, see Garry et al. (1996) and Goff and Roediger (1998). I thank Manya Koetse for drawing my attention to this strand of research. She explored collective remembering in her graduate thesis (Koetse 2012).
6. Dayan and Katz (1992) have examined how live broadcasting establishes events as 'historic' (see, in particular, their ch.6).
7. In fact, as I pointed out in the introduction of this book, claims about how nations 're-member' or 'forget', how they have been 'traumatized' or suffer 'amnesia', are themselves discursive moves that deploy the metaphor of personal memory in order to configure historical scripts for political purposes (see also Wertsch 2002: 553).
8. See Hargittai and Shaw (2015) on the gender and skill gap among Wikipedia contributors. Reagle (2011) provides an overview of the debates surrounding Wikipedia, and of the hyperbole that often accompanies it.
9. For an overview, see the various contributions in Lovink and Tkacz (2011). Rogers (2013: ch.8) examines the potential uses of Wikipedia for research purposes.
10. For studies of online encyclopaedias in China and Taiwan, see the seminal work by Liao Han-Teng and Thomas Petzold (Petzold et al. 2012; Liao 2013; Liao & Petzold 2014).
11. The issue of digital labour, particularly the corporate exploitation of user participation, is increasingly receiving scholarly attention, for instance in the various contributions to Scholz (2013). Christian Fuchs (2014) has provided a Marxist interpretation of such developments.
12. Note that the Baidu entry has been revised since I analysed it in 2015. It has been thoroughly reworded to include references (to PRC state media resources) and has adopted a more confident, less nuanced tone. For instance, in May 2017, the opening paragraph stated that the Japanese troops had 'organized, planned, and premeditated' the murders, rapes, arson, and plunderings that they committed at the time, providing no reference for this assertion. While these edits do not refute the general findings regarding the 2015 entry outlined below, they do raise the question of whether Baidu's entries are generally more recent sites of construction and development that may be less stable than Wikipedia's established entries on the same topics—a question that I am not in a position to answer here. The changes also draw attention to a general methodological problem of analysing digital materials: their changeable nature. The internet archive's Wayback Machine, for instance, maintains no record of this Encyclopaedia Baidu entry and its changes over time, making it very difficult to reproduce discourse analyses of such web articles without editorial access to the site's earlier contents. A copy of the entry in its 2015 and 2017 states is available from

me upon request. I thank one of the anonymous reviewers of this book for pointing the re-cent edits out to me.

13. These quotes are taken from the Nanjing Massacre web portal of the *Global Times*, avail-able at http://history.huanqiu.com/special/2012-02/2465037.html (last accessed 1 July 2017).

14. As Sven Saaler (2013: 140) points out, Sino-Japanese collaboration on issues of history is indeed extensive, ranging from 'official bodies at the government level' to 'private initiatives by universities, non-governmental organizations (NGOs) and historians' groups', and resulting 'in dozens of bilateral and multilateral symposia, in addition to a number of publications ranging from conference proceedings to the first supplementary textbooks on East Asian history to be published by a multinational group of authors'.

15. Note that both sites had moved between the original study of 2013 and the time of writing. In March 2018, Leiting's Nanjing Massacre website was available at http://www.leitingcn.com/huati/nanjingdts/, and Tiexue's site had moved to http://data.tiexue.net/view/8436#.

16. This derogatory phrase is used to make Japan appear morally small; it is a recurring phrase throughout the discourse, also in its official instantiations. The PLA website Tiexue, for in-stance, has a sub-domain dedicated to discussions about 'little Japan' (Tiexue 2014).

## Chapter 6

1. For accounts and assessments in English, see for example, Choong (2014) and Hagström (2012). Earlier assessments are available by Blanchard (2000) and Shaw (1999). For studies of media coverage in various contexts, see the contributions in Hollihan (2014).

2. The non-profit Internet Archive has set up the Wayback Machine (https://archive.org/web/) to help trace past changes to websites around the world.

3. A third-party service that checks sites for their 'backlinks' is the Open Site Explorer, which includes the free browser tool that I have used here (https://moz.com/researchtools/ose).

4. Encyclopaedia Baidu, in its 'Diaoyu Island' entry, asserts that the Japanese government started naming names first, on 29 January 2012, but the site does not corroborate this assertion with a reference.

5. See also Schoenhals (1992). Leibold (2016b: 427) has covered terminological rectification with regard to ethnic categories in China.

6. The original reads: 钓鱼岛海域是中国的传统渔场，中国渔民世世代代在该海域从事渔业生产活动。

7. It should be pointed out that international law currently favours the Japanese interpreta-tion of the dispute. This reference to the law likely means PRC law. In fact, the Chinese authorities would reject the idea that the island dispute is a matter of international law, preferring to interpret the issue as domestic.

8. The Nationalist Party (KMT) on Taiwan seems to have contributed significantly to naturalizing such conceptual overlap during its recent two terms in government (2008–2016). In particular, former ROC president Ma Ying-jeou has repeatedly evoked a common Chinese historical and cultural heritage across the Straits—a political strategy particularly visible for the case of contested territories, for instance in the South China Sea (see Wu 2016).

9. Xilu frequently reproduces other Chinese-language media, but notably copies materials from mainland sources. The site at times *references* outlets in Taiwan or Hong Kong, but it takes the texts that describe such news reports from official mainland sources like the *Global Times*, changes their titles, and re-brands them with the in-house logo to suggest that these texts were authored for the Xilu website itself.

10. For additional discussion of how 'Chineseness' is constructed in different contexts, see the various contribution in Jurriëns and De Kloet (2007).

11. The cipher 918 refers to the so-called Manchurian Incident (see Mitter 2013: 877), a staged attack on Japanese railway lines in Manchuria that served as the pretext for Japan's invasion and subsequent annexation of the region. The event took place on 18 September 1931, and the date still provides a powerful symbol for national humiliation within Chinese discourse.

12. As Johnston (2016: 35) has shown in his survey work on Beijing, 'Chinese youth are less nationalistic, not more nationalistic, than older respondents across all measures of nationalism'. Findings by Qian et al. (2017) further strengthen this impression that China's youth may not be as nationalist as is often assumed; importantly, young students appear to be quite critical of the Japan image that is conveyed through official patriotic education materials. Finally, recent assumptions about young nationalist women in digital China seem to also be based on misperceptions, providing a convenient label ('little pinks'; *xiao fenhong* 小粉红) for seemingly authentic, bottom-up nationalist activism, but ultimately not representing the views of actual young women (see Fang & Repnikova 2017).

## Chapter 7

1. A number of scholars have studied the blogging phenomenon in detail, for example, Barlow (2007), Dean (2010), Farrell and Drezner (2008), Johnston et al. (2011), Lovink (2008), and Walker Rettberg (2014). Specifically on blogs in China, see for example, Barmé et al. (2012), Gao and Martin-Kratzer (2011), and MacKinnon (2005).

2. An ardent critic of the Web 2.0 idea is Jaron Lanier (2011: 421), who provocatively views the associated design and business practices as part of a 'digital Maoism' in which 'people define themselves downward' into hive-like collective intelligences, reducing their individuality and ultimately changing 'the very idea of what it is to be a person'. For a more favourable assessment, see the tongue-in-cheek discussion by Bruce Sterling (2009). For a discussion of the Web 2.0 paradigm, see Beer and Burrows (2007).

3. The Chinese government and state media use the English term 'netizen' to cover two separate Chinese terms: 'net citizen' (*wangmin* 网民) and 'net friend' (*wangyou* 网友). The encyclopaedia here opts for the second term.

4. The corpus is part of the 'Weiboscope' project that Fu King-wa and his colleagues (2013) have assembled at Hong Kong University.

5. For recent scholarly discussions of Sina Weibo, see Svensson (2014) and Sullivan (2014). Benney (2014) has explored specifically how the Weibo interface might guide communication on the platform.

6. Indeed, as a foreign researcher, I have found it prohibitively difficult to receive access to Weibo's API. Access to the API requires an accredited account, and for reasons that remain obscure to me, my own attempts to submit my account for such accreditation have only yielded rejections from Sina's byzantine bureaucratic system.

7. The charts are available at Sina (2016); a Weibo user account is required to access the page.

8. The original post from 18 September, 18:10, reads: 北京的日本店一样的装饰。The image has since been deleted by Sina.

9. The originals: 爱国，请从爱每一人开始！(17:47) and 这就是国耻！(21:54).

10. The original: 人渣！干了鬼子曾经干过的事，畜生！(26 September, 22:56).

11. It is relatively common to connect such sociality in Chinese online spheres with presumably 'Chinese' cultural characteristics. Wang and Gu (2015: 25) suggest that rhetorical styles in digital China are 'deeply rooted in two dominant philosophical traditions of Chinese culture: Confucianism and Taoism'. Chen et al. (2017: 3) explain the social processes that Weixin usage facilitates in terms of ostensibly Chinese concepts like guanxi-relationships (*guanxi* 关系), face (*mianzi* 面子), and various affective concerns (e.g., *renqing* 人情 and *ganqing* 感情), which they, in turn, believe are anchored in Confucianism. While such studies point out important social dynamics, I am not convinced that these dynamics are in any meaningful way 'Chinese'. Like Zhou et al. (2017: 6), I would argue that alleged cultural preferences, such as the supposed popularity of video chatting among 'Asian' users, are

ultimately not shaped by collective 'cultures'. In fact, the kind of cultural essentialism and exceptionalism that informs such assertions often reflect an uncritical commitment to community narratives themselves, potentially helping construct precisely the kind of imagined community assumptions I have studied throughout this book.

## Chapter 8

1. For an earlier translation than mine, see the China Real Time report on this song (Chin & Wong 2015).
2. The quote is from a speech that Xi (2014) gave at the opening of the CAC. In its original, it reads: 没有网络安全就没有国家安全。没有信息化就没有现代化。努力把我国建设成为网络强国。
3. For detailed discussions of the PRC's political system, its revolutionary legacies, the challenges it faces, and the governing mechanisms it adopts, see Burns (2003), Lieberthal (2003), Saich (2015), Shirk (2007: ch.3), Pieke (2016), and the various contributions in Heilmann and Perry (2011) and Joseph (2010). Specifically on the workings of the CCP, see Shambaugh (2008) and the contributions in Brodsgaard and Zheng (2006).
4. This discourse, and in particular its implicit assumption that democratic systems are inherently superior to authoritarian polities, has come under attack from neo-authoritarianists, who claim that liberal democracies are ill-equipped to make tough decisions and enforce them effectively; see Fewsmith (2008: ch.3) and Van Dongen (2009) for discussions of neo-authoritarianism in China. A recent example of this line of reasoning comes from the entrepreneur Eric X. Li (2013). The economist Huang Yasheng (2013) has provided a critique of Li's TED-talk. A scholarly discussion of the perceived benefits of authoritarian meritocratic leadership has been put forward by Daniel Bell (2015). Andrew Nathan (2015) has provided a critical review of Bell's arguments.
5. I have discussed these practices in the context of China's broadcasting system in Schneider (2016b). The present account of the logic behind such practices largely follows that book chapter. For more comprehensive discussions of how the CCP manages China's media, see Zhao Yuezhi's work (1998, 2000, and 2008). My colleague Rogier Creemers, who edits the substantive web database China Copyright and Media with its many authoritative translations of Chinese policy documents, has contextualized issues of privileged speech in China within their historical contexts, starting from the 19th century and moving through China's revolutions to contemporary attempts to manage digital media (Creemers 2016b).
6. Barmé (2013) provides a useful introduction to how civility is engineered in China. Andrew Kipnis (2011) has examined 'education for quality' in PRC classrooms, and Gary Sigley (2009) has analysed historically how the 'quality' discourse connects with what he calls 'technoscientific reasoning'. On attempts by the CCP to boost its 'social engineering' capacities through new and improved administrative techniques, see Pieke (2012).
7. On censorship and propaganda in China, see Brady (2008), Chan (2007), Deibert, Palfrey, Rohozinski, and Zittrain (2010: 449–487), Esarey (2005), Hassid (2008), Zhang (2009), and Zhao (1998). Pye (2008) provides an overview of traditional political culture in China. See Munro (1969) on officially sanctioned role models of political behavior in premodern China, and Idema and Haft (1997: 47–60) on the moral obligation of earlier states to engage in censorship.
8. Such network structures were first conceptualized by Paul Baran (1964) as part of a collaborative Cold War project by the libertarian RAND Corporation and the US Air Force. The project aimed to construct communication networks that could survive a nuclear attack. Baran's vision of distributed information came to form the basis of the ARPANET, which later became the internet. See also Walker Rettberg (2014: 1140).
9. See the various contributions in the 2015 special issue of the *Journal of Peace Research* (52/3), especially Weidmann's introduction to politics and network properties (2015a: 265) and his analysis of how ICT-enabled communication across borders 'adds a new layer of

interstate linkages' that amplifies 'society-level grievances as drivers of ethnic violence' (2015b: 293–294). Warren (2015: 300) has provided an intriguing study of how classic mass-media technologies and social ICT each have a very different 'capacity to systematically alter the incentives facing competing producers of political ideas', with traditional mass media generally facilitating stability whereas social media create conflict. Note, however, that the studies in the special issue take somewhat different positions to those I have taken in this book regarding the usefulness of dichotomies such as democratic systems versus authoritarian regimes, and that they generally assume that technologies are value-free, a notion I have criticized in chapter 2.

10. On the 'internet superpower' strategy, see People's Net (2015b). The 'national big data strategy' and its position in the 13th Five Year Plan is discussed on the cadre-training website Study China (2015). The 'Internet Plus' plan is laid out by the PRC State Council (2015). Creemers (2015) has provided a full English translation.

11. The following example comes from personal correspondence with Christian Göbel, who has explored the various dimensions of e-government, participation, and shifting policy priorities in Göbel (2014, 2015). On e-government, see also Schlæger (2013).

## Chapter 9

1. Smith's argument about ICT and their potential to spread ideas across traditional borders seemed to be meant as a critique of the potential cultural imperialism to which such communication patterns give rise, for example in the form of Hollywood's near-global cultural hegemony. Smith also recognizes that dissatisfaction with this kind of imperialism may re-invigorate the nation and its state. Nevertheless, he overall seems to view ICTs as challengers to nationalism.

2. This is not to say that processes of meaning-making, such as collective remembering, are a 'free-for-all': meanings do indeed often emerge in new and unexpected ways, but they do so systematically, based on predefined 'input spaces' of meaning, and following established patterns in human cognition and communication (see Fauconnier & Turner 2002); this is precisely why it remains important to pay attention to mainstream discourse. It is through such discourse that we can trace the common conceptual frameworks and shared semiotic resources that provide the markers for how people make sense of the world.

3. Li et al. (2012) have provided a study of African communities in Guangzhou. On the reality TV show contestant Lou Jing and the debates she elicited, see Frazier and Zhang (2014) and Leung (2015).

4. See the various contributions in Jenner and Thuy (2016) for a state-of-the-field overview of the conflicting claims in the South China Sea.

5. Based on an analysis of cases from 2010, Johnston (2013) has challenged the idea that Chinese foreign policy has generally become more assertive, arguing that ill-informed claims about such ambitions narrow potential policy options, for example, with regard to the South China Sea. Zhou (2016) similarly questions whether Chinese foreign policy is increasingly 'assertive', making the case that the South China Sea overall ranks relatively low on policy-makers' agenda, leading to measured and pragmatic behaviour on the part of PRC actors. Such depictions do not fit easily with the frequent hyperbole the issue elicits, for example in the wake of the 2016 ruling by the Permanent Court of Arbitration in The Hague (PCA 2016), which sparked strong nationalist indignation across digital China.

6. For a discussion of Friedman's misrepresentation of McLuhan's 'global village' as a 'flat' earth, see Pariser (2012: 281).

7. Blyth and Matthijs (2017) have argued that much of the 'surprise' surrounding global populism stems from a failure to assess the macroeconomic dynamics that have created populist dissatisfaction with wealth inequalities. For an excellent critique of the seeming 'implausibility' of Brexit from a feminist perspective, see Hozić and True (2017).

8. On Donald Trump's hijacking of the Republican Party, see Ware (2016). Schmidt (2017) has linked Brexit and Trumpism in her discursive institutional study of populist developments across the Atlantic.

9. Note how certain commentators in China have been quick to claim that the PRC's extensive information and communication controls should be considered a prescient and much-needed policy for effectively preventing 'fake news' from spreading, and that China's media logic demonstrates the ostensible superiority of Chinese governance over 'Western' approaches (e.g., Ran 2017). Such accounts fail to mention the many high-profile cases of Chinese citizens falling prey to so-called online rumours, the degree to which such cases are made possible by the very insecurities that information controls in China have generated, and the amount of anxiety that these cases generate among Chinese leaders. Clearly the PRC is far from exempt when it comes to the effects of viral misinformation. Conveniently, such accounts also omit that the CCP itself has perfected the practice of astroturfing and 'fake news' circulation, reportedly creating about 448 million fabricated social media comments each year (King et al. 2017).

# Glossary of Technical Terms

**Authoritarian technic:** any mechanisms aimed at organizing a social process by emphasizing centralization of power and compliance with decisions.

**Betweenness:** a measure of a node's centrality that represents its power within a network, based on the number of times that the node acts as a connection along the shortest path between other nodes.

**Bias:** a distorted perspective, based on material, social, and/or subjective factors. Bias is negative when its selection mechanism relies on counterfactuals that other actors have intentionally manipulated, e.g., for personal gains. Bias is positive when its selection mechanism relies on facts that confirm expectations.

**Censorship:** any authoritative act that intentionally influences the production, release, or circulation of information, based on a claim to protect the public interest.

**Centrality:** a measure of a node's importance within a network.

**Community network:** a network of nodes in which each node maintains connections with at least two other members of the network.

**Complexity:** any system of interlinking components that exhibits non-trivial adaptive, emergent, and self-organizing behaviours.

**Cultural governance:** the process of indirectly regulating society by regulating culture, that is: any authoritative action that aims to manage the symbolic context within which a political issue is situated.

**Data:** sets of signifiers that have been assigned value and can be selected and combined in ways that carry potential meaning.

**Degree:** the number of connections that a node maintains with other nodes in a network.

**Democratic technic:** any mechanisms aimed at organizing a social process by emphasizing egalitarian participation and consensus-building.

**Digital bias:** the provision of selective information by digital media technologies that systematically draw on and assess the salience of data, based on algorithmic interpretations of material, social, and subjective biases.

**Digital China:** all digital information and networks in the People's Republic of China, including the digitally enabled actors who access and interact in these networks.

**Discourse:** communication practices that systematically construct our knowledge of reality as commonly accepted truths.

**Edge:** the link or tie between two nodes in a network. Edges can be unidirectional (pointing from one node to another) or bidirectional (pointing back and forth between two nodes). An edge's 'rank' measures its strength, that is: the number of links between the two nodes.

**Eigenvector centrality:** a measure of a node's centrality that represents its authority within a network, calculated as a function of the connections the node maintains with other authoritative nodes.

**Executive permission:** the ability to execute scripts in networks and assign network permissions to other actors.

**Framing:** using sets of signs to force a particular code onto a communication process, thereby guiding the perception, understanding, or interpretation of the communicated information.

**Governance:** any attempt to govern by reaching beyond the level of the state and including private institutions and actors in the process, usually in ways that re-define the governing process in terms of cost-effective and efficient market exchanges.

**Hyperlink:** a digital object that points a browser to a specific file on the internet.

**Imagined community:** any group of human beings with a common belief in a collective purpose, culture, history, or ancestry, in which some members do not maintain direct personal ties with each other.

**Information:** any piece of data to which a sentient being has attributing meaning.

**Medium:** the container or conduit through which data and information are transmitted or stored.

**Media ecology:** the complex systems of people, hardware, and software that create and spread discourse in various media, according to the logic inherent to the system and its institutions.

**Multi-modal communication:** communication that combines different levels of symbolic representation to relay its messages, for instance by stacking both visual and acoustic signs in the service of the same communication process.

**Nation/national community:** any group of people who imagine themselves as a territorially bound community, based on a belief in a collective purpose, shared history, culture, language, and/or ethnic ancestry, and aspiring to maintain or establish political autonomy (i.e., a nation state).

**Nationalism:** the sentiment and cognitive framework in which the nation features as a major element of personal identity and as the primary locus of political organization.

**Nation state:** any polity of a territorially defined, imagined community that claims political autonomy.

**Needs:** psychological mechanisms that motivate humans to satisfy perceived requirements in their lives.

**Network:** a system of interconnected actors or things, each represented as a node and connected to other network elements through edges.

**Network permission:** a set of rules that determine access to a network, assigned to actors or groups of actors on the basis of previous social processes. Network permissions include (combinations of) the ability to read objects, write or modify them, execute their functions, or alter the permissions of other actors.

**Node:** an actor or object in a network.

**Pathos formula:** a recurring pattern of symbols that, based on a previously established social convention, is connected to a specific emotional response.

**Patriotic community:** any group of people who imagine themselves as a community, based on a belief in a collective purpose, shared history, culture, language, and/or ethnic ancestry that is associated with a specific territorially defined homeland.

**Patriotism:** the sentiment and cognitive framework in which a territorially defined imagined community features as a major element of personal identity.

**Polity:** any formal set of political institutions that regulate human behavior.

**Priming:** the act of anchoring meanings, associations, and emotions through continuous exposure to certain signs.

**Programming power:** the ability to set the values of a network by infusing it with specific discourses.

**Read permission:** the ability to access the information contained in a networked object.

**Search engine:** an algorithm designed to systematically screen data, filter that data based on user queries and digital biases, and return the result to users as actionable information.

**Small-scale community:** any group of human beings with a common belief in a collective purpose, culture, history, or ancestry, in which the members maintain direct personal ties with each other.

**State:** any polity of a territorially defined community.

**Switching power:** the ability to establish or interrupt links within a network.

**Technology:** any systematic, practical application of human knowledge.

**Write permission:** the ability to modify the information contained in a networked object.

# References

Ahlers, Anna L., Heberer, Thomas, & Schubert, Gunter (2015), '"Authoritarian Resilience" and Effective Policy Implementation in Contemporary China: A Local State Perspective'. *Duisburg Working Papers on East Asia*, 99, 1–27.

Allan, George (1972), 'Croce and Whitehead on Concrescence'. *Process Studies*, 2(2), 95–111.

An, Shanshan & Yang, Boxu (2010), 'Zhongguo wangluo yulunzhong minzu zhuyi de chengxian tezheng ji yingxiang—yi Zhongwen BBS luntan she ri yiti wei kaocha duixiang de shizheng yanjiu' (Nationalism in Chinese Online Opinion, Its Rise and Its Impact: An Empirical Study of Anti-Japanese Discussions in Chat-Forums). *MediaResearch.cn*, retrieved 1 September 2017 from http://xinwen.cssn.cn/xmtyj/xmt/201009/t20100911_1967998.shtml.

Anderson, Benedict (2006), *Imagined Communities* (3rd ed.). London & New York: Verso.

Armstrong, Gary & Giulianotti, Richard (eds.) (1999), *Football Cultures and Identities*. London: Palgrave Macmillan.

Arora, Payal (2012), 'The Leisure Divide: Can the "Third World" Come out to Play?' *Information Development*, 28(1), 93–101.

Austin, Greg & Harris, Stuart (2001), *Japan and Greater China—Political Economy and Military Power in the Asian Century*. London: Hurst & Co.

Bai, Daijin (2015, February 18), 'Weibo Is Dying Out'. *MCLC Resource Centre*, retrieved 1 September 2017 from http://u.osu.edu/mclc/2015/02/18/weibo-is-dying-out/.

Bao, Peng, Shen, Hua-Wei, Huang, Junming, & Cheng, Xue-Qi (2013), 'Popularity Prediction in Microblogging Network: A Case Study on Sina Weibo'. Paper presented at the 22nd International World Wide Web Conference, retrieved 1 September 2017 from http://arxiv.org/abs/1304.4324.

Baran, Paul (1964), *On Distributed Communications*. Santa Monica, CA: The RAND Corporation.

Barbalet, Jack M. (2001), *Emotion, Social Theory, and Social Structure*. Cambridge: Cambridge University Press.

Barefoot, Peter (2012, August 23), 'Japanese Nationalists on Diaoyu Islands, Netizen Reactions'. *chinaSMACK*, retrieved 1 September 2017 from http://www.chinasmack.com/2012/pictures/japanese-nationalists-on-diaoyu-islands-chinese-netizen-reactions.html.

Barlow, Aaron (2007), *The Rise of the Blogosphere*. Westport: Greenwood Publishing.

Barmé, Geremie (2009), 'China's Flat Earth: History and 8 August 2008'. *The China Quarterly*, 197, 64–86.

Barmé, Geremie (2013), 'Introduction: Engineering Chinese Civilisation'. In Barmé, Geremie & Goldkorn, Jeremy (eds.), *Civilizing China: China Story Yearbook 2013*. Canberra: Australian Centre on China in the World (pp. x–xxix).

Barmé, Geremie, Goldkorn, Jeremy, Cartier, Carolyn, & Davies, Gloria (2012), 'Voices from the Blogosphere'. In Barmé, Geremie (ed.), *China Story Yearbook 2012: Red Rising: Red Eclipse* (online ed.). ANU: Australian Centre on China in the World. Retrieved 1 September 2017 from https://www.thechinastory.org/yearbooks/yearbook-2012/.

Baudrillard, Jean (1983), *Simulations*. Los Angeles: Semiotext(e).

BBC (2011, June 5), 'Could London Declare Independence and Leave the UK?' *BBC Online*, retrieved 1 September 2017 from http://www.bbc.com/news/uk-politics-13661001.

BBC (2014, February 25), 'China Mulls Holiday Marking Japanese Defeat and Nanjing Massacre'. *BBC Online*, retrieved 1 September 2017 from http://www.bbc.com/news/world-asia-26342884.

BBC (2017, May 12), ' "Proud to Be Japanese" Posters Star Chinese Woman'. *BBC News*, retrieved 1 September 2017 from http://www.bbc.com/news/world-asia-39880212.

Beaulieu, Anne (2005), 'Sociable Hyperlinks: An Ethnographic Approach to Connectivity'. In Hine, Christine (ed.), *Virtual Methods—Issues in Social Research on the Internet*. Oxford & New York: Berg (pp. 183–197).

Beck, Ulrich (1992), *Risk Society: Towards a New Modernity*. Los Angeles et al.: Sage.

Beck, Ulrich (2007), *Power in the Global Age*. Cambridge & Malden: Polity Press.

Becker, Konrad & Stalder, Felix (eds.) (2009), *Deep Search: The Politics of Search Engines Beyond Google*. Edison, NJ: Transaction.

Beech, Hannah (2015, December 9), 'Xi Jinping, Leader of World's Largest Online Censor, to Address World Internet Conference'. *Time*, retrieved 1 September 2017 from http://time.com/4142305/xi-jinping-china-censorship-world-internet-conference/.

Beer, David & Burrows, Roger (2007), 'Sociology and, of and in Web 2.0—Some Initial Considerations'. *Sociological Research Online*, 12(5), retrieved 1 September 2017 from http://www.socresonline.org.uk/12/5/17.html.

Beijing Time (2003, December 5), 'Toyota Apologizes to Chinese Consumers for Improper Ads'. *People's Daily Online*, retrieved 1 September 2017 from http://en.people.cn/200312/05/eng20031205_129766.shtml.

Bell, Daniel A. (2015), *The China Model: Political Meritocracy and the Limits of Democracy*. Princeton: Princeton University Press.

Benkler, Yochai (2006), *The Wealth of Networks—How Social Production Transforms Markets and Freedom*. New Haven and London: Yale University Press.

Benney, Jonathan (2014), 'The Aesthetics of Chinese Microblogging: State and Market Control of Weibo'. *Asiascape: Digital Asia*, 1(3), 169–200.

Billig, Michael (2009), *Banal Nationalism* (9th ed.). London et al.: SAGE.

Billig, Michael (2013), *Learn to Write Badly: How to Succeed in the Social Sciences* (Kindle ed.). Cambridge et al.: Cambridge University Press.

Bingdou Linglong (2013, April 11), 'Taiwan xiading maiguo juexin: Hui quli Diaoyudao shuiyu dalu yuchuan' (Taiwan Presents as Its Bride-Price a Resolution That Sells Out the Country: May Expel Mainland Fishing Vessels Entering Diaoyu Island Waters). *Xilu*, retrieved 1 September 2017 from http://www.xilu.com/20130411/news_933_344176.html.

Blanchard, Jean-Marc F. (2000), 'The U.S. Role in the Sino-Japanese Dispute over the Diaoyu (Senkaku) Islands, 1945–1971'. *The China Quarterly*, 161, 95–123.

Bolter, David & Grusin, Richard (2000), *Remediation—Understanding New Media*. Cambridge MA: MIT Press.

Bondes, Maria & Schucher, Günter (2014), 'Derailed Emotions: The Transformation of Claims and Targets during the Wenzhou Online Incident'. *Information, Communication and Society*, 17(1), 45–65.

Brady, Anne-Marie (2008), *Marketing Dictatorship—Propaganda and Thought Work in Contemporary China*. Lanham & Plymouth: Rowman & Littlefield.

Branigan, Tania (2014, November 28), 'China Bans Wordplay in Attempt at Pun Control'. *The Guardian*, retrieved 1 September 2017 from http://www.theguardian.com/world/2014/nov/28/china-media-watchdog-bans-wordplay-puns.

Braun, Kathryn A., Ellis, Rhiannon, & Loftus, Elizabeth F. (2002), 'Make My Memory: How Advertising Can Change Our Memories of the Past'. Cornell University, School of Hospitality

Administration, retrieved 18 March 2018 from http://scholarship.sha.cornell.edu/articles/332.

Breslin, Shaun & Shen, Simon (2010), 'Online Chinese Nationalism'. *Chatham House Asia Programme Paper ASP PP 2010/03*, retrieved 1 September 2017 from: https://www.chathamhouse.org/sites/files/chathamhouse/public/Research/Asia/0910breslin_shen.pdf.

Breuilly, John (1993), *Nationalism and the State* (2nd ed.). Chicago: The University of Chicago Press.

Breuilly, John (ed.) (2013), *The Oxford Handbook of the History of Nationalism.* Oxford: Oxford University Press.

Britannica (n.d.), 'Technology'. *Encyclopaedia Britannica online*, retrieved 1 September 2017 from http://www.britannica.com/topic/technology.

Brodsgaard, Kjeld Erik & Zheng Yongnian (eds.) (2006), *The Chinese Communist Party in Reform.* London: Routledge.

Bruns, Axel (2007), 'Methodologies for Mapping the Political Blogosphere: An Exploration Using the IssueCrawler Research Tool'. *First Monday*, 12(5), retrieved 1 September 2017 from http://eprints.qut.edu.au/7832/1/7832.pdf.

Bullingham, Liam & Vasconcelos, Ana (2013), '"The Presentation of Self in the Online World": Goffman and the Study of Online Identities'. *Journal of Information Science*, 39(1), 101–112.

Burke, Peter (2013), 'Nationalisms and Vernaculars, 1500–1800'. In Breuilly, John (ed.), *The Oxford Handbook of the History of Nationalism.* Oxford: Oxford University Press (pp. 21–35).

Burnett, Dean (2013, April 9), 'The Only Susan Greenfield Article You'll Ever Need'. *The Guardian*, retrieved 1 September 2017 from http://www.theguardian.com/science/brain-flapping/2013/apr/09/susan-greenfield-article-how-to-guide.

Burns, John P. (2003), '"Downsizing" the Chinese State: Government Retrenchment in the 1990s'. *The China Quarterly*, 175, 775–802.

Buruma, Ian (2002), 'The Nanjing Massacre as a Historical Symbol'. In Li, Feifei, Sabella, Robert, & Liu, David (eds.), *Nanking 1937: Memory and Healing.* Armonk, NY: M.E. Sharpe (pp. 1–9).

Callahan, William A. (2006), *Cultural Governance and Resistance in Pacific Asia.* Abingdon & New York: Routledge.

Callahan, William A. (2010), *China—The Pessoptimist Nation.* Oxford: Oxford University Press.

Callahan, William A. (2013), *China Dreams: 20 Visions of the Future.* Oxford et al.: Oxford University Press.

Carr, Nicholas (2010), *The Shallows: How the Internet Is Changing the Way We Think, Read and Remember.* New York: W.W. Norton.

Carrico, Kevin & Gries, Peter (2016), 'Race, Knowledge Production and Chinese Nationalism'. *Nations and Nationalism*, 22(3), 428–432.

Carroll, Noël (1998), *A Philosophy of Mass Art.* Oxford et al.: Oxford University Press.

Carter, Liz (2015), *Let 100 Voices Speak—How the Internet Is Transforming China and Changing Everything.* New York: I.B. Tauris.

Castells, Manuel (2001), *The Internet Galaxy—Reflections on the Internet, Business, and Society.* Oxford et al.: Oxford University Press.

Castells, Manuel (2009), *Communication Power.* Oxford et al.: Oxford University Press.

Castells, Manuel (2010), *The Information Age* (2nd ed.). Oxford et al.: Wiley-Blackwell.

Cave, Peter (2012), 'Japanese Colonialism and the Asia-Pacific War in Japan's History Textbooks: Changing Representations and Their Causes'. *Modern Asian Studies*, 47(2), 542–580.

Central Propaganda Department (2013), 'Jiang wenming, shu xinfeng—gongyi guanggao' (Discussing Civilization, Cultivating New Trends—Public Service Announcements). CCP Central Civilization Office, retrieved 1 September 2017 from http://www.wenming.cn/jwmsxf_294/zggygg/.

CERNET (2001, January 1), 'Evolution of Internet in China'. *China Education and Research Network*, retrieved 1 September 2017 from http://www.edu.cn/introduction_1378/20060323/t20060323_4285.shtml.

Ceruzzi, Paul E. (2012), *Computing—A Concise History*. Cambridge MA: MIT Press.

CFDD (2007, December 12), 'Shi er yue shi san ri, ta shi Zhongguo zui meili de nühai' (On 13 December, she was China's most beautiful girl). *Chinese Federation for Defending the Diaoyus*, retrieved 18 March 2018 from https://web.archive.org/web/20080629032414/http://www.cfdd.org.cn:80/html/76/n-476.html.

Chabert, Jean-Luc (ed.) (2013), *A History of Algorithms: From the Pebble to the Microchip*. Berlin et al.: Springer.

Chadwick, Andrew (2013), *The Hybrid Media System—Politics and Power*. Oxford: Oxford University Press.

Chan, Alex (2007), 'Guiding Public Opinion Through Social Agenda-Setting: China's Media Policy since the 1990s'. *Journal of Contemporary China*, 16(53), 547–559.

Chang, Iris (1997/2012), *The Rape of Nanking: The Forgotten Holocaust of World War II* (Kindle ed.). New York: Basic Books.

Chao, Eveline (2016, April 4), 'A Week Behind the Great Firewall of China'. *Fast Company*, retrieved 1 September 2017 from http://www.fastcompany.com/3056721/most-innovative-companies/a-week-behind-the-great-firewall-of-china.

Chen, Lisha, Chin, Fei Goh, Sun, Yifan, & Amran, Rasli (2017), 'Integrating Guanxi into Technology Acceptance: An Empirical Investigation of WeChat'. *Telematics and Informatics*, ahead of print, retrieved 1 September 2017 from http://www.sciencedirect.com/science/article/pii/S073658531630524X.

Chen, Te-Ping (2014, November 28), 'Nowhere to Pun amid China Crackdown'. *The Wall Street Journal China Real Time*, retrieved 1 September 2017 from http://blogs.wsj.com/chinarealtime/2014/11/28/chinas-latest-crackdown-puns/.

Chen, Xiaojin (2016), *The Effects of the Internet on Collective Democratic Action in China*. PhD Thesis. London: King's College.

Chen, Yashu (2017), 'WeChat Use Among Chinese College Students: Exploring Gratifications and Political Engagement in China'. *Journal of International and Intercultural Communication*, 10(1), 25–43.

Cheung, Anne S. Y. (2009), 'A Study of Cyber-Violence and Internet Service Providers' Liability: Lessons from China'. *Pacific Rim Law and Policy Journal*, 18(2), 323–346.

Chhabra, Deepak, Healy, Robert, & Sills, Erin (2003), 'Staged Authenticity and Heritage Tourism'. *Annals of Tourism Research*, 30(3), 702–719.

Chilton, Paul (2004), *Analysing Political Discourse—Theory and Practice*. New York: Routledge.

Chin, Josh (2013, September 9), 'China Tightens Grip on Social Media – 'Slanderous' Content Reposted 500 Times Will Result in Charges'. *Wall Street Journal*, retrieved 18 March 2018 from http://www.wsj.com/articles/SB10001424127887324549004579065113098846226.

Chin, Josh & Wong, Chun Han (2015, February 12), 'China's Internet Censors Now Have Their Own Theme Song, and It Is Glorious'. *China Real Time*, retrieved 1 September 2017 from http://blogs.wsj.com/chinarealtime/2015/02/12/chinas-internet-censors-now-have-their-own-theme-song-and-it-is-glorious/.

China Daily (2005, May 18), 'Hong Kong Marshal Jackie Chan to Boost Chinese Nationalism'. *China Daily News*, retrieved 1 September 2017 from http://www.chinadaily.com.cn/english/doc/2005-05/18/content_443738.htm.

China Daily (2016, February 22), 'State Media Should Play Due Role in Properly Guiding Public Opinion'. *China Daily*, retrieved 1 September 2017 from http://www.chinadaily.com.cn/opinion/2016-02/22/content_23580181.htm.

ChinaFile (2016, March 15), 'What's Driving the Current Storm of Chinese Censorship? A ChinaFile Conversation'. *Asia Society Center on US-China Relations*, retrieved 1 September 2017 from http://www.chinafile.com/conversation/whats-driving-current-storm-chinese-censorship.

China News (2014, August 1), 'Riben jueding gei 158 ge li dao mingming—han Diaoyudao fushu daoyu' (Japan Decides to Name 158 Separate Islands, Including Subsidiary Islets of the Diaoyu Islands). *Zhongguo xinwen wang*, retrieved 1 September 2017 from http://news.china.com.cn/2014-08/01/content_33116940.htm.

Chomsky, Noam (2013), *On Anarchism*. New York & London: The New Press.

Choong, William (2014), 'The Senkaku/Diaoyu Dispute'. *Adelphi Series*, 54(445), 59–92.

Chubb, Andrew (2012, September 23), 'A Cautionary Tale from the Beijing Youth Daily: Misfortune of One Driver in the Xi'an Anti-Japanese Protests'. *Southseaconversations*, retrieved 1 September 2017 from https://southseaconversations.wordpress.com/2012/09/23/a-cautionary-tale-from-the-beijing-youth-daily-misfortune-of-a-xian-car-driver-in-the-xian-anti-japanese-protests/.

Chun, Allen (1996), 'Fuck Chineseness: On the Ambiguities of Ethnicity as Cultural Identity'. *boundary 2*, 23(2), 111–138.

Clinton, Hillary R. (2010, January 21): 'Remarks on Internet Freedom'. Speech delivered at *The Newseum*, Washington DC. Retrieved 1 September 2017 from https://2009-2017.state.gov/secretary/20092013clinton/rm/2010/01/135519.htm.

Clinton, William J. (2000, March 8), 'Full Text of Clinton's Speech on China Trade Bill'. *The New York Times*, retrieved 1 September 2017 from http://partners.nytimes.com/library/world/asia/030900clinton-china-text.html.

CNNIC (2009), '1997 nian–1999 nian hulianwang dashiji' (Internet Event Chronicle, 1997–1999). *China Internet Network Information Centre Online*, retrieved 1 September 2017 from http://www.cnnic.cn/hlwfzyj/hlwdsj/201206/t20120612_27416.htm.

CNNIC (2015), '35th Statistical Report on Internet Development in China (January 2015)'. *China Internet Network Information Centre Online*, retrieved 1 September 2017 from https://cnnic.com.cn/IDR/ReportDownloads/201507/P020150720486421654597.pdf.

CNNIC (2016), '38th Statistical Report on Internet Development in China (July 2016)'. *China Internet Network Information Centre Online*, retrieved 1 September 2017 from .

CNNIC (2017), '39th Statistical Report on Internet Development in China (January 2017)'. *China Internet Network Information Centre Online*, retrieved 18 March 2018 from https://cnnic.com.cn/IDR/ReportDownloads/201706/P020170608523740585924.pdf.

CNZZ (2014), 'Suosuo yinqing shiyong qingkuang fenxi baogao' (Report on Search Engine Usage). Retrieved 19 October 2015 from http://engine.data.cnzz.com/.

Coates, Jamie (2014), 'Rogue Diva Flows: Aoi Sola's reception in Chinese Media'. *Journal of Japanese and Korean Cinema*, 6(1), 89–103.

Cohen, Paul (2002), 'Remembering and Forgetting: National Humiliation in Twentieth-Century China'. *Twentieth-Century China*, 27(2), 1–39.

Colbert, Stephen (2006, July 31), 'The Wørd: Wikiality'. *The Colbert Report*, retrieved 1 September 2017 from http://www.cc.com/video-clips/z1aahs/the-colbert-report-the-word---wikiality.

Cole, Michael J. (2014, March 5): 'Kunming Massacre Sparks Media War'. *China Policy Institute Blog*, retrieved 1 September 2017 from http://blogs.nottingham.ac.uk/chinapolicyinstitute/2014/03/05/kunming-massacre-sparks-media-war/.

Conover, Michael D., Ratkiewicz, Jacob, Francisco, Matthew, Goncalves, Bruno, Menczer, Filippo, & Flammini, Alessandro (2011), 'Political Polarization on Twitter'. Paper presented on 5 July 2011 at the *Fifth International AAAI Conference on Weblogs and Social Media*, retrieved on 1 September 2017 from: https://www.aaai.org/ocs/index.php/ICWSM/ICWSM11/paper/view/2847.

Creemers, Rogier (2015, July 1), 'State Council Guiding Opinions Concerning Vigorously Moving Forward the 'Internet Plus' Plan', *China Copyright and Media* translation of State Council document 2015(40), retrieved 1 September 2017 from https://chinacopyrightandmedia.wordpress.com/2015/07/01/state-council-guiding-opinions-concerning-vigorously-moving-forward-the-internet-plus-plan/.

Creemers, Rogier (2016a), 'Internet Plus'. Paper prepared for Leiden University conference *Digital Disruption in Asia*.

Creemers, Rogier (2016b), 'The Privilege of Speech and New Media: Conceptualizing China's Communications Law in the Internet Age'. In deLisle, Jacques, Goldstein, Avery, & Yang, Guobin (eds.), *The Internet, Social Media, and a Changing China*. Philadelphia: University of Pennsylvania Press (pp. 86–105).

Cruz, Consuelo (2000), 'Identity and Persuasion: How Nations Remember Their Pasts and Make Their Futures'. *World Politics*, 52(3), 275–312.

Damasio, Antonio (2010), *Self Comes to Mind—Constructing the Conscious Brain*, London: Random House.

Damm, Jens & Thomas, Simona (eds.) (2006), *Chinese Cyberspaces: Technological Changes and Political Effects*. London & New York.

Dayan, Daniel & Katz, Elihu (1992), *Media Events: The Live Broadcasting of History*. Cambridge, MA: Harvard University Press.

De Seta, Gabriele (2015), *Dajiangyou: Media Practices of Vernacular Creativity in Postdigital China*. PhD thesis, Hong Kong Polytechnic University.

Dean, Jody (2003), 'Why the Net Is Not a Public Sphere'. *Constellations*, 10(1), 95–112.

Dean, Jody (2010), *Blog Theory: Feedback and Capture in the Circuits of Drive*. Cambridge & Malden, MA: Polity Press.

Deibert, Ronald, Palfrey, John, Rohozinski, Rafal, & Zittrain, Jonathan (eds.) (2010), *Access Controlled: The Shaping of Power, Rights, and Rule in Cyberspace*. Cambridge, MA: MIT Press.

Denton, Kirk A. (2014), *Exhibiting the Past—Historical Memory and the Politics of Museums in Postsocialist China*. Honolulu: University of Hawai'i Press.

Derczynski, Leon (2017a, April 3), 'Pathology of a Fake News Story'. *Thoughts on Journalism*, retrieved 1 September 2017 from https://medium.com/thoughts-on-journalism/pathology-of-a-fake-news-story-aa572e6764e8.

Derczynski, Leon (2017b, April 7), 'Four Ways to Spot Fake News Accounts'. *Politics Means Politics*, retrieved 1 September 2017 from https://politicsmeanspolitics.com/four-ways-to-spot-fake-news-accounts-d23098d93350.

Diamond, Jared (1999), *Guns, Germs, and Steel—The Fate of Human Societies*. New York & London: Norton.

Diamond, Larry (2010), 'Liberation Technology'. *Journal of Democracy*, 21, 69–83, retrieved 1 September 2017 from http://www.journalofdemocracy.org/articles/gratis/Diamond-21-3.pdf.

DiNucci, Darcy (1999), 'Fragmented Future'. *Print*, 53(4), 32, 221–222, retrieved 1 September 2017 from http://darcyd.com/fragmented_future.pdf.

Dirlik, Arif (2015, July 29), 'Born in Translation: "China" in the Making of "Zhongguo"'. *Boundary 2*, retrieved 1 September 2017 from http://boundary2.org/2015/07/29/born-in-translation-china-in-the-making-of-zhongguo/.

Dörner, Dietrich (1996), *The Logic of Failure: Recognizing and Avoiding Error in Complex Situations*. New York: Basic Books.

Dörner, Dietrich (2001), *Bauplan für eine Seele (Blueprint for a Soul)*. Hamburg: Rowohlt.

Drummond, David (2010, March 22), 'A New Approach to China: An Update'. *Google Official Blog*, retrieved 1 September 2017 from https://googleblog.blogspot.nl/2010/03/new-approach-to-china-update.html.

Druxes, Helga (2016), '"Montag ist wieder Pegida-Tag!" Pegida's Community Building and Discursive Strategy'. *German Politics and Society*, 34(4), 17–33.

Duara, Prasenjit (2015), 'The Agenda of Asian Studies and Digital Media in the Anthropocene'. *Asiascape: Digital Asia*, 2(1), 11–19.

Duara, Prasenjit (2016), 'The Temporal Analytics of Nationalism'. *Nations and Nationalism*, 22(3), 419–423.

Eagleton, Terry (1991/2007), *Ideology—An Introduction*. London & New York: Verso.

Eco, Umberto (1979), *A Theory of Semiotics*. Bloomington, IN: Indiana University Press.

Economist (2013, April 6), 'The Machinery of Control: Cat and Mouse'. *The Economist*, retrieved 1 September 2017 from http://www.economist.com/news/special-report/21574629-how-china-makes-sure-its-internet-abides-rules-cat-and-mouse.

Edelman, Benjamin (2011), 'Bias in Search Results? Diagnosis and Response'. *The Indian Journal of Law and Technology*, 7, 16–32.

Ellison, Nocle B., Vitak, Jessica, Gray, Rebecca, & Lampe, Cliff (2014), 'Cultivating Social Resources on Social Network Sites: Facebook Relationship Maintenance Behaviors and Their Role in Social Capital Processes'. *Journal of Computer-Mediated Communication*, 19(4), 855–870.

Elmer-DeWitt, Philip (1993, June 12), 'First Nation in Cyberspace'. *Time Magazine*, 142(24), 62–64.

Engesser, Sven, Ernst, Nicole, Esser, Frank, & Büchel, Florin (2017), 'Populism and Social Media: How Politicians Spread a Fragmented Ideology'. *Information, Communication and Society*, 20(8), 1109–1126.

Esarey, Ashley (2005), 'Cornering the Market: State Strategies for Controlling China's Commercial Media'. *Asian Perspective*, 29(4), 37–83.

Esarey, Ashley, & Qiang, Xiao (2008), 'Political Expression in the Chinese Blogosphere—Under the Radar'. *Asian Survey*, 48(5), 752–772.

Esarey, Ashley, & Qiang, Xiao (2011), 'Digital Communication and Political Change in China'. *International Journal of Communication*, 5, 298–319.

EU SME Centre (2015), 'The ICT Market in China'. *EU SME Centre and China Britain Business Council*, retrieved 1 September 2017 from http://www.ccilc.pt/sites/default/files/eu_sme_centre_report_-_the_ict_market_in_china_update_-_july_2015.pdf.

Evans, Richard J. (2003), 'Introduction: Redesigning the Past: History in Political Transition'. *Journal of Contemporary History*, 38(1), 5–12.

Fairbank, John K. & Goldman, Merle (2006), *China—A New History* (2nd ed.). Cambridge MA & London: Belknap Harvard.

Fairclough, Norman (1995), *Critical Discourse Analysis: The Critical Study of Language*. Harlow: Pearson Education Limited.

Fang, Kecheng (2015), 'Weibo, WeChat and the Chinese Culture of Connectivity'. Paper presented at the *International Conference on Communication and the Public: Social Media and Public Engagement* in Hangzhou on 13 June 2015.

Fang, Kecheng & Repnikova, Maria (2017), 'Demystifying "Little Pink": The Creation and Evolution of a Gendered Label for Nationalistic Activists in China'. *New Media and Society*, ahead of print.

Farrell, Henry & Drezner, Daniel W. (2008), 'The Power and Politics of Blogs'. *Public Choice*, 134, 15–30.

Farrell, Henry & Newman, Abraham (2017), 'BREXIT, Voice and Loyalty: Rethinking Electoral Politics in an Age of Interdependence'. *Review of International Political Economy*, 24(2), 242–247.

Fauconnier, Gilles & Turner, Mark (2002), *The Way We Think—Conceptual Blending and the Mind's Hidden Complexities*. New York: Basic Books.

Feng, Miao & Yuan, Elaine J. (2014), 'Public Opinion on Weibo: The Case of the Diaoyu Island Dispute'. In Hollihan, Thomas A. (ed.), *The Dispute over the Diaoyu/Senkaku Islands: How Media Narratives Shape Public Opinion and Challenge the Global Order*. New York: Palgrave Macmillan (pp. 119–140).

Feuz, Martin, Fuller, Matthew, & Stalder, Felix (2011), 'Personal Web Searching in the Age of Semantic Capitalism: Diagnosing the Mechanisms of Personalisation'. *First Monday*, 16(2). Retrieved 1 September 2017 from http://firstmonday.org/ojs/index.php/fm/article/view/3344/2766.

Fewsmith, Joseph (2008), *China Since Tiananmen* (2nd ed.). Cambridge et al.: Cambridge University Press.

Fisher, Max (2013, January 10), 'The Anti-Americanism of Jackie Chan'. *The Washington Post*, retrieved 1 September 2017 from https://www.washingtonpost.com/news/worldviews/wp/2013/01/10/the-anti-americanism-of-jackie-chan/.

Fogel, Joshua A. (ed.) (2000), *The Nanjing Massacre in History and Historiography*. Berkeley: University of California Press.

Foucault, Michel (1965/1988), *Madness and Civilization–A History of Insanity in the Age of Reason*. New York: Vintage Books.

Foucault, Michel (1978/1995), *Discipline and Punish: The Birth of the Prison*. New York: Vintage Books.

Foucault, Michel (1978/2009), *Security, Territory, Population—Lectures at the College de France, 1977–1978*. Hampshire & New York: Palgrave Macmillan.

Frater, Patrick (2013, December 19), 'Li Ruigang's CMC Buys Stake in Caixin Media'. *Variety*, retrieved 1 September 2017 from http://variety.com/2013/biz/news/li-ruigangs-cmc-buys-stake-in-caixin-media-1200978643/.

Frazier, Robeson Taj & Zhang, Lin (2014), 'Ethnic Identity and Racial Contestation in Cyberspace: Deconstructing the Chineseness of Lou Jing'. *China Information*, 28(2), 237–258.

Freeden, Michael (2017), 'After the Brexit Referendum: Revisiting Populism as an Ideology'. *Journal of Political Ideologies*, 22(1), 1–11.

Friedman, Edward (1995), *National Identity and Democratic Prospects in Socialist China*. Abingdon & New York: Routledge.

Frith, Chris (2007), *Making Up the Mind—How the Brain Creates Our Mental World*. Malden, MA, et al.: Blackwell Publishing.

Frost, Catherine (2006), 'Internet Galaxy Meets Postnational Constellation: Prospects for Political Solidarity after the Internet'. *Information Society*, 22(1), 45–49.

Fu, King-wa, Chan, Chung-hong, & Chao, Michael (2013), 'Assessing Censorship on Microblogs in China: Discriminatory Keyword Analysis and Impact Evaluation of the "Real Name Registration" Policy'. *IEEE Internet Computing*, 17(3), 42–50. Retrieved 1 September 2017 from http://papers.ssrn.com/sol3/papers.cfm?abstract_id=2265271.

Fuchs, Christian (2014), *Digital Labour and Karl Marx*. New York & London: Routledge.

Fuchs, Christian (2015), 'Baidu, Weibo and Renren: The Global Political Economy of Social Media in China'. *Asian Journal of Communication*, First View.

Fuller, Matthew (2005), *Media Ecologies: Materialist Energies in Art and Technoculture*. Cambridge, MA & London: MIT Press.

Gan, Chunmei (2017), 'Understanding WeChat Users' Liking Behavior: An Empirical Study in China'. *Computers in Human Behavior*, 68, 30–39.

Gang, Qian & Bandurski, David (2011), 'China's Emerging Public Sphere: The Impact of Media Commercialization, Professionalism, and the Internet in an Era of Transition'. In Shirk, Suzan L. (ed.), *Changing Media, Changing China*. Oxford: Oxford University Press (pp. 38–76).

Gao, Fangfang & Martin-Kratzer, Renee (2011), 'Gender Differences in Chinese Journalists' Blogs'. *Chinese Journal of Communication*, 4(2), 167–181.

Gao, Helen (2015, February 2), 'China Sharpens Its Censorship Blade'. *The New York Times*, retrieved 1 September 2017 from http://mobile.nytimes.com/2015/02/03/opinion/china-sharpens-its-censorship-blade.html.

Garry, Maryanne, Manning, Charles G., Loftus, Elizabeth F., & Sherman, Steven J. (1996), 'Imagination Inflation: Imagining a Childhood Event Inflates Confidence That It Occurred'. *Psychonomic Bulletin and Review*, 3(2), 208–214. Retrieved 17 March 2018 from http://faculty.washington.edu/eloftus/Articles/Imagine.htm.

Gellner, Ernest (1983/2006), *Nations and Nationalism* (2nd ed.). Oxford: Blackwell.

Gernet, Jacques (1972/2002), *A History of Chinese Civilization* (2nd ed.). Cambridge et al.: Cambridge University Press.

Geuss, Raymond (1981), *The Idea of a Critical Theory—Habermas and the Frankfurt School*. Cambridge: Cambridge University Press.

Gibson, William (1984/1995), *Neuromancer*. London: HarperCollins.

Giddens, Anthony (1985/2002), *The Nation-State and Violence*. Cambridge & Oxford: Polity Press.

Giddens, Anthony (1991), *Modernity and Self-Identity: Self and Society in the Late Modern Age*. Stanford: Stanford University Press.

Giese, Karsten (2003), 'Construction and Performance of Virtual Identity in the Chinese Internet'. In Ho, K. C., Kluver, Randolph, & Yang, Kenneth C. C. (eds.), *Asia.com—Asia Encounters the Internet*. New York & London: RoutledgeCurzon (pp. 193–210).

Gilmore, John (2013), 'Things I've Said (That People Sometimes Remember)'. Retrieved 1 September 2017 from http://www.toad.com/gnu/.

Gluck, Carol (2011), 'The End of Elsewhere: Writing Modernity Now'. *American Historical Review*, 116(3), 676–687.

Göbel, Christian (2011), 'Authoritarian Consolidation'. *European Political Science*, 10, 176–190.

Göbel, Christian (2014), 'Government Complaint Websites: Function, Contents, Effects'. In Kaminski, Gerd (ed.), *Wer hört auf die Bürger? Beschwerdewesen in China und Europa* (Who Listens to Citizens? Complaint Systems in China and Europe). Vienna: Österreichisch-Chinesische Gesellschaft (pp. 229–245).

Göbel, Christian (2015), 'Why Does China Have Internet? Contagion, Contingency and Strategy in China's ICT Management'. Conference Paper presented at *Multiple Futures—Africa, China, Europe*. Freiburg: University of Freiburg, retrieved 17 March 2018 from https://www.researchgate.net/publication/282817659_Why_does_China_Have_Internet_Contagion_contingency_and_strategy_in_China%27s_ICT_management.

Goff, Lyn M. & Roediger, Henry L. (1998), 'Imagination Inflation for Action Events: Repeated Imaginings Lead to Illusory Recollections'. *Memory and Cognition*, 26(1), 20–33.

Goffman, Erving (1959), *The Presentation of the Self in Everyday Life*. New York: Anchor Books.

Goldbeck, Jennifer (2013), *Analyzing the Social Web* (Kindle ed.). Amsterdam et al.: Morgan Kaufmann.

Goldman, David (2015, January 4), 'Google: The Reluctant Censor of the Internet'. *CNNMoney*, retrieved 1 September 2017 from http://money.cnn.com/2015/01/04/technology/google-censorship/index.html.

Goldman, Eric (2006), 'Search Engine Bias and the Demise of Search Engine Utopianism'. *Yale Journal of Law and Technology*, 8, 188–200.

Gong, Haomin & Yang, Xin (2010), 'Digitized Parody: The Politics of Egao in Contemporary China'. *China Information*, 24(1), 3–26.

Goto-Jones, Christopher (2015), 'Playing with Being in Digital Asia: Gamic Orientalism and the Virtual Dōjō'. *Asiascape: Digital Asia*, 2(1–2), 20–56.

Graeber, David (2004), *Fragments of an Anarchist Anthropology*. Chicago IL: Prickly Paradigm Press.

Graeber, David (2011a), *Revolutions in Reverse: Essays on Politics, Violence, Art, and Imagination*. New York: Autonomedia.

Graeber, David (2011b), *Debt: The First 5,000 Years* (Kindle ed.). Brooklyn & London: Melville House.

Granka, Laura A. (2010), 'The Politics of Search: A Decade Retrospective'. *The Information Society*, 26(5), 364–374.

Greenfield, Susan (2015), *Mind Change: How Digital Technologies Are Leaving Their Mark on Our Brains*. New York: Random House.

Gries, Peter Hays (2004), *China's New Nationalism—Pride, Politics, and Diplomacy*. Berkeley et al.: University of California Press.

Gries, Peter Hays (2005), 'China's "New Thinking on Japan"'. *The China Quarterly*, 184, 831–850.

Gries, Peter Hays (2009), 'Problems of Misperception in U.S.–China Relations'. *Orbis*, 53(2), 220–232.

Gries, Peter Hays (2014), *The Politics of American Foreign Policy: How Ideology Divides Liberals and Conservatives over Foreign Affairs*. Stanford: Stanford University Press.

Gries, Peter, Steiger, Derek, & Tao, Wang (2016), 'Social Media, Nationalist Protests, and China's Japan Policy: The Diaoyu Islands Controversy 2012–13'. In deLisle, Jacques,

Goldstein, Avery, & Yang, Guobin (eds.), *The Internet, Social Media, and a Changing China*. Philadelphia: University of Pennsylvania Press (pp. 161–179).

Guibernau, Montserrat (2004), 'Anthony D. Smith on Nations and National Identity: A Critical Assessment'. *Nations and Nationalism*, 10(1/2), 125–141.

Guibernau, Montserrat (2013), *Belonging: Solidarity and Division in Modern Societies*. Cambridge: Polity Press.

Guo, Zhenzhi & Wu, Mei (2009), 'Dancing Thumbs—Mobile Telephony in Contemporary China'. In Zhang, Xiaoling & Zheng, Yongnian (eds.), *China's Information and Communications Technology Revolution: Political Impacts and State Responses*. New York et al.: Routledge (34–51).

Gustafsson, Karl (2014), 'Memory Politics and Ontological Security in Sino-Japanese Relations'. *Asian Studies Review*, 38(1), 71–86.

Guthrie-Shimizu, Sayuri (2012), *Transpacific Field of Dreams: How Baseball Linked the United States and Japan in Peace and War*. Chapel Hill: University of North Carolina Press.

Habermas, Jürgen (1962/1990), *Strukturwandel der Öffentlichkeit—Untersuchungen zu einer Kategorie der bürgerliche Gesellschaft* (The Structural Transformation of the Public Sphere: An Inquiry into a Category of Bourgeois Society). Frankfurt a.M.: Suhrkamp.

Habermas, Jürgen (2001), *The Postnational Constellation*. Cambridge, MA: MIT Press.

Hagström, Linus (2012), ' "Power Shift" in East Asia? A Critical Reappraisal of Narratives on the Diaoyu/Senkaku Islands Incident in 2010'. *The Chinese Journal of International Politics*, 5, 267–297.

Halavais, Alexander (2009), *Search Engine Society* (Kindle ed.). Cambridge & Malden, MA: Polity.

Halbwachs, Maurice (1992), *On Collective Memory*. Chicago & London: University of Chicago Press.

Han, Gang & Wang, Wen (2015), 'Mapping User Relationships for Health Information Diffusion on Microblogging in China: A Social Network Analysis of Sina Weibo'. *Asian Journal of Communication*, 25(1), 65–83.

Han, Qiao (2012, November 6), 'China Builds Up New Pillar Industries'. *Xinhua News*, retrieved 1 May 2016 from http://news.xinhuanet.com/english/china/2012-11/06/c_131954795.htm.

Han, Rongbin (2013), 'Adaptive Persuasion in Cyberspace: The "Fifty Cents Army" in China'. Paper Submitted for the 2013 Annual Meeting of the America Political Science Association.

Hardin, Russell (1995), *One for All—The Logic of Group Conflict*. Princeton & Chichester: Princeton University Press.

Hargittai, Eszter & Shaw, Aaron (2015), 'Mind the Skills Gap: The Role of Internet Know-How and Gender in Differentiated Contributions to Wikipedia'. *Information, Communication and Society*, 18(4), 424–442.

Hargittai, Eszter (2007), 'The Social, Political, Economic, and Cultural Dimensions of Search Engines: An Introduction'. *Journal of Computer-Mediated Communication*, 12, 769–777.

 Harwit, Eric (2017), 'WeChat: Social and Political Development of China's Dominant Messaging App'. *Chinese Journal of Communication*, 10(3), 312–327.

Hassid, Jonathan (2008), 'Controlling the Chinese Media—An Uncertain Business'. *Asian Survey*, 48(3), 414–430.

Hawkins, Amy (2017, May 24), 'Chinese Citizens Want the Government to Rank Them'. *Foreign Policy*, retrieved 1 September 2017 from http://foreignpolicy.com/2017/05/24/chinese-citizens-want-the-government-to-rank-them/.

He, Baogang & Warren, Mark (2011), 'Authoritarian Deliberation: The Deliberative Turn in Chinese Political Development'. *Perspective on Politics*, 9(2), 269–289.

He, Qinglian (2008), *The Fog of Censorship: Media Control in China*. New York: Human Rights in China.

He, Yinan (2007a), 'Elite Mythmaking, Mass Reaction, and Sino-Japanese Relations 1950–2006'. *History and Memory*, 19(2), 43–74.

He, Yinan (2007b), 'History, Chinese Nationalism and the Emerging Sino–Japanese Conflict'. *Journal of Contemporary China*, 16(50), 1–24.

Heberer, Thomas & Schubert, Gunter (2008), *Politische Partizipation und Regimelegitimität in der VR China. Band I: Der urbane Raum (Political Participation and Regime Legitimacy in the PR China. Volume 1: Urban Spaces)*. Wisbaden: FS Verlag für Sozialwissenschaften.

Heilmann, Sebastian & Perry, Elizabeth J. (eds.) (2011), *Mao's Invisible Hand: The Political Foundations of Adaptive Governance in China*. Cambridge, MA: Harvard University Press.

Held, David & McGrew, Anthony (eds.) (2000), *The Global Transformations Reader: An Introduction to the Globalization Debate*. Cambridge et al.: Polity Press.

Henochowicz, Anne (2015, February 6): 'I Love the Chinese Dream; A Coffee, Please, and Cream'. *China Digital Times*, retrieved 1 September 2017 from http://chinadigitaltimes.net/2015/02/love-chinese-dream-coffee-please-cream/.

Herman, Edward S. & Chomsky, Noam (1988/2002), *Manufacturing Consent: The Political Economy of the Mass Media*. New York: Pantheon Books.

Herold, David K. (2011), 'Human Flesh Search Engines: Carnivalesque Riots as Components of a "Chinese Democracy"'. In Herold, David K. & Marolt, Peter (eds.), *Online Society in China: Creating, Celebrating, and Instrumentalising the Online Carnival*. London & New York: Routledge (pp. 127–145).

Herold, David K. (2012), 'Through the Looking Glass: Twenty Years of Research into the Chinese Internet'. Paper presented at the *11th Chinese Internet Research Conference* on 15 June 2015 at the Oxford Internet Institute, retrieved 1 September 2017 from http://repository.lib.polyu.edu.hk/jspui/bitstream/10397/5789/1/Herold_Through_Looking_Glass.pdf.

Herold, David K. (2014), 'Users, Not Netizens: Spaces and Practices on the Chinese Internet'. In Marolt, Peter & Herold, David K. (eds.), *China Online: Locating Society in Online Spaces*. Abingdon: Routledge (pp. 20–30).

Herold, David K. & Marolt, Peter (eds.) (2011), *Online Society in China: Creating, Celebrating, and Instrumentalising the Online Carnival*. London & New York: Routledge.

Hindman, Matthew (2010), *The Myth of Digital Democracy*. Princeton: Princeton University Press.

Hjorth, Larissa (2014), 'Locating the Social and Mobile: A Case Study of Women's Use of Kakao Social Mobile Media in Seoul'. *Asiascape: Digital Asia*, 1(1–2), 39–53.

Hobsbawm, Eric (1990), *Nations and Nationalism Since 1780: Programme, Myth, Reality*. Cambridge: Cambridge University Press.

Hoffman, Donald D. (1998), *Visual Intelligence—How We Create What We See*. New York & London: W.W. Norton.

Holbig, Heike & Gilley, Bruce (2010), 'Reclaiming Legitimacy in China'. *Politics and Policy*, 38(3), 395—422.

Holbig, Heike (2009), 'Remaking the CCP's Ideology: Determinants, Progress, and Limits Under Hu Jintao'. *Journal of Current Chinese Affairs*, 38(3), 35–61.

Hollenbaugh, Erin (2010), 'Personal Journal Bloggers: Profiles of Disclosiveness'. *Computers in Human Behavior*, 26, 1657–1666.

Hollihan, Thomas A. (ed.) (2014), *The Dispute over the Diaoyu/Senkaku Islands: How Media Narratives Shape Public Opinion and Challenge the Global Order*. New York: Palgrave Macmillan.

Hoofd, Ingrid M. (2012), *Ambiguities of Activism: Alter-Globalism and the Imperatives of Speed*. New York & Abingdon: Routledge.

Hoopes, James (ed.) (1991), *Peirce on Signs—Writings on Semiotic by Charles Sanders Peirce*. Chapel Hill & London: University of North Carolina Press.

Howarth, David (2000), *Discourse*. Buckingham & Philadelphia: Open University Press.

Howland, Douglas (2012), 'Popular Sovereignty and Democratic Centralism in the People's Republic of China'. *Social Text*, 30(1–110), 1–27.

Hozić, Aida A. & True, Jacqui (2017), 'Brexit as a Scandal: Gender and Global Trumpism'. *Review of International Political Economy*, 24(2), 270–287.

Hu, Henry L. (2011), 'The Political Economy of Governing ISPs in China: Perspectives of Net Neutrality and Vertical Integration'. *The China Quarterly*, 207, 523–540.

Huang, Ronggui & Sun, Xiaoyi (2014), 'Weibo Network, Information Diffusion and Implications for Collective Action in China'. *Information, Communication and Society*, 17(1), 86–104.

Huang, Yasheng (2013, July 1), 'Why Democracy Still Wins: A Critique of Eric X. Li's "A Tale of Two Political Systems"'. *TED Blog*, retrieved 1 September 2017 from http://blog.ted.com/ why-democracy-still-wins-a-critique-of-eric-x-lis-a-tale-of-two-political-systems/.

Huang, Zheping & Horwitz, Josh (2016), 'Always Vigilant: China Is Using Mr. Bean and Batman to Help Explain the Importance of Protecting State Secrets'. *Quartz*, retrieved 1 September 2017 from http://qz.com/662802/china-is-using-mr-bean-and-batman-to-help-explain-the-importance-of-protecting-state-secrets/?utm_source=The+ Sinocism+China+Newsletter&utm_campaign=8116d9df9f-Sinocism04_18_164_18_ 2016&utm_medium=email&utm_term=0_171f237867-8116d9df9f-29665325&mc_ cid=8116d9df9f&mc_eid=8298647a14.

Huddy, Leonie (2003), 'Group Identity and Political Cohesion'. In Sears, David O., Huddy, Leonie, & Jervis, Robert (eds.), *The Oxford Handbook of Political Psychology*. Oxford et al.: Oxford University Press (pp. 511–558).

Hughes, Christopher R. (2006), *Chinese Nationalism in the Global Era*. London: Routledge.

Hung, Ho-Fung (2016), 'From Qing Empire to the Chinese Nation: An Incomplete Project'. *Nations and Nationalism*, 22(4), 660–665.

Huntington, Samuel P. (1991), 'Democracy's Third Wave'. *Journal of Democracy*, 2(2), 12–34.

Hutton, Eric L. (2014), *Xunzi: The Complete Text*. Princeton NJ: Princeton University Press.

Idema, Wilt L. & Haft, Lloyd L. (1997), *A Guide to Chinese Literature*. Ann Arbor: University of Michigan Press.

Information Office (2010, June 8), 'The Internet in China'. *White Paper*, Information Office of the State Council of the People's Republic of China, retrieved 1 September 2017 from http:// www.china.org.cn/government/whitepaper/node_7093508.htm.

ISC (2002, March 26), 'Zhongguo hulianwang hangye zilü gongyue' (Public Pledge of Self-Regulation and Professional Ethics for China Internet Industry). *Internet Society of China*, retrieved 1 September 2017 from http://www.isc.org.cn/hyzl/hyzl/listinfo-15599.html (Chinese) and http://www.isc.org.cn/english/Specails/Self-regulation/listinfo-15321. html (English).

Ito, Mizuko, Horst, Heather, Bittanti, Matteo, Boyd, Danah, Herr-Stephenson, Becky, Lange, Patricia G., Pascoe, C. J., et al. (2008), *Living and Learning with New Media: Summary of Findings from the Digital Youth Project*. Chicago: The MacArthur Foundation. Retrieved 1 September 2017 from http://digitalyouth.ischool.berkeley.edu/files/report/digitalyouth-WhitePaper.pdf.

Iyengar, Rishi (2015, June 4), 'The Tiananmen Massacre Has Created Division in the Only Chinese City Able to Commemorate It'. *Time Magazine*, retrieved 1 September 2017 from http://time.com/3908551/tiananmen-massacre-june-4-1989-hong-kong-vigil-hkfs/.

Jäger, Siegfried (2004), *Kritische Diskursanalyse: Eine Einführung* (Discourse Analysis: An Introduction) (4th unabr. ed.). Münster: UNRAST-Verlag.

Jenkins, Henry (2008), *Convergence Culture: Where Old and New Media Collide*. New York: New York University Press.

Jenkins, Henry (2013), 'Counterpublics: Self-Fashioning and Alternate Communities'. Podcast recorded on 6 May 2013 at *Media in Transition 8: Public Media, Private Media, Massachusetts Institute of Technology*. Retrieved 1 September 2017 from: http://cmsw.mit.edu/ media-in-transition-8-counterpublics.

Jenkins, Henry, Ford, Sam, & Green, Joshua (2013), *Spreadable Media: Creating Value and Meaning in a Networked Culture* (Kindle ed.). New York & London: New York University Press.

Jenner, Christopher John & Thuy, Tran Truong (eds.) (2016), *The South China Sea: A Crucible of Regional Cooperation or Conflict-Making Sovereignty Claims?* Cambridge: Cambridge University Press.

Jiang, Min (2010a), 'Authoritarian Informationalism: China's Approach to Internet Sovereignty'. *SAIS Review of International Affairs*, 30(2), 71–89.

Jiang, Min (2010b), 'Authoritarian Deliberation on Chinese Internet'. *Electronic Journal of Communication*, 20(3–4). Retrieved 1 September 2017 from http://www.cios.org/EJCPUBLIC/020/2/020344.html.

Jiang, Min (2014), 'The Business and Politics of Search Engines: A Comparative Study of Baidu and Google's Search Results of Internet Events in China'. *New Media and Society*, 16(2), 212–233.

Jiang, Min & Okamoto, Kristen (2014), 'National Identity, State Ideological Apparatus, or Panopticon? A Case Study of Chinese National Search Engine Jike'. *Policy and Internet*, 6(1), 89–107.

Jiang, Ying (2012), *Cyber-Nationalism in China: Challenging Western Media Portrayals of Censorship in China*. Adelaide: University of Adelaide Press.

Jie, Dalei (2016), 'Public Opinion and Chinese Foreign Policy: New Media and Old Puzzles'. In deLisle, Jacques, Goldstein, Avery, & Yang, Guobin (eds.), *The Internet, Social Media, and a Changing China*. Philadelphia: University of Pennsylvania Press (pp. 150–160).

Jin, Xuelian (2015), *Towards Democratisation? Understanding University Students' Internet Use in Mainland China*. PhD Thesis, University of Sheffield.

Jingbao (2012, July 6), 'Tai bao diao renshi Diaoyudao qian liang wuxing hongqi xuanshi zhuquan' (Taiwanese Protect the Diaoyus Activists Raise the Five-Starred Red Flag Before the Diaoyu Islands to Proclaim Sovereignty). *Jingbao*, retrieved 1 September 2017 from http://news.ifeng.com/history/zhongguojindaishi/special/diaoyudao/detail_2012_07/16/16061254_0.shtml.

Johnson, Gary R. (1997), 'The Evolutionary Roots of Patriotism'. In Bar-Tal, Daniel & Staub, Ervin (eds.), *Patriotism in the Lives of Individuals and Nations*. Chicago: Nelson-Hall (pp. 45–90).

Johnston, Alastair Iain (2013), 'How New and Assertive Is China's New Assertiveness?' *International Security*, 37(4), 7–48.

Johnston, Alastair Iain (2016), 'Is Chinese Nationalism Rising? Evidence from Beijing'. *International Security*, 41(3), 7–43.

Johnston, Anne, Friedman, Barbara, & Peach, Sara (2011), 'Standpoint in Political Blogs: Voice, Authority and Issues'. *Women's Studies*, 40, 269–298.

Jones, Ron (1976), 'Learning from The Third Wave'. *The Wave Home*, retrieved 17 March 2018 from http://www.thewavehome.com/1976_The-Third-Wave_story.htm.

Jordán, Ferenc (2008), 'Predicting Target Selection by Terrorists: A Network Analysis of the 2005 London Underground Attacks'. *International Journal of Critical Infrastructures*, 4(1–2), 206–214.

Joseph, William A. (2010) (ed.), *Politics in China—An Introduction*. Oxford et al.: Oxford University Press.

Jurriëns, Edwin & De Kloet, Jeroen (eds.) (2007), *Cosmopatriots—On Distant Belongs and Close Encounters*. Amsterdam & New York: Rodopi.

Kaiman, Jonathan (2013, September 10), 'China Cracks Down on Social Media with Threat of Jail for "Online Rumours"'. *The Guardian*, retrieved 19 March 2018 from http://www.theguardian.com/world/2013/sep/10/china-social-media-jail-rumours.

Keane, Michal (2013), *Creative Industries in China—Art, Design and Media*. Cambridge & Malden, MA: Polity Press.

Kelly, Kevin (2010), *What Technology Wants*. New York et al.: Viking.

King, Gary, Pan, Jennifer, & Roberts, Margaret (2013), 'How Censorship in China Allows Government Criticism but Silences Collective Expression'. *American Political Science Review*, 107(2), 1–18.

King, Gary, Pan, Jennifer, & Roberts, Margaret (2017), 'How the Chinese Government Fabricates Social Media Posts for Strategic Distraction, Not Engaged Argument'. *American Political Science Review*, retrieved 1 September 2017 from https://gking.harvard.edu/50c.

Kingston, Jeff (2007), 'Awkward Talisman: War Memory, Reconciliation and Yasukuni'. *East Asia*, 24(3), 295–318.

Kipnis, Andrew B. (2011), 'Subjectification and Education for Quality in China'. *Economy and Society*, 40(2), 289–306.

Kluver, Randolph (2005), 'The Architecture of Control: A Chinese Strategy for E-Governance'. *Journal of Public Policy*, 25(1), 75–97.

Knight, Simon (2014), 'Finding Knowledge: What Is It to "Know" When We Search?' In König, René & Rasch, Miriam (eds.), *Society of the Query Reader—Reflections on Web Search*. Amsterdam: Institute of Network Cultures (pp. 227–238). Retrieved 1 September 2017 from http://networkcultures.org/wp-content/uploads/2014/04/SotQreader_def_scribd.pdf.

Knox, John S. (2009), 'Punctuating the Home Page: Image as Language in an Online Newspaper'. *Discourse and Communication*, 3(2), 145–172.

Koetse, Manya (2012), *The 'Magic' of Memory—Chinese and Japanese Re-Remembrances of the Sino-Japanese War (1937–1945)*. MPhil Thesis Asian Studies, Leiden University. Retrieved 1 September 2017 from http://www.manyakoetse.com/wp-content/uploads/2012/12/the-magic-of-memory-manyakoetse.pdf.

Koetse, Manya (2015, July 9), 'Beware: 10 Scams in China to Watch Out For'. *What's on Weibo*, retrieved 1 September 2017 from http://www.whatsonweibo.com/10-scams-in-china-to-watch-out-for/.

Koetse, Manya (2016a, September 25), 'Leaving Water Taps Running in Japanese Hotels—Controversial "Act of Patriotism" Fuels Debate'. *What's on Weibo*, retrieved 1 September 2017 from http://www.whatsonweibo.com/leaving-hotel-water-taps-running-japan-controversial-act-patriotism-fuels-debate/.

Koetse, Manya (2016b, December 18), '"I Wish We Never Bought a Japanese Car"—Lasting Scars of Anti-Japanese Demonstrations'. *What's on Weibo*, retrieved 1 September 2017 from http://www.whatsonweibo.com/wish-never-bought-japanese-car-lasting-scars-anti-japanese-demonstrations/.

Koetse, Manya (2017, March 1), 'Video of Far-Right Japanese Kindergarten Recital Sparks Controversy in China'. *What's on Weibo*, retrieved 1 September 2017 from http://www.whatsonweibo.com/video-controversial-japanese-kindergarten-recital-sparks-controversy-china/.

König, René & Rasch, Miriam (eds.) (2014), *Society of the Query Reader—Reflections on Web Search*. Amsterdam: Institute of Network Cultures, retrieved 1 September 2017 from http://networkcultures.org/wp-content/uploads/2014/04/SotQreader_def_scribd.pdf.

Kress, Gunther & Van Leeuwen, Theo (2001), *Multimodal Discourse—The modes and Media of Contemporary Communication*. London: Arnold.

Lagerkvist, Johan (2010), *After the Internet, Before Democracy: Competing Norms in Chinese Media and Society*. Bern et al.: Peter Lang.

Lai, Chih-Hui (2014), 'Can Our Group Survive? An Investigation of the Evolution of Mixed-Mode Groups'. *Journal of Computer-Mediated Communication*, 19(4), 839–854.

Lakoff, George (2002), *Moral Politics: How Liberals and Conservatives Think*. Chicago & London: The University of Chicago Press.

Lanier, Jaron (2011), *You Are Not a Gadget: A Manifesto* (Kindle ed.). New York: Vintage Books.

Latour, Bruno (2005), *Reassembling the Social—An Introduction to Actor Network Theory*. Oxford: Oxford University Press.

Lavin, Frank (2016, November 15), 'Singles' Day Sales Scorecard: A Day in China Now Bigger Than a Year in Brazil'. *Forbes Asia*, retrieved 1 September 2017 from https://www.forbes.com/sites/franklavin/2016/11/15/singles-day-scorecard-a-day-in-china-now-bigger-than-a-year-in-brazil/#e283cbf1076e.

Lee, Hong Yung (1978), 'The Politics of Cadre Rehabilitation Since the Cultural Revolution'. *Asian Survey*, 18(9), 934–955.

Leibold, James (2007), *Reconfiguring Chinese Nationalism: How the Qing Frontier and Its Indigenes Became Chinese*. New York & Basingstoke: Palgrave Macmillan.

Leibold, James (2010), 'More Than a Category: Hand Supremacism on the Chinese Internet'. *The China Quarterly*, 203, 539–559.

Leibold, James (2011), 'Blogging Alone: China, the Internet, and the Democratic Illusion?' *The Journal of Asian Studies*, 70(4), 1023–1041.

Leibold, James (2016a), 'Han Cybernationalism and State Territorialization in the People's Republic of China'. *China Information*, 30(1), 3–28.

Leibold, James (2016b), 'The *Minzu* Net: China's Fragmented National Form'. *Nations and Nationalism*, 22(3), 423–428.

Leung, Wing-Fai (2015), 'Who Could Be an Oriental Angel? Lou Jing, Mixed Heritage and the Discourse of Chinese Ethnicity'. *Asian Ethnicity*, 16(3), 294–313.

Li, Eric X. (2013), 'A Tale of Two Political Systems'. *TED Global*, retrieved 1 September 2017 from http://www.ted.com/talks/eric_x_li_a_tale_of_two_political_systems.

Li, Fengru & Shooshtari, Nader H. (2007), 'Multinational Corporations' Controversial Ad Campaigns in China—Lessons from Nike and Toyota'. *Advertising and Society Review*, 8(1).

Li, Hongmei (2011), 'Parody and Resistance on the Chinese Internet'. In Herold, David K. & Marolt, Peter (eds.), *Online Society in China: Creating, Celebrating, and Instrumentalising the Online Carnival*. London & New York: Routledge (pp. 71–88).

Li, Jingke (2014), *Diaoyudao dongwu he zhiwu* (The Flora and Fauna of the Diaoyu Islands). Xiamen et al.: World Chinese Alliance in Defence of the Diaoyus.

Li, Ran (2012, September 21), 'Xi'an rixi che chezhu yu shiwei renqun bei zhongji toubu zachuan lugu' (Xi'an Nissan Driver from Xi'an Encounters Crowd of Demonstrators, Has His Skull Smashed). *Beijing Youth Daily*, retrieved 1 September 2017 from http://news.sina.com.cn/c/2012-09-21/092225223127.shtml.

Li, Xiguang, Xuan, Qin, & Kluver, Randolph (2003), 'Who Is Setting the Chinese Agenda? The Impact of Online Chatrooms on Party Presses in China'. In Ho, K. C., Kluver, Randolph, & Yang, Kenneth C. C. (eds.), *Asia.com—Asia Encounters the Internet*. New York & London: RoutledgeCurzon (pp. 143–158).

Li, Zhigang, Lyons, Michal, & Brown, Alison (2012), 'China's 'Chocolate City': An Ethnic Enclave in a Changing Landscape'. *African Diaspora*, 5(1), 51–72.

Liang, Lawrence (2011), 'A Brief History of the Internet from the 15th to the 18th Century'. In Lovink, Geert & Tkacz, Nathaniel (eds.) (2011), *Critical Point of View: A Wikipedia Reader*. INC Reader No.7, Amsterdam: Institute of Network Cultures, retrieved 1 September 2017 from http://www.networkcultures.org/_uploads/%237reader_Wikipedia.pdf (pp. 50–62).

Liao, Han-Teng (2013), 'How Does Localization Influence Online Visibility of User-Generated Encyclopedias? A Case Study on Chinese-Language Search Engine Result Pages (SERPs)'. In *Proceedings of the 9th International Symposium on Open Collaboration*. New York: ACM.

Liao, Han-Teng & Petzold, Thomas (2014), 'Geographic and Linguistic Normalization: Towards a Better Understanding of the Geolinguistic Dynamics of Knowledge'. *Opensym*, 14. Retrieved on 1 September 2017 from http://www.opensym.org/os2014/proceedings-files/p611.pdf.

Lieberthal, Kenneth (1992), 'Introduction: The 'Fragmented Authoritarianism' Model and Its Limitations'. In Lieberthal, Kenneth & Lampton, David M. (eds.), *Bureaucracy, Politics, and Decision Making in Post-Mao China*. Berkeley, CA: University of California Press (pp. 1–32).

Lieberthal, Kenneth (2003), *Governing China* (2nd ed.). New York: W.W. Norton.

Lien, Che Hui & Cao, Yang (2014), 'Examining WeChat Users' Motivations, Trust, Attitudes, and Positive Word-of-Mouth: Evidence from China'. *Computers in Human Behavior*, 41, 104–111.

Lim, Louisa (2014), *The People's Republic of Amnesia: Tiananmen Revisited*. Oxford: Oxford University Press.

Lin, Hsiao-Ting (2009), 'The Tributary System in China's Historical Imagination: China and Hunza, ca.1760–1960'. *Journal of the Royal Asiatic Society of Great Britain and Ireland*, 19, 489–507.

Lindtner, Silvia & Szablewicz, Marcella (2011), 'China's Many Internets: Participation and Digital Game Play Across a Changing Technology Landscape'. In Herold, David K. & Marolt, Peter (eds.), *Online Society in China: Creating, Celebrating, and Instrumentalising the Online Carnival*. London & New York: Routledge (pp. 89–105).

Linenthal, Edward T. (1995), *Preserving Memory—The Struggle to Create America's Holocaust Museum*. New York & Chichester: Columbia University Press.

Linenthal, Edward T. (1996), 'Anatomy of a Controversy'. In Linenthal, Edward T. & Engelhardt, Tom (eds.), *History Wars: The Enola Gay and Other Battles for the American Past*. New York: Holt (pp. 9–62).

Lipton, Zachary C. (2017, January 23), 'Is Fake News a Machine Learning Problem?' *Approximately Correct*, retrieved 1 September 2017 from http://approximatelycorrect.com/2017/01/23/is-fake-news-a-machine-learning-problem/.

Liu, Jing & Li, Shijun (2015), 'Characteristics Study of Weibo Users' Interactions'. *Wuhan University Journal of Natural Sciences*, 20(6), 499–504.

Liu, Jun (2014), 'Mobile Communication and Relational Mobilization in China'. *Asiascape: Digital Asia*, 1(1–2), 14–38.

Liu, Kun (2013, April 11), 'Tai guanyuan: Taifang jiang quli jinru Diaoyudao shuiyu dalu yuchuan' (Taiwanese Official: The Taiwanese Side May Expel Mainland Fishing Boats Entering Diaoyu Island Waters). *Global Times Web*, retrieved 1 September 2017 from http://mil.huanqiu.com/china/2013-04/3822205.html.

Liu, Lydia H. (2004), *The Clash of Empires: The Invention of China in Modern World Making*. Cambridge, MA & London: Harvard University Press.

Llinás, Rodolfo R. (2001), *I of the Vortex—From Neurons to Self*. Cambridge, MA & London: MIT Press.

Lollar, Xia Li (2006), 'Assessing China's E-Government: Information, Service, Transparency and Citizen Outreach of Government Websites'. *Journal of Contemporary China*, 15(46), 31–41.

Lovink, Geert (2008), *Zero Comments: Blogging and Critical Internet Culture*. New York: Routledge.

Lovink, Geert & Tkacz, Nathaniel (eds.) (2011), *Critical Point of View: A Wikipedia Reader*. INC Reader No.7, Amsterdam: Institute of Network Cultures. Retrieved 1 September 2017 from http://www.networkcultures.org/_uploads/%237reader_Wikipedia.pdf.

Lu, Wei (2016, February 3), 'Jianchi zunzhong wangluo zhuquan yuanze, tuidong goujian wangluo kongjian mingyun gongtongti' (Insist on Respecting the Principle of Internet Sovereignty, Promote the Establishment of a Mutual Destiny for Internet Spaces). *Chinese Communist Party News Network*, retrieved 1 September 2017 from http://theory.people.com.cn/n1/2016/0302/c83846-28165695.html.

Lukes, Steven (2005), *Power: A Radical View* (2nd ed.). London & New York: Palgrave MacMillan.

Macartney, Jane (2008, May 31), 'War Memories Sink Plan for Japan's Military to Help China'. *The Times*, 39.

MacDonald, David B. (2005), 'Forgetting and Denying: Iris Chang, the Holocaust and the Challenge of Nanking'. *International Politics*, 42, 403–427.

MacFarquar, Roderick & Schoenhals, Michael (2006), *Mao's Last Revolution*. Cambridge, MA & London: Belknap Harvard.

MacKinnon, Rebecca (2005, November 7), 'Chinese Bloggers: Everybody Is Somebody'. *RConversation*, retrieved 1 September 2017 from http://rconversation.blogs.com/rconversation/2005/11/page/2/.

MacKinnon, Rebecca (2009, February 2), 'China's Censorship 2.0: How Companies Censor Bloggers'. *First Monday*, 14(2), retrieved 1 September 2017 from http://firstmonday.org/htbin/cgiwrap/bin/ojs/index.php/fm/article/view/2378/2089.

MacKinnon, Rebecca (2012), *Consent of the Networked: The Worldwide Struggle for Internet Freedom*. New York: Basic Books.

Mann, Michael (1997), 'Has Globalization Ended the Rise and Rise of the Nation-State?' *Review of International Political Economy*, 4(3), 472–496.

Manovich, Lev (2013), *Software Takes Command*. New York & London: Bloomsbury Academic.

Mao, Zedong (1942), 'Zai Yan'an wenyi zuotanhui de jianghua' (Talks at the Yan'an Forum on Literature and Art). Speech held in Yan'an on 2 May 1942, retrieved 1 September 2017 from https://www.marxists.org/chinese/maozedong/marxist.org-chinese-mao-194205.htm.

Marolt, Peter (2011), 'Grassroots Agency in a Civil Sphere? Rethinking Internet Control in China'. In Herold, David K. & Marolt, Peter (eds.), *Online Society in China: Creating, Celebrating, and Instrumentalising the Online Carnival*. London & New York: Routledge (pp. 53–68).

Marvin, Carolyn & Ingle, David W. (1999), *Blood Sacrifice and the Nation: Totem Ritual and the American Flag*. Cambridge et al.: Cambridge University Press.

Maslow, Abraham H. (1943), 'A Theory of Human Motivation'. *Psychological Review*, 50, 370–396.

McCombs, Maxwell (2004), *Setting the Agenda: The Mass Media and Public Opinion*, Malden: Blackwell.

McCurry, Justin (2008, May 30), 'Japan Drops Plans to Use Military to Deliver Aid to China'. *The Guardian*, retrieved 1 September 2017 from http://www.theguardian.com/world/2008/may/30/china.

McDonald, Tom (2015), 'Affecting Relations: Domesticating the Internet in a South-Western Chinese Town'. *Information, Communication and Society*, 18(1), 17–31.

McDonald, Tom (2016), *Social Media in Rural China*. London: UCL Press.

McLuhan, Marshall (1964/2001), *Understanding Media: The Extensions of Man*. London & New York: Routledge.

McPherson, Miller, Smith-Lovin, Lynn, & Cook, James M. (2001), 'Birds of a Feather: Homophile in Social Networks'. *Annual Review of Sociology*, 27, 415–444.

Medaglia, Rony & Yang, Yang (2017), 'Online Public Deliberation in China: Evolution of Interaction Patterns and Network Homophily in the Tianya Discussion Forum'. *Information, Communication and Society*, 20(5), 733–753.

Meltzer, Hannah (2013, February 6), 'Are the French Right to Ban the Word 'Hashtag'?' *New Statesman*, retrieved 1 September 2017 from http://www.newstatesman.com/business/2013/02/are-french-right-ban-word-hashtag.

Memorial Hall (2005a), 'Nanjing datusha yunan tongbao jinianguan guoji youhao guan (tu)' (The Memorial Hall for the Victims of the Nanjing Massacre's Institutions of International Friendship [figure]). *Never Forget*, Sina.com, retrieved 1 September 2017 from http://neverforget.sina.com.cn/pl/p/2005-03-25/2214152.html.

Memorial Hall (2005b), 'Riben dabanfu Ri-Zhong youxie nüxing weiyuan daibiaotuan lai guan zuotan' (Japanese 'Peace Tourism' Friendship Delegation to China Visits Memorial to Mourn). *The Memorial Hall for the Victims of the Nanjing Massacre Committed by the Invading Japanese Forces*, retrieved 1 May 2016 from http://www.nj1937.org/cn/2015-07/21/c_134432439.htm.

Memorial Hall (2005c), 'Riben "heping zhi you" youhao fanghuatuan lai guan canguan daonian' (Female Representatives of Japan's Osaka Society for Sino-Japanese Friendship Visit Memorial for Informal Discussion). *The Memorial Hall for the Victims of the Nanjing Massacre Committed by the Invading Japanese Forces*, retrieved 1 May 2016 from http://www.nj1937.org/cn/2015-05/14/c_134239360.htm.

Memorial Hall (2005d), 'Riben Limuxian Ri-Zhong youxie lai guan canguan daonian' (Japan's Tochigi Prefecture Society for Japanese-Chinese Friendship Visit Memorial to Mourn). *The Memorial Hall for the Victims of the Nanjing Massacre Committed by the Invading Japanese Forces*, retrieved 1 May 2016 from http://www.nj1937.org/cn/2015-05/26/c_134272020.htm.

Meng, Na & Mou, Xu (2012, November 12), 'Xinhua Insight: China Never to Copy Western Political System'. *Xinhua*, retrieved 1 September 2017 from http://english.cntv.cn/20121112/107203.shtml.

Meng, Bingchun (2011), 'From Steamed Bun to Grass Mud Horse: E Gao as Alternative Political Discourse on the Chinese Internet'. *Global Media and Communication*, 7(1), 33–51.

Mertha, Andrew (2009), '"Fragmented Authoritarianism 2.0": Political Pluralization in the Chinese Policy Process'. *The China Quarterly*, 200, 995–1012.

MIIT (2016, February 14), 'Wangluo chuban fuwu guanli guiding' (Stipulation on the Management of Internet Publishing Services). *Ministry of Industry and Information Technology of the People's Republic of China*, retrieved 1 September 2017 from http://www.miit.gov.cn/n1146295/n1146557/n1146619/c4639081/content.html.

Miller, Daniel, & Slater, Don (2000), *The Internet—An Ethnographic Approach*. Oxford & New York: Berg.

Millward, Steven (2015, December 8), '20 Amazing Things That Chinese People Do in WeChat'. *Tech in Asia*, retrieved 1 September 2017 from https://www.techinasia.com/how-wechat-is-really-used-in-china.

Mirani, Leo (2015, February 9), 'Millions of Facebook Users Have No Idea They're Using the Internet'. *Quartz*, retrieved 1 September 2017 from http://qz.com/333313/milliions-of-facebook-users-have-no-idea-theyre-using-the-internet/.

Mitchell, Melanie (2009), *Complexity—A Guided Tour*. Oxford: Oxford University Press.

Mitter, Rana (2003), 'Old Ghosts, New Memories: Changing China's War History in the Era of Post-Mao Politics'. *Journal of Contemporary History*, January, 117–131.

Mitter, Rana (2004), *A Bitter Revolution: China's Struggle with the Modern World*. Oxford et al.: Oxford University Press.

Mitter, Rana (2013), *Forgotten Ally: China's World War II, 1937–1945* (Kindle ed.). New York: Penguin Books.

MOE PRC (2016, January 26), 'Zhong-Gong Jiaoyubu dangzu guanyu jiaoyu xitong shenru kazhan aiguo zhuyi jiaoyu de shishi yijian' (Views of the Central Ministry of Education's Party Group on the Educational System Implementing Patriotic Education in a Deep-Going Way). *Ministry of Education of the People's Republic of China*, retrieved 1 September 2017 from http://www.moe.edu.cn/srcsite/A13/s7061/201601/t20160129_229131.html.

Moeke-Pickering, Taima Materangatira (1996), 'Maori Identity Within Whanau: A Review of Literature'. Working Paper, Hamilton: University of Waikato. Retrieved 1 September 2017 from http://researchcommons.waikato.ac.nz/handle/10289/464.

MOFA Japan (2014), 'Japanese Territory: Senkaku Islands'. *Ministry of Foreign Affairs of Japan*, retrieved 1 September 2017 from http://www.mofa.go.jp/region/asia-paci/senkaku/index.html.

MOFA ROC (2012), 'East China Sea Issue'. *Republic of China (Taiwan) Ministry of Foreign Affairs*, retrieved 1 September 2017 from http://www.mofa.gov.tw/en/theme.aspx?s=780E70E6D142B833&sms=BCDE19B435833080.

MOFA ROC (2013, November 25), 'The Republic of China's Sovereignty Claims over the Diaoyutai Islands and the East China Sea Peace Initiative'. *Republic of China (Taiwan) Ministry of Foreign Affairs*, retrieved 1 September 2017 from http://www.mofa.gov.tw/Upload/WebArchive/1384/a5646805-7335-43ea-b4b6-71d7058aa055.PDF.

Morozov, Evgeny (2011), *The Net Delusion: How Not to Liberate the World* (Kindle ed.). London: Allen Lane.

Morris, Andrew D. (2011), *Colonial Project, National Game: A History of Baseball in Taiwan*. Berkeley et al.: University of California Press.

Müller, Marion G. & Kappas, Arvid (2011), 'Visual Emotions—Emotional Visuals. Emotions, Pathos Formulae, and Their Relevance for Communication Research'. In Doveling, Katrin, von Scheve, Christian, & Konijn, Elly A. (eds.), *The Routledge Handbook of Emotions and the Mass Media*. Oxford: Routledge (pp. 310–331).

Mullaney, Thomas (2011), *Coming to Terms with the Nation: Ethnic Classification in Modern China*. Berkeley et al.: University of California Press.

Mumford, Lewis (1964), 'Authoritarian and Democratic Technics'. *Technology and Culture*, 5(1), 1–8. Retrieved 1 September 2017 from http://www.nyu.edu/projects/nissenbaum/papers/authoritarian.pdf.

Mumford, Lewis (1966), *Technics and Human Development—The Myth of the Machine* (Vol. 1). San Diego et al.: Harvest/HBJ.

Munro, Donald J. (1969), *The Concept of Man in Early China*. Stanford: Stanford University Press.

Nathan, Andrew (2003), 'Authoritarian Resilience'. *Journal of Democracy*, 14(1), 6–17.

Nathan, Andrew (2015, October 22), 'Beijing Bull: The Bogus China Model'. *The National Interest*, retrieved 1 September 2017 from http://www.nationalinterest.org/feature/beijing-bull-the-bogus-china-model-14107.

Ng, Jason Q. (2013), *Blocked on Weibo: What Gets Suppressed on China's Version of Twitter (and Why)*. New York: New Press.

Ng, Jason Q. (2015), 'Politics, Rumors, and Ambiguity: Tracking Censorship on WeChat's Public Accounts Platform'. *Citizenlab*, retrieved 1 September 2017 from https://citizenlab.org/2015/07/tracking-censorship-on-wechat-public-accounts-platform/.

Ng, Teddy (2014, January 14) '"Cultural Threats" Among Five Focuses of New National Security Panel, Colonel Says'. *South China Morning Post*, retrieved 1 September 2017 from http://www.scmp.com/news/china/article/1404926/cultural-threats-among-five-focuses-new-national-security-panel-colonel.

Nie, Hongping Annie (2013), 'Gaming, Nationalism, and Ideological Work in Contemporary China: Online Games Based on the War of Resistance Against Japan'. *Journal of Contemporary China*, 22(81), 499–517.

NMDIS (2014), 'Diaoyu Dao: The Inherent Territory of China'. *National Marine Data and Information Service of the People's Republic of China*, retrieved from http://www.diaoyudao.org.cn/en/index.htm.

Nordin, Astrid & Richaud, Lisa (2014), 'Subverting Official Language and Discourse in China? Type River Crab for Harmony'. *China Information*, 28(1), 47–67.

Nordin, Astrid (2014), 'Bordering on the Unacceptable in China and Europe—"Cao ni ma" and "nique ta mère" '. In Liu, Joyce C. H. & Vaughan-Williams, Nick (eds.), *European-East Asian Borders in Translation*. London: Routledge (pp. 166–181).

Novick, Peter (1999), *The Holocaust in American Life*. Boston & New York: Mariner Books.

Nyíri, Pál, Zhang, Juan, & Varrall, Merriden (2010), 'China's Cosmopolitan Nationalists—"Heroes" and "Traitors" of the 2008 Olympics'. *The China Journal*, 63, 25–55.

Nysted, Dan (2006, August 6), 'Wikipedia Attacks Chinese Search Engine'. *PC Advisor*, retrieved 1 September 2017 from http://www.pcadvisor.co.uk/news/internet/wikipedia-attacks-chinese-search-engine-10304/.

NYT (2010, March 21), 'What Chinese Censors Don't Want You to Know'. *The New York Times*, retrieved 1 September 2017 from http://www.nytimes.com/2010/03/22/world/asia/22banned.html.

O'Barr, William M. (2007), 'Advertising in China'. *Advertising and Society Review*, 8(3).

Oreglia, Elisa, Qiu, Jack Linchuan, Bu, Wei, Schulte, Barbara, Wang, Jin, Wallis, Cara, & Zhou, Baohua (2015), 'Studying the Sent-Down Internet: Roundtable on Research Methods'. *Chinese Journal of Communication*, 8(1), 7–17.

O'Reilly, Tim (2005, September 30), 'What Is Web 2.0? Design Patterns and Business Models for the Next Generation of Software'. O'Reilly Media, retrieved from http://www.oreilly.com/pub/a/web2/archive/what-is-web-20.html.

O'Sullivan, Dan (2011), 'What Is an Encyclopedia? A Brief Historical Overview from Pliny to Wikipedia'. In Lovink, Geert & Tkacz, Nathaniel (eds.), *Critical Point of View: A Wikipedia Reader*. INC Reader No.7, Amsterdam: Institute of Network Cultures. Retrieved 1 September 2017 from http://www.networkcultures.org/_uploads/%237reader_Wikipedia.pdf (pp. 34–49).

Owen, Taylor (2015), *Disruptive Power: The Crisis of the State in the Digital Age*. Oxford: Oxford University Press.

Pariser, Eli (2012), *The Filter Bubble: How the New Personalized Web Is Changing What We Read and How We Think* (Kindle ed.). New York et al.: Penguin Books.

Park, Han Woo & Thelwall, Mike (2003), 'Hyperlink Analyses of the World Wide Web: A Review'. *Journal of Computer-Mediated Communication*, 8(4). Retrieved 1 September 2017 from http://onlinelibrary.wiley.com/doi/10.1111/j.1083-6101.2003.tb00223.x/full.

Pauwels, Luc (2005), 'Websites as Visual and Multimodal Cultural Expressions: Opportunities and Issues of Online Hybrid Media Research'. *Media Culture Society*, 27(4), 604–613.

PCA (2016, July 12), *South China Sea Arbitration Award*. Case No. 2013–19 of the Arbitral Tribunal Constituted under Annex VII to the 1982 United Nations Convention on the Law of the Sea, retrieved 1 September 2017 from https://pca-cpa.org/wp-content/uploads/sites/175/2016/07/PH-CN-20160712-Award.pdf.

Peng, Yuzhu (2017), 'Affective Networks: How WeChat Enhances Tencent's Digital Business Governance'. *Chinese Journal of Communication*, 10(3), 264–278.

People's Daily (2016, February 17), 'Zunzhong guojia wangluo zhuquan' (Respect National Internet Sovereignty). *State Council of the People's Republic of China*. Retrieved 1 September 2017 from http://www.gov.cn/zhengce/2016-02/17/content_5042042.htm?utm_source=The+Sinocism+China+Newsletter&utm_campaign=e50e7d87aa-The_Sinocism_China_Newsletter_02_16_162_16_2016&utm_medium=email&utm_term=0_171f237867-e50e7d87aa-29670273&mc_cid=e50e7d87aa&mc_eid=af39f883fb.

People's Net (2015a), 'Zong-Ri lianhe xiufu Nanjing chengqiang 20 zhounian jinian huodong zai Nanjing juxing' (Nanjing Holds Activities Celebrating the 20-Year Anniversary of the United Sino-Japanese Renovation of Nanjing's City Wall). *The Memorial Hall for the Victims of the Nanjing Massacre Committed by the Invading Japanese Forces*, retrieved 1 May 2016 from http://www.nj1937.org/cn/2015-05/17/c_134245890.htm.

People's Net (2015b, August 12), 'Xi Jinping de "wangluo guan": Nuli jiancheng wangluo qiangguo, rang fazhan chenggou huiji renmin' (Xi Jinping's 'Internet Views': Work Hard to Build an Internet Superpower; Let Developmental Achievements Extend to the People). CCP News Net, retrieved 1 September 2017 from http://cpc.people.com.cn/xuexi/n/2015/1208/c385474-27901830.html.

Petzold, T., Liao, Han-Teng, Hartley, J., & Potts, J. (2012), 'A World Map of Knowledge in the Making: Wikipedia's Inter-Language Linkage as a Dependency Explorer of Global Knowledge Accumulation'. *Leonardo: Art, Science and Technology*, 45(3), 284.

Phillips, Tom (2016, February 28), 'Love the Party, Protect the Party: How Xi Jinping Is Bringing China's Media to Heel'. *The Guardian*, retrieved 1 September 2017 from http://www.theguardian.com/world/2016/feb/28/absolute-loyalty-how-xi-jinping-is-bringing-chinas-media-to-heel.

Pieke, Frank (2012), 'The Communist Party and Social Management in China'. *China Information*, 26, 149–165.

Pieke, Frank (2016), *Knowing China: A Twenty-First Century Guide* (Kindle ed.). Cambridge et al.: Cambridge University Press.

Pierson, Emma (2014, November 25), 'See How Red Tweeters and Blue Tweeters Ignore Each Other on Ferguson'. *Quartz*, retrieved 1 September 2017 from http://qz.com/302616/see-how-red-tweeters-and-blue-tweeters-ignore-each-other-on-ferguson/.

Pinker, Steven (2002), *The Blank Slate—The Modern Denial of Human Nature*. New York et al.: Penguin Books.

Pinker, Steven (2012), *The Better Angels of Our Nature: Why Violence Has Declined*. New York et al.: Penguin Books.

Pissin, Annika (2015), 'Growing Up in Mommy's Blog: Raising Girls' Voices in China'. *Asiascape: Digital Asia*, 2(3), 213–237.

Poell, Thomas, de Kloet, Jeroen, & Zeng, Guohua (2014), 'Will the Real Weibo Please Stand Up? Chinese Online Contention and Actor-Network Theory'. *Chinese Journal of Communication*, 7(1), 1–18.

Praemium Erasmianum (2015), 'Erasmus Prize 2015 Awarded to Wikipedia'. Amsterdam: Praemium Erasmianum Foundation, retrieved 1 September 2017 from http://www.erasmusprijs.org/?lang=en&page=Erasmusprijs.

PRC State Council (2015, July 1), 'Guowuyuan guanyu jiji tuijin "hulianwang+" xingdong de zhidao yijian' (State Council Guiding Opinions Concerning Vigorously Moving Forward the 'Internet Plus' Plan). *State Council of the People's Republic of China*, retrieved 1 September 2017 from http://www.gov.cn/zhengce/content/2015-07/04/content_10002.htm.

Pye, Lucian W. (2008), 'Political Culture'. In Leese, Daniel (ed.), *Brill's Encyclopaedia of China*. Leiden: Brill.

Qian, Licheng, Xu, Bin, & Chen, Dingding (2017), 'Does History Education Promote Nationalism in China? A "Limited Effect" Explanation'. *Journal of Contemporary China*, 26(104), 199–212.

Qiu, Jack Linchuan & Bu, Wei (2013), 'Chinese ICT Studies: A Review of the field 1989–2012'. *The China Review*, 13(2), 123–52.

Qiu, Jack Linchuan (2003), 'The Internet in China: Data and Issues'. Working Paper prepared for the *Annenberg Research Seminar on International Communication*, retrieved 1 September 2017 from https://pdfs.semanticscholar.org/be2e/119cee731c5ff5a2aa9c0c2827f7b3ac9 6fc.pdf.

Qiu, Jack Linchuan (2009), *Working-Class Network Society: Communication Technology and the Information Have-Less in Urban China*. Cambridge, MA: MIT Press.

Qiu, Jack Linchuan (2015), 'Go Baobao! Image-Driven Nationalism, Generation Post-1980s, and Mainland Students in Hong Kong'. *Positions*, 23(1), 145–165.

Quiroga, Alejandro (2013), *Football and National Identities in Spain: The Strange Death of Don Quixote*. London: Palgrave Macmillan.

Ramirez, Artemio, Sumner, Erin M. Bryant, Fleuriet, Christina, & Cole, Megan (2015), 'When Online Dating Partners Meet Offline: The Effect of Modality Switching on Relational Communication Between Online Daters'. *Journal of Computer-Mediated Communication*, 20(1), 99–114.

Ran, Jijun (2017, March 15), 'American Unrest Proves China Got the Internet Right: Beijing Has Been Criticized for Its Great Firewall and Online Censorship. Now It's Looking Prescient'. *Tea Leaf Nation*, retrieved 1 September 2017 from http://foreignpolicy.com/2017/03/15/ american-unrest-proves-china-got-the-internet-right-beijing-great-firewall-censorship-trump/.

Reagle, Joseph (2011), 'The Argument Engine'. In Lovink, Geert & Tkacz, Nathaniel (eds.) (2011), *Critical Point of View: A Wikipedia Reader*. INC Reader No.7, Amsterdam: Institute of Network Cultures. Retrieved from http://www.networkcultures.org/_uploads/ %237reader_Wikipedia.pdf (pp. 14–33).

Reilly, James (2012), *Strong Society, Smart State: The Rise of Public Opinion in China's Japan Policy*. New York: Columbia University Press.

Repnikova, Maria (2017), *Media Politics in China: Improvising Power Under Authoritarianism*. Cambridge et al.: Cambridge University Press.

Reuters (2011), 'China Sets Up Agency to Tighten Grip on Internet'. *Reuters Technology*, retrieved 17 March 2018, from http://www.reuters.com/article/ us-china-internet-idUSTRE7436SA20110504.

Rogers, Everett M. (2003), *Diffusion of Innovations* (5th ed., Kindle). New York et al.: Free Press.

Rogers, Richard (2010), 'Mapping Public Web Space with the Issuecrawler'. In Brossard, Claire & Reber, Bernard (eds.), *Digital Cognitive Technologies: Epistemology and Knowledge Society*. London: Wiley (pp. 115–126).

Rogers, Richard (2013), *Digital Methods*. Cambridge MA: MIT Press.

Rosen, Jay (2006), 'The People Formerly Known as the Audience'. *PressThink*, retrieved 1 September 2017 from http://archive.pressthink.org/2006/06/27/ppl_frmr.html.

Rosen, Stanley (2009), 'Contemporary Chinese Youth and the State'. *The Journal of Asian Studies*, 68(2), 359–369.

Ruan, Lotus, Knockel, Jeffrey, Ng, Jason Q., & Crete-Nishihata, Masashi (2016), 'One App, Two Systems: How WeChat Uses One Censorship Policy in China and Another Internationally'. *Citizenlab*, retrieved 1 September 2017 from https://citizenlab.org/2016/11/wechat-china-censorship-one-app-two-systems/.

Saaler, Sven (2005), *Politics, Memory and Public Opinion: The History Textbook Controversy and Japanese Society*. Munich: Deutsches Institut fur Japanstudien.

Saaler, Sven (2013), 'Bad War or Good War? History and Politics in Post-War Japan'. In Kingston, Jeff (ed.), *Critical Issues in Contemporary Japan*. London & New York: Routledge (pp. 137–148).

Saich, Tony (2015), *Governance and Politics of China* (4th ed.). London: Palgrave Macmillan.

Salmenkari, Taru (2006), *Democracy, Participation, and Deliberation in China: The Discussion in the Official Chinese Press, 1978–1981*. Helsinki: Finnish Oriental Society.

Sandby-Thomas, Peter (2011), *Legitimating the Chinese Communist Party since Tiananmen: A Critical Analysis of the Stability Discourse*. Abingdon & New York: Routledge.

Sandby-Thomas, Peter (2014), 'How Do You Solve a Problem Like Legitimacy? Contributing to a New Research Agenda'. *Journal of Contemporary China*, 23(88), 575–592.

SAPPRFT (2014, November 27), 'Zongju fachu "Guanyu guangbo dianshi jiemu he guanggao zhong guifan shiyong guojia tongyong yuyan wenzi de tongzhi"' (State Administration Issues 'Notification regarding the Standard Usage of the National Common Language and Script in Radio and Television Programmes and Advertisings'). Beijing: State Administration of Press, Publication, Radio, Film and Television of the People's Republic of China. Retrieved 1 September 2017 from http://www.sarft.gov.cn/art/2014/11/27/art_113_4781.html.

Sautman, Barry (1994), 'Anti-Black Racism in Post-Mao China'. *The China Quarterly*, 138, 413–437.

Schiller, Dan (1999), *Digital Capitalism—Networking the Global Market System*. Cambridge, MA & London: MIT Press.

Schiller, Dan (2014), *Digital Depression: Information Technology and Economic Crisis*. Urbana et al.: University of Illinois Press.

Schlæger, Jesper (2013), *E-Government in China: Technology, Power and Local Government Reform*. London: Routledge.

Schmidt, Vivian A. (2017), 'Britain-out and Trump-in: A Discursive Institutionalist Analysis of the British Referendum on the EU and the US Presidential Election'. *Review of International Political Economy*, 24(2), 242–247.

Schneider, Florian & Hwang, Yih-jye (2014a), 'The Sichuan Earthquake and the Heavenly Mandate: Legitimizing Chinese Rule Through Disaster Discourse'. *Journal of Contemporary China*, 23(88), 636–656.

Schneider, Florian & Hwang, Yih-jye (2014b), 'China's Road to Revival: "Writing" the PRC's Struggles for Modernisation'. In Cao, Qing, Tian Hailong, & Chilton, Paul (eds.), *Discourse, Politics and Media in Contemporary China*. Amsterdam & Philadelphia: John Benjamins (pp. 145–170).

Schneider, Florian (2012), *Visual Political Communication in Popular Chinese Television Series*. Leiden & Boston: Brill.

Schneider, Florian (2014a), 'Reconceptualizing World Order: Chinese Political Thought and Its Challenge to International Relations Theory'. *Review of International Studies*, 40(4), 683–703.

Schneider, Florian (2014b), 'It's a Small World After All? Simulating the Future World Order at the Shanghai Expo'. In Cao, Qing, Tian Hailong & Chilton, Paul (eds.), *Discourse, Politics and Media in Contemporary China*. Amsterdam & Philadelphia: John Benjamins (pp. 97–120).

Schneider, Florian (2015), 'Searching for "Digital Asia" in Its Networks: Where the Spatial Turn Meets the Digital Turn'. *Asiascape: Digital Asia*, 2(1–2), 56–91.

Schneider, Florian (2016a), 'China's 'Info-Web': How Beijing Governs Online Political Communication About Japan'. *New Media and Society*, 18(11), 2664–2684.

Schneider, Florian (2016b), 'The Cultural Governance of Mass Media in Contemporary China'. In Keane, Michael, Hemelryk Donald, Stephanie, & Qiu, Zitong (eds.), *Handbook of Cultural Industries in China*. Cheltenham & Northampton, MA: Edward Elgar (pp. 189–206).

Schneider, Florian (2017), 'China's "Big V" Bloggers: How Celebrities Intervene in Digital Sino-Japanese Relations'. *Celebrity Studies*, 8(2), 331–336.

Schneider, Florian (2018), 'Mediated Massacre: Digital Nationalism and History Discourse on China's Web'. *Journal of Asian Studies*, 77(2), 429–452.

Schneier, Bruce (2012, November 26), 'When It Comes to Security, We're Back to Feudalism'. *Wired*, retrieved 1 September 2017 from https://www.schneier.com/essays/archives/2012/11/when_it_comes_to_sec.html.

Schneier, Bruce (2015), *Data and Goliath—The Hidden Battles to Collect Your Data and Control Your World*. New York & London: W.W. Norton.

Schoenhals, Michael (1992), *Doing Things with Words in Chinese Politics: Five Studies*. Berkeley: Institute of East Asian Studies, University of California.

Scholz, Trebor (ed.) (2013), *Digital Labor: The Internet as Playground and Factory*. New York & Abingdon: Routledge.

Schubert, Gunter & Heberer, Thomas (2009), *Politische Partizipation und Regimelegitimität in der VR China. Band II: Der urbane Raum* (Political Participation and Regime Legitimacy in the PR China. Volume 2: Rural Spaces). Wisbaden: FS Verlag für Sozialwissenschaften.

Schubert, Gunter (2008), 'One-Party Rule and the Question of Legitimacy in Contemporary China'. *Journal of Contemporary China*, 17(54), 191–204.

Schubert, Gunter (2014), 'Political Legitimacy in Contemporary China Revisited: Theoretical Refinement and Empirical Operationalization'. *Journal of Contemporary China*, 23(88), 593–611.

Schwartz, Raz & Halegoua, Germaine R. (2015), 'The Spatial Self: Location-Based Identity Performance on Social Media'. *New Media and Society*, 17(10), 1643–1660.

Scott, John (2012), *Social Network Analysis* (3rd ed.). Los Angeles et al.: Sage.

Shambaugh, David (2007), 'China's Propaganda System: Institutions, Process, and Efficacy'. *China Journal*, 57 (January), 25–60.

Shambaugh, David (2008), *China's Communist Party—Atrophy and Adaptation*. Berkeley et al.: University of California Press.

Shani, Giorgio (2008), 'Toward a Post-Western IR: The Umma, Khalsa Panth, and Critical International Relations Theory'. *International Studies Review*, 10(4), 722–734.

Shapiro, Michael J. (2004), *Methods and Nations: Cultural Governance and the Indigenous Subject*. New York & London: Routledge.

Shaw, Han-yi (1999), *The Diaoyutai/Senkaku Islands Dispute: Its History and an Analysis of the Ownership Claims of the P.R.C., R.O.C., and Japan*. Baltimore: University of Maryland, retrieved 1 September 2017 from http://digitalcommons.law.umaryland.edu/cgi/viewcontent.cgi?ar ticle=1151&context=mscas.

Sheehan, Matt (2015), 'Here's How China's Trying to Rewrite the Rules of the Global Internet— "Cyber Sovereignty" Lets Censors Fence off Online Content'. Interview with Jeremy Goldkorn, *The World Post*, retrieved 17 March 2018 from http://www.huffingtonpost.com/entry/china-cyber-sovereignty_566bc51be4b0fccee16ec083.

Shen, Simon (2008), 'Alternative Online Chinese Nationalism: Response to the Anti-Japanese Campaign in China on Hong Kong's Internet'. *Intercultural Communication Studies*, 17(3), 155–168.

Shen, Simon & Breslin, Shaun (eds.) (2010), *Online Chinese Nationalism and China's Bilateral Relations*. Lanham: Lexington.

Shih, Chih-yu (2012), 'Assigning Role Characteristics to China: The Role State Versus the Ego State'. *Foreign Policy Analysis*, 8, 71–91.

Shirk, Susan L. (2007), *China—Fragile Superpower*. Oxford et al.: Oxford University Press.

Shirky, Clay (2003), 'Power Laws, Weblogs, and Inequality. Clay Shirky's Writings About the Internet'. *Clay Shirky's Writings About the Internet*, retrieved 1 September 2017 from http://www.shirky.com/writings/powerlaw_weblog.html.

Shirky, Clay (2008), *Here Comes Everybody—The Power to Organize Without Organizations*. New York et al.: Penguin Books.

Shirky, Clay (2010), *Cognitive Surplus: Creativity and Generosity in a Connected Age* (Kindle ed.). New York: Penguin.

Shirky, Clay (2015), *Little Rice: Smartphones, Xiaomi, and the Chinese Dream* (Kindle ed.). New York: Columbia Global Reports.

Shue, Vivienne (2004), 'Legitimacy Crisis in China?' In Gries, Peter Hays & Rosen, Stanley (eds.), *State and Society in 21st-Century China: Crisis, Contention, and Legitimation*. New York & London: RoutledgeCurzon (pp. 24–49).

Sigley, Gary (2009), '*Suzhi*, the Body, and the Fortunes of Technoscientific Reasoning in Contemporary China'. *Positions: East Asia Cultures Critique*, 17(3), 537–566.

Silbert, Sean (2014, December 3), 'No Laughing Matter: China's Media Regulators Ban Puns'. *Los Angeles Times*, retrieved 1 September 2017 from http://www.latimes.com/world/asia/la-fg-china-bans-puns-20141203-story.html.

Sina (2005a), 'Lishi burong cuangai' (History Does Not Brook Distortion). *Sina.com*, retrieved 18 March 2018 from http://neverforget.sina.com.cn/distort/index.shtml.

Sina (2005b), 'Youhao guan jiaoliu' (Friendship Exchange). *Sina.com*, retrieved 18 March 2018 from http://neverforget.sina.com.cn/place/intercourse/index.html.

Sina (2016), 'Mingxing shili bang' (Star Power Charts). *Sina Weibo*, retrieved 1 May 2016 from http://chart.weibo.com/?rank_type=5.

Smith, Anthony D. (1991), *The Ethnic Origins of Nations*. Oxford & Malden, MA: Blackwell.

Smith, Anthony D. (1993), *National Identity*. Reno: University of Nevada Press.

Smith, Anthony D. (1998), *Nationalism and Modernism*. London & New York: Routledge.

Sohu (2010), 'Zhongguo yuchuan yu Riben xunluochuan fasheng xiangzhuang' (Chinese Fishing Boat and Japanese Patrol Boat Collide). *Sohu News*, retrieved 18 March 2018 from http://news.sohu.com/s2010/yuchuan/.

Sperber, Dan (1996), *Explaining Culture—A Naturalistic Approach*, Oxford & Malden, MA: Blackwell Publishing.

Steinkraus, Warren E. (1980), 'Socrates, Confucius, and the Rectification of Names'. *Philosophy East and West*, 30(2), 261–264.

Sterling, Bruce (2009, March 1), 'The Brief but Glorious Life of Web 2.0, and What Comes After'. *Wired*, retrieved 1 September 2017 from http://www.wired.com/2009/03/what-bruce-ster/.

Stevenson, Michael (2012), 'After Virtuality: A Postmortem on Early Internet Culture'. *Blind*, 28, retrieved 1 September 2017 from http://www.ziedaar.nl/article.php?id=413.

Stevenson, Neil (1992), *Snow Crash*. London et al.: Penguin Books.

Stevenson, Neil (1999), *Cryptonomicon* (Kindle ed.). New York: Avon Books.

Stevenson, Neil (2014), *The Baroque Cycle: Quicksilver, The Confusion, and The System of the World* (Kindle ed.). New York: HarperCollins.

Stockmann, Daniela (2010), 'Who Believes Propaganda? Media Effects During the Anti-Japanese Protests in Beijing'. *The China Quarterly*, 202, 269–289.

Stockmann, Daniela (2013), *Media Commercialization and Authoritarian Rule in China* (Kindle ed.). Cambridge: Cambridge University Press.

Stockmann, Daniela (2014, August 14), 'Authorit@rianism 2.0: About the Project'. Retrieved 1 September 2017 from http://www.authoritarianism.net/about-the-project/.

Strafella, Giorgio & Berg, Daria (2015), 'The Making of an Online Celebrity: A Critical Analysis of Han Han's Blog'. *China Information*, 29(3), 352–376.

Strange, Susan (1996), *The Retreat of the State: The Diffusion of Power in the World Economy*. Cambridge: Cambridge University Press.

Strasser, Todd (1981/2013), *The Wave* (Kindle ed.). New York: Dell.

Study China (2015, November 12), 'Guojia dashuju zhanlüe—Xi Jinping yu "shi san wu" shisi da zhanlüe' (National Big Data Strategy—Xi Jinping and the 14 Grand Strategies of the '13th Five-Year Plan'). *Xuexi Zhongguo*, retrieved 1 September 2017 from http://www.ccln.gov.cn/hotnews/160487.shtml.

Sudworth, John (2013, May 17), 'Chinese Web Activists See New Pressure from Censors'. *BBC News*, retrieved 1 September 2017 from http://www.bbc.com/news/world-asia-china-22566821.

Sullivan, Jonathan (2014), 'China's Weibo: Is Faster Different?' *New Media and Society*, 16(1), 24–37.

Sullivan, Jonathan & Sapir, Eliyahu V. (2013), 'Strategic Cross-Strait Discourse: A Comparative Analysis of Three Presidential Terms'. *China Information*, 27(1), 11–30.

Surowiecki, James (2005), *The Wisdom of Crowds*. New York: Anchor Books.

Suzuki, Takeshi & Murai, Shusuke (2014), 'How the Japanese Legacy Media Covered the Senkaku Controversy'. In Hollihan, Thomas A. (ed.), *The Dispute OVER the Diaoyu/Senkaku Islands: How Media Narratives Shape Public Opinion and Challenge the Global Order*. New York: Palgrave Macmillan (pp. 141–168).

Svensson, Marina (2014), 'Voice, Power and Connectivity in China's Microblogosphere: Digital Divides on SinaWeibo'. *China Information*, 28(2), 168–188.

Swaminathan, Ramanathan (2015), 'The Emergent Artificial Intelligence of Green Spaces'. *Asiascape: Digital Asia*, 2(3), 238–278.

Szablewicz, Marcella (2014), 'The "Losers" of China's Internet: Memes as "Structures of Feeling" for Disillusioned Young Netizens'. *China Information*, 28(2), 259–275.

Tai, Zixue (2006), *The Internet in China: Cyberspace and Civil Society*. New York & London: Routledge.

Tang, Kevin (2013, August 9), 'How Jackie Chan Became the Most Hated Celeb on the Chinese Internet'. *BuzzFeedNews*, retrieved 1 September 2017 from http://www.buzzfeed.com/kevintang/jackie-chan-offends-chinese-netizen#.ux60YXgoM.

Tang, Nancy (2015, February 5), '"Straight Man Cancer": Sexism with Chinese Characteristics'. *The Diplomat*, retrieved 1 September 2017 from http://thediplomat.com/2015/02/straight-man-cancer-sexism-with-chinese-characteristics/.

Tavor, Ori (2014), 'Naming/Power: Linguistic Engineering and the Construction of Discourse in Early China'. *Asian Philosophy*, 24(4), 313–329.

Taylor, Alan (2012, September), 'Anti-Japan Protests in China'. *The Atlantic*, retrieved 1 September 2017 from http://www.theatlantic.com/photo/2012/09/anti-japan-protests-in-china/100370/.

Teets, Jessica C. (2013), 'Let Many Civil Societies Bloom: The Rise of Consultative Authoritarianism in China'. *The China Quarterly*, 213, 19–38.

Ter Haar, Barend J. (2010), *Het hemels mandaat: De geschiedenis van het Chinese Keizerrijk* (The Heavenly Mandate: The History of the Chinese Empire). Amsterdam: Amsterdam University Press.

The Japan Times (2017, January 25), 'Despite Calls for Boycott, Apa Hotel Chain Will Keep Books Denying Nanjing Massacre'. Retrieved 1 September 2017 from http://www.japantimes.co.jp/news/2017/01/25/national/despite-calls-boycott-apa-hotel-chain-will-keep-books-denying-nanking-massacre/#.WSEtamiGOUm.

Thelwall, Mike (2004), *Link Analysis: An Information Science Approach*. San Diego: Academic Press.

Thompson, John B. (1995), *The Media and Modernity: A Social Theory of the Media*. Stanford: Stanford University Press.

Thompson, Simon & Hoggett, Paul (eds.) (2012), *Politics and the Emotions: The Affective Turn in Contemporary Political Studies*. New York & London: Continuum.

Tianfu Morning News (2012, August 17), 'Yi ge daoguo de yexin' (Ambitions of an Island Nation). *Tianfu zaobao*, retrieved 1 September 2017 from http://www.morning.sc.cn/new/html/tfzb/20120817/tfzb608005.html.

Tiexue (2014), 'Little Japan'. *Tiexue.net*, retrieved 11 December 2015 from http://data.tiexue.net/view/13680.

Tilly, Charles (2005), *Identity, Boundaries, and Social Ties*. Boulder & London: Paradigm.

Timmons, Heather (2016, February 4), 'Losing the Plot: As China's Economy Unravels, Beijing's Attempts at Damage Control are Growing Increasingly Desperate'. *Quartz*, retrieved 1 September 2017 from http://qz.com/596745/beijing-controls-the-largest-most-powerful-propaganda-team-on-the-planet-so-why-is-chinas-pr-suddenly-so-awful/.

Tomasello, Michael (2008), *Origins of Human Communication*. Cambridge, MA: MIT Press.

Tong, Jinrong & Zuo, Landong (2014), 'Weibo Communication and Government Legitimacy in China: A Computer-Assisted Analysis of Weibo Messages on Two "Mass Incidents"'. *Information, Communication and Society*, 17(1), 66–85.

Tsang, Steve (2009), 'Consultative Leninism: China's New Political Framework'. *Journal of Contemporary China*, 18(62), 865–880.

Tu, Fangjing (2016), 'WeChat and Civil Society in China'. *Communication and the Public*, 1(3), 343–350.

Turkle, Sherry (2011), *Alone Together: Why We Expect More from Technology and Less from Each Other* (Kindle ed.). New York: Basic Books.

Turner, Fred (2008), *From Counterculture to Cyberculture: Stewart Brand, the Whole Earth Network, and the Rise of Digital Utopianism*. Chicago, IL: University of Chicago Press.

Turner, Mark (2001), *Cognitive Dimensions of Social Science—The Way We Think About Politics, Economics, Law, and Society*. Oxford et al.: Oxford University Press.

Van Dijk, José & Poell, Thomas (2013), 'Understanding Social Media Logic'. *Media and Communication*, 1(1), 2–14.

Van Dongen, Els (2009), *'Goodbye Radicalism!' Conceptions of Conservatism Among Chinese Intellectuals During the Early 1990s*. Doctoral Thesis, Leiden: Leiden University.

Van Leeuwen, Theo (2008), *Discourse and Practice—New Tools for Critical Discourse Analysis*. Oxford et al.: Oxford University Press.

Vander Wal, Thomas (2007, February 2), 'Folksonomy Coinage and Definition'. *Vanderwal.net*, retrieved 1 September 2017 from http://www.vanderwal.net/folksonomy.html.

Volland, Nicolai (2011), 'Taking Urban Conservation Online: Chinese Civic Action Groups and the Internet'. In Herold, David K. & Marolt, Peter (eds.), *Online Society in China: Creating, Celebrating, and Instrumentalising the Online Carnival*. London & New York: Routledge (pp. 184–199).

Vossen, Koen (2017), *The Power of Populism: Geert Wilders and the Party for Freedom in the Netherlands*. London & New York: Routledge.

Wahba, Mahmoud A. & Bridwell, Lawrence G. (1976), 'Maslow Reconsidered: A Review of Research on the Need Hierarchy Theory'. *Organizational Behavior and Human Performance*, 15(2), 212–240.

Wakabayashi, Bob Tadashi (2007a), 'The Nanking 100-Man Killing Contest Debate, 1971–75'. In Wakabayashi, Bob Tadashi (ed.), *The Nanking Atrocity, 1937–38: Complicating the Picture*. New York & Oxford: Berghahn Books (pp. 115–148).

Wakabayashi, Bob Tadashi (ed.) (2007b), *The Nanking Atrocity, 1937–38: Complicating the Picture*. New York & Oxford: Berghahn Books.

Wakefield, Bryce & Martin, Craig (2014), 'Reexamining "Myths" About Japan's Collective Self Defense Change—What Critics (and the Japanese Public) Do Understand About Japan's Constitutional Reinterpretation'. *The Asia Pacific Journal, Japan Focus*, retrieved 1 September 2017 from http://apjjf.org/-Bryce-Wakefield/4803/article.html.

Walker Rettberg, Jill (2014), *Blogging*. Cambridge: Polity.

Wallace, Jeremy, & Weiss, Jessica Chen (2015), 'The Political Economy of Nationalist Protest in China: A Subnational Approach'. *The China Quarterly*, 222, 403–429.

Wallis, Brian (1997), 'A Forum, Not a Temple: Notes on the Return of Iconography to the Museum'. *American Literary History*, 9(3), 617–623.

Wang, Chunhui (2015, December 18), 'Wuzhen Fenghui zhuanjia tan: Hulianwang zhili si xiang yuanze jiyu guojifa liying cheng quanqiu zhunze' (Wuzhen Summit Expert Talk: On the Basis of International Law, the Four Principles of Internet Governance Should Become Universal Norms). *Legal Daily*, retrieved 1 September 2017 from http://www.legaldaily.com.cn/commentary/content/2015-12/18/content_6405668.htm.

Wang, Fang (2011), *'Wang' shi zhi duoshao: wangluo xinli yu chengyin jiexi* ('Net' Know-How: Analysis of Internet Psychology and Addiction). Shanghai: Fudan daxue chubanshe.

Wang, Hui (2008), *Xiandai Zhongguo sixiang de xingqi* (The Rise of Modern Chinese Thought). Beijing: Shenghuo, dushu, xinzhi sanlian shudian.

Wang, Hui (2014), *China from Empire to Nation-State*. Translated by Michael Gibbs Hill. Cambridge, MA & London: Harvard University Press.

Wang, Mingde & Okano-Heijmans, Maaike (2011), 'Overcoming the Past in Sino-Japanese Relations?' *The International Spectator*, 46(1), 127–148.

Wang, Xiaobo & Gu, Baotong (2015), 'The Communication Design of WeChat: Ideological as well as Technical Aspects of Social Media'. *Communication Design Quarterly*, 4(1), 23–35.

Wang, Zheng (2012), *Never Forget National Humiliation—Historical Memory in Chinese Politics and Foreign Relations*. New York: Columbia University Press.

Ware, Alan (2016), 'Donald Trump's Hijacking of the Republican Party in Historical Perspective'. *The Political Quarterly*, 87(3), 406–414.

Warren, T. Camber (2015), 'Explosive Connections? Mass Media, Social Media, and the Geography of Collective Violence in African States'. *Journal of Peace Research*, 52(3), 297–311.

WCADDL (2014, December 27), 'Diaoyudao xinnian de heli "Diaoyudao dongwu he zhiwu" shuji zhengshi faxing' (Diaoyu Island New Year's Gift 'The Flora and Fauna of the Diaoyu Islands' Has Officially Been Published). *World Chinese Alliance in Defence of the Diaoyus*, retrieved 1 September 2017 from http://www.wcaddl.org/news/?82.html.

WCADDL (2015, August 2), 'Jiaoyubu guanyu "chenqingshu" de huifu' (The Ministry of Education's response to the 'petition letter'). *World Chinese Alliance in Defence of the Diaoyus*, retrieved 1 September 2017 from http://www.wcaddl.org/news/?198.html.

WCADDL (n.d.), '"Diaoyudao—jiaokeshu". Qianglie yaoqiu Jiaoyubu chongxin zengbu, xiuding Diaoyudao zai jiaokeshu li de kemu, ji neirong!' (Diaoyu Islands—Textbooks. Strongly Demand That the Ministry of Education Again Augment and Revise the Subject and Content of the Diaoyu Islands in Textbooks!). *World Chinese Alliance in Defence of the Diaoyus*, retrieved 1 September 2017 from http://www.wcaddl.org/textbook.asp.

Weber, Max (1980), *Wirtschaft und Gesellschaft* (Economy and Society) (5th rev. ed.). Tübingen: Mohr Siebeck.

Wei, Chengsi (2011), 'Di yi wei bao diao lieshi: Xianggang tongbao Chen Yuxiang xianchu shengming' (The First Protect the Diaoyus Martyr: Hong Kong's Chen Yuxiang Dedicated His Life). *Nanfang renwu zhoukan*, retrieved 1 September 2017 from http://news.ifeng.com/history/zhongguojindaishi/special/diaoyudao/detail_2012_07/16/16061983_0.shtml.

Weidmann, Nils B. (2015a), 'Communication, Technology, and Political Conflict: Introduction to the Special Issue'. *Journal of Peace Research*, 52(3), 263–268.

Weidmann, Nils B. (2015b), 'Communication Networks and the Transnational Spread of Ethnic Conflict'. *Journal of Peace Research*, 52(3), 285–296.

Weiss, Jessica Chen (2014), *Powerful Patriots: Nationalist Protest in China's Foreign Relations*. New York: Oxford University Press.

Welitzkin, Paul (2014, December 3), 'China May Take Global Lead in IT by Its Sheer Size'. *China Daily USA*, retrieved 1 September 2017 from http://usa.chinadaily.com.cn/business/2014-12/03/content_19020669.htm.

Weller, Robert P. (2008), 'Responsive Authoritarianism'. In Gilley, Bruce & Diamond, Larry (eds.), *Political Change in China: Comparisons with Taiwan*. Boulder, CO: Lynne Rienner (pp. 117–133).

Wertsch, James V. (2002), *Voices of Collective Remembering*. Cambridge: Cambridge University Press.

Westcott, Ben & Ge, Celine (2016, March 31), 'A4 Waists, iPhone Legs: Chinese Women Set Bizarre New Standards for Beauty on Social Media'. *South China Morning Post*, retrieved 1 September 2017 from http://www.scmp.com/news/china/society/article/1932291/a4-waists-iphone-legs-chinese-women-set-bizarre-new-standards.

White, Hayden (1987), *The Content of the Form: Narrative Discourse and Historical Representation*. Baltimore: Johns Hopkins University Press.

Wikimedia (2015), 'Baidu Baike dui Weiji Baike de qinquan' (Baidu Baike's Infringements Against Wikipedia). *Wikipedia*, retrieved 1 May 2016 from https://zh.wikipedia.org/wiki/Wikipedi a:%E7%99%BE%E5%BA%A6%E7%99%BE%E7%A7%91%E5%B0%8D%E7%B6%AD%E5%9F%BA%E7%99%BE%E7%A7%91%E7%9A%84%E4%BE%B5%E6%AC%8A.

Wilkinson, Charles F. (2005), *Blood Struggle: The Rise of Modern Indian Nations*. New York: W.W. Norton.

Wodak, Ruth & Krzyzanowski, Michal (eds.) (2008), *Qualitative Discourse Analysis in the Social Sciences*. Basingstoke & New York: Palgrave Macmillan.

Wodak, Ruth & Meyer, Michael (eds.) (2009), *Methods of Critical Discourse Analysis* (2nd ed.). Los Angeles et al.: Sage.

Wong, Chun Han (2016, February 16), 'In Rare State Media Tour, Xi Jinping Takes the Anchor's Chair'. *The Wall Street Journal's China Real Time Report*, retrieved 1 September 2017 from http://blogs.wsj.com/chinarealtime/2016/02/19/in-rare-state-media-tour-xi-jinping-takes-the-anchors-chair/.

World Bank (n.d.), 'Data: China'. *The World Bank World Development Indicators*, retrieved 1 September 2017 from http://data.worldbank.org/country/china.

Wright, Joss (2014), 'Regional Variation in Chinese Internet Filtering'. *Information, Communication and Society*, 17(1), 121–141.

Wu, Angela Xiao (2014), 'Ideological Polarization over a China-as-Superpower Mind-set: An Exploratory Charting of Belief Systems Among Chinese Internet Users, 2008–2011'. *International Journal of Communication*, 8, 2650–2679.

Wu, Shang-su (2016, February 12), 'Taiwan's South China Sea Dilemma'. *The Diplomat*, retrieved 1 September 2017 from http://thediplomat.com/2016/02/taiwans-south-china-sea-dilemma/?utm_content=buffer21672&utm_medium=social&utm_source=twitter.com&utm_campaign=buffer.

Wu, Yanfang (2015), 'Incivility on Diaoyu Island Sovereignty in Tianya Club: A Case Study of Comments in an Online Public Sphere'. *The Journal of International Communication*, 21(1), 109–131.

Xi, Jinping (2014, February 27), 'Nuli ba woguo jianshe chengwei wangluo qiangguo' (Work hard to turn our country into an internet superpower). Speech held at the opening of the CCP's Central Leading Group of Cyberspace Affairs, retrieved 1 September 2017 from http://cpc.people.com.cn/xuexi/n/2015/0720/c397563-27331860.html.

Xin, Xin (2006), 'A Developing Market in News: Xinhua News Agency and Chinese Newspapers'. *Media Culture Society*, 28(1), 45–66.

Xinhua (2007, December 13), 'Nanjing datusha 70 zhounian jinian huodong xianchang tupian' (Images Depicting the Commemoration of the Nanjing Massacre's 70-Year Anniversary). *iFeng*, retrieved on 1 September 2017 from http://news.ifeng.com/photo/news/detail_2007_12/13/554903_0.shtml.

Xinhua (2009, March 9), 'China Will Never Copy Western Political System: Top Legislator'. *China Net*, retrieved 1 September 2017 from http://www.china.org.cn/government/NPC_CPPCC_2009/2009-03/09/content_17406822.htm.

Xinhua (2014, May 10), '"Chinese Dream" to Benefit China, World'. *Global Times*, retrieved 1 September 2017 from http://www.globaltimes.cn/content/859590.shtml.

Xinhua (2015, December 16), 'Highlights of Xi's Internet Speech'. *World Internet Conference—Wuzhen Summit*, retrieved 1 September 2017 from http://www.wuzhenwic.org/2015-12/16/c_47742.htm.

Xinjingbao (2015, December 17), 'Jiedu Xi Jinping de hulianwang fazhan si xiang yuanze he wu dian zhuzhang' (Deciphering Xi Jinping's Four Principles and Five Propositions of Internet Development). *Tencent Tech*, retrieved 1 September 2017 from http://tech.qq.com/a/20151217/027535.htm.

Xiong, Xiaobing, Zhou, Gang, Huang, Yongzhong, Chen, Haiyong, & Xu, Ke (2013), 'Dynamic Evolution of Collective Emotions in Social Networks: A Case Study of Sina Weibo'. *Science China*, 56(July), 1–18.

Xu, Wu (2007), *China's Cyber Nationalism—Evolution, Characteristics, and Implications*. Lanham: Lexington.

Yan, Lianke (2013, April 1), 'On China's State-Sponsored Amnesia'. *New York Times*, retrieved 1 September 2017 from http://www.nytimes.com/2013/04/02/opinion/on-chinas-state-sponsored-amnesia.html?_r=1.

Yang, Guobin (2009), *The Power of the Internet in China—Citizen Activism Online*. New York: Columbia University Press.

Yang, Guobin (2014), 'Political Contestation in Chinese Digital Spaces: Deepening the Critical Inquiry'. *China Information*, 28, 135–144.

Ye, Wei Ming, Sarrica, Mauro, & Fortunati, Leopoldina (2014), 'Two Selves and Online Forums in China'. *Asian Journal of Social Psychology*, 17(1), 1–11.

Ying, Li & Yue, Xiaodong (2008), *E hai taosheng—wangluo chengyin ji kefu* (Farewell to Internet Addiction). Beijing: Gaodeng jiaoyu chubanshe.

Yoshida, Takashi (2006), *The Making of the 'Rape of Nanking': History and Memory in Japan, China, and the United States*. Oxford et al.: Oxford University Press.

Young, James E. (2000), 'Germany's Holocaust Memorial'. Lecture at University of California in December 2000. Retrieved 1 September 2017 from https://www.youtube.com/watch?v=GmxyYXtf_vw.

Yu, Guoming (2014) (ed.), *Zhongguo shehui yuqing niandu baogao* (Annual Report on Public Opinion in China). Beijing: Remin University Press.

Yu, Haiyang (2014), 'Glorious Memories of Imperial China and the Rise of Chinese Populist Nationalism'. *Journal of Contemporary China*, 23(90), 1174–1187.

Yuan, Ye (2010a), 'Bao diao yundong de qiyuan' (Origins of the Movement to Protect the Diaoyus). *San lian shenghuo zhoukan*, 49. Retrieved 1 September 2017 from http://news.ifeng.com/history/zhongguojindaishi/special/diaoyudao/detail_2012_07/16/16061689_0.shtml.

Yuan, Ye (2010b), 'Di er bo Taiwan bao diao yundong' (The Second Wave of Taiwan's Protect the Diaoyus Movement). *San lian shenghuo zhoukan*, 49. Retrieved 1 September 2017 from http://news.ifeng.com/history/zhongguojindaishi/special/diaoyudao/detail_2012_07/17/16085918_0.shtml.

Zarrow, Peter (2004), *China in War and Revolution, 1895–1949*. London & New York: Routledge.

Zeng, Jinghan (2014), 'Bridging the Wide Gulf Between Western and Chinese Scholarship: The Debate on Regime Legitimacy in China', *Journal of Contemporary China*, 23(88), 612–635.

Zhang, Chenchen (2017, May 11), 'The Curious Rise of the "White Left" as a Chinese Internet Insult'. *Open Democracy*, retrieved 1 September 2017 from https://www.opendemocracy.net/digitaliberties/chenchen-zhang/curious-rise-of-white-left-as-chinese-internet-insult.

Zhang, Ning (2014), 'Web-Based Backpacking Communities and Online Activism in China: Movement Without Marching'. *China Information*, 28(2), 276–296.

Zhang, Xiaoling (2009), 'From "Foreign Propaganda" to "International Communication": China's Promotion of Soft Power in the Age of Information and Communication Technologies'. In Zhang, Xiaoling & Zheng, Yongnian (eds.), *China's Information and Communications Technology Revolution: Political Impacts and State Responses*. Oxon & New York: Routledge (pp. 103–120).

Zhang, Xiaoling (2011), *The Transformation of Political Communication in China—From Propaganda to Hegemony*. Singapore: World Scientific.

Zhang, Xiuming (2005), 'Zhongguo dalu minjian "bao diao" shouhang he shoudeng Diaoyudao' (The Maiden Voyage and First Landing on the Diaoyu Islands by Mainland China's Non-Governmental 'Protect the Diaoyus'). *iFeng*, retrieved from http://news.ifeng.com/history/zhongguojindaishi/special/diaoyudao/detail_2012_07/16/16062326_0.shtml.

Zhang, Yongjin (2001), 'System, Empire and State in Chinese International Relations', *Review of International Studies*, 27, 43–63.

Zhang, Zhan (2014), 'Fanning the Flames of Public Rage: Coverage of Diaoyu Islands Dispute in the Chinese Legacy Media'. In Hollihan, Thomas A. (ed.), *The Dispute over the Diaoyu/Senkaku Islands: How Media Narratives Shape Public Opinion and Challenge the Global Order*. New York: Palgrave Macmillan (pp. 81–118).

Zhao, Suisheng (2004), *A Nation-State by Construction: Dynamics of Modern Chinese Nationalism*. Stanford: Stanford University Press.

Zhao, Suisheng (2016), 'The Study of Chinese Nationalism: Theoretical Engagement, Empirical Testing and Influence on Chinese Foreign Policy'. *Nations and Nationalism*, 22(3), 436–441.

Zhao, Yuezhi (1998), *Media, Market, and Democracy in China: Between the Party Line and the Bottom Line*, Urbana and Chicago: University of Illinois Press.

Zhao, Yuezhi (2000), 'From Commercialization to Conglomeration: The Transformation of the Chinese Press Within the Orbit of the Party State'. *Journal of Communication*, 50(2), 3–26.

Zhao, Yuezhi (2008), *Communication in China—Political Economy, Power, and Conflict*. Lanham & Plymouth: Rowman & Littlefield.

Zheng, Yongnian (2008), *Technological Empowerment—The Internet, State, and Society in China*. Stanford: Stanford University Press.

Zheng, Yongnian (2010), *The Chinese Communist Party as Organizational Emperor*. London & New York: Routledge.

Zhi, Zhenfeng (2016, February 17), 'Tuidong hulianwang quanqiu zhili tixi biange de shouyao yuanze' (Promote the Chief Principle for Reform of the Internet Governance System). *People's Net*, retrieved 1 September 2017 from http://opinion.people.com.cn/n1/2016/0217/c1003-28128800.html.

Zhou, Fangyin (2016), 'Between Assertiveness and Self-Restraint: Understanding China's South China Sea Policy'. *International Affairs*, 92(4), 869–890.

Zhou, Laura (2013, January 16), 'Businesspeople Top Weibo Microbloggers List'. *South China Morning Post*, retrieved 1 September 2017 from http://www.scmp.com/news/china/article/1128952/businesspeople-top-weibo-microbloggers-list.

Zhou, Ping, Zu, Xinning, & Leydesdorff, Loet (2010), 'A Comparative Study of Communication Structures of Chinese Journals in the Social Sciences'. *Journal of the Association for Information Science and Technology*, 2010, 61(7), 1360–1376.

Zhou, Rui, Wen, Zhonghe, Tang, Muchao, & DiSalvo, Betsy (2017), 'Navigating Media Use: Chinese Parents and Their Overseas Adolescent Children on WeChat'. Paper presented at the *2017 ACM Conference on Designing Interactive Systems* in New York, retrieved 1 September 2017 from https://www.researchgate.net/publication/316635752_Navigating_Media_Use_Chinese_Parents_and_Their_Overseas_Adolescent_Children_on_WeChat.

Zubrzycki, Genevieve (2009), 'National Culture, National Identity, and the Culture(s) of the Nation'. In Hall, John R., Grindstaff, Laura, & Lo, Ming-cheng (eds.), *Handbook of Cultural Sociology* (Kindle ed.). Oxon & New York: Routledge (pp. 514–525).

Zuckerman, Ethan (2013), *Rewire: Digital Cosmopolitans in the Age of Connection* (Kindle ed.). New York & London: Norton.

# Index